Follow Me
Up Fools Mountain
Korea, 1951

Follow Me
Up Fools Mountain
Korea, 1951

dudley c gould

A www.war-books.com story of courage from
Southfarm Press, *Publisher*
Middletown, Connecticut

Southfarm Press, *Publisher*
Publishing Imprint of Haan Graphic Publishing Services, Ltd.
P.O. Box 1296, Middletown, Connecticut 06457
(860) 346-8798; Fax: (860) 347-9931
ISBN: 0-913337-47-1

Full color art on book jacket by Emily Stelea
Photograph on book jacket courtesy of Steven E. Danish

Printed in The United States of America

Contents

COMBAT NURSE
by Mary E. Hill Arthur
Army Nurse, WWII

I will not fail you, fall or crumble
At the sight and smell and touch of blood
Open cavities or missing limb or mind
I will not cry when you have to die
I wrap wounds, medicate, inject
And hold your hand
To let you know I understand
I will change you, turn you like a baby
Call the OD and Chaplin on the double
Stay after hours to help write to your true love
If it be your struggle is over, it is your last fight
I will gently close your eyes and
Prepare you for your next flight
As your young weary soul takes wing
Into the subtle shadows
Of this cold unending pain-filled night
I must not crumble, I must not cry,
That would not do at all
I keep hearing yet another frantic call
And though at times it seems
My fluttering heart may faint, I know that
Someone needs my cool hand, needs my clear head
So Lord help me keep my wits together
Keep my heart rhythm steady, keep it strong
Lest my senses fail me and I fall
I cannot crumble, I will not cry
No, that would not do at all

Time to relax and clean up. One Mash tent hospital in the Second Division area treated seven hundred wounded in one week of the May Massacre.

To Kitty
and forty years
that were

Follow Me Up Fools Mountain is not hearsay. It is the real thing from the memory of an infantry veteran of two wars and two armies. Survivor of the Second Infantry Division during the May Massacre in Korea, 1951, Gould recalls crying "Follow Me!" many times. He especially remembers yelling "Follow Me!" that proud day he led two rifle companies taking the highest ground of the infamous Punchbowl, hundreds of meters above both Bloody and Heartbreak Ridges.

Preface

I was advised by two publishers not to bother to write this book. "Nobody wants to hear about the Korean War." And Ernest Hemingway should not have written about World War One. This work, however, is no more about the Korean War than *Farewell to Arms* was about the war to end all wars. It is what happened to men in the throes of battles, primarily about this rifle platoon leader and the tragedy of his defenseless wife.

Why should the war and the infantry that remains in place to guarantee the peace of Asia ever be forgotten? The war is not forgotten by America's fighting men. Only in abeyance is the war that has already wounded 103,000 American soldiers, taken 7000 prisoners of war, half of whom vanished in miserable deaths, 8177 still missing in action and 54,246 killed outright, compared to the very well-remembered and advertised controversial war that followed in Vietnam, that in one way or another disgusted American civilians, that lasted six years longer than the Korean War with only 4,000 more killed. Counting buddies of mine, our foreign battalions, civilians, ROKS, Republic of Korea, and enemy, some 4,000,000 died in South and North Korea; 42,000 tons of bombs dropped on one small area the first seven months heavy on artillery, 3,000 tons more than we used on Nazis in all 1942.

Korea was particularly heavy on artillery, 11,800 howitzer rounds one night by the 38th Field Artillery Battalion alone on one small area in an eleven-hour TOT, time on target; and the longest linear ground combat ever endured, twice as long as in either world war, leaving some of us stranded, engaged in firing positions somewhere

9

across the 150-mile front until fatigue uniforms gave in to the moldy rot of bunkers.

The Korean War is forgotten by civilians because it was only five years after the largest, most costly war in history. For a frightful year after our entire Pacific Navy was sunk at Pearl Harbor, a seemingly unwinnable war, who, having lived through that trying period, can forget how emotionally drained and involved everyone was? War was dragged right into your home, with hundreds of deaths on newspaper pages daily, strict rationing, buying war bonds, saving grease from your frying pan, tinfoil from gum wrappers.

Following that impossible-to-forget war by only a few years occurred a tank-led blitzkrieg invasion into the southern half of a small politically divided country in far away Asia. One should not ever forget this war is still smoldering, especially when the aggressor threatens us with the fifth largest Army in the world, benefiting from short supply lines, brought up-to-date with the latest nuclear armament.

Korea was already forgotten when the highly publicized, bitterly denounced Vietnam War took over the news. When the Korean War broke out less than a fourth of Americans had television. Eighty percent saw the Vietnam War, bringing the fury of combat into living rooms everywhere by the latest broadcasting device. Of even greater sustained fear and interest, also brought to the home front, was the stealthy terror of the up-and-down Cold War with constant threats of worldwide destruction, individual gas masks, backyard bomb shelters, enemy missiles ninety miles from Miami, intercontinental ballistic missiles prepared to blast the nation's capitol. Korea, what's that?

What follows is not about nations at war. It is a down-to-earth rifle platoon leader's journal begun in 1952 while memory was still exciting but put away for what I felt was the need for collaboration. In truth I had not been able to settle my troubled mind nor had I learned to write. That was half a century ago when I decided this must not be a one-sided account. For instance, it was embarrassing and seemingly untrue to state, as I found myself doing, even though justified by enormous pride, that I took Fools Mountain (Hill 1179) on the Punchbowl in the south of North Korea. Although no other officer other than fellow platoon leaders can boast of having been there that day, Artillery and

10

Air softened the objective to the extent that the press nicknamed it the Five-million Dollar Hill, before men of my company and I overran it.

Having since 1994 located survivors of that uphill battle, nameless they need no longer be. Together we conquered 1179 on the Punchbowl, and two even more difficult ones.

Pride it rightfully is, for this platoon leader had the responsibility as acting company commander to line up attackers to make the assault; supervise supporting artillery, mortars, heavy machine guns, recoilless rifles, large and small, whatever could be thrown against enemy positions, positioning himself close behind the lead platoon where he could inspire and control upward progress and momentum and assess continually the whole ever moving operation, stopping occasionally to advise the battalion commander trying to follow us with his powerful BC, battalion commander's scope.

On this particular attack on Hill 1179, alias Taeusan, Gateway to the Orient, on the early morning of 29 July 1951 Korean time, in desperation I doubled and wrapped a bright red air panel around my helmet and tied it with commo wire for there was some confusion as to whether or not we would be getting an air strike whether we wanted one or not. In May 1952, it was my word alone that this unusual event occurred, but since 1994 men who recall my bright red hat are resurrected by name.

In 1994 I discovered by accident the Second Division Association and its Korean War Alliance with a roster of survivors. Although WWII vets like me are dropped every printing or so, others, via telephone-tracking computer were being located. Only then, when I contacted more than a dozen buddies who shared memories of combat with me was I confident to sit again at a typewriter and arrange what we all recalled, as accurately as we can after half a century of forgetting.

Most veterans were of no help since they spent the intervening years trying to forget; others had little to relate because they had simply outlived their memories. A minority, like me, nurtured memories over time with great pride and retained good, often vivid, memories of the bulk of what transpired.

Example of the former: John W Glisson, Andrews, South Carolina, who packed a SCR 300 (Signal Corps Radio) in February

11

1951 for F Company at Hoengsong, being overrun in summer uniforms by Chinks in the terrible cold; later, hit bad on Heartbreak, spent time in the 278th Osaka General Hospital before being reassigned to artillery. John got out of the Army just as soon as duration allowed and went to work for the International Paper Company until retiring in 1988. He told me how anxiously he examines each *Morning Report* survivor roster from the Korean War Alliance, searching for a name he can recall. So far, he says he's sad not to recognize any of the buddies he suffered so much with and would I mind, when contacting Fox Company men of 1951, asking if any remember Johnny Glisson who packed the company 300. I don't remember Johnny myself but I was in Fox a very short while and the only company radioman I remember there was killed early one morning with Captain Poston.

The survivor roster grew slowly and also shrank as I was forced to commiserate with new widows, learning sorrowfully of buddies during the dying years of eighties and nineties succumbing to cancer, strokes, or overtired hearts, pining to hear from comrades in arms. We, all of us hoary veterans near to life's ending, are being reacquainted with Death, who once needed no introduction.

At least two buddies died at Audie Murphy VA Hospital unknown to me, although only a few miles from where I live. I cry for them belatedly, in vain and apologize over and over. We just didn't know how near we were to one another and so reachable. None of us knew how to find the sequence of numbers that could bring us together again.

"How Johnny would have loved to hear your voice," Mrs. Warnock of Kansas City remarked one painful night over the phone. "I wish you'd called a month sooner, before Johnny's stroke; he often talked about you, Lieutenant Gould.... I'm so awfully sorry."

"I'm more sorry, Mrs. Warnock."

I was in much better shape in 1994 than 1952 to write this chronicle for I retired from the Army and after fifteen years as publications editor of a large Chicago-based technical society, retired on Social Security. I became a widower hermit in 1985 with enough physical disability to keep me in a wheelchair researching and writing memoirs of my days in combat and colonial American military histories.

With living buddies to jiggle my memory and back me up, I

pulled out the yellowing copy of the 1952 draft and banged away at a substantiated journal on a more modern typewriter, spending hours and hours on the telephone, which, though up to $400 a month, is cheap research for such a book as this.

I served in Fox and Love companies of the 38th, Rock of the Marne, and was P&A, pioneer and ammunition, platoon leader at Third Battalion headquarters, in all but Love Company briefly.

Forty-five years erodes lots of memory and there were bound to be polite misunderstandings. Example: A Bobby Estes of Magolin, California, retired Air Force E-8, fellow Korean War Veterans Alliance member, tells me that he was acting platoon leader of my platoon, the Third Platoon of Love while I led Love Company to take 1179. We argued back and forth a bit and gave up. I don't doubt Bobby's word but do not recall him. We are even—he doesn't remember me though I led the company that bloody day. His is among many episodes I and my correspondents evidently did forget, for such is the cursed memory loss in the passing of half a century. Then, too, my attention the day of that great battle was directed elsewhere than on my old platoon.

Facts are facts and they come forth directly, uncontrived, only by the angle of delivery sometimes altered a little. Except for composites for readability, I need not substitute pseudonyms for enlisted men I knew, who served magnificently, at times maligned.

I am lucky to work closely with wonderful guys from all over the country who, knowing full well the odds were that they had a good chance of ending up in one of the large American military cemeteries in Korea decided in their honor they would put on a noble performance en route, and I have been blessed to reclaim friendship with two of my platoon medics over there, one being, before he was promoted to SFC and moved up to battalion, survivor Bill Maddox of North Little Rock, Arkansas; and one of my best riflemen, Bill Miller, retired truck driver of Clarence, Oklahoma. Also on the survivor *Morning Report*, among others, is West Pointer, US Navy seaman in World War II, then infantry lieutenant, John Fox, retired colonel, loving life and teaching college at Trenton, New Jersey. He inadvertently saved my life with his evasion and escape lecture, although he has no reason to remember me. And there is Tom M Miller, Oakmont, Pennsylvania, no relation to Bill, a brave young private who earned a Silver Star the hard way as only enlisted men did.

There to exchange happy greetings over the phone was former SP4 Myles Carlson, lucky of luckies, my last medic. Doc recalls one of our living nightmares during the monsoon when, after the machine gunner's bunker caved in, I pushed broken ribs into his lungs—gurgling, bloody foam from his nostrils—as I used the old manner of artificial respiration trying to resuscitate him, laid out on his stomach on the litter in the rain near my bunker. I'll never forget that crime, particularly since Myles warned me against it. No consolation, but Ich's neck was broken anyway, which I would have noticed had there been more light. Surely, it seems some days, given the prolonged tragedies we survived, too many of us are here to answer the morning report.

At thirty-one, a recalled reservist, I was the oldest in my company to climb mountains, dodge enemy fire, and rove the line with my platoon sergeant nights and days and it has been near half a century since I led the Third Platoon, Love Company, and Love Company itself, 38th Infantry Regiment, US Second, Second to None (Indianhead) Infantry Division, X Corps, US Eighth Army, Korea (EUSAK), United Nations Command, good guys, determined volunteers of the Regular Army, recalled Reserves, National Guardsmen and unhappy, sacrificing draftees, lined up over hills, mountains and valleys against those who 'statesmen' under Washington's domes warned were bad, gooks and Chinks. We called the Chinese "Chinks."

We found them touchy, bad as we were bad, taught to kill and never yield, men of a so-called yellow complexion, initially innocent as were we when we arrived, my men and I, enlisted, drafted or recalled against our wishes; forced like us to become hardened murderers.

So dramatic were the days of *Follow Me Up Fools Mountain,* there's no need to exaggerate. In any event, there is enough unintended disinformation in the pages of our official blue-bound history book to fulfill that need for fiction wherein our battalion was concerned. Printed in Japan, the *Second to None History of the US Army Second Division 1950-51 in Korea*, specifically quotes from X Corps exaggerating the numbers we were supposed to have killed with small arms.

Some old-timers wanted replacements to think they were calloused, desensitized to death; personally, I continued to be shocked every time at life's most violent ending, the absolute appalling, instantaneous difference between life and death in the same man's face drained of blood. In two wars I never became inured to or felt at ease in the presence of combat's horrible crimes. Facing uncomfortably the hideous frozen smirk of a guy lying broken on the ground, I would glance for a fast identification and more quickly look away and start talking about something else and was never one to coldly examine a corpse, especially a guy I knew. He died there for me; let him be, is there no dignity? To me, cadavers I was forced to look at in civilian life, our neighbor Mr. Easton and my mother, were cruel caricatures; horrible interruptions to living. But there also seems a quiet comfort in the death of old ones, an unquestionable necessity in death's termination, when led that way by the determined life span of man. Those who die peaceful deaths get there on their own.

Most field grade officers I served were somewhat older and crossed over the river some time ago. I've been able to contact two. One I knew casually as Lieutenant Colonel Edward L Rowny, 38th regiment exec, now of Alexandria, Virginia, who once sent me a personal note of congratulation telling me what a good platoon leader I was as he stepped in to endorse my Silver Star. I was greeted on the phone by a butler: "Good evening, sir. This is the residence of Ambassador, retired Lieutenant General Edward L. Rowny. Who may I say is calling?"

Rowny and I talked stiff-legged very briefly, an ambassador to a former lieutenant, after he lied how good it was to hear from an 'old comrade in arms.' As far as I can remember, Rowny never carried arms. He always seemed, since Lieutenant General Almond sent him to regiment from X Corps for combat on his record, to have been only diplomatic. After about three minutes on both calls, he cut me off, apologizing for being so preoccupied. I could tell he hadn't recalled me at all, nor made any effort to.

As for combat buddies, I spent more than half an hour at a time on the phone with terrific sixty- and seventy-year-old PFCs and sergeants. We'd suffered combat together on the wild ridges and held it in common to reminisce, trying almost desperately to be young again. "Well, Bill, enjoyed our chat, be hearing from me."

15

"Say, lieutenant, how about Woody? Remember him?"

"I'll say I do. I'm putting him in *Follow Me.*"

"Don't forget that ball-busting climb from the Pia-ri Valley."

"Sh-e-e-it, who could?"

Meshed with my personal rifle platoon leader's journal are pertinent excerpts passed along from the official history of the Second Division to give it backbone, but which, among other things, ommissively perpetuates the lie that our battalion of the 38th was withdrawn before 15 May 1951 from our outpost-patrol base, even though it's a depressing fact Chinese overran us. I should know, I was forced to play dead on that tragic knob as buddies in two companies were viciously gunned down after surrendering. If an order to withdraw ever was sent, it got no further than battalion. The cruel fact is that although both battalion and company headquarters pulled back the three miles to the MLR (main line of resistance) without loss, we were left in the open, a long nail on a sore thumb.

Infantry combat is a rapid series of still pictures strung together, one etched cruelly in the memory of former rifleman Joe Layne, retired truck driver of Coalmont, Tennessee. On 29 August 1951, a perimeter guard on Fool's Mountain on the Punchbowl, he and his holemate were wounded by a gook hand grenade just after dawn, he in the guts, his buddy in the chest. Lying there bleeding internally, Joe has no memory of being placed on a litter. The last he recalls is holding his buddy's hand in the slowly growing light, patting the back of it, assuring him as he himself drifted in and out of consciousness, that everything would be all right, until the hand grew cool and stiff.

Buddy of ours, Master Sergeant Elmer L Falconburg of Jerome, Idaho, communications chief at Headquarters Company, third Battalion, was taken by Chinks near Hoengsong, along with thirty or so comrades, all of whom were released and herded south. For two nights they were corraled under a threatening machine gun and on the third day reached the US Marines. Elmer could never figure out why such good treatment, enemy guiding and guarding their march some forty miles to freedom, finally standing on a knoll above them gesturing where their friends would be found.

Contrast this with the experiences of Corporal Bernard Goldman, radioman, of Milwaukie, Oregon, taken with other Love Company men the same frozen day near Hoengsong, lined up along a gully by a Chinese colonel, a graduate of the University of Washington he bragged, who solved his prisoner burden a different way, telling them in perfect English, "I am sorry, men, we do not have food or men to guard you, so we will shoot every other one of you." Whereupon, the man on either side of Bernard was shot in the face with a captured US Army forty-five pistol, reloaded as the executioner strode down the ranks. Weak, frightened, half-starved, half-frozen survivors, Bernie and his remaining buddies were deserted the following day by their reluctant captor, withdrawing in a hurry from the clank, clank tread rattle of our tanks.

Combat was like that—and many other things.

Most of my older fellow officers and sergeants have passed on but not only did I take notes of phone conversations with twenty-seven survivors, I mailed drafts of *Follow Me* to buddies who shared combat and the in-between-times with me; who made suggestions and corrections to keep this story especially true and complete. They were Karl Eppler of Venice, Florida, retired procurement officer of Chrysler Corporation, my former platoon sergeant; Myles Carlson, my last platoon medic, retired school teacher at Joliet, Illinois; Conely Clarke, author and gentleman farmer from Hickory, South Carolina, whose POW experiences, *Journey Through Shadow*, were so controversial and true, written right after POWs got home, he had to publish it on his own. From his moment of capture to release, it is far and away the best unexpurgated account I have read of the adventures of POWs anywhere.

Another reviewer is John Pater who fought King Company while I fought Love, relieving one another on the Punchbowl through several important attacks. John was invalided out of the service in '51 after being sorely wounded. He is now 85, living in pain south of me at Weslaca, Texas. I hope he lives to read this.

Friends and relatives of those young warriors who served the Indianhead unto death in faraway Korea, those long, frightful days and ever-watchful nights, so cruelly shortened, work hard to understand that they remain spiritually alive in an energy linked to the great power of

17

cosmoses; physically, in atoms here and there and everywhere part of the divine force that sends worlds whirling through black-velvet space, stars zipping across our lefts and our rights; brilliant lights through our dark age of mankind, living things on our tiny earth, bound to atomic nuclei, producing vast new sets of catapulting quantum-jumping particles, forms of matter never registered, never sensed, made of yet more fundamental particles than we know of, and have departed from here to everywhere with their souls; gone forever, echoing forever and ever away, soldiers of the Forgotten War who live forever.

—dudley c gould, 2002
San Antonio, Texas
Silver Star, Soldier's Medal,
Bronze Star, Purple Heart

1
Baptism

As a reserve infantry officer I did nothing until December 1949 when I was told by letter in so many words to shit or get off the pot. Commit myself; if I didn't attend weekly classes at the Army Reserve Center, take extension courses to bring myself up-to-date on Infantry matters. I was working second shift at a foundry in Syracuse, building a house part-time and subscribed to a military justice correspondence course, for which, because of absolute lack of interest, I was graded unsatisfactory. There were months when I did nothing to satisfy my obligations, neither took courses from Fort Benning or attended classes at the reserve center, and I was threatened with expulsion, which failed to motivate me; after all, Army plans for us Reserves were dulled by peace, and for reasons favorable to the US Army expulsion never came about. Kitty took a very mild interest in my tenuous association with the Army and considered it a waste of time.

"All those bad things you told me, didn't you get enough in World War II?"

As the war, excuse me, Police Action, in Korea progressed unsatisfactorily for our side, I attended eight weekly classes in a row. Per diem pay wasn't high enough to attract any below master sergeant and almost all of us were low-ranking officers and master sergeants. Some would come at seven in the evening, sign in for the pay, sip a coffee, gossip and take off with a couple doughnuts provided generously by our Regular Army instructor.

Paid reserve meetings were supposed to last two hours one night a week but usually broke up or faded away after an hour. Most field grade officers, scheming for promotion or potential politicos, were businessmen or local leaders, as Lieutenant Colonel Persons, AFL union boss.

Most supported rather large bellies that made it awkward to appear in uniform any more, as our Regular Army man, Major Fryer, begged us to do at meetings. "Act like soldiers," he whined. In their tight uniforms were minor businessmen and petty executives, officious and self-important shop owners, insurance salesmen, attorneys, and a couple of bank employees. Only two wore combat infantryman badges.

There were two aside from me who hadn't gone soft in civilian life, who engaged in physical work and were therefore unpromotable officers.

I trained some weeks and then did not for several months. Beginning in 1950, those of us whose MOS, military occupational specialty, was 1542, infantry unit commander, began soon to receive a letter a week from the First Army Reserve Center, 90 Church Street, New York, telling us how badly we were needed in Korea and, with the Puson perimeter only thirty-five miles from the Pusan seaport, would we please apply for active duty.

As I struggled to make a home of the unpainted walls and second-hand furniture of our house, I reacted to what had, without me really knowing it, become my hope for a return to what I never accomplished in WW II: proving myself a man, at least earning a combat infantryman badge. So, in response to weekly pleas by the Army Reserve I broke down a week after returning from summer camp and wrote a letter volunteering to return to active duty.

With my first application, I took Major Fryer's advice and began looking for a buyer for our unfinished house.

"You'll get orders any day, lieutenant. They need you Reserve guys bad over there."

"Don't I know. I get letters from the Reserve Center at 90 Church Street and Benning all the time, and look how the Chinese shot through Seoul. They might drive us off the peninsula."

"Sell our home, you crazy?" Kitty cried. "Sell our home after all that separation and scrimping and hard work; you're out of your head."

When she found out why I wanted to sell so soon, she broke out sobbing and turned away. "You've changed since summer camp," she sobbed. I never dreamed in my worst nightmare you'd do anything like this. Not without saying a thing to me; without thinking of Dickie and me, what we'd think. You must have gone crazy. One minute you loved us and the very next you want to get away from us. Don't you love Dickie and me?"

She paused, sobbing, wiping tears on the back of her arm. "Dudley, I don't understand why you prefer the Army to us and your home; didn't you get enough in the Army killing all them people?"

"It wasn't that bad," I confessed. "I laid it on a little, actually I didn't get to kill very many, well, to be honest, none. As to preferring the Army and the guys, you're a woman and wouldn't understand."

It was hard to sell our house, hard to find a buyer, but eventually we did and then moved in with my inlaws

While waiting for the late New York Central Empire Express headed west to Buffalo, Kitty and I sat on her mother's davenport drinking, listening to the big bands on the late night radio, kissing, hugging and feeling each other. When her folks went upstairs, at one point we tore off a piece and swore undying allegiance to each other as I formally charged her with the responsibility of missing me.

"We can get along without you," I was informed.

After a few more drinks, she started sobbing, blaming me for wanting to go, volunteering without talking it over and deserting her and our eleven-month-old son. I explained what could I do. I was recalled involuntarily and we argued a little and then kissed and made up and then argued some more and, half polluted on vodka collins, kissed and made up and tore off another piece.

At Lawton I turned in my bag and civilian clothes and drew infantry field garb and as our bags were secured by metal tape and locked in storage, we said good bye to civilization. Here I go to the war in Korea, in a class of thirty-five recalled reservists collected at Fort Lawton, Seattle for processing and refresher infantry training at nearby Fort Lewis prior to shipping to Korea.

The group included a Signal Corps captain who amazed us with tales of bouncing radio waves from cloud formations behind Japanese lines in China, a Baptist captain chaplain who borrowed ordnance brass before hitting a neighborhood bar every night and a short, fat draftee doctor pediatrician from Washington, D.C. we nicknamed Cannonball.

On arriving at the end of the line in Korea, I was assigned to Fox Company, 38th Infantry, US Second Infantry Division, West Pointer Captain Poston commanding and two weeks later transferred to L Company, then short of officers.

We were in division reserve training and for reasons unknown, I was selected over nominated officers from the two sister regiments for duty at division forward as liaison officer to the Seventh Division headquarters, thirty kilometers on our right flank.

I wrote Kitty I had the war knocked, which I did for nine days until the Seventh, the Hour Glass Division, headed out west overnight to block for the US Marines after the breakthrough of the defenses of the British Commonwealth 27th Brigade on their west. Then the Fifth ROKs pulled west to guard our flank and a KMAG, Korean Military Advisory Group—what they themselves called Kiss My Ass Goodbye— captain took over my liaison job.

My job was to worm my way up to the Seventh's huge plastic situation overlay maps in the Seventh's war room tent showing the fighting front fifty miles east and west, a smaller map for intelligence reports and incidents, and make my own scaled-down overlay of pertinent information, showing positions of all known units, Chinese, ROK and American. When map changes were being made, I stood back out of the way and watched and listened. All-in-all, what with the drive each way over a dirt road, it was a tough job.

Driving my jeep back to the Second Division late one afternoon, I ended up somehow in a convoy of a battery of the big tractor-drawn pieces of the 555th, all-black 155mm artillery who lost their guns twice in furious combats. With the enormous weight and vibrations on the makeshift Korean back road, they not only threw dirt clods high into the air but such a thick cloud of red dust I was hardly able to see the tail light of the piece in front of me, none of it if I dropped back a few feet. I know this fact all too well for I scared the hell out of myself once by dropping back too far leaving nothing but a cloud to follow. The huge artillery tractor drivers' seats were five feet higher than in my jeep, my windshield covered with red dust and I was forced to peek around it, which, even with road goggles, was hard on the eyes. And I had to steer with one hand, wiping my goggles with the back of the other.

The road was newly rough-graded by Army engineers and like so many in wild Korea, a cliff was on one side and a drop-off to a small river on the other. Our convoy rattled along at 55 mph, headlights and tail lights on, twisting and sometimes turning rather suddenly and had one of the Black drivers slowed a bit too much, he'd lose his bearings and go off the road, either into the drainage ditch on our right or through the air way down to the river. Had he suddenly exceeded 55 mph, the huge tractor following might have lost the sole guidance of his taillights and would at the first unpredictable road bend have shot into the air out over the river far below.

The race went on about four miles and when we finally slowed, the monsters pulled to the side of a wider valley road. I stopped on the shoulder about a quarter of a mile ahead of the first vehicle, shut off my engine and shook uncontrollably on the steering wheel for a good five minutes. Brother Dante had no worse a ride in hell.

Another day, about a mile from the turnoff to the Second Division forward command post, I entered a wide ford, shallow except in the very middle. The three or four days I made the trip I'd been lucky enough to draft one supply truck or another, that is, get in close enough to his rear to ride through the more shallow water produced by his wake. This time, I went charging alone over the ford until my foot, with all the distracting bumpity bumping over rocks, slipped off the accelerator and stalled the engine smack in the middle with water running over the top of my seat. I sat there for two hours while one truck after another, about six in all, bypassed me, saluting sarcastically, "Hi lieutenant!" Finally, a 2½-ton pulled in front and its driver jumped down, sloshing through the water to run a large hook over my front bumper and pull me to freedom. I couldn't thank him enough. He explained I had to run the ford at a steady rate to keep the water blown out of the exhaust pipe and first disconnect the fan belt. (After Korea the M38 jeep was built with a snorkel to prevent water blocking the exhaust.)

I was half an hour late for the general's briefing, still obviously wet from the waist down, and caught angry looks from Lieutenant Colonel Foster, my G2 boss.

Object of my liaison trips was to keep Major General Clark Ruffner, division commander of the Second, informed daily of the situation, operations and intelligence, and all major plans to his right flank. I was part of the 1800 hour briefing by his staff. Neither division was engaged with enemy and the most exciting matters to report were sightings of Chinese line crossers, spies and saboteurs disguised in the white garb of Korean civilians. Once I was handed a button for Colonel Foster, which enemy agents in Korean garb sewed certain places to authenticate one another.

War began for me with a Chinese buildup after I returned from my liaison job to Love Company, Third battalion of the 38th Regiment. Some readers may recall the first step of the enemy's Fifth Phase to re-capture Seoul and cut off United Nations troops. Seoul was saved but the eastern flank of Eighth Army's line across Korea was forced to pull back. Roll with the punch, they said.

Only for the days when I was liaison to the Seventh Division did I glimpse the big picture, otherwise every setback or success to our division plans, unless we were in it, was a total surprise. To strengthen my personal account and support it with an official chronology, I will quote now and then from our division official, blue-bound history book, from July 1950 to October 1951, printed in Japan in November 1951, referred to from here on as the Blue Book, my corrections or comments in brackets —

General James A. Van Fleet assumed command of the Eighth Army on 13 April, relieving Lieutenant General Matthew B. Ridgway who had gone to Tokyo to become Supreme Commander of Allied Powers, following the dismissal of General Douglas MacArthur by President Truman.

Preparation and occupation of the Noname Line was complete on 30 April. The Third, Blue Battalion, of the 38th, in order to keep contact with the enemy, moved forward of the line and set up an advance patrol base [my battalion three miles in front of the MLR, main line of resistance] with L and K companies reporting minor contacts during that time. To the west of the Second Division sector, were strong spearheads of communist buildup areas, particularly in the Iron Triangle. The 9th and 23rd continued training and girding themselves for the test which seemed imminent. Preparation of defenses on the Noname Line began on 27 April as the 38th Infantry moved into position. And, although pressure against the entire front began slacking off on the 27th all nontactical equipment impedimenta was sent south. Division artillery moved up into new positions from which it could mass its fires anywhere in front of the new defensive line.

The 23rd Regiment commenced its withdrawal on 28 April together with the elements of Task force Zebra, passing through the 38th Infantry which had its First, Second and Dutch battalions on the Noname Line with the third battalion in reserve. The 9th moving from Corps and Division reserve went forward to the 38th.

Further knowledge of enemy movements was limited as haze and smoke from grass fires continued to obscure the vision of air observers. Division liaison pilots, ranging far behind enemy lines in their thin metal-covered L-19 Piper Cubs had little to report.

April closed with the Division digging into position to meet whatever new moves might be brewing under screening smog which blanketed movements of the enemy lurking, still powerful, in the north.

The Division front on the night of 13 May was manned, from left to right, by the 9th Infantry, two battalions of the 38th Infantry and Task Force Zebra. [Our battalion still on outpost three miles ahead of this line.] The 23rd Infantry designated as Corps Reserve, had its French Battalion at Hangye as Division Reserve, prepared to counterattack anywhere in the Division sector. The second Battalion was with Task Force Zebra, having *relieved the French Battalionon 12 May.*

Patrols continued throughout the 14th with stiff resistance encountered in the vicinity of Hill 699. Air observers, late in the afternoon of the 14th, reported masses of enemy troops moving southeastward along a trail between Nae-yongni and Saojti-ri, headed for the Second Division positions. Immediately the entire 503d Artillery Battalion, two batteries of the 196th and one battery of the 38th Field Artillery Battalion were shifted to cover the area and opened fire with heavy concentrations.

The CCF, Chinese Communist Forces, a peasant Army of illiterates, a *jen hai*, human sea, endless columns of earth-brown, cotton, padded-quilt figures turning back from their overall unsuccessful attacks were spotted dog-trotting on mountain valley roads north and east of Seoul out of range of heavy artillery, headed our way, leaving thousands of dead, gunned down from the air, poorly concealed in hastily scraped graves on the fast-warming hill and mountain sides.

A grim joke went the rounds: "A worried Chinese top general, Lin Piao, head of the Fourth Field Army's eighteen divisions, reported to Mao Tse-tung, 'We lost 5000 men today, a regiment and a half.' 'And how many Americans were killed?' Mao asked. 'Five hundred,' was the reply. This went on several weeks, every day thousands of Chinks killed to a few hundred Americans, until the end of the month when the figure for their dead was 50,000 to 1800 Americans. 'Good,' smiled Mao, 'soon no more Americans.'"

Second Division claimed to have inflicted 37,750 casualties on the enemy by May 21, while understating our own losses at 900. Such claims were accepted uncritically by the eye-to-Congress Pentagon. At a military briefing of ambassadors of those nations with forces in Korea, the Pentagon officially put enemy losses for the three-day period May 17 to May 20 at 67,800, of which, the Pentagon briefer stated, 36,000 were killed and 31,800 wounded. This proportion is impossible, close to one-to-one, when the average in a bitterest close-in combat through history is seldom more than one-killed-to-four-wounded, as in the extremely bitter battle on Breed's (Bunker) Hill.

The Blue Book—

The 20th and 27th Armies of Ninth Army Group of a 400,000-man Chinese Communist Fourth Field Army shifted eastward from positions west of Chunchon in the early days of May, moving well-indoctrinated yellow men from the wide plains of China, heavily laden, obedient animals on two legs. Three more powerful armies, the 12th, 15th and 60th of the Third CCF Army Group poured into newly captured Chorwan as weary GIs watched from afar wormlike columns crawling fast through mountain valleys; long lines of dilapidated trucks captured from Chiang Chek's Army and lately Americans in Korea, and supplies on bicycles and the backs of hairy Mongolian ponies. Repeated airings of the Peking radio bragged that this time the Indianheads would be annihilated, even as the Gloucesters. Political leaders, lower echelon commissars, peddled alongside those pushing burdened bicycles, haranguing, telling of great victories soon to come, warning them to conserve their light rations of dried corn, fried flour cakes, kaoliang and rice; hardening their resolves with lies of upcoming fleets of airplanes, masses of tanks soon to support their drive.

Our men, 'the good guys,' dug in along the crest of a great rugged hill mass separated by the Hongchon and Soyang rivers; part of the left flank, with lower trails level enough to introduce tanks. The First Battalion of the 38th occupied part of the left flank, extending about two miles to the Second Battalion anchored on Hill 809.

Battalion outpost bases were established on salient positions ahead of the MLR to push combat patrols ten miles north to the Soyang river. When I returned to Love Company, our Third Battalion was pulling this outpost duty, with a platoon from each company alternating daily combat patrols.

From 8 May on, the Chinks showed increasingly more reluctance to withdraw and disperse as we called in heavy long-range artillery and air strikes to blast their underwater bridges. By 10 May the buildup increased dramatically and they resisted our combat patrols aggressively. Air reported much greater enemy traffic. Chink patrols behind our lines were numerous and dangerous and there came to us a sudden flow of

27

terrified white-clad civilian refugees, intermingled with white-clad line crossers.

From this time on to the bitter end of my service in Korea, in our rugged, isolated, roadless mountain terrains, all equipment, tools, barbed wire, mines, commo wire, etc., along with weapons, ammunition, C rations and water, had to be backpacked or A-framed up often very slippery and dangerous foot paths from hills into mountains over half a mile high. The Blue Book states—

Harried intelligence officers at every level struggled to piece together the puzzle which faced them. Curling east and south through the rugged hills and mountains our Air Force reported a great buildup and Peking radio increased its boasts to wipe out the Indianheads. Feverish preparations were made to place the Division into positions from which to absorb the coming attack. The 155 mm 96th Field Artillery battalion was put in direct support of the Division and operation plans at all levels based on every conceivable emergency. A special Roger Line was established 4000 yards forward of the constantly improving Noname Line of Eighth Army. The 9th made company-size attacks from the Roger Line and, meeting practically no resistance, occupied Hill 899 five miles from Chunchon.

Old timers worried we'd be clobbered good this time, harder even than at Kunu-ri where the Second Division took 5000 casualties and had to be pulled behind Army reserve areas and rebuilt. That was November 1950 after Chinks first appeared in North Korea. Intelligence told us that this time there were twice as many. Night reconnaissance planes, crisscrossing X Corps's front, flying low, returned film that revealed traffic of heavy wheeled vehicles, many taken from UN positions, particularly ROKs, whereas last November supplies of forward units were almost all carried on bicycle trailers or Mongolian ponies. Air was unable to pierce the heavy morning fogs and mists covering deep valleys that the sun wouldn't light until high noon. After the fogs lifted, Chinks fired smoke pots, lit grass fires and repaired low bombed-out bridges overnight.

In mid-May there was thrown at Eighth Army the heaviest assault of the war, 762,000 infantry and artillery, 551,000 Chinks, 211,000 gooks—96,000 Chinks against the 38th and our Dutch Battalion alone. Unknown to us, the 15th division of the Fourth CCF Field Army was to make a frontal assault on our battalion outpost. We wouldn't have worried had we known, for we had every right to assume we'd pull back and indeed it was made known that our outpost, with no more patrolling to do, would soon be pulled in as had all outposts west of us with the massive enemy thrust rolling our way.

The Blue Book continues—

The Chinese decided to open a wide breech in Noname Line stretching across the Korean neck and the 60th Army would pass through in column and fan out to the flanks in a thundering assault, hammering with its 12th Army—twelve full-strength infantry divisions screaming out of the night in a concentrated move to annihilate the Indianheads. Following them were 4th, 35th, 44th, 181st, 80th and 81st divisions. After it was over, dead from the Chinese 29th, 179th, 180th and 79th divisions were also identified.

By 0230 hours, 15 May 1951, reckless attacks by the enemy overwhelmed positions of Love and King companies of the 38th Infantry, a regiment of the US Army Second Infantry Division, X Corps, Eighth US Army of the United Nations Command in Korea (EUSAK). [Unmentioned was the fact that we were still on an outpost three miles in front of the MLR.] As dusk began to settle, the tempo of the battle sharpened as reports from across the front revealed increasingly numerous clashes and focused attention on the worsening situation to the east where units of the Fifth ROKs were falling back.

The daylight hours of 15 May saw all the usual signs of impending enemy attack, including an increased number of enemy agents trying to slip through the lines. Air patrols reported more bridge construction, and enemy probing attacks grew more numerous. Van Fleet's command made ready to stand firm. The night of 15-16 May, Communists launched a preliminary attack

29

against the Fifth ROK Division on the Second Division's right flank. An enemy force, trying to infiltrate between Task Force Zebra and the 38th Regiment, walked directly into the blocking positions of the Ivanhoe Security Force. And, although the determined Chinese pressed their attack until daylight, they were forced to withdraw and were observed moving into the village of Hachon which was immediately subjected to a heavy artillery concentration.

The attack in the ROK sector was launched at 0300 hours on the 15th and continued throughout the day. By 1800 hours, the entire ROK front was under heavy attack and all units forced from their positions. Withdrawing south of the Inje-Hongchon road, ROKs laid bare the entire east flank of the Second Division, and as this threat developed, contact patrols from the 38th Infantry and Task Force Zebra, reaching out after beating off attacks of the previous night, quickly encountered enemy groups, withdrew and called for artillery to break up the concentrations they had discovered.

By nightfall of the 15th it was apparent the long-expected offensive had begun. Later intelligence reports revealed the full extent of the assault. Three Chinese Armies rolled forward in the Second Division zone. The 12th aimed to penetrate the ROK positions on the right then turned in behind the Indianhead Division and enveloped the right flank. The 15th Chinese Army was to make the frontal assault then split and move onto the flanks while the 60th CCF Army passed through in a column of divisions.

On 15 May 1951, the day we were overrun, hauling heavy loads of ammo both ways, it was our platoon's turn to try to keep Chinks from finishing an underwater bridge over the shallow Soyang-gang (Soyang river) where I had my first taste of abject fear.

Combat, I found, is a shock every time, never to become more familiar than an unexpected ice cold shower. A battle, combatants working hard to kill each another, is always routine hysteria evoked by sheer terror and threat of harm and death causing bodily malfunctions.

30

It begins with complete surprise no matter how long before you knew it was coming. Terror to your entire person, fatal to your faltering ego, your little entirety; no way to prepare for such emotional commotion, what Karl von Clausewitz called realm of confusion. Suddenly, too late, you discover there is no preparation for this debilitating horror, the strange, ugly, all-powerful sensations. You stand, if your rubbery legs will allow, or crouch shaking, seeming naked there in a faraway land; the why escapes you, feeling you have to do with what you were trained all your young years not to do, piss or shit your pants, crawl into a hole and hide, scream and throw away your rifle that attracts them to you and run like hell for the safety of the rear, behind the tanks and artillery, way back down the main supply road somewhere where the big tents are.

Suddenly you are alone with no way to understand what is the powerful paralyzing happening or do nothing but call God, whose main job now is serving you; none but Him to listen as you beg for your life; nothing but keep calling on God. God help me! No appeal to anyone lower will help. Obviously your platoon leader is not up to it. It takes a god to get you out of this terrible thing. Call for God, if you have one and if you are Agnostic like me, appeal to your lucky stars or some all-powerful force as yet undisclosed. Then when you're actually penetrated by a bullet or hunk of shrapnel, skip God and yell for your on-hand savior, the platoon medic. "MEDIC! MEDIC! God's sake, DOC, save me! Stop my blood!"

Soon as this ripping electricity you never suspected existed has torn and shocked your body, somehow you must remind yourself you are *the* rifle platoon leader on whom others depend, supposedly their leader because they are even less prepared than you who has studied all about it at infantry OCS. Everything but how to control fear reaction.

"C'mon guys, c'mon, let's go!" Run that ugly gauntlet of debilitating fear, let's go! Safeties off, one in the chamber, let's get 'em. "Get 'em. Careful they don't get you first."

Approaching our objective, our platoon was caught by a Chink machine gun in an open field away from cover. We hit the dirt; that is, pressed down as low as possible and every time one of us made a visible move, the gunner let loose, sweeping back and forth to cut the weeds above our heads. You could reach up your helmet and scoop it full of bullets. Good for us the gunner couldn't lower his muzzle and swerve down to our level.

My body trembled helplessly, anticipating a blow from what whizzed and whined over my head, a sudden fearful sound to end me. I froze as low as I could, learning what an earthworm does, understanding for the first time the protection and comfort Mother Earth offers the desperate; hugging her without moving any of me up an eighth of an inch; unable even to think of giving orders, praying without thought as, I confess, properly frightened Agnostics do from habit acquired in childhood. Sergeant Ulriche would emerge as our leader, which, of course, he actually would have to be until I learned to control my fear reaction and got some combat under my belt, should I live that long.

Fully frightened, the guys hugged the bottom of what scant declination each had, some old-timers turning around low down accusingly on elbows to appraise me. When my brain was able to work, it was to express my helplessness over and over to myself with the phrase, 'What to do? What to do?' Not until I sensed the guys were thoroughly disgusted with their new officer could I force control over my automatic violent fear reaction with Ulriche's help as he shouted from a hundred yards behind, testing me, "What you want us to do?"

God, what a joy hearing his confident, commanding voice.

"Hell, man, you're the veteran. What *do* we do?"

"Yeah, Lieutenant, but I ain't in charge." Then having established supremacy, he went on, "Now if I was you, with that there radio, I'd get some artillery. If I'm not mistaken, we got 155s on call that can reach past us. Have them throw over a few. Give the underwater bridge azimuth, concentration one zero, first and then FO (forward observer) it back, bring it in twenty-five increments at a time. Have them throw a few and walk them back toward us, and while the Chinks are busy we'll bug out."

"Git some good news on that thing of yours," he ordered our radioman.

Hearing Sergeant Ulriche, the guys relaxed, cat-calling around to their buddies, discharging the energy that stunned them, dammed up by fear.

Half an hour later, being registered correctly, 155mm shells came overhead like hot, deep-treaded rubber tires of heavily-loaded 18-wheelers purring 80 mph on a midsummer, tar-bubbling macadam mid-day roadway and, like Sergeant Ulriche said, the machine gun quieted and we chogeed out of there. I mean we slid away low and got up staying low, running hunched over back, our equipment jingle-jangling like we were junk men. Running dogfaces, scared shitless, an ungainly sight to see, holding rifles tightly to a high port, everything bouncing from the waist up, reaching one hand to hold a side of their helmets lest they bounce out of the chin straps.

Assembling in a hollow behind a grove of pine trees, I felt wonderful, completely self-controlled, primarily, I believe, by the exercise and, refreshed, I was cleansed of fear; baptized; born to live again. I stood shouting hackneyed orders, first to one and then another squad leader – "What, you guys think this is, a picnic? Shape up and get ready to move back. Right, Sergeant Ulriche?"

Jesus, what a powerful, brave, clean feeling. A thoroughly baptized man! Damn it, mister, I made it. I'm still alive, by God. I'm still alive. I behaved! Hand me my combat infantry badge.

While returning up the valley floor, Chinks followed on a ridge and we got into a real hot scrape. One guy caught a fragment and the medic's tag – Private Perkins – who was carried immediately toward the rear with what we all prayed was a stateside wound; hopefully no bone to cripple him but maybe a large enough nerve in the hip to get home.

For the first time I watched with interest and admiration an enlisted physician, nurse and specialist in many branches of medicine; in fact, our sole salvation, at work. First he assured the frightened young private that he was in good, experienced hands (Doc was all of sixteen) and would have no difficulty living through it and then went quickly to work to stop the bleeding.

He directed Perkins to drop his fatigue pants and underwear shorts and worked on two large pressure bandages applied under two-inch-wide adhesive tape to dam the bleeding long enough to thicken and coagulate ... no place to apply a tourniquet.

No man in our platoon but Doc could have done it right. Doc Lynch was able to determine that no artery was hit although from the pain exhibited he believed Perkins's right pelvis was penetrated. Asking again how painful it was, Doc broke the front of the needle and stabbed him with a little plastic, morphine ampule which he pinched to dry and helped him pull up his bloody shorts and fatigue pants, staying close to him all the way back, stopping occasionally to check for dripping blood, keeping up a running query—how Perkins felt, was he dizzy, more pain, less pain, etc.

It takes twenty minutes before morphine stops pain. Pity the Chink who, even for those lucky enough to have glass vials of raw, waxlike opium, would take an hour, for the pain-deadening effect of opium is due to morphine, only ten percent of its bulk.

Blood flowing away must be stopped or the biggest cause of death in combat, irreversible shock from loss of blood pressure and circulation, will collapse too many small blood vessels; with sufficient pressure no longer coming from the heart pump, blood seeps back into the major arteries and unless pressure is soon reestablished, the smaller vessels cannot be reinflated or expanded and the average guy of about 170 pounds will die if he loses fifteen pints of blood unless given an IV (intravenous infusion of a saline solution) to inflate minor blood vessels. When Doc got Perkins to the aid station, the surgeon shot him with a syringe of penicillin and gave him a transfusion of whole blood.

If Doc wasn't smooth, fast and very capable, the guy's blood pressure was apt to drop below 80, diastolic count, when he loses consciousness, his pulse flutters, he breathes rapidly, shallowly, his temperature falls away fast, lips turn blue, jaw drops, skin turns a pale blue-green-yellow, and the sweat of death lies over him. God, how I learned to hate that cheap, certain way of dying.

We spent over an hour without luck trying to get an air strike on the underwater bridge. On the return we caught up to Perkins and three of his squad and Doc Lynch taking turns carrying him on their backs. They could make a chair from two rifles and a buttoned fatigue jacket but because his wound was on his ass, it was better to ride belly to back. It was good that he was lighter than most. Don't ask me why we never took a litter. Perhaps psychologically a bad omen. I packed Perkins about half a mile myself and the rest of the platoon took turns without having to be named.

34

This day the Chinks were especially mean and didn't disengage at the big hill coming in. My platoon sergeant and I, Master Sergeant Onis L Ulriche, took rear guard, prodding stragglers, the few times necessary, for the Chinks were a pack of wolves 500 yards back on a ridgeline taking pot shots, throwing captured 60mm mortar shells, getting a couple almost to us. They'd tossed the tripods and base plates to sit down with the tube between their legs, estimating range by raising or lowering it, pointing it on-line-target, dropping in rounds one after the other. They had a lot of our ammo.

For a few miles hauling Perkins, a little blood dripped on the back of our legs although the wound was mostly clotted. My over-tired brain played tricks on me, or I daydreamed, that we should have gutted Perkins as we did deer in the deep woods before dragging them out. I tried to squelch this ugly comparison but was too fatigued to control my thoughts. You bleed pretty bad in the ass, but every two or three miles our medic, Doc Lynch, helped ease him down to check the heavy bandage the adhesive tape was keeping tight. Until we got Perkins to the aid station, stopping the blood and easing his pain was all he could do.

The sun was dropping of its own weight behind a mountain miles and miles west of us when the tail end of the platoon climbed with the help of knotted ropes on the bare, steep rise to the top. With ropes under his armpits, we pulled Perkins on his stomach. It was an 800-yard, 30-degree descent down the back side to the litter jeep dismount point where Doc Lynch snapped on high above Perkins a gravity feeding I V saline bag, and then made the shaky four-mile ride to battalion aid station.

There was a listening post run by battalion about 100 yards lower than our ridge, down a wooded finger, likely avenue of approach leading north from Love and King Company. Being on the enemy side behind a hill mass, radios couldn't read. I was told by our company commander, First Lieutenant I B Foney, to get a squad over to man the listening post. I was told to get a squad down to the listening post and didn't have to lead them like I did after trying to change Foney's mind.

"My guys are plain pooped," I argued. "We just came in from Soyang and there's plenty of battalion headquarters never seen a patrol.

How about Major Wilkes's personal shotgun guard? It's not legal anyway, and how about reconnaissance sitting on their ass at regiment all the time. What they paid for?"

"Want to tell Major Wilkes it's illegal? And stop crying over those guys; you don't have to go so why worry?"

True, I didn't have to go, it was Sergeant Dorn's turn, his second tour. But why, I thought, couldn't I ever win an argument with Foney? He was a Reserve like me, manager of a Safeway grocery store in Chicago, bucking for promotion and a commission in the Regulars.

Returning from the listening post, I checked the yellow strand of wire, the right one of the four various-colored wires strung by previous units on this outpost. We'd say they could get through our tactical barbed wire but not our commo wires.

I was bushed and once the sun was down, chilly in my sweaty fatigues. I flopped into my hole. If I took off my boots to massage my feet I'd perk up some but the rest of me ached so I decided to forget it. Redoing the laces would be a chore. A rock stuck in my back. It had projected there from the bottom since my runner, J J, and I and our medic dug our CP, command post, two days before. We'd been away much of that time.

Beat up though I was, I couldn't fall asleep; some guys whose tense voices I couldn't identify were yakity-yaking a few yards toward the ridge trail above. It wouldn't have been so bad if I could have made out something they were saying, even the topic, for that matter. I rested, an OD (olive drab) wool Army blanket doubled about my shoulders, ears ringing from fatigue, eyes so dry they scratched when I blinked, irritable from lack of a good sleep for two days and nights, chainsmoking, trying to disregard what they were talking about—more arguing than anything. I asked, J J lying half upright against a tree near our hole, "find out who's yappin' up there."

"Sergeant Miller, sir, company commo, and some new guy on their way to check the line to Dorn. Nobody's heard from them."

Sergeant E-5 Chuck Dorn, leader of the third squad, had the listening post end of a battery-operated EE-8 field phone line directly through our position to company and the Battalion S-3. Starting at dark the listening post was supposed to call in a situation report every half-

36

hour like night watchmen in a spooky factory.

Our battalion was especially vulnerable for we were the most advanced outpost patrol base across Eighth Army front, in fact by that night, the 15th of May, although we didn't know it at the time, the only outpost remaining. The Marines to our left pulled in theirs on 13 May as waves of Chinks approached and, I learned much later, tragically much too late, ours was supposed to be in also.

Logically, and from common sense, one should withdraw a battalion from an unnecessary outpost patrol base three miles ahead of the main line of resistance when exposed to the great peril of being surrounded. Withdrawal, when it came, however, did not occur in response to an order, but in complete disorder, deserted after Lieutenant Foney and Major Wilkes and his staff sneaked away to the MLR, ending in a terrible bugout of frightened riflemen, every man for himself, hysterical.

Again, from the official Division Blue Book history—

A special Roger Line was established by the Second Division 4000 yards forward of the constantly improving Noname Line, and from it the 38th Infantry sent patrols which met little resistance from enemy groups who seemed prone to turn and flee at the approach of the friendly force.

On the 15th the 38th Infantry stemmed repeated attacks early in the night with the Third Battalion coming under the brunt of the enemy effort together with a company which clung to its positions atop Hill 1051, a main anchor on the Noname Line. Through the darkness, the confident enemy masses broke their endless columns against the positions of the 38th with L and K Companies [note: no mention made of being on an outpost] fighting to hold their positions. Artillery, crashing into the ground forward of the lines, took a terrific toll of the attackers while other hundreds died in the mine fields checkered with barbed wire. The groans of the wounded, screams of the attackers and the blast of bugles mingled with the clattering roar of battle as waves of Chinese pushed against the lines.

Searchlights were turned on by the Second Engineers to illu-

minate the battle area and aid the defenders in locating and slaughtering onrushing Chinese.

By 2030 hours, 15 May, bloody, reckless attacks by the Chinese had overwhelmed the positions of K and L Companies of the 38th Infantry and the entire Third Battalion was under extreme pressure and ordered to pull back. [Orders which my platoon never received.]

This official combat operation description contains a blatant omission. I would very much like to know who in our history section was ordered to cover for the commanders from Major General Clark Ruffner on down because we were never withdrawn from the outpost, Or, possibly, the order to withdraw did come down and our Major Wilkes did not receive it because he was already bugging and out of contact.

Someone blundered on our sad night of May 15, 1951. On our hill of death were left two rifle companies on outpost three miles ahead of the main line of resistance as on, and on, and on, ever on that screaming hill of death they died.

If such withdrawal orders were indeed ever issued, it was too late for our dead and dying. Apparently battalion headquarters and Love Company CPs withdrew soon after dark some time before our platoons were bloodied and surrounded.

What the American Press called the May Massacre began in late April with the annihilation of the Gloucester Battalion of the 27th British Brigade beyond our First Marines to our left. Many of their men were found shot in the neck after surrendering, hands raised above them as they fell, 1000 casualties in all; thirty-nine reached friendly lines and 830 became POWs.

Not long before Sergeant Ulriche and I brought back the platoon from the Soyang river, X Corps Intelligence phoned a scrambled message classified top secret for morale that enemy forces in excess of 200,000 were bouncing rapidly across the Corps, penetrating where they could, raising hell with the rear, killing and taking no prisoners, building for a massive breakthrough.

Suddenly sharp whistles came one after another over our platoon's sound-powered phone, First Squad leader Sergeant J C Rodriguez whistling loudly for attention—whistle! CP? . . . whistle! CP? . . . whistle! CP? Damn it, somebody answer!"

"Lieutenant Gould here."

"J C, lieutenant. There's something fishy out there!"

"What do you mean, fishy?"

"Better come up, sir, there's lots of lights or something and funny noises from the hill we was at today."

As I started up to the ridgeline to the combat positions facing Chinks, I passed the two wiremen who kept me awake and told Sergeant Miller to get down there and check the wire to Dorn. Neither Miller nor his young assistant said anything.

J C Rodriguez was standing beside his hole pointing north, "See 'em, those weird lights I was telling you about. Look, look up there!"

About ten miles due north, straight across a large valley on a hillside finger parallel to our outpost, piercing the darkness were irregular lines of lights twinkling in the twilight. They made the Korean mountain wilderness seem heavily overrun. As I stared, a light on the far left blinked out and then another and another and hundreds of them from left to right with increased rapidity; then they came on again, or maybe Chinese, someone suggested, holding lights, turning their backs to us in rotation. It continued so fast you couldn't begin to count all that went on and off, on-and-off, on-and-off, on-and-off, on-and-off, on-and-off; on-and-off like thousands of busy fireflies. There wasn't any counting or even estimating how many; the whole mountainside blinked on and off and gave you the jitters.

"God Almighty!" someone swore. "Look at all them. What're they up to?"

I shuddered.

In the fearful dark that night the Chinese became forever damn Chinks. They were for the first time real to us. All the bad stories by old timers about the Japs and stinking Krauts in World War II combined to prejudice me with fear and hate against the Chinks and later against the North Korean gooks.

"What they doing?" someone asked.

There were no guesses.

39

"Must be crazy. What do you think, lieutenant?"

"Beats me," I said. "Never heard tell of anything like this." It made me more than a little uneasy. Some trick they've read in the Bible, I thought. What kind of psychological warfare is that?

"Listen!" J C continued, holding a cupped hand to his ear.

We cocked our heads listening. Whenever an evening breeze came from the north up toward the Soyang where all the strange lights were, we heard fragments of sounds wavering in and out – sounds being torn apart by the wind.

"Chinks blowing bugles," J C concluded.

"Listen to them drums," someone said. "Just listen."

I looked sideways both ways. Eight or ten of my guys were out of their holes to see what the confab was about.

"Hey, you guys, get some shuteye," I told them. "Keep the racket down, we're trying to hear."

We listened carefully and heard screaming, broken and fragmented, wavering to us in and out and high-pitched gibberish and occasionally clanging of cymbals. Our veteran platoon sergeant, Master Sergeant Ulriche, came up and after listening a second, swore, "Dammit! We're getting it tonight!"

"Those instruments," he told us, "are looted from bands they overran."

Sergeant Rodriguez and I stared at him.

"What're all them lights for?" J J asked.

"Dunno; they had them at Kunu-ri last November after they got in Korea. We saw and heard them our last night at Kunu-ri – rice paper lanterns running all over the hills on either side of us blowing bugles and after we saw them, they got closer and we couldn't get out fast enough. Line crossers blew the only bridge on the road south and everyone and the officers stood around talking in low voices waiting for orders, and turned out it was too long. Even nurses in a MASH hospital were taken there at Kunu-ri. I took out remnants of four platoons and we hid in a gully until the shooting died down and the bugles and horns and I'll tell you, we bugged! I'm telling you, nobody, but nobody, could've done better and lived to tell about it and I led guys cross country to a ROK outfit. They didn't bother ROKs then; they was after the Indianheads."

"What are they, flashlights?" someone asked and quickly answered, "Hell no, they're too soft."

"I heard they was rice paper lanterns," Ulriche said. "They even had Halloween racket makers, clackers, those wooden things on a handle we used to whirl in the air."

My guys and I reflected for a time, looking through the gloaming past the valley toward the strange lights wavering and blinking on and off, on-and-off, listening to the night wind blow down snatches of sounds of yelling and bugle calls and cymbals, as if the horde of Chinks were celebrating. Not really bugle calls, sort of urgent, sustained ta-ta! ta-ta! Most of the Chinks couldn't play bugles; they just blew into them as hard as they could, trying to sing at the same time like a kazoo. After listening a bit more, I skuddled down to the platoon CP and cranked my EE-8 magneto phone to Dorn and company and battalion all the way back at the jeep dismount point. The field first SFC Roy Martin answered.

"I'm trying to raise Sergeant Dorn," I told him.

"Hang on, lieutenant, the lieutenant's on with S3; wants to talk to you."

"Anyone heard from Dorn?" I asked.

"That's what S3's asking. Not since their second call after dark. Miller's on his way laying new wire. Battalion was supposed to send their own wire team this time, it's their listening post, but you know battalion, they shoved it on us. . . . Just a minute, hang on, lieutenant. I've got to raise the other platoons."

When we were all on conference call, Foney told us to be on the ball because eight Chinese heavily armed, dressed in white Korean civilian clothes, were killed an hour earlier all the way back at regiment forward. "Don't tell your men, keep that poop to yourselves and third platoon!" he said, catching me before I could hang up, "make sure those wiremen get to the listening post; it's critical, we could get hit any time in the next five hours. Battalion's on my ass; haven't heard from your man Dorn or the wiremen in over an hour. They've been told to carry a spare phone. Bastards, that's battalion's baby, not mine."

I heard the wiremen still yakking near our hole. They weren't arguing anymore; reassuring each other how dangerous it was. I called them down and told them what the CO said and in the sternest command voice I could muster, ordered them to get crackin'. They stood to me silent, heads hanging.

"Sir," Sergeant Miller pleaded in a low, respectful voice, "It's awful dark down that saddle, can't see your dick."

"The Chink moon'll be up soon."

"That's what we know, that's when they hit."

"Christ!" the young wireman swore, "they got the nerve. Got good wiremen at battalion sitting on their asses all the time. What do they ever do but run wire to regiment where it's safe. Dorn and his guys must be sound asleep down there or a thumb screw's loose on their battery or something."

Sergeant Miller joined in. "We should've buried our wire. But lieutenant, there ain't been mortar or artillery or nothing along that trail. Nothing wrong except they're not on the ball. You know how pooped your guys are."

"Yeah," reflected the young one, "unless some Chinks cut the line or let the guys have it."

"If there was even one shot we'd heard it," I rationalized.

Miller, quickly, "I know there's other ways," and he and the wireman gave each other anxious stares and shook their heads.

A single airplane came over fast headed north toward the strange lights. It was unusual to hear a plane after dark, except the Chinese's Washing Machine Charlie routinely trying to reconnoiter in the dark, and this was an entirely different sound, a prop job, definitely a bomber. The wiremen and I were quiet, searching the night sky, trying to follow the path of the sound back up to the source. It sounded to me like a medium twin-engine prop job.

"Probably one of them black Douglas B26 Invaders running no lights," I said.

"Wish I was up there," the young wireman mumbled.

The EE-8 rang angrily. It rang twice and twice more, all three rifle platoons and weapons platoon, another conference call.

"First Platoon," Lieutenant Hollingsworth acknowledged.

A long pause.

42

"Is there a second platoon?" Foney asked sarcastically.

"Second Platoon, sir," Second Lieutenant Fred Hurtz, a New York City ROTC officer, answered a little unconvincingly. His platoon sergeant was killed three days before.

"Third Platoon here," I checked in.

"Fourth Platoon, sir," Master Sergeant Billson of weapons platoon answered.

"This is Lieutenant Foney. Listen good. Battalion says there's a big buildup this side of the Soyang-gang and we should get hit some time after false dawn. They're ahead of schedule and will have their moon nearly full. They've got infiltrators everywhere. Two cooks were killed outside their mess tent all the way back to division forward just two hours ago; they were after General Ruffner. According to Air they're pouring over that damn underwater bridge. Gould, you were supposed to knock it out." I shivered at all the bad news. A pause, "Gould, you got air strikes. How come you didn't knock it out? By the way, did Miller get off?"

He didn't wait for answers; Baker company behind us on the MLR, the Noname Line, was reporting on the radio that mines began detonating the hard way within shadows of the sinking sun. Then our outpost mines, the few we were allowed, began exploding one after another. We counted twenty of the thirty Second Division Engineers planted for us.

We argued with the engineer master sergeant who laid and mapped our field just two days before with the very likely avenue of approach up the finger between us and King Company, we needed four times as many. Sergeant Ulriche and I did our best to get him to plant at least a dozen more and Ulriche had insisted we needed fifty-five gallon drums of fugasse and primer cord to wrap around trees down the saddle, to say nothing of barbed wire.

"We aren't in fighting positions," Foney reminded us, defending the engineer sergeant. "Don't even have clear fields of fire, nor covered bunkers so we can call for air bursts," Fact was, we were not even supposed to be exposed to an enemy.

Later, we were informed that the mines we heard popping one after another were detonated by volunteer Chinese National soldiers of

43

Chiang Kai-shek who, after volunteering, were allowed to select one of three styles of caskets displayed back at their division rear and were promised to be classed and treated as loyal, reliable communist soldiers if they survived. With no time to probe for the mines, they walked steadily upright on the trails to clear safe approaches; every explosion a dead or badly wounded Chink.

As near as I can reconstruct it from surviving eyewitnesses, this is about time the company CP began pulling back.

There was a loud, sharp cracking explosion in the air to the north. It came from the valley a few miles south of the Soyang river where the Chink buildup was behind the row of lights.

"What the hell was that?" J J asked loudly.

"That bomber got hit," Doc Lynch offered.

"No," Sergeant Ulriche corrected, "that's butterfly bombs. Whole package explodes after it leaves the bomber and scatters little cans all over. They lie dormant until you pick one up; blow off hands, not kill."

He returned to his hole on the right. I handed the phone to J J, and turned to Sergeant Miller standing outside the hole.

"What was that?" he asked, "bomber blow up? Lieutenant," he paused before going on in a humble low voice, "would you send just two guys like this? Plain crazy for just two down there. Couldn't you talk the lieutenant out of it? It's battalion's job and Dorn can take care of himself. There ain't a better fighter in the company, you know that. Would've heard if something bad happened."

The young wireman sounded off. "I wouldn't mind going so much, personally, if there was about six of us at least. At least six, maybe a dozen. We need a BAR, Browning automatic rifle, and some rifles, you know that, lieutenant. We're only commo, not supposed to be fighting like riflemen. Right? That's not our MOS." He paused, listening for an answer that didn't come. "Look, we got pea shooters," he said, raising his voice, holding out his single-shot M1 carbine.

"What can I do?" I asked. "You're making too much of this whole thing. You'd been back if you hadn't balked so long. There's nothing between here and there can hurt you. I know, I came back from there a couple hours ago and the wire was okay. I double-checked coming back. I'd notice if it was cut; now calm down."

"That's just it, the wire *was* okay," the young wireman said. "Me and Sergeant Miller heard they caught a squad of line crossers south of regiment just yesterday. Them Chinks got suicide squads. They ain't scared to go no place. Probably cut the wire after you passed. Wonder they didn't jump you and that's probably what happened to Dorn and his men later."

Suddenly he burst out, "Hell with it! Miller, let's chogee and get it over with!"

They started for the ridge trail. I watched for a few minutes without saying anything, worrying about how pooped I was and started to pick up the EE-8 to ring Foney then threw the receiver into the dirt. "Sh-e-ee-it!" I lay back as fatigue made a heavy attack on me and had nodded off good when Miller and the young wireman came scuttling down to my hole, Miller hissing fearfully, "Lieutenant! Lieutenant! He can't order us down there alone. Damn it, that's suicide down that saddle path, just two of us with pea shooters."

The excited young wireman exclaimed, "That's right, sir. Gonzales heard them jabbering down there. Lieutenant, you ought to talk to your guys down the ridge, they're plain scared. Gonzales heard Chinks arguing. We're walking right into them."

I was worried. If Speedy heard something, it wasn't just nerves. For all his surliness he was an *ichibon* fighter, *numero uno*. I went to Gonzales' hole.

"Going to call you," Gonzales hissed at me. "Did those guys tell you there's *takuson* Chinks down the saddle path? Flashed a light; them crazy hombres got flashlights."

They can have anything they overrun, I told myself.

Suddenly all hell broke loose at Baker Company about three miles southwest on the main line behind us; a rash of rapid popping small arms. We heard the sharp snappy thwaps of hand grenades and hollow thu-umps, thu-umps and muffled crunch of 60 and 81mm mortars and the even, steady rat-tat-tat of a Browning 30 caliber machine gun through the cool mountain air, each weapon identified by its own characteristic sound.

Russian burp guns reached rapid crescendos instantaneously—

heavy canvas ripping, r-r-r-r-r-r-ept! Salvo after salvo and a number of deep throated w-o-o-oumpts of Russian 120mm mortars in battery and then high velocity 76mm SP, self-propelled artillery ka-pow! ka-pow! terrific velocity like kraut 88s, and our familiar 105 and 155mm howitzer and long tom cannons replying, while parachute artillery flares lighted the night sky so brightly for miles around you could read a newspaper as everyone describes it. Zipping dots, little balls of burning yellow-orange thirty calibre machine gun bullets strung outward like fiery beads, one burning every fifth round tracing the way to targets, occasionally bouncing off rocks, dancing straight lines high into the air.

I lay on my stomach peering down the steep, dark saddle path and heard dead branches snapping and other accidental sounds of movement, even over the distracting noises of the firefight behind us— excited, high-pitched jabbering in a sing-song rhythm, a Chink argument or heated discussion. Trip flares closer to our position began popping high into the air, especially in front of King Company on the left flank of our outpost and red Chink attack flares giving the trees below a fiery glow and the soft crackling and white smoke in darkness of random grass and brush fires.

I took the wiremen back to my CP and got Foney on the EE-8. "I don't think you ought to send just two wiremen down that path. We need a combat patrol at least, maybe some of the reserve platoon. They hear Chinks down that saddle. I heard them too, and they're pretty sure of themselves."

Foney, obviously fighting to control his voice, scared as were all of us and angry at losing control, talked too fast in a high, shrill voice. "Goddammit, Gould! Get on the ball. Hasn't that wire been checked? I just told battalion it was! Regiment's getting into it now and the reserve platoon is on its way to help King Company. It might be too late for anything. Your men know the escape route. Stop crying over those characters. I've had enough trouble with Miller; tell that coward if he doesn't get cracking and hightail it to the listening post with new wire, I'll see he gets a court-martial. What're you so worried about anyway, letting them eightballs scare you? You don't have to go."

No, I didn't have to go, they're his own company wiremen, I slammed the phone at its leather case swearing to myself, "And you sonofabitch, he's not a coward!"

"What did the commander say?" Sergeant Miller asked.

"Never mind what he said. Listen, you guys are getting on my nerves. You belong to company headquarters and you got your orders direct from the company commander to get over with new wire. I'm not telling you anymore. I'm ordering you, understand? Get chogeeing . . now . . . NOW!"

I sounded mad and I was, at that bastard Foney. Ordering two defenseless guys to certain death. Nobody's getting wire down to that listening post alive. Dorn must've been jumped, gagged and cautioned to be quiet. Sh-e-e-it! Nobody can help him now.

Both wiremen glared angrily at each other and me. They didn't say a word, just gave me dirty looks in the dark and then the young wireman slung the wire reel on his back with Miller's help and hitched over his left shoulder the strap of his single-shot carbine, the weapon most support troops were armed with. The young soldier had the issue M1 carbine with fifteen-round magazines instead of an M2 with automatic selector switch, single shot or automatic, and a number of thirty-round banana magazines taped together upside down for fast recharging.

"Jesus!" the young wireman swore, pleading hopelessly. "If asshole thinks for one friggin' minute I'm yellow, he's full of shit! It's plain suicide, that's all, but if you order me to go, I'll goddamn go, all right. Won't we, Miller. Lieutenant, you and asshole divvy up my Medal of Honor; hope you're goddamn proud."

"Who's ordering you to go?" I asked. "Let's get one thing straight. You're not my concern; all I'm doing is passing along orders as I'm told to do. It's not my idea; you heard me talk to the guy."

"He's all right," Sergeant Miller told the young wireman. "The lieutenant's okay. It's that chickenshit Foney; he's a first class prick. He's buckin' for captain, won't say shit if he had a mouthful; not to battalion. Probably even volunteered to run battalion's wire. Who's ever heard of asshole being anywhere there's Chinks?" After a long pause, "Well, as the man says, when you got to go, ya gotta' go. So long lieutenant, you tried."

The wiremen moved slowly, reeling out the new wire, heads down, up towards the saplings to Gonzales's hole; certain they were being fed to a monster, the private bending slightly under his load. When they were almost dissolved by darkness, I caught up. "Hold a minute," I growled and took a man apiece from the first three holes. They bitched but hurried after us with their standard five grenades, double bandoliers and rifles with bayonets fixed. One, a PFC Philip Funaro, pleaded he lost part of his M1 in his dark hole trying to clean it. No time to argue, I took his holemate instead, whose name I don't recall. He pleaded he was scared, but came on anyway.

"How come I get it?" he complained. "Nothing wrong with Funaro he's a coward. Lieutenant, you picked him first, give him my rifle. Honest, sir, I've been trembling half an hour. Can't get control of myself."

There was no time then to consult a conscience like the one nagging ever since. I salute that nameless young hero, and, I suppose to relieve the pressure of my guilt, still must believe that Funaro's holemate was taken POW and survives. I hope he will read this and help me feel better. I'll try to make it up to him but of course he won't be a kid anymore.

I stopped at Gonzales' hole and got J J on the sound-powered platoon phone at our CP to tell him that I was heading toward the battalion listening post to check Dorn and for him to call Sergeants Ulriche and Karl Eppler, our guide, if they heard shooting toward the listening post, warn company and right away take the platoon out the evacuation trail we rehearsed.

"I haven't received word," I told J J, "from anyone but we're sure we're infiltrated and now company won't answer their phone or the 536, walkie-talkie. Whatever happens at the listening post, we'll try to cut sharp left to get to either the company or battalion CP. Quick, questions?"

"I tried to raise Ulriche," J J told me, "but I think the bulk of the platoon has already gotten out. Good luck, sir, I'll wait for you."

"No," I shouted, "get out *now*!"

Except for company headquarters, down the jeep trail, our platoon escape route was the best on the outpost.

No matter what happened, Master Sergeant Ulriche, RA 35968263, was much better qualified than me. He earned two Purple

Hearts and a Silver Star at Guadalcanal and was commissioned in the field fighting Japs. It was he who knew of what he talked about who named our third platoon banzai.

In 1948 he resigned in lieu of a court-martial for slugging a drunken rear echelon bird colonel for pinching his wife's butt at an officers' club and was allowed to enlist as a master sergeant. In Korea he was awarded a cluster to his Silver Star leading remnants of several companies out of Kunu-ri. Colonel Coughlin, regimental commander, desperate for officers he could trust, twice asked him to accept another field commission, guaranteeing he would make first lieutenant within a month. This was again discussed by Major General Clark Ruffner who personally presented the cluster to Ulriche's Silver Star, assuring him that Lieutenant General Almond, CO of X Corps, would make it automatic. Ulriche, however, remained bitter that the colonel who insulted his wife was not even reprimanded. If he wasn't good enough for a peacetime officers' club, he'd stay with the guys.

Everyone on the outpost listened in dread to the firefights behind him on the MLR moving relentlessly company to company up the line, from Baker to Charley. At the close sounds of battle, with voices yelling, Chink and American, more and more audible under great stress, I shuddered from the base of my spine, vibrating between my shoulder blades, short hairs standing on my neck as I shivered, shook.

"Geezus crise!" a rifleman muttered.

When our makeshift patrol arrived at Gonzales' hole, he said, "They're down there all right; anybody hear anything from Dorn and his men? There's movement at the bottom of the saddle, lieutenant. It sure ain't Dorn."

Suddenly a hot firefight blazed in King Company on our outpost. Bullets snipped in low overhead; those headed straight at you made loud crack sounds. Two riflemen tried to squirm into Gonzales' hole, others flattened and slid on their bellies over the ground like snakes to get behind a large tree stump. Sandy Opoulus, King Company's new CO, commanding officer, was heard yelling through the black air, "Watch it! Watch it! Dammit, watch it! They want us out of ammo."

Other GI voices joined with Sandy's and King's fire lessened;

not so burp guns and screaming Chinks building to a fury. We searched the hill trail under the daylight of chandelier flares, four tiers of magnesium candles from an eight-inch cannon swinging back and forth high above us, as busy little men in padded earth-colored clothes trod toward us searching King for a spot to break through. It was recorded in the Blue Book —

The 38th Infantry stemmed repeated attacks early in the night with the First Battalion on H 1051 coming under the brunt of the enemy effort together with Charlie Company which clung to its positions. Through the darkness the confident enemy masses broke their endless columns against the positions of the 38th with Baker Company fighting to hold its positions.

This took place three miles behind us on the MLR. According to our Blue Book, our outpost had been withdrawn prior to 15th of May mass attack. Not true, it was never withdrawn, brutally overrun and scattered and the more phoning I did in my research for this journal, the more I heard of men deserted wholesale by their companies and battalions, not privates bugging out but majors and light colonels fleeing in jeeps to avoid Chinks, and, in our case, a Major Wilkes and Lieutenant Foney deserting hundreds of faithful, obedient enlisted men and a few lieutenants; left helpless, but for the little ammo they owned, each tragically had to face individually the loss of their place on this earth.

One, Staff Sergeant Jerry Sperbeck of Utica, New York, with whom I recruited three years, was positioned in another division at twilight by his weapons platoon leader with a 57mm recoilless rifle at an intersection to try to hold back the enemy and his company left without contacting him. The next man he saw, in dim light of dawn, was a quilted stranger motioning him to leave his weapon and surrender.

Jerry was lucky to survive two years of Death Camp 5, Pucktong on the Yalu, where, in his three-year captivity, he helped bury hundreds of buddies with no funeral service or word of kindness, no covering or casket, half naked in unmarked graves on a barren hillside. I often feel for them, cast into a cold, cruel wilderness, stripped of humanity, among evil savages, Chinks and gooks. Fuck them all.

2
Don't Worry Honey

"The rifleman fights without promise of either reward or relief. Behind every river there's another hill — and behind that hill, another river. After weeks or months in the line, only a wound can offer him the comfort of safety, shelter, and a bed. Those who are left to fight, fight on, evading death but knowing that with each day of evasion they have exhausted one more chance for survival. Sooner or later, unless victory comes, this chase must end on the litter or in the grave."

—General Omar Bradley

I led our impromptu wire patrol past a thin roll of concertina barbed wire, whispering hoarsely to step over a trip wire I pointed to, and to pass the warning back, stepping high, as a brilliant rising Chinese moon freed itself of witch's arms, the bare, black branches of leafless saplings.

Once I stopped, demanding to know what in hell I was doing. Who ordered me here? How'd I get suckered into this crazy thing? Company's responsible for commo I explained to myself but the guys down there on the listening post are mine.

A terrible silence hung over the listening post and vicinity. Aside from one partly concealed rifle, the circular trench emplacement was empty. There were no bodies nor signs of struggle and it seemed evident that the six men had been surprised before they could get off a shot. Years later, Conley Clarke told me he thinks he remembers the name Charles Dorn written in charcoal on the wall of one of the prison camps he passed through, but despite my most strenuous efforts researching this book, searches by computer and telephone, I have been unable to locate Sergeant Dorn. VA could tell me only he was dropped

KIA after carried MIA for a year. They have no record of his imprisonment.

I learned it was not unusual for small units to disappear this way. General Marshall, in his *The River and the Gauntlet,* has Lieutenant Robert H Rivet at Kunu-ri radioing the Second Battalion 38th that a force of an estimated 2000 Chinese was coming against his platoon from the east.

Lieutenant Colonel Skeldon asked, "What are you going to do about it, Bob?"

Rivet answered, "I will take them under fire as soon as they get close enough."

This was the last Colonel Skeldon or anyone heard of Lieutenant Rivet or any of his men; their fate unknown to this day.

I tried to raise company and battalion on Dorn's EE-8 to no avail and after a few rings to my CP heard J J's voice.

"Lieutenant?" he said. "Get back fast! Company and Battalion pulled out. Chinks overrunning King Company, headed our way. A King Company guy here with me says there're thousands."

Red and white flares rose from the valleys around us; undoubtedly Chinks for their white flares had a reddish cast.

"Can't get back; we're cut off," I told J J. "Raise Ulriche again and Eppler and have them take the platoon back our withdrawal route."

"No need, sir, Ulriche's gone and Eppler called ten minutes ago to tell me to let you know they would make it okay and you to take care of yourself."

"Good luck, J J. I'm ordering you *again,* stop fooling around; take off *now,* we're going to try to take a shortcut to company CP and on out the jeep trail. Good luck, buddy."

J J made it out alone minutes before the entire outpost was surrounded. The following is from a letter from my platoon guide at the time, Sergeant Karl Eppler —

I'll never forget the reassuring sound of King's 30-cal. machine guns and how I held my breath for them to continue. The Chinese hit our company in at least four separate attacks, all of which were repulsed, while our unit sat and waited. I heard

52

noise in front of my position and several land mines were deto-
nated, but I never saw anything or fired a shot.

Somewhere around midnight I was told by J J that Lieutenant
Gould was on his way to check on Dorn and the Third Platoon
was to leave its position and withdraw. Knowing the trail and
location of the flares, I was point man. We had to walk through
an open field, down a hill, and then up the next hill toward
King's position. I remember every time an artillery flare went
off illuminating us we drew small arms fire from the top of the
hill. At the time I didn't know if this was friendly fire or not.

As I approached the bottom of our hill and started up the
next, I met two GIs from King Company running down saying
their position had been overrun and we should get the hell out
of there. I started back to report this to you when it really hit the
fan.... Chinese had come in behind us as we pulled out and
were now shooting up the people behind me very seriously. I
couldn't tell our people from theirs, but as I had been point, I
was not directly engaged.

A sadness overcomes me to recall that hour; a strange bitterness, deep hurt that never left me. The world came to end that night and
for a second I was five again losing my mother. "Mommy, mommy,"
I pleaded, "mommy don't let it happen," and just as suddenly I was
returned to the present and dropped the phone and scrambled out of the
listening post trench to get the guys going, only to discover they'd taken
off while I was on the phone. Which way I never learned. A burp gun
fluttered its short blue flame a few feet down the ridge. I headed away,
south, down a wild brush-covered finger without a trail and in a few
minutes came across Sergeant Miller, desperately pawing at someone's
fatigue top, popping buttons trying to find where the man was hit. I
grabbed the guy squirming sideways right and left and held him to ease
Miller's job as the wounded man rolled his eyes, frothed at the mouth
and convulsed. A flare light disclosed a large goiter about the size of a
billiard ball growing on his throat. Then I realized I was holding
Miller's young assistant. "You and asshole divvy up my Medal of
Honor. . . ." Bullets were zipping in close to us and I ordered Sergeant

Miller to drop his man before we were hit and follow me as I bolted down the finger.

Later, Miller told me he disregarded my orders and stayed with his young assistant a few more minutes before taking off after me. Like J J, he miraculously escaped by the same route I took, only with enough stamina to make it through, apparently not far behind J J. He must have passed close to where I was to lie.

Sergeant Miller's fingers felt some slippery blood and a small puckered hole behind each ear where a bullet passed, evidently from a burp gun at close range, unable to find much blood, our battalion surgeon explained because his man bled internally. I asked if I could have saved his life by cutting open the goiter to relieve pressure but the major didn't think so.

During our long reserve in June, Sergeant Miller and I were called to the battalion adjutant's office to sign sworn statements that we saw his assistant, so-and-so (I can't recall his name) dead at such-and-such a place. I swore, assuming his death because of the large internal bleeding and Miller believed he was gone before he left in haste. Otherwise, the kid would have to be carried MIA, missing in action, for a year. This way it was KIA, killed in action, allowing his next of kin to receive his GI insurance and begin a closure. As soon as the territory in which he fell was retaken, as it was two days later by US Marines, a search would be made to recover his remains which, in his case, I doubt were ever found without dogs and I don't recall there being any canines in the Second Division at that time.

Although by necessity sometimes left lying where they fell zeroed in, our dead were treated with more respect than in any previous war, beginning in the War for Independence when corpses of soldiers after a battle were stripped of clothing for sale and reuse and naked bodies assembled and lowered together in mass graves, or buried individually beside rough roads they'd been traveling. Only when they died near their homes were their bodies turned over to relatives and friends fully clothed to be interred in local graveyards. The morning after Lexington, mothers sent their sons searching for fathers and older brothers. British dead were buried in graves earmarked for Massachusetts' 5000 slaves.

After the battle of Monmouth, reacting to accusations of insubordination, Major General Charles Lee, retired British officer, second in command to George Washington, angrily belittled the General by complaining that while he was risking his life in battle, Washington "had nothing to do but disrobe the dead."

In the world wars, bodies were pushed into mattress covers, in Korea black plastic body bags that today are nylon with plastic liners and carrying loops, two at either end and two in the middle, in case of a heavy body.

After being shipped to an Army mortuary in Japan in body bags for embalming, they were returned and buried in U.N. cemeteries at Pusan, Seoul, some at Taegu, and when, after the war, remains were requested by next of kin in writing, were shipped home in all-metal transfer canisters and into brown Army-issue metal caskets. Those not claimed remained in Korea until sometime after the war when they were reburied, as was Ernie Pyle after WWII, in American soil in the National Cemetery on a hilltop in Hawaii. UN Forces dead, other than Americans, not requested and sent home, remain in Korea in cemeteries tended by the United Nations.

I fled crashing down the brushy finger and with no hope of holding off the horde, tossing my heavy helmet, discarding my carbine and pistol belt and chogeed, a badly frightened animal, in the direction of the jeep dismount point and trail leading to the MLR. Burp guns and grenades sounded everywhere in front, behind and to the sides, and hard-blown crude bugle blasts, screaming Chinks shouting to one another and American voices in great alarm issuing violent, agonized curses and desperate pleas. "SARGE! SARGE! WHERE ARE YOU? LIEUTENANT! LIEUTENANT, HELP ME. I'M HIT BAD! MEDIC! MEDIC! PLEASE, PLEASE, SOMEONE PLEASE! And among it all, calm, hardly audible resignations, "Oh, my God. My God. My God, this is it," and for all I ever found out they were talking directly.

A diabolic fury in a small area of a Korean ridgeline, our underworld above ground, its own terror equal to when Hercules hurled boulders, Spartacus defied Rome, Attila swept across Europe and General Benedict Arnold spurred his charger hell bent into the German nobleman Breyman's redoubt at Saratoga. God only knows what unsung heroes went straight to soldier's heaven that horrible night of our forgotten war.

As I reached a dry, rocky creek bed at the foot of the finger, short of the company CP, our 105s began landing rapid fire on the ridge above three minutes apart. Then as stragglers radioed more accurate information to the guns, they dropped round after round in three-gun salvos without letup into an impact area behind me, sometimes burning barrels, joined by the heavies, 155mm howitzers, and later, those throaty monsters, eight-inchers, 200mm, the largest cannon in Korea in 1951, before the 240mm and 280mm atomic cannons President Eisenhower sent over to end the war.

Suspicious of the open jeep trail, I ran on the east side of the small valley, which in more peaceful surroundings one might call a glen, and as I climbed desperately, suddenly my legs simply gave out, dropping me flat on my stomach unable to move, completely exhausted, aching all over and gasping like a stricken asthmatic with a raw throat. Scared shitless was the only expression close to describing it, understood only by those of us who have literally had shit scared out of us. I remembered an evasion and escape lecture several weeks earlier and decided I'd have to try playing dead. There was no alternative but one form or another of suicide.

Two weeks earlier, during a short reserve, young First Lieutenant John Fox, mentioned in the preface, gave the battalion an escape and evasion lecture (after the war, changed to evasion and escape, the preferred order), ending it with the advice: "If everything else fails, don't hesitate to pretend you're dead."

I approached him after the class to express my doubts. "C'mon, Fox, don't tell me you've got the nerve to just lie there with them all around and pretend you're dead. Crimus!"

Fox, who doesn't recall me at all, was aware that at one time about then he went around companies giving all kinds of lectures. I remember him as a bright, young-looking guy, he tells me he was only twenty-six, out of West Point that year, who took time to show me in the manual where it was written, making no effort to defend the advice.

"Don't know, Gould, never met anyone who's gone through it."

Except for rare, slowly-brought-about sideways peeks, everything I experienced from that moment until the next afternoon came either through my ears or sixth sense, intuition, which I had no means of verifying but trusted unquestionably. Chinks came suddenly then and dug shallow foxholes about thirty feet on either side as I hugged mother earth as close as possible and strained with my tongue and lips to suppress noisy gasping as much as I could, but continued to puff along like a run-away steam engine making a hill.

By then the Triple Nickel, Heavy Artillery Battalion of 155s who gave me the hellacious ride, and Wyoming National Guard powerful eight-inch 'persuaders' were tearing up the rocks and bushes around me. The only thing that saved my Chink neighbors and me was the fact that we were in a depression on the hillside. Shrapnel, miniature sirens, whirred overhead. The Blue Book explained —

As night fell in the vicinity of Hill 699 on 15 May air observers reported masses of enemy headed for the Second Division. Immediately the entire 555th and 503d Field Artillery, two batteries of the 196th, X Corps' 155s, and one battery of the 38th's 105mm field artillery were shifted to cover the area and opened fire with heavy concentrations with the kind of monumental artillery support which helped to create the so-called ammunition shortage that later was the subject of public debate and a Congressional investigation in the United States. All UN artillery units were firing the 'Van Fleet load,' five times larger than the ammunition allowance previously in use. The Van Fleet load, together with a shortage of motor transport and the difficulties of supply inherent in mountain warfare, was largely responsible for the much-publicized shortage.

Van Fleet authorized Almond's 105mm howitzers to fire 250 rounds per gun per day. Maintaining that rate required twenty heavy ordnance truckloads of artillery ammo per hour, but managed only twelve until Van Fleet directed his G-4 to fire more and by daybreak they did.

As I lay there in perpetual terror, I must have heard every one of the 11,800 rounds, the 38th Field Artillery's record, that landed behind me in an area slightly larger than a football field. I later learned that this was an all-time world record for an eleven-hour period for 105 howitzers, but because of the nearness and the massing of men in earlier wars, perhaps less lethal and frightening than fighting man-to-man with swords or the short range of muskets.

We and the Chinks never sought to fight man-to-man, for modern combatants plan on doing major damage with long-range artillery and Air. Only when mistakes are made is there close combat, as not being pulled in from off that damn knob of an outpost when there was no longer patrolling to do, that sort of mistake bringing man-facing-man. Otherwise, when outmaneuvered or outnumbered, threatened by superior firepower and mass attack, we simply "pulled back to strengthen our line" and at times, as during the May Massacre, pulled back to draw the enemy further from his supply base, an old tactic of Genghis Khan.

Tanks of regimental tank company and the division's 72d Tank Battalion were employed in direct fire missions. Together with other available supporting weapons, 200 artillery pieces were brought to bear on the Second Division front, much of it directed directly behind me. In addition were the quad fifty caliber revolving four-gun mounts of the 82d antiaircraft battalion half tracks which could be hulled down and lowered in the rear to fire like long-range mortars over a ridge.

I gagged quietly many times and almost puked from cordite fumes settling into our depression. One descending 155mm flare swung so violently in such a wide arc it caught its parachute on fire and came down sizzling loudly. Chinks to my right yelled warnings before it landed, I guessed about fifty yards away, and started a small brush fire which they extinguished.

I lay there still for hours with nothing to defend me but a hidden grenade from which I'd pulled the cotter pin, when I don't recall. It remained in the grip of my tightly closed fingers of my right hand for about seventeen hours, most of which time I was not conscious, but the grenade remained locked in my right hand. I crawled the fingers of my left hand forward under my head and using neck muscles to press my head down on my left hand to give it weight, dug a hole in soft woods dirt to hide the grenade and my right hand under my head. I slowly pulled up my right leg in an awkward position I imagined a dead man might appear and then remembered I had written down the code, HOT CARBINE, for the grids on our 1:50,000 combat maps, one through ten, H being numeral one, O two, T three and so on, and very slowly worked it with my left hand out of my inner jacket pocket to wad it and push it under the grenade in my hidden right hand. Even slight movements were risky and I felt enormously proud of myself.

At one point I made a joke, "the next war I'm invited to, I'm hiring a stunt man like they do for big movie heroes."

In the record-breaking cannonading that followed, VT and proximity shells burst in the air to send large hunks of shrapnel thudding into the ground around me and once during the long night, one Chink cried out in pain. "Good," I thought, "hit him again." Countless light and heavy artillery flares swung back and forth in the sky, which I clearly experienced through half buried, closed eyelids but mainly through their sizzling noises as they descended. A number were chandelier flares exposing all about me, throwing long, dark, shaking shadows of trees and boulders as flares swayed back and forth above, sizzling loudly. I was further lighted by the full Chinese moon and I learned later a C-47 Firefly made several passes dropping huge parachute flares whose wide canopies allowed fifteen minutes of brilliant 1,000,000 kilowatt candlepower turning night into day. I heard it passing over but had no inkling what it was doing, hoping whatever it was it wouldn't bomb me.

I sensed from a rustling sound and an angry exclamation in Chinese from what was apparently a leader, that a scavenger was scooting over to me. In my fear fantasy I seemed to actually see the soldier as he quickly yanked the watch from my limp, exposed left wrist without changing my position. I thanked my lucky stars I wore a loose expansion bracelet. The scavenger's leader hissed at him and the man hesitated as he gave me a push with one foot meaning to roll me over, I suppose, for my wallet. My body was halfway up and I had to use poorly responsive muscles to cause it to drop slowly back. I didn't worry about the whiteness of my face for I'd smeared it well with black

59

woods dirt and it was half buried. His squad leader spoke in an authoritative voice and the looter replied a few rapid words in Chinese, and returned. I felt confident then that I was doing a good job of pretending.

I tried to think of ideas to make me look more like a dead man. Unfortunately, a rock pressed against my bladder and I had to piss badly for several hours and tried constantly to put it out of mind. A frightened young man ran down the rocks of the dry creek bed below yelling, "Sarge, sarge, you said you'd wait. Where are you? You didn't let me know. They got Bob. Bob's dead, sarge. . . . Hey, sarge, where are you guys?" Chinks jabbered and answered b-r-r-r-rpt! b-r-r-r-rpt! with burp guns to his cry, and he was heard no longer. I learned that the vanguard sweeping through us were ordered not to take prisoners, they didn't have the wherewithal to feed or guard us.

I had to piss so badly tears came to my eyes. The night air grew chilly as I agonized about having to take a piss in my pants. I had to go so badly my bladder ached. I considered digging a hole down there for it but knew there would be too many movements of my body to a watchful Chink.

An authoritative loud voice sounded off below and behind me, evidently on a radio, distracting me momentarily: "Hey, you guys, for Christ's sake lift the damn stuff. You're killing us. This is Lieutenant Baker. I repeat, Bill Baker. Lift the damn artillery. It's smack on top of us. Lift the stuff; the Chinks have gone; you're killing your own men. Lift the stuff!"

Damn traitor, I thought.

With the theft of my watch, I lost all understanding of time. Soon the need to piss was my total concern; tears dropped from my eyes; never had I disregarded the need so long and suddenly I chuckled quietly to myself: "Here in your own graveyard afraid to piss your pants," and so let it go. Letting it go out of control wasn't that easy and it shut off automatically several times, not consciously for fear of making a mess, but because I'd been trained long ago not to pee my pants. The hot liquid flowed unpleasantly around the upper parts of my thighs and made me uncomfortable, dirty and guilty and as the temperature cooled, more uncomfortable.

I began to catalog the pains, fears and miseries that beset me inside and out and I lay in constant dread of the curious Chink's return. I felt pity for the deserted young man they murdered down behind me. Even in war, how can they be so callous, or are they hop heads? Doc Lynch, our medic, once showed me a little glass vial of waxlike lumps some of their riflemen carried. Just knowing they had opium gave us the willies, feeding rumors that this is why they are so wild when they attack and scream and yell, forgetting we did the same. They were fanatic little devils.

At what I guessed from the lessened intensity and low angle of the Chinese moon whose light I sensed was about four-thirty in the morning, I raised my head slowly, deciding I couldn't take fear any longer, there'd be no happy end no matter what and I was convinced the Chinks were there to stay; why extend myself for their ultimate pleasure? If this is where I'm supposed to die, so be it; I will fear no longer. No reason to hang on miserably in the short time left, better die a soldier than prolong what would most certainly be my life's end when the light of day came.

I fretted that the sun would be up in a couple of hours and they'd see me for sure and the guy who got my watch, or one of his buddies, would roll me all the way over for my wallet and see the grenade in my hand and finish me off, lying there entirely helpless—hopelessly helpless. Better the end be my doing.

I was conscious of that grenade for the first time all night and tried to remember if I'd pulled the ring. Something told me to be careful in case I had. Fingers that held it were unable to stretch to an open position. All this time I held down the spring handle mainly by the dead weight of my head resting on my tight hand grip and now felt nothing in that hand. I could sense that my cocked leg was asleep, also without the usual tingling feeling; certainly, I thought, my right hand was past tingling. I would flex the muscles in my legs from the inside to get blood flowing and work all my muscles from inside without outward movement, working them from inside to get blood circulating, smear dirt again ever so slowly over my head and face for more camouflage, crawl slowly to get close as possible to the bastards on my right, then jump up, toss the grenade in the middle and scramble on hands and knees to the ridge trail above. Should the shock be enough, I might possibly make it. Fortunately, the Chinese moon had set behind the ridge, flares were no longer falling and the shadows were dark in our little woods.

My legs balked at such unexpected duty. Break them in more slowly, I told myself. By knowledge garnered by my ears I knew that Chinks were passing intermittently all night in groups along the ridge about forty feet above and I'd be damn lucky not to get it before I made ten feet. Nevertheless, call it a death wish if you will, I decided to go and was flexing muscles internally preparing to move when Kitty, a bold, glowing vision in color, came floating down. A shimmering Kitty, just head and shoulders, came down from the ridgetop. My face buried, I saw her plainly through the top of my head.

Kitty came down to me as an icon that troubled night, her hair worn down to her shoulders as she appeared our first week together, after which she had it cut shorter and always wore it very becomingly up in back. Through the top of my head I watched her floating down from the ridge, so realistic I worried the Chinks would shoot her. She shimmered slowly below me out of 'sight' and after I believed her gone, stroked the back of my head tenderly and said soothingly, "Don't worry, honey, everything will be all right," and vanished, or melted away.

I immediately fell into what I can describe only as a coma—somehow initially revisiting the horrible reality of the week of my mother's death when I was five. I cried hard that terrible time her casket was wheeled into our parlor, before my father told me sentimentality was wrong, weakening the mind, leaving it more vulnerable to pain. He told me that sentimentality is not felt by lower animals nor hardworking, honest, primitive people, who, in their miserable lives, face death young and frequently and do not have the luxury to dream while awake; not those busy with constant grief and danger, but when I tried to act blasé about her death it wouldn't work. Later he explained he was so rough with me (today, tough love) to prepare me for her death. I recall, however, the night he kissed me and held me and told me she was gone and not to cry that every night for a week from the big bedroom came my father's sobs of self-pity.

I woke from my coma, or whatever, as suddenly as it came, sometime in the afternoon. My ears told me I was alone and I slowly, cautiously lifted my head to make certain with my eyes. The Chinks were gone all right and I learned later that even before first light this crack assault unit and many thousands of their swarm had dogtrotted east to cave in the Fifth ROKs. I stood slowly, looking around, trying to feel my right hand with the grenade, and, listening carefully, with my movable left hand massaged my right thigh and leg, which at first collapsed as I put weight to them, and drew myself up again favoring that side, stumbling uphill until the leg and thigh finally worked.

On the ridgetop a few yards overlooking my platoon's withdrawal route, I saw a large lump of fatigues on a litter, an image I'll never be free of. Another soldier, half sitting, slumped forward on the ground beside the man on the litter. In one agonizing flash, my spirit cried out, "God make them alive." For a long moment I stood staring transfixed at the pitiful scene; a badly wounded man, bleeding his life away by now certainly dead, being carried on a litter by a wounded man now slumped and also dead, or would soon be that, and I thought of another soldier, missing, who obviously left his buddies at the collapse of the other carrier, took off running to save himself.

It was too far to be sure but I believed, because my platoon among others must have passed this way, that at least I might be able to identify these guys. As I turned to go over to check if there was life left in either of them, I was shot at by a small Chink patrol coming up the trail behind. I took off, crazed, a wild thing, down across a highland wheat field toward the jeep trail, hurling myself through the air like a suicide-bent acrobat, down a plowed hillside, each leap forward landing me many feet down the steep slope. I did not count the times I was shot at until I was able to slide to my right into a bushy gully and get behind rock formations.

When I got down to the jeep trail, I could hear them jabbering somewhere above me but at no time did I see them. I ran pell mell into my second wind and loped easily, thanking me for saving me, three miles to the MLR. As I approached M Company's barbed wire concertina rolls across the jeep trail, I was shot at by a trigger-happy guy who was immediately admonished, "Don't shoot, he might be GI." I had a short crewcut, about half an inch and with wood dirt smeared over my face and head must have resembled a wild man.

I yelled the only thing that came to mind: "It's me! Don't shoot, it's me! It's me! It's me!" A soldier came forward to separate the concertina wire as another man yelled, "Is there a pin in that grenade? Get rid of that grenade!" For the first time in hours I was aware of it in my seemingly frozen right hand. I saw the ring was gone and all I had to do to arm it was to let go of the handle. I tried to get my fingers to open by themselves to throw it in the stream that ran to the right of the trail but they refused to move and I twisted my whole torso facing away from the stream to move my entire right arm and shoulder back, keeping it straight at the elbow as far as it could go through an arc and like a discus thrower swung the grenade sideways, centrifugal force taking the heavy grenade from my fingers through the air into a pool of the stream that flowed by the jeep trail. As guys manning the roadblock scurried for cover, I stood watching it blow up a small geyser.

Safe among my own, I began to quiver all over and laugh uncontrollably, and shudder deeply, then suddenly sob loudly, pitifully, like a badly hurt child, changing back and forth that way, laughing and crying, my emotions gone wild—laughing and crying, laughing and crying and sobbing. Captain George Brownell, a big guy, put his arm around my shoulder and escorted me to his jeep, saying all the while, "C'mon, buddy. Now c'mon, buddy, you're out of it now, buddy. Get hold of yourself, lieutenant. C'mon now." To a sergeant staring at me, "He's hysterical, out of control."

I was the last man to get off the outpost alive and Brownell drove me six miles to the door of the large squad tent that was the 38th regimental forward CP war room, and ushered me inside to be debriefed by General Ruffner, Colonel Coughlin and two full birds from X Corps. After answering several questions and blabbing the little I knew of interest to them, and being escorted away by a major, I recalled the traitor in the middle of the night trying to lift our artillery. Ruffner had his back to me talking to the colonels as I rushed back, grabbed his shoulder and spun him around. He was built solid, an all-American lineman at VMI, Virginia Military Institute. Fortunately, my uncontrolable anxiety was quite obvious.

"Baker's turned traitor," I told him. "Lieutenant Baker, Bill Baker, kept yelling over the radio, 'lift the artillery ... lift the artillery!'"

General Ruffner gave a cold stare and ordered me to get hold of myself. "Calm down, lieutenant. We've checked that out. There was no Lieutenant Baker up there but they've got plenty of intelligence officers educated in the States. Had a Lieutenant Baker's tags."

Other escapees had been debriefed before me and the Baker incident already noted.

Remembering how I, at some risk of being seen, had protected our top secret map coordinate code, I explained proudly how I risked my life burying it. "They'd never learn our secret code from me." The general was annoyed rather than pleased and reminded me, "*Gould,* those codes are changed every day," and gave a hand sign for the major to move me out.

Ruffner made a searching second look as I turned, glancing at my still wet pants, perhaps recalling the fact that, for a short while the previous month, I gave part of his daily briefing, perhaps linking my piss wet pants then with how wet they were after that incident at the ford sitting in my stalled jeep. If he did, he failed to acknowledge it.

I was just as happy that the general chose not to recognize me, for late one dark, rainy afternoon, relieving myself before the briefing, daydreaming about how important I was associating with the brass, in turning quickly, shaking off the drops, I bumped smack into him. I was using what, unbeknown to me, was the commanding general's private piss tube, an empty 155mm cardboard shell container slanted into the ground with small stones and a sprinkle of lime around the base. Next morning, Lieutenant Colonel Foster warned the enlisted staff as he stared over at me, that someone illegally used the general's private pissoir, almost knocked him down.

Lower ranks I passed by at regiment seemed properly awed and I overheard an observant PFC say respectfully, "That's the last guy to escape from the outpost!"

I was anxious to reach Love company and find out if the rest of my guys made it. Again the man prone on the litter and the pathetic shape of the one half-sitting beside the litter revisited me, as it has many times over the years. Was either of them alive; could I have saved one?

Of course not, but my conscience was never reasonable.

I was escorted to the transient officers' mess tent where I gulped down what the mess sergeant handed me on a tray, and leaned over outside and violently released it. On the way to where they said Love was, I spied a form I recognized from the rear, chubby Father Carl Carrol (having left the priesthood, now married living in Roswell, Georgia), one of our regimental chaplains. He was stepping his way carefully flat rock to flat rock over a makeshift ford and, splashing through the foot-deep stream, I grabbed his elbow and blurted: "Boy, have I got religion now."

He turned trying to recognize me, which he never had any reason to do.

"Good," he said. "I'm holding a special mass in half an hour, although most have already left."

"Oh, no," I told him, "I'm Agnostic."

I hadn't attended church or Sunday School willingly since my mother died.

When dying suddenly in combat, like being hit by a car, one hasn't energy or time to waste crying out anything more than *medic,* and *my God.* Nor conjure up calculated pathetic looks; unthinking, thoroughly frightened cornered animals like I once saw in the face of a wounded doe, silently pleading please don't kill me. Deers don't know God, not that we know of, but in our many hunting days in Korea the name of God bursts forth as a hard, vindicative curse or threat, rather than a pious supplication or simple proper noun.

Most of my guys died not begging or soliciting any supernatural thing, but hurling their last dire expletives at our enemy, bottled-up fear suddenly released to anger. God was mentioned alright. "Goddammit! Goddamn Chinks! Oh, my God, I've had it!" God is the most anguished verbal expression associated with the most violent surprise that you can ever get, the strongest expletive intended as such in our limited infantry combat vocabulary, limited at the final moment to the greatest mystery of all, God, whose great power remains a supposition to the very end. Where are you God? God, stop sliding around up there and hear me! You got to listen to me! I need you badly, God. Now! Now!

Catch me, I'm falling to Hell!

The sudden realization to young men crouching near the end of their lives on a dark mountain ridge facing heartless reality, shocked by the violent death of buddies, fearful that they too are going to be killed, is a hell of a demoralizing blow to their egos, not an indication of religious neglect. They might answer this fierce, frightening realization with a very short, desperate prayer of sorts, but one's pending, premature death is contrary to things one was taught to believe in church, besides, they are too young to die. "Me? Not me, I just prayed."

They immediately find that praying doesn't work. It may have once got them a new bicycle should their parents overhear them, but they need something more bulletproof than prayers to cover their trembling bodies, something to comfort their minds, like the sweet warmth from memories of family dependencies and affections, thoughts of home, a religion more powerful than any supposedly revealed or organized.

Some more philosophical who, with sophistic presence of mind when hard hit, yell out the real root of life—SHIT! Hear me foul excrement that was muscles, leftovers of living, the ugly remainders we shed each day and one day, embalmed or not, will return into.

Again, from the Blue Book—

After darkness fell on the night of 15-16 May, an estimated twenty-one Chinese divisions, flanked by three North Korean divisions in the west and six in the east, struck down the center of the peninsula against X Corps and the ROK III Corps in the Naep'yong-ni-No-dong area. To the right was the US Second Division, with the ROK Fifth and Seventh Divisions on its right, and the ROK III Corps to their right. Chinese units crossed the Pukhan River west of Chunchon, and on 16 May other units struck hard against the ROK Fifth and Seventh Divisions. The patrol base regiment [only us terrified survivors] fell back to Noname Line, and by 1930 hours of 16 May the two ROK divisions were heavily engaged along a twenty-mile front in the vicinity of Hangye-ri, a village ten miles northeast of Inje. The two divisions held their ground for a time, then fell back, disor-

ganized and broken.

On the left [west] shoulder of the enemy salient, the Second Division, including the French and Dutch Battalions, withstood resolute enemy attacks until 18 May, and then, together with the First Marine Division, moved right to fill the gap left by the two ROK divisions. IX Corps extended its front to the right to cover the area left by the Second Division and the marines. Van Fleet raced the 15th RCT [regimental combat team] of the US Third Division from Seoul to bolster the west face of the salient, and sent the Seventh and 65th Infantry [Puerto Rican Regiment, Third Division], to blocking positions at the southernmost part of the penetration. The swarming columns of Chinese and North Koreans soon almost surrounded the Second Division, pushing against its front, right, and rear. The Chinese even blocked the Second's main supply route, but a coordinated attack by the 9th Infantry driving northward, and the 23d and 38th Infantry Regiments attacking southward along with their French and Dutch contingents, regained control of the route. The Second Division stood fast and punished the enemy heavily.

Was ever a civilian uniformed to fight made aware of what total fear would do to his mind and body? If fear was mentioned at all, it was the disgraceful motivation of a coward. And did any Army official ever tell him what made him a coward and what a hero? Hell no, all left to chance in the most terrifying seconds of his life.

Combat fear is often totally disorganizing and demands the best of esprit de corps and training to counteract, which Marines advertise they have in abundance. What they find at last, however, is that it is more basic and necessary to know the awful truth beforehand than to simply be told you're invincible.

The sudden shock of a burp gun fired by a hidden infiltrator in the dead of night makes those who have heard it before have an instantaneous, uncontrollable recognition, the prime signal for fear reaction, for the sound is a peculiarly rapid, tearing, ripping sound that automatically affects your need to shit as the suddenly bloodless sphincter muscles around your asshole and your mouth react to loss of blood and your bladder is suddenly too full, and cause you to babble like an idiot when you mean to give firm orders. One must wait a few minutes to regain at least part control of the rushing blood flow that by then is strumming violently across his temples.

I reviewed what was done and said, especially by me, before and after the overrunning of our outpost. The first mistake I made was tip-toeing around the holes whispering, asking if anyone had spotted anything and were they all right. I learned later from J J that Sergeant Ulriche said I was spooking the guys. "Christ, you don't talk to men as though they was scared kids."

Fred Hurtz, Second Platoon, suggested that we humans, especially Westerners, have unnatural, artificial fear, that other animals whose brains are free from worry aren't burdened with, fear of failure and death and we have no reason to fear death either unless we have no belief in the soul, which is the real us. Way too much attention is given to our fragile, short-lived physical bodies which we know very well are transitory. Fear of the natural transformation of one's body to shit—or clay—is no reason to fear the extinction of us, the real us, souls.

The combat men of Love company had left the kitchen train by the time I arrived. None of the rear echelon, supply, morning report clerks who jotted me down MIA, mess personnel, etc. acted as though they recognized me. Grapevine preceded me from regiment that I was back alive and I wondered what sort of a virus made people unable to recognize a former acquaintance merely because of a rumor that he might be out of favor. Crimus, for no reason I was made to feel like a rogue elephant cast out of the herd. "I deserve a medal if anything."

I felt like Ulysses after all I'd been through when I reported to the company CP, exec officer Lieutenant Roy Carse and he gave me the cold shoulder.

"What's wrong with everyone?" I demanded.

"Everyone knows," Carse said.

"Knows what?"

"You bugged out. Lucky you don't get a court-martial."

Roy Carse was one of the very few friends I made in Korea. He

69

was a year older than me, a cop from Maplewood, New Jersey. Most of the company didn't know it, but Roy was a rifle platoon leader in Love Company, 38th in WWII from the landing on D Day plus one, through the Bulge where he got hit in the leg. He volunteered to waive a disability pension to return to combat if he could be in the same unit. His offer was accepted and processed that way and although he didn't suspect it a hold in his personnel records at division saw to it that he wouldn't be in combat again. Perhaps because of two Purple Hearts.

"My God, Roy" I swore. "After what's happened to me, what's wrong with everyone? I've been thorough hell and you guys think I bugged?"

"C'mon, Gould," Roy said. "Sergeant Ulriche says you took off to save your skin without telling anyone . . . but never mind the talk, get something to fight with and we'll see you catch up to company. Lieutenant Foney will have something to say later. Right now we got a fight coming."

Lieutenant Foney's first words were, "Gould, you'll have a chance to explain your actions."

"Accusing me of bugging?"

"I didn't say you bugged; said you've got explaining to do."

"Lookit, Goddammit, I may be junior in grade around here but if there's anyone to be blamed for anything, it's you sending two poorly armed guys down that path after you learned Chinks were all over the place."

"I didn't know anything for sure."

"You still don't; I warned you and did you have any reason to think it was safe. . . . You know, Foney, I'm a recalled Reservist like you but without a chance of becoming RA no matter how hard I try, and frankly, I don't give a shit what I say. You think you're John Wayne just because you're tall and grunt short answers because you don't have a damn thing to say that's worth listening to."

"Keep it up, Gould, you'll get your court martial. I'm company commander and don't forget it."

"I hear you put yourself in for the DSC, Distinquished Service Cross X Corps has handed out to each company on the outpost. True?"

"None of your business."

"I'd like to read the citation . . . for pulling your phone and radio without notifying the platoons and being right on Wilkes' ass getting off the outpost? C'mon, Foney, let's see the citation. Opoulus put in real heroes who died on their machine guns—Sergeants Erasmo G Lopez and Robert K Imrie."

Foney and I had a whizzer of a personality conflict. I was honest, forward, talkative and friendly; medium height and all. He was the so-called strong-silent type, about 6'2". I have in mind several examples of why he had to be smart enough to keep his mouth shut, but since John Knight (colonel retired, San Jose, California) told me that Foney died several years after the war from a rare form of sleeping sickness, of all things picked up in Korea, I'll refrain from relating them, even though I don't use his real name.

I was a pariah without knowing why, but like Carse said, we had a fight coming and pooped as I was, I was part of it. The supply sergeant gave me a surprisingly warm greeting.

"Hi, Lieutenant Gould. See you made it; a guy's got to watch out for himself. I know just how you feel. I was cut off from the guys of my rifle platoon at Kunu-ri. Lucky to be alive. Don't worry, sir. They'll come around."

"What do you mean, come around?"

"You know, lieutenant; they'll get over it."

"Never mind the talk," I told him. "Get me outfitted."

I gathered that the supply sergeant didn't appreciate my aloofness, as though I owed him a little more friendliness because we had some failing in common. He handed me an old steel helmet someone had been driving pickets with, an M1 rifle with a chipped stock and a frayed pistol belt with a battered canteen.

"Out of ammo belts and carbines," he said, handing me the one-bandage medical pouch and one bandolier of M1 clips. I was too tired to argue but found the chance a week or so later to tell him off and was able to sign out an army watch, along with an illuminated dial wrist compass. "Sergeant Ulriche has your platoon binoculars," I was told.

"Honest, lieutenant, you weren't the only one threw away equipment. I haven't had the opportunity to resupply. You're lucky I had this

71

stuff to turn in."

The motor pool sergeant jeeped me five miles down a bumpy road parallel to what had been the front, now penetrated in several places to where Love Company was chogeeing along bent over, either sad or real tired or perhaps both. Sergeant Ulriche grunted acknowledgment as I fell in behind leaving him at the head of the Banzai Third Platoon and I said hi to several others I was glad to see, but it was a long march following a frightening night for survivors and nobody was talkative or glad to see me, glad for anything. I was ignored except by J J Jenkins who saw me get out of the jeep and came running up.

"Lieutenant! Boy am I glad to see *you*! I heard we lost Dorn and his guys along with that wire patrol you made up. Speedy Gonzales made it out okay although nicked in the left arm. He'll be back in a few days."

I was the only one not hauling a pack which was just as well because I was too pooped to carry one anyway, or talk. I'd gone through every type of fear and worry known to infantrymen, plus great energy lost escaping and running three miles to the MLR, fast as I could without stopping, later tossing my cookies, as well as two almost sleepless nights on the patrol base outpost, but, bushed though I was, I was happy to discover how well the platoon made out without me.

We were on a twenty-mile forced route march to the northeast where Chinks caved in the Fifth ROKs. All available trucks in X Corps were dispatched to move ammunition and the US Third Infantry Division's 15th Infantry motored over to back up our old positions, even as ten-ton trailers were borrowed from Eighth Army Quartermaster to haul ammo from the docks at Inchon. Hiking relentlessly along, I asked J J why Sergeant Ulriche and Lieutenant Carse thought I'd bugged and he said he didn't rightly know. He told the platoon sergeant how I was drawn away trying to help the wiremen. Sergeant Ulriche seemed to prefer to believe I was a coward and deserter, I think, simply because I hadn't cleared with him personally as if he was still the acting platoon leader. I was hoofing in my place beside him but too pooped to explain and he never even glanced my way and it grew dark.

Before he died, I'm happy to say my platoon sergeant and I got to talk it over and he apologized for jumping to conclusions not knowing the real sequence of events. I was right, worrying about Dorn and his men but I didn't have to guard those company wiremen. He told me accusingly that wasn't my job and we didn't have to lose the three guys I ordered along on wire patrol. There was no reason they had to get it and custom was, he explained, not to pick riflemen on my own; first ask squad leaders for volunteers.

All I had to do was follow back out the withdrawal route with the platoon altogether, particularly with Master Sergeant Onis L Ulriche. They made it out, even as he led out the scattered men at Kunuri. I let him know I made a mistake and was sorry and Sergeant Ulriche finally told me, begrudgingly it seemed, that it was a fine thing I'd tried to do, but next time take care of our own men and don't risk them in such a hairy enterprise. If they needed help, it was Foney's job.

"But he . . ." I started to explain to myself, but we were bushed and it was over and another battle maybe worse down the way.

We marched wearily, faced away from the rising Chinese moon, until 2200 hours when we quit the main road and headed due east single file down a mere pathway. Much later during a ten minute break at a road junction and an artillery aid station, I showed them my swollen left thumb, infected from a cut on a C ration can the day before, the very day we were overrun. A medical sergeant gave me a shot of something and a little glass vial of Benzedrine something or other which he warned me to use sparingly — tiny hard white pills.

"Maybe they'll keep you going," he said.

We went another four or five miles up a different trail and mounted a small steep foothill of about 500 meters. Almost to the top we started digging holes and waited. It began to pour and turn cold — mid-May in the South Korean east central mountains — and I ached all over. Stupid, I forgot to draw a blanket and poncho and the supply sergeant hadn't volunteered them. I was never so conscious of my age. Knuckles of my right hand were blue holding the rifle sling and I transferred the piece to my left shoulder and got my left knuckles blue; the scab over the infected thumb, whitened in the cold rain, softened and the Band Aid loosened and slipped off. That thumb continued bothering me for several days off and on, throbbing and jumping. I tried to force my teeth from chattering. Counting out three of the little pills,

73

I remember thinking, "You'll need a dozen next time," but thought better of it. J J eyed me a bit, then reached under his poncho pointing to his blanket covering his shoulders, motioning that I could borrow it. I thanked him, but declined. I was already soaking wet. My lower teeth beat against uppers in noisy percussion like what would one day be called rock 'n roll. I played a game making rhythms from otherwise uncontrollable shivering and shaking, managing a staccato Clementine. I was about as miserable as animals get and for the first hour I sucked in my breath every ten minutes or so and held it as I tried to make myself stop shivering, my teeth from chattering.

We backtracked down to a valley and marched and at about 2400 stopped for a long rest and I bent down and put frozen hands in my crotch tight under my balls until I got tired bending and then tight under each arm pit, and then alternatingly under my balls again, which heaters were my only sources of warmth. I told Sergeant Ulriche to take over the platoon. He grumbled something. We both knew that I joined his platoon, officerless for the past four months, and it was very unnecessary to tell him anything. I went through the formality anyway, too pooped to argue with myself. If anything happened, I told him, I'd be out of it; do my best to take care of myself.

A secret voice within me jumped up and down clapping hands: "Boy, oh boy, are we ever lucky; we've got it good this time. We're no good to anyone anymore; when a surgeon sees us in the morning we'll be evacuated all the way to the States." I had wished shamelessly since my first patrol that, like most guys I knew on the job, I'd soon get a stateside wound; now I was contracting pneumonia, or worse, hopefully ambulatory so I could still otherwise get around.

I shivered badly through the night not knowing whether I was getting any sleep or not. I must have, for in the morning, as the sun exploded over the eastern mountains, things around me steamed, including me, I blew hard and hawked lumps of yellow-green stuff up from my chest, which became much less tight—I took deep breaths without hurting and the swelling and throbbing subsided in my thumb. The medic's shot was a winner.

To the dismay of the little voice that assured me we'd be evacuated, instead of quitting I began to feel I had the making of some heroic

74

rifle platoon leader all right; could really take it. Crimus, in the past few days; I'd taken more than a young George Patton his first time out or, further back and better yet, Napoleon. Napoleon Gould standing on the banks of the Neman, or maybe, to be patriotic, twenty-one-year-old George Washington trudging knee deep through cold west Pennsylvania swamps in that miserable winter weather, warning young French Lieutenant Jumonville to get his ass off British property.

From our division Blue Book—

By early morning of 18 May, the situation in the sector of the 38th Infantry had become critical with many of the units fighting Chinese on all sides. The First Battalion of the 38th was in particularly dangerous shape with the main enemy penetration between A and B companies [where friend Conley was taken away POW]. It was evident that help would have to be provided, so, at first light the Second Battalion of the 9th shifted eastward behind the 38th and attacked northeastward while the Third Battalion of the 9th launched a drive to the north. The purpose was to seal off the enemy who had succeeded in bursting through the lines.

As there was no reserve available to the 23rd, the Division commander attached the strongest company remaining in the Third Battalion of the 38th to the 23rd as reserve, it was Item Company, then composed of one officer and 94 enlisted men. The enemy hurled fresh waves of troops at the modified Noname line shortly after midnight on 19 May. The fire of battle raged for 90 minutes with the Third Battalions of both the 9th and 38th bearing the brunt of the attack.

By 1030 hours, 18 May, communications were reestablished with the First and Third Battalion of the 38th and arrangements made to air-drop urgently needed supplies to the units that had been cut off. Both battalions had suffered heavy casualties and were extremely short of ammunition and rations.

That night, the first after being overrun, we hit it lucky and found no Chinks. We passed a warm day in sunshine and took a hot

75

meal from insulated marmite cans brought to us by Carse in a Love Company jeep trailer. Having been informed of my plight over the radio, Roy saw that I got a poncho and blanket, a field jacket (a bit too large), an M2 carbine with three thirty-round magazines, carbine knife (bayonet) and an entrenching tool.

I listened to battle tattle of some of the guys, especially Sergeant E-5 Raymond Roundtree, who, as Lawrence 'Pop' Miller's assistant replacing Dorn's lost Third Squad. Pop, was back to sergeant E-5, on his way up again to E-6, which stripe he lost in March for telling off a rear echelon officer, Tree, with us by mistake, was the first Black assigned to the 38th until August when all segregated Black combat units in Korea were disbanded and some assigned to the 38th Infantry. Tree had a great sense of humor, so typical of his race, greeting us in the Banzai Third as he reported in slave jargon with a grin: "Here's yo token nigger."

Late in the day trucks came to pick us up. I rode in the cab of one containing half of the Banzai Third, Ulriche in the other cab. It was an all-colored trucking company (despite the Truman Executive Order for all to integrate) of the Transportation Corps. My driver chattered like the proverbial monkey—"I'se sure glad I wasn't with youse guys. Man, I heerd youse clobbered bad. I mean bad bad." I dropped off half asleep half daydreaming, in which this time I threw my grenade to kill the Chinks and busted through and rescued the man slumped beside the litter. Unfortunately the guy on the litter was dead, bled to death as I presumed but I packed his buddy on my shoulders for he had a chance and he turned out to be the great hero, Master Sergeant Ulriche, former first lieutenant, two Silver Stars and Purple Heart, veteran of Guadacanal and Kunu-ri, North Korea. He kept telling me, "Let me down Dud, can't make it with me, let me down, get out yourself."

"Nothing doing, sarge, it's both of us or none."

I stumbled with him on my shoulders and he was a couple inches taller than me, to the MLR and a movie cameraman took our picture and got a shot of me easing Sergeant Ulriche down on a litter carried by two medics with red crosses on their helmets, as they wore only in World War II before Japs and krauts used them as aiming stakes. A well-lighted photo showed my sweaty face, dirty beard and firm jaw.

Man, it would be in all the papers and the Watertown Times, me covered with blood, beaten, staggering through a mine field in spite of everyone yelling to set him down and save yourself. And Ulriche would have a young, beautiful sister and. . . .

Motoring along we passed small bands of ROK soldiers strolling along, deserters of the Fifth ROK Division which unit also bugged out at Wonju in February 1951, exposing an American flank to be overrun. They were silent, guilt-ridden, smiling nervously, too broadly. Some very few wore bandages and a few limped, all hurrying south unarmed toward safety, smirking with what seemed luminous smiles in the darkness. We Americans stared back in disgust.

"Your goddamn country we're fighting for," a soldier called out in the dark.

"Hey, Kim," another called. "Where you go, Pusan? Suck a hatchi."

Matthew B Ridgway, commanding general, Eighth Army—

I drove out north of Seoul and into a dismaying spectacle. ROK soldiers by truckloads were streaming south, without order, without arms, without leaders, in full retreat. Some came on foot or in commandeered vehicles of every sort. They had just one aim—to get as far away from the Chinese as possible. They had thrown their rifles and pistols away and had abandoned all artillery, mortars, machine guns, every crew-served weapon.

And on one of his visits to Korea after the second fall of Seoul, General MacArthur complained of the mass desertion of ROK units; "I haven't seen a wounded man yet."

The Chinese moon popped up as the convoy made a sharp turn off the MSR, main supply route, and pulled up in the middle of a large treeless valley. Hopping down, the guys lined a ditch, then hurriedly zipped up their flies to go looking for buddies. Lifetimes were shortened, and they sought to fraternize with guys among them they felt comfortable with before they, too, were gone forever. No one mentioned that, but all felt the need for close association. Me? No one but J J and

Sergeant Roundtree looked my way. Five Black drivers made a tight, intimate group, joking and laughingly poking one another on the arm, stabbing playfully at one another, kidding because this or that individual had been hard to overtake motoring down the undeveloped oxen roads as they lifted off what was left of the Second Battalion the night before.

"Woo-heee! man! I'se seen folks move, man. You was movin'. Hear what I say, man, you was long gone."

"Say I was skeered? Sh-e-e-et, man, I ain't the onliest one," laughing and rolling his eyes. "Ain't nothin' slow about Jesse, man. You ain't the onliest one."

God, I thought, guys like that can't ever be lonely.

French Legionnaires were grouped loosely at the truck dismount point waiting for a ride, talking in low voices in broken English with survivors of King Company. Around the corner 105s fired frantically answering trouble in the hills to our right front. Nearby a battery of their big cousins, 155mm long toms, longer barrels than ordinary howitzers, sent out volleys and after the initial smoke blows out behind their shells large blue-white smoke rings floated up lazily from their barrels high into the clear air through moonlight. As each smoke ring dissipated, wisps of residual blue smoke, seemingly an afterthought, came up lazily from the barrels for night breezes to whisk away—bad-ass Wild West gunfighters puffing to clear powder smoke from the barrels of eight-ton six shooters.

A crowd of ROKs, fully equipped, uniformed in fatigues like us—from a little distance the same as us—bustled and jabbered, gesticulating excitedly in clusters of two and three, as an American KMAG advisor, a major, pushed through trying to get them to assemble. "Hey!" he shouted at his ROK lieutenant interpreter. "Let's get some organization around here. Line them up!"

"Them ROKs bugging on us?" a voice demanded.

"What's it to you?" came an angry reply.

Mike Company, battalion's heavy weapons, was seating 81mm mortar base plates for tubes over to the left. In the center of activity nearer to the road a hamlet of primitive huts thatched with bundles of aged rice straw rested behind light green, double-walled arctic tents for battalion staff officers and across from Mike Company CTC (civilian

78

transportation corps) laborers were boiling huge fire-blackened pots of daikons (large elongated white radishes) and rice.

A KMAG captain, on the defensive for the misbehavior of his ROK unit, demanded somewhat aggressively of Lieutenant Fred Hurtz: "What unit you with?" Fred told him "Second Platoon, Love of the 38th" the officer asked, "Where's the rest?" When told, "This is all that's left," the captain shut his eyes hard and turned away.

The Chinese moon was straight up when Foney caught up to us in his jeep. Peering nervously at his watch, he demanded of no one in particular: "Why hasn't the company fallen in?" Spotting me, he ordered, "Gould, get on the ball; fall them in."

"All right," I yelled. "The company commander wants you to fall in. Let's get on the ball."

After Love fell in, First Sergeant, Master Sergeant, James B Luther, RA16230326, marched us out to the road and up a valley leading to where more artillery was firing. A zig-zag file of French Foreign Legionnaires passed us boot-sloshing wet, headed to the dismount point we just left. A chance meeting of Caucasians in that Asian wilderness. It seemed obvious to some of us they were quitting the fight, while we were being committed. Private First Class Kiezlowsky, Ski, whose first name was Spudacus, whatever that means, sounded off: "Hey, Frenchy, no Chinks that way."

"They're lovers not fighters," snapped another.

"Yeah, frogs are funny people," Private Funaro sounded off for those who understood English. "Fight with their feet, fuck with their face."

"Shut up!" Sergeant Ulriche snarled.

Bringing up the rear of the weary French column were five Legionnaires shrouded motionless on litters.

A few miles north we watched red flares sailing along on low sky winds, and tracers bouncing off Hill 442, small seemingly redhot balls, as units of the 23rd Infantry attacked, and across a narrow valley was H 710 where the French Battalion had been repulsed after forty casualties. The fatigued silent Legionnaire company that passed us had gone back with litters to retrieve the last of its dead.

Seeing us headed for their old objective, a small group of 23rd's walking wounded waiting for ambulances or litter jeeps cheered us on in low, subdued voices, offering what little ammunition they were carrying away, holding out grenades and taking off over their helmets olive drab cloth bandoliers, drab necklaces of M1 clips.

We route-marched at ease, in spooky moonlight, beat up and silent, behind a handful of headquarter's platoon and First Sergeant Luther. Next came the Fourth, weapons platoon, led by Master Sergeant Darrow Billson; then our Third Platoon, Sergeant Ulriche and me; the Second Platoon, ROTC Second Lieutenant Fred Hurtz was last; a nice guy, Hurtz, very intelligent but a sheltered city-bred young man; a bit naive about nonintellectual ways, the only Jew I got to know personally; and the young battlefield-commissioned Second Lieutenant Dale Hollingsworth with the First Platoon. I got real close to Fred, as with no one before; for my money he was one of us; whatever was obviously Jewish, that irritated gentiles, he left at home.

Beaten though we were, and in this condition like every platoon across the line, looking around I felt we were still a good match for Chinks. Or maybe it was only my confidence growing for some reason. I hadn't actually killed anyone yet but I'd been shot at enough to call myself veteran, earned a combat infantryman's badge of honor. At last I was an unmistaken machismo man not to be trifled with. As we marched along I checked our strength. Aside from the small arms we packed on us were the real powerful weapons carried by quarter ton jeep trailers, the larger in battalion weapon carriers: 57mm recoilless rifles that replaced the WWII 57mm cannon company at regiment and the old one-pounder, 37mm cannon company at battalion. The 3.5-inch hand-held rocket launcher replacing the WWII 2.5-inch bazooka, and there were 60mm mortars of company weapons platoon and the 81 mortars of weapons company at battalion, with the 4.2-inch 105mm chemical mortar company at regiment, so-called in WWI designed for throwing poison gas shells. Light 30 caliber machine guns were carried on marches in company trailers and the heavies of weapons companies, water-cooled for steady overhead firing, in weapons carriers.

Ammunition for all was hauled behind the column in battalion's 3/4-ton P&A pioneer and ammunition weapon carriers, or in company quarter-ton jeep trailers. On our long marches guys with truly handicapping afflictions, still-draining nonvital wounds, rode in weapons carriers or jeep trailers as they could find room.

By the time I got to Korea, Chinks, with all the American stuff they'd captured, especially out West and North, were as well armed as we were, and we all knew only too well they had something that we could not count on—an avowed necessity to die before their ever-present commissars who very vehemently declared at every opportunity the obvious lie that they all were happy volunteers defending their homeland.

Compare those persistent, narrow-minded assholes with a rather easy-going platoon leader like me. After Ulriche left, I seldom ordered my guys around. Chinese writers may have boasted of their soldiers' willingness to die but, aside from those Nationals who stepped on mines, I never heard of one going that far, nor any chronicler of modern military history being able to say he was told by a Chink he was *willing* to die. I've been close enough to enough Chink soldiers to think otherwise. I suggest that they are no more weary of life than we; though we were all guilty, one way or another, of being there to die—a long way from being willing to die. Trained to obey like animals performing in a circus maybe, but sealed in one-way kamikazes, no!

I felt much closer to my guys, even the hero Onis L Ulriche. I decided that in the next battle that seemed about to happen, I'd take over and show everyone how brave I really was, that is, granted the circumstances were right. Of course, I could never supplant Sergeant Ulriche in the eyes of the guys and I wouldn't want to; he'd already proven so much to them. In the first place, I tended to be a little round-shouldered and only five feet, eight and a half inches, although I could bench press ninety and was as wiry as they come. Much as I aspired to be a professional writer, I had always to do hard physical labor for a living.

Slogging along, it hurt to realize I'd never see the platoon together again. Dorn and his six-man squad and three from Pop Miller's gone forever. One thing for sure, I'd never be separated from the guys again. I couldn't understand how they might think I deserted them looking out for my own hide by the very hazardous path I took if nothing else. Seemed obvious to me, and mentioned once to J J that if anything, I should get a medal. After all, nobody ordered me to do such a

dangerous thing. I was an asshole for sure. If it happened to some photogenic Limey leftenant, they'd call it noble, no greater love and all that,
not that Love wasn't involved – a pun or something.

At the least I guess I should have let Sergeant Ulriche know
where I was going because I felt so sorry for those wiremen but it was
kind of spontaneous. I never decided anything; just got sucked along.
He probably would have talked me out of it as suicidal, which is a hell
of a lot different than heroic. At least J J and Gonzales knew the truth.

As a combat veteran, at last I sensed an opportunity to be a
winner. If only I could survive long enough. "Boy," I thought, "we're
the Banzai Third all right." Company, battalion and regiment were all
out of my perspective. Of the combined effort, all that mattered was our
platoon. I'd get them to like me as they do Sergeant Ulriche, at least
show me some respect. I'd stick out my neck on purpose and do something foolishly reckless to prove how brave I was; maybe Onis would get
to like me, or grow to respect me. How to do that I decided was to rush
right into things without worrying what could happen to me; maybe
knock off fifteen or twenty Chinks. I'd need a BAR for that, and maybe
yank a burp gun from one of them and turn it around.

As we continued our slow climb up a valley, I couldn't believe
my eyes. There up ahead were Chinks, silhouetted against distant flares,
on the skyline about two miles to our left front where, I estimated, the
French had been. My eyesight seemed superior to everyone's, for on
several other occasions I spotted Chinks or gooks before others did.
Some might not think it a manly thing to do, look all over like that all
the time. Maybe I was more apprehensive, or worried, or concerned as
a leader; or, hell, let's be frank, more scared than most. I tried to get
the message passed up the file ahead of me but my message died a few
men away so I hightailed it up the rocky trail pushing guys out of the
way when necessary to reach Lieutenant Foney, practically shouting for
him to stop and have a good look. When I got to him, military deco-
rum, hell, I grabbed his left arm to turn him around and pointed to
where I saw Chinks as their legs showed in the flare light, snipping dots
under the lowest branches of pine trees, more visible as they crouched
over to run across a clearing to the next group of trees. Hundreds of
busy ants flanking us.

Foney halted the column and finally after making out the Chinks called for his radio and soon we were ordered to retrace our steps to battalion headquarters. I returned to the platoon and fell in in the lead with Sergeant Ulriche feeling important. Someone was rewarded for listening to me. Probably saved battalion headquarters.

We retraced our steps and took the left turn in a fork in the foothill trail, wading a small stream grown uncomfortably deep from spring rains. Cold water came to my knees, the footing was difficult and later clammy water sloshing and squishing inside my boots for miles made my toes sore where they rubbed against wet leather despite our socks.

"Man," Pop said in a low voice, "seems I washed dishes with them feet; toenails limber as rubber."

Our eyes focused on H 710, in plain view from a slightly different angle this time. We stopped for a ten-minute break, filling canteens, supposedly after dropping in a little Halazone pill of tasteless water purifier that supplanted the strongly flavored chlorine tablets of WWII. Few used them, subconsciously, I suppose, preferring to get sick enough to be sent home; at least back to the rear for a while, like a self-inflicted wound.

We gathered in small bunches, speculating about the heavy firefight we heard going on to our left in the black of night lit here and there by magnesium flares, criss-crossed by tracers. Although they were used by us for tracing lines to targets, correcting sightings, the enemy never used anything to give a fix on their starting points, nor willie peter (wp, white phosphorus) hand grenades or 60mm mortar shells, unless taken from us. Holly, Sergeant Billson, Hurtz, Sergeant Ulriche and I were called by Foney who pointed to his map lit by his flashlight, at one hill, 442, one in a group of foothills between us and H 710 and told us we were ordered to fortify it and remain there until further notice. Sergeant Ulriche still used our platoon map without inviting me.

We began to climb a finger leading to 442. Someone grouched, "Look, it's 0100 already," and I looked in vain at my left wrist for confirmation. A couple of guys pooped out on the first ascent, up the last of what seemed to be a perpendicular climb. Our soaking wet boots seemed made of limber lead and all that drew us along was the persistence of the lead man and the necessity to maintain the regulation five yards apart. "Keep up. Keep up," we nagged one another. "Don't bunch up." "Crimus," I muttered. "Don't lag."

Carbine strapped cater-corner over my back, I learned to remove my steel helmet, piss pot, carrying it under one arm to relieve my neck muscles or held by the brim, swinging it low to my side back and forth steadily as a pendulum to keep me moving at even pace. I learned to walk sideways flat-footed up steep inclines, to stomp my feet down heavily, digging with the sharp outside of the soles of my boots at an angle, followed by a stomping out with the outside of my other foot for better traction. Sometimes we moved on hands and knees and, when we stood did so slowly, experimentally, leaning forward to prevent ourselves from being pulled backward. It was impossible always to resist the sliding down pull unaided, and we searched ahead as we climbed for large rocks or shrubs, or even better, low-growing gnarled mountain trees to cling to or brace our feet against. At rest our bodies had to work against gravity.

Starting up each time I carried myself low, zig-zagging like the others back and forth on the trail up the slopes. It was better to move steadily, deliberately, planting your feet heavily on their sides stomping one foot after the other; better to take plenty of two-minute breaks than fewer longer ones . . . get you out of rhythm.

Foney called so many halts and lit his map so often we got the impression we might be on the wrong finger. Good or bad, one had to trust his superior. After coming down on the other side, we soon found ourselves climbing up from another saddle.

"Crimus," I thought.

"Will someone make up his friggin' mind?" one complained behind me.

"Who's in charge of this mob?" another groaned loudly.

Funaro added his bit, "Suck a hatchi."

Others snickered, "S-s-h-h-e-e-it!"

"We're trying to confuse enemies," Sergeant Roundtree explained.

Suddenly, two, three, four, up to six three-round vollies of 'friendly' 105 artillery exploded proximity shells fifteen feet in the air just beyond the company command group and lead rifle platoon, luckily catching our platoon on the protecting side of a gully. We 'heard' each other yell my God only by seeing open-mouthed, strained expressions as chunks of meteors, hunks of almost red-hot shrapnel showered down, crackling and sizzling on the damp ground, zinging through trees and bushes, dropping leaves of one tree like heavy hail. Proximity are shells, still a top secret to the end of WWII, in the nose of which a tiny radar reckons the distance to objects exploding at a preset footage from any solid object to get an airburst that would reach men cowering in the bottom of their holes. VT, variable time, shells, fuze timers set by artillerymen for air bursts, in which the time in flight to a target would be known and a nose fuze set to explode after a certain time in the air so many feet above.

Guys slid downhill on their bellies, propelling themselves pushing off with their hands; others dropped their rifles, stood panic-stricken with arms over their faces as though to ward off the cutting steel fragments, and ran stumbling into one another. Our company lost two KIA and three WIA, ambulatory. As I said, the Banzai Third was spared.

"Gawd!" someone growled. "My gawd, this is awful!"

I was left shuddering with hunched shoulders as a weird feeling came over me. What was this strange primeval dread I felt? Surely, something that wasn't supposed to happen to civilized men. 'Friendly' fire they always admitted was a sorry accident and yet it happened on and off in all wars. Obviously not intentional, although Chinks were known to have overrun artillery batteries and turned cannon on us. To me there was no explanation; no excuse at all. It was a sinister thing with deeper meaning of self-destruction, assisted suicide of a strange sort. But I had no time to dwell on the feeling other than record the impression.

The US government has always softpeddled, even denied, as late as 2001 in the terrorist war in Afghanistan, the occurrence of short rounds killing friendly troops. But its existence cannot be denied as is admitted in the following note in Training Bulletin 2, 14 March 1952, Office of Chief Army Field Forces, Fort Monroe, Virginia dispensed to all US Army infantry and artillery units down to company—

It was observed on numerous occasions that frontline commanders hesitated to call for close artillery support because of a frequently justified fear of short rounds. It is important that constant attention be directed to elimination of faulty range estimation and firing techniques. They can spell the difference between an easy victory and a costly defeat (Comd Rept - 2d Inf Div)

The faulty sighting was corrected and the next salvo went sailing high over us to the hill we faced. We were called to order again.

"Okay, fall in; on the ball; let's chogee."

"It's all over men. Second platoon here, fall in on me," I heard Fred Hurtz yell.

"Okay," I yelled. "Third platoon on me."

Instead, they sought Master Sergeant Ulriche.

Foney started us up 442 again from a different finger with a much easier-going trail. We bent forward, once more climbing until we reached the summit unopposed. Straight ahead, lighted by the full Chinese moon, was H 710, Chinks swarming all over it—thousands.

"Crazy," Tree moaned. "All them enemies crawlin' 'round."

"Plain suicide!" someone insisted. "They'll pick us off like flies."

Given rest, we were allowed to mill around our peak as freely as the Chinks and our guys soon became more curious than frightened; first time I observed enemy without being shot at, or so I hoped. I borrowed the platoon binoculars from Sergeant Ulriche and focused to see what I thought was an officer, some kind of honcho because he had binoculars too and was watching me. Most probably captured from us. After a bit, both let our binoculars drop on their straps to our chests and then, disappointed with what little we could see without them, put them to our eyes and observed one another once more. I wondered about him; was he as amazed as I was at this harmless sport?

Our excuse for avoiding making an attack, I learned later, was sudden lack of artillery preparation and air support, it being night. What, I wondered, was their excuse? Certainly they could have clobbered us. Their ammo, of course, was much more difficult to replace than ours and they were in retrograde.

I had to shit urgently. I asked myself why, since I'd eaten so little the past four days. Pissing my pants and now having to go to the bathroom. At a time like this, I scolded, should have gone before you left this afternoon. Like the stone pressing against my bladder, I couldn't put it off forever. Going behind a large boulder, I dropped my fatigue pants and shorts and let it drop. Fortunately it was hard in one piece for there was no ass wipe in the helmet given me. Prefolded tissues come with C rations and normally I'd have a few leaves in my upper fatigue jacket pocket or, most often, under my helmet liner.

When I came back from the bushes, a private next to me was shivering as though cold, not that it was exactly mild.

"Sir," he asked hoarsely, "Goin' to make us go up there?"

"Expect so," I answered and to myself, "somebody do something, do something — get us out of here."

Then, as though the private's God took pity on him and me, battalion radioed they couldn't get artillery so we should hold up until plans were made. How rumor starts, I don't know, but it went around that we were not going further, probably that whole night. Rumor or not, we were ordered to take over Chink holes and make them deep enough. We knew Chinks had been there recently from the strong odor of garlic. It was difficult scratching and trying to shovel the stony earth with little collapsible entrenching tools. What we needed were pick axes. We had a few and D handle engineer shovels as well, in jeep trailer number four, not enough to go very far.

Once again I realized how damn pooped I was. J J sensed it and offered, "Just sit there, Lieutenant, I'll dig a CP, you take it easy. I know what you've been through."

I thought this was the nicest thing anyone said to me since I got to the asshole of the world. As he chopped at the hard dirt, he sang low and soft, "O'ver the moun-tain, o-ver the see-ah-ee. Bring back . . . oh bring back . . . oh bring back my baby to me. O-o-over thee-e ocean, o-v-er the s-e-a . . . bring back my bonnie to me."

Fog that rose from the ground on rainless nights effused moonlight in great empty expanses of valleys, swirling around below hilltops of that eerie world of hills and mountains as the flickering light of flares in our small portion of a great battlefield showed down, reflected from black night clouds. Our position on the hill, 442 meters, was quite low for the average Korean hill in the east central mountain spine, and fog and mists of the night reached up from valleys almost to us. Far west an angry storm flashed and sounded its artillery. Valleys were bottomless, only surrounding hilltops visible, stepping stones across an endless fluffy white river, marked by Chinese retreat flares, huge green blobs thrown into the sky.

Under each misty hole or valley we worried were ghastly secrets, battalions of enemies lining up to get at us.

At about 0330 tracers drew our eyes to two firefights progressing at levels lower even than 442; one, we worried, from the direction of our battalion command post. Fog obscured the red tracers from one anxious machine gun that sent ricocheting rounds long distances through the free air above the white screen, burning brightly; at other times striking the ground near their starting points, angling into the night air in rapid red streaks, little burning balls bouncing off boulders, disappearing, burning out to mere wisps high above. Here and there from other valleys came Chink signal flares from captured Very pistols and, from an engagement miles to our west, chandelier flares swinging back and forth delivered high above by our heavy artillery pieces. The Chink light bursts we wanted to see were green Very flares that signaled retreat — pull back from an objective.

Company CP was under an overhanging rock shelf out of sight of Chinks as the yellow horde stopped digging to watch the rest of us and, as though by tacit agreement and being out of easy small arms range, neither side fired a shot until one asshole from the First Platoon turned loose his automatic rifle. The Chinks scurried for cover and a sergeant down the line roared, "Can it! Damn it, can it! Dumb sonofabitch want to fan things up? We ain't lookin' for medals, pinhead!"

Rain water still dripped from the rocks an hour later when bugles and flares came against the forward, northern, part of our loose company perimeter, a sharp reply to the pinhead BAR hero. No warning shots, no warning at all, and there was Death spread out wholesale once more, going down the ranks flipping coins — Mongolian death makers and slightly taller, less high cheek bones and lighter colored death-

death-dealers from the ricelands of China in their winter quilted jackets, rapidly penetrating between two of our platoons. Sergeant Ulriche quickly had the guys in a tight, self-supporting, criss-crossing fire plan and the Banzai Third, spitting out a hateful volley at one Chink effort was left alone, although our position was threatened overhead by a captured 60mm mortar not far away.

A kid from one of the other platoons with a jammed automatic rifle scrambled panicky into the hole with Sergeant Ulriche who worked out a torn, separated cartridge case with his pocket knife like the proverbial thorn in the lion's paw and sent him rearmed back to his platoon. Before the furious attack was over, which it was as suddenly as it began, three guys lay bloodied and limp in the first platoon, five altogether, high price for such a brief attack and withdrawal, and seven wounded. Afterward, guys scooted from hole to hole, checking on buddies, drying off, congratulating one another on a questionable victory, thankful the Chinks disengaged. Our platoon was alerted by Pop Miller to look for Ski.

"Missing all right, upstairs," one said.

"Might know it would be Ski," another piped up.

It became one of the platoon jokes how Ski, in the midst of the action jumped up, followed the guy with the jammed rifle back to his hole and, deciding to stay put until the fight was over, and fell sound asleep.

Our brief, bloody engagement that night was lost in bigger, more tragic battles as splintered, stubborn companies, battalions and regiments of the US Second Infantry Division, the Indianheads, took on the many enemy units let into our rear by the wide breech opened in the Fifth ROK Division. Loss of the good men in Love Company was painful but little compared to some units as together we halted the last of the Chink offensive starting them in a grand retreat north across the 38th Parallel.

Sad news over the SCR 300 back-pack company radio to battalion, from 38th Regimental Tank Company, our battalion CP was overrun and, among others, replacement battalion executive Captain Tracey marched off POW. Grapevine was that Colonel Coughlin was furious when he learned of Tracey's fate. Not just that he was a likeable young officer, but the fact that Major Wilkes, battalion commander, remained safe in the kitchen trains and let his executive go forward. Such procedure was unheard of, unexplainable and outrageous and should have resulted in Wilkes immediate removal. The fact that Tracey, a West Pointer new to Korea, eagerly volunteered was no excuse.

As we neared the valley where battalion set up headquarters, two of our regimental tanks came roaring ingloriously from out a side valley—whipped elephants shaking their big butts taking evasive actions—running from trouble, making gruff, mechanical growling noises, shifting, gear-meshing, pouring it on, spewing black puffs of diesel smoke. We discovered why when a strange, startling new sound made us pull our heads deep under our helmets and down under our collars—Chinks halfway down a neighboring finger throwing low velocity shells at the tanks from a 75mm recoilless rifle captured from the heavy weapons company of a ROK regiment.

L. B. Bounds of Fort Worth, commo officer, fellow member of our Korean War Veterans Alliance, was taken prisoner on a short mission to aid Company A, First Battalion nearby on Wilkes's order and ended up a long-term companion of our buddy Conley Clarke in several Chinese POW camps. Ask *him* about Major Wilkes, despised by practically every officer who served under him.

My platoon was put out to scout and as daylight prevailed, we had plenty sightings of Chinks on ridges around us. Our heavy artillery had landed on a long finger to our right front on the white-clothed Chink scouts disguised as Korean civilians who overran battalion headquarters and slunk off the skyline headed north with a squad of prisoners.

I saw Chinks on a hill ahead of us pointing our way excitedly and as our mountain domain was lighted by the sun, we located six sets of identifying air panels, four laid down by the enemy correctly to conform to the day's secret code to protect them from air strikes, yellow shank, red-top design pointing north.

We returned to where we left battalion before midnight at a crossroad. I sauntered over to a group of officers where Captain Brownell was explaining what happened. He greeted me, "Hi Gould, doin' better?" Set up with his heavy weapons company across from battalion's forward CP, he witnessed what went on by gunflashes when the CP was clobbered. "Just an hour after King, the last rifle company left, Chinks came through our Civilian Transportation Corps across from where our heavy machine guns were sand bagged. Like a streak of shit through the dark they were, well rehearsed, screaming, 'Don't shoot! CTC, don't shoot!' Them little bastards had regular CTC shoulder patches pinned to their white civilian sleeves and had been taught those two words in English, 'Don't shoot!' When we opened up we had to kill CTC as well. We killed a few Chinks and eight CTCs and a number wounded.

"Lieutenant Carr, motor pool officer, came over with the outfit, did his best to line up jeeps to pull them out when a burp gunner caught him low at close range shattering his shin bones. When he stumbled down, another bastard walked over and shot him in the head. So many things happened, I can't remember all. It was dark, of course, and I was busy as a cat covering shit on a hot tin roof. It was mass confusion. Not the Chinks; they'd been trained as a raiding party to hit us. Seemed only a second before they were gone, taking about ten of our guys, including the new exec, Captain Tracey. With the Fifth ROKs collapsed, they were taking POWs again.

"Molinsky, you know Molinsky, the new supply officer. He dropped into a hole with wireman Sergeant Kramer and pretended he was dead. Kramer was hit already and unconscious and a goddamn Chink heard him groan and worked a barrel into his mouth and pulled the trigger. Molinsky said he liked to shit his pants. Then that dirty little cocksucker stepped on Molinsky's stomach, bent down and grabbed both their wristwatches.

"With the exception of Molinsky, all officers on the battalion staff were killed, badly wounded or led off POW. Captain Marcy, Battalion Surgeon, got it from a grenade as he was examining a guy. Others said they could never find his body and it was likely he was led off POW."

Tankers reported to regiment that King Company and Item, too, then assigned to the 23d, had been wiped out to a man. We knew it wasn't quite that bad; the further to the rear, the more absurd are worries. Less confident than we dogfaces of their strength, they had doom on their minds always. Those not directly involved always expect the worst, fear more than us warriors, and we found that our sister company, Item, had not been engaged at all that night due to sudden rains and shortage of artillery ammo which precluded them from attacking. Besides, she had less than a hundred survivors.

We grabbed a quick breakfast of C Sixs. In reserve we got B rations—in barracks A rations—three hot meals at regular stateside times, 0700, 1200 and 1730 after daily retreat when we stood to lower and salute the national flag that flew over us in reserve. Old Glory to riflemen. There was never a special time to eat in a combat situation; whenever we felt the urge and had Cs.

Sergeant LaPlace, our mess stewart, ran herd on a gang of lost Korean boys, ages eight to probably twelve. Where they came from no one knew; they just staked out Frenchy's warm mess tent last winter at Hoengsong for temporary room and board purporting to be his essential helpers. Taking turns, all they did was wash pots and open cans. Potato peeling was passé in the Army and everything came in cans or waxed boxes. All you did was open them. Every time we got wind of an inspection, the entourage, at times as many as twelve youngsters, was shooed away.

Every once in a while, Lieutenant Foney had a mean spell and told Frenchy to get rid of at least half of them. The interlopers would lie low for a day to humor him. Occasionally, Frenchy's GI cooks complained that the 'little bastards' got in their way and on their nerves and didn't do anything told to do. Especially the many rainy days the whole jabbering bunch would be in a corner of the large company mess tent squatting on the ground, completely wrapped up in some kind of a gambling game they played wherein they shouted at each other, held up cards with strange figures, and exchanged paper money, sometimes shouting like on the floor of a stock exchange.

There were always problems and arguments as the babble would rise to an irritating degree and when it got too noisy out would come Frenchy in his white mess coat and apron, sleeves rolled up, swinging a meat cleaver, yelling in Korean to get out cudda cudda, bali bali, and they'd hightail in mock terror. During our long reserve he periodically chased them down to the main road that ran past our camp, swearing at them in a mixture of Korean and English colored with French-Canadian.

"Catch a bus or something . . . take a tank, *alle sortir!* and don't come back begging no more. Chogee! I like a daddy you boys."

They would leave in a bunch bawling like babies and each time, before dusk, infiltrate back under the broad canvas where it was dry and warm, where unlimited food, which they grew to prefer to rice, could be had.

Out of sight down the long valley parallel and to our left, an early-morning air strike by South African F-51s (formerly P-51) made repeated passes. Although the target was out of our sight, we could see they were Mustangs as they zoomed up fast into the open sky after dropping their loads, on the first pass five-inch HVAR rockets, second napalm, and final four fifty-caliber machine guns each. I thought they zoomed up into the air away from the targets dangerously sharp and warned them, "Level off! Level off!"

Other air strikes came from Shooting Stars, F-80 jets, and F-86 Sabre jets but most all jets flew over targets delivering their loads too fast to be very effective. The marine/navy Corsair, F4Ws, a prop job, on the other hand, had ground support down to a T. Normally they supported the First, Fifth and Seventh Marine regiments of the First Marine Division and knew well how foot slogging dogfaces wanted the ridges worked. It angered and frustrated us to watch the high-speed jets zip in after Chinks, who early on, spotting Mosquito Air circling waiting for fighter bombers, ran over the ridge to hide behind rocks below to avoid all three terrible passes. Marine Corsairs, on the other hand, lowered their big flaps to slowly rake both sides of the ridgetop; first a plane on, say, the right just off the ridge with rockets, his mate following, slanting to the left just off the ridgeline to where the Chinks had vanished, and the flight of usually four planes would alternate this way through rockets, machine gun and napalm running Chinks back and forth.

Although no platoon leader was in on the secret movement orders arrived from regiment for us to proceed to Hongchon for hasty reorganization, absorb newcomer replacements and supplies. More than bloodied, we were half drained. The battalions would be shuttled in the order White, Red and Blue, second, first and third, we to do the most hoofing, the last to ride out alive.

Our dead were rolled in pup tent halves, ponchos, blankets or slid into black plastic body bags if and when we had extras. Regimental graves registration wouldn't be on the scene for several days, if the Noname Line was reestablished. However, three officers of the battalion staff and the sergeant major were rolled up and taken out on a battalion headquarters 2½-ton truck with the wounded to the nearest helicopter pad.

Regiment assumed battalion forward headquarter's work and radioed for an ambulance and three machine-gun-toting armored reconnaissance jeeps from regimental Recon platoon for guard while retrieving and assembling the dead. Name, rank and serial number of KIAs, WIAs, and MIAs were radioed as soon as possible to their company headquarters clerks where they'd be noted on the morning report. Thus an official record was kept of what goes on personnelwise every day of the war. Through them division knew its real tactical strength; how deployable its units were in that sector.

Cadavers were usually gathered by Korean labor teams of graves registration and delivered in the backs of trucks, or, if only a few, in a jeep trailer, weapons carrier or ambulance to one of four platoons of two companies of the 23d Graves Registration Group. The 148th Graves Registration Company headquarters was at Wonju, the 293d at Seoul. When up to strength, each platoon had thirty men, including my contact for this journal, Corporal Lynn Hahn of Whitehall, Michigan, trained for the grisly job at the Fort Lee, Virginia Quartermaster Graves Registration School where he was taught such depressing, earnest business as handling bodies and proper maintenance of soldiers' graves.

With transportation engaged in supporting fighting all over the map, moving priority supplies, food, water, ammo and troops to engage the enemy, units had to recover their dead as best they could and pile them at crossroads for Graves Registration recovery teams to collect and ship to the large Army mortuary in Japan for embalming before returning to the fast expanding American cemetery near Seoul or one of the other American cemeteries.

Where we failed to hold ground or lost it for days, enemy were depended upon to bury our guys, at least put them under out of sight. When that land was retaken, dead buddies were supposed to be located using campaign maps to pinpoint where bodies had to be left and might have been buried. None of the Grave Registration people in a division is formally quartermaster-trained to recover and handle dead and none but cemetery workers allowed to bury them.

A reported 8,600 or more remains will never be recovered, a fact not publicized until the nationwide protests by gold star mothers of the Vietnam War.

Those of us not burdened with dead and wounded pushed through a small river and over a dirt road, jostling, shouting back and forth until we were worked by First Sergeant Luther into a presentable column of twos on opposite shoulders of the roads, on trails single file in proper position in relation to organization and we hoofed a couple more miles.

"Hey, lieutenant, how you doin'?" some rifleman shouted.

I tried to smile. I'd hardly slept three days and nights and occasionally quivered in spasms from fatigue. I stumbled a lot because my muscles seemed to be becoming flaccid, rubbery, aching, harder to control, which worried me.

"Yah, lieutenant, what you think of Korea now?" an old-timer shouted.

"Yeah," was all I could answer rather weakly. Were they beginning to respect me now that J J was spreading the truth?

Rumor matured that we were headed for division reserve for, with the outpost tragedy, we were widely acclaimed a badly mauled battalion. Man oh man, anywhere there were no Chinks would be home. We laughed at nothing, using our hands for emphasis as we filed into a large assembly area of dry rice paddies, and one guy ran over to waiting tanks to give an iron hulk a big kiss.

"Baby, baby, am I glad to see you."

"Yeah?" he was warned from the open hatch. "Not when Chinks are on us."

Guys ran around stowing what was allowed on company trailers. "Load up! Load up!" a tank sergeant mimicked. "You heard the boss

95

man, chogee! What outfit's that?"

"Mushroom Company," Pop Miller answered. "Fed bullshit and kept in the dark!"

Lieutenant Carse led a convoy of company jeeps with trailers and Lieutenant Foney did something seldom seen—he smiled broadly. "Let's get at it," he shouted. "Let's go now. Fall in." So saying, he mounted the lead jeep and turned the company over to First Sergeant Luther who had already quietly fallen us in.

We were charged with a strange animal electricity, alert and expectant. We heard we were going all the way back to Pusan; one of the guard divisions on its way from Japan would take our place and the way things were, we'd probably hoof it all the way.

The 40th California National Guard and the Oklahoma Thunderbirds 45th, were both federalized and sent to Korea. Two more National Guard divisions, the 28th Pennsylvania 'Bucket of Blood,' and the 43d Connecticut, Rhode Island and Vermont, were brought on active duty in general reserve and then committed to West Germany to strengthening NATO and discouraging Soviets from jumping in.

Replacements for active duty with the Regular Army were drawn from Reserves, unsuspecting guys like me not active in units and from the standby federalized National Guard units, backing us up in Korea. After Chinks entered the Police Action, the 31st Alabama and Mississippi, the 37th Ohio, the 44th Illinois and the 49th Minnesota and North Dakota National Guards entered federal service on a standby basis. My last medic, Doc Carlson, Joliet, Illinois, was transferred to the active Regular Army from the 44th. Some 244,300 Reserve officers and men were called on active duty to join the 43,000 Reserve officers already on active duty when the war began.

"Where's John Wayne?" someone suggested.

"Fuck Wayne."

"Forty-eight, forty-nine, fifty!" my guys shouted in unison. "Fuck Wayne!"

"Yah," I told them. "That'll be the day." glancing around for appreciation and feeling just a little warmer.

A tanker said he heard we were slated for some prison island off the south coast where gook POWs were rioting . . . Koje-do Island.

"What?" Sergeant Burris asked unbelievingly. "Rioting? Prisoners? Mow the bastards down. Don't play with them."

"Forty-eight, forty-nine, fifty, s-o-o-me s-h-e-e-e—it! Mow 'em down!"

"That'll be the day," I joined in. Several of the guys gave me a cold stare and I realized I was pushing for acceptance maybe a little too fast.

"Hey, foot sloggers!" a tanker called. "What's that, sick call?" His buddies snickered.

"You tell 'em horseshit, you been on the road," Private Funaro yelled back.

"Fuck you! Got any friends? Fuck 'em. They got friends, fuck 'em too."

"Y-a-h," Ski sounded off. "You tell 'em Kotex, you been up against it," looking around laughing heartily because he knew what Kotex was.

"Twenty years in the cavalry, ain't stepped in horseshit yet," added a tanker master sergeant.

Funaro again with the familiar widespread Eighth Army threat, "Suck a hatchi!"

We fell in to march as far as we could to meet trucks returning for us. Drivers on QM heavy-duty trucks got as little sleep as we did and time was saved this way by marching for we released hard-run trucks to haul emergency ammo and supply runs during the hectic May Massacre. Besides, time saved could be used to move some other beat-up unit some other place. Along with what was left of battalion forward, we dragged our feet on down the weird Korean mountain valley road, sand-dancing, stomp-shuffling, wearing down the soles of combat boots; as Kipling complained: "boots! boots! Sloggin', movin' up and down again, there's no discharge in the war." Different war, same problem, Rudyard.

Behind survivors of battalion headquarters the little group of two depleted rifle companies moved out tediously, battle weary, leather slings slapping against hard-used rifle stocks. Happy to leave Death behind, the guys began to shout, "When this bloody war is over we will all enlist again...like so much shit we will...like so much shit we will."

97

Leaving, we passed where battalion CP had been where the dead were piled conveniently for Graves Registration, passed silently as our eyes went to them humbly, sorrowfully, deeply appreciative, it hurt like we were them.

"There's Captain Allen," his S-2 clerk, a corporal, said in a low voice. "Bye, sir," handing out a sweeping salute. Allen, already stiffened, was easy to spot, tall and thin; wrapped tight in a pup tent half tied with commo wire like a rolled-up, misshapen rug.

"Good day for murder," someone observed wryly, meaning, I guessed, that the sky threatened another rain. Lifting his head, heavy with fatigue, swinging his battered steel helmet to his side and rear, J J began: "Over the moun-tain . . . ov-er the see-ah-ee, oh ma baa-bee-ee come back to mee-ah-ee. Oh honey, bring back my bonnie to me."

"What's that mean?" he was asked.

"Scotch, where mom's from."

"Where's them damn trucks!" came an empty demand.

Changing shoulders frequently, the guys decided neither would do, that old M1 was too heavy no matter where you laid it—nine pounds grown to fifty. For short time relief, many laid them casually over their forearms, like dirty, bearded deer hunters or grabbed them by the small of their stocks, swinging them along their thighs front to rear, back and forth as we often did our piss pots for pendulum thrust momentum.

We infantrymen, whom Western Indians called 'walk-a-heaps,' trudged ten miles more. Me? I counted footsteps one to a hundred, starting over again and again and again, one to a hundred, one to a hundred, etc, etc, etc, but despite good intentions lost count of how many hundreds by the time a halt was called. Sweat, rain and water of the fords last night softened blisters on my feet and mashed them into weeping sores. Fatigue silenced songs except a soft, lonely, lament from Tree, whose throaty, very Black voice, was soothing as a lullaby: "Is I blue . . . Is I blue . . . Tell everyone 'round de place, I is blue . . . Is I blue. . . .," taken over twenty feet up ahead by J J's perpetual wail: "O-ver the moun-tain, o-ver the sea, o-ver the moun-tain all the way." Just as we all felt ourselves soft and whimsical, purified by physical weakness and were falling asleep marching, some asshole of the Second Platoon assailed our reveries with the shouted vulgar Marine chant: "If

I die on the Russian front, bury me in a Russian cunt!"

"Yah," someone sneered among laughter, "beats this shit!"

We were awake a few more miles until hiking along I fell in a trance, sleep-walking. Some oldtime soldiers told me it's possible to fall sound asleep route marching, especially when you've been run hard and have made over ten miles already. I used to think they were full of crap.

Thinking no longer about all the bodies I'd seen and would certainly see, and dead Chinks, not neatly piled but tossed in heaps to be bulldozed under, and having to attack or be attacked by those persistent little guys and possibly, very possibly, getting it this time—I mean getting it, killed, like the young wireman and Captain Allen and others. "My God! there's too much exposure, too many ways of dying."

During our first ten-minute break, worrying that blood poisoning might set in in my infected thumb, I faced away and pissed on it. It smarted some, which gave me confidence and I did it on the march whenever I had to go. I read somewhere, Lawrence of Arabia I think, that piss was a good disinfectant, but the thumb continued to swell and throb worse than ever. Adding to my discomfort, my asshole both smarted from sweat and itched from hemorrhoids beginning to protrude again, rubbed almost raw from chaffing. Fortunately, they never swelled critically. My athlete's foot squished. It's possible in such a situation, your thighs rubbing your sweaty crotch up and down hundreds and hundreds of times to have knots in your pubic hairs, someone once told me.

It seemed that each time we had just collapsed beside the road the break was over. A wave of grumbling answered. "Hit the road!" I noticed grenades, bandoliers of M1 clips, and other equipment, even bayonets left lying each time we moved.

One gripped, "Here we go already."

Private Philip Funaro was still lying down. His squad leader, Pop Miller, yelled from up the road; "C'mon, Funaro, catch up! Cut a chogee!"

"Can't go no farther," Funaro whined. "Lung's paining me."

"That's not all going to pain you," Pop threatened, walking backward slowly.

Tree, Pop's assistant squad leader, snickered. "Sh-e-e-eit!" and several joined in: "Sh-e-e-eit!" "Sh-e-e-eit!"

"Nobody can make me go," Funaro threatened. "I ain't RA; I never signed up for this horseshit. I got rights to see a lawyer."

"Lawyer?" Pop laughed loudly, "There ain't no law around here! This is the wild, Wild West, man" Everyone snickered sharply, "Shit!"

"Them's guardhouse lawyers; ain't no guardhouse here," someone explained.

"Nobody asked you how you got here," Pop said, "now chogee."

"How about it, lieutenant, can I wait for the ambulance?"

"They tell me the ambulance is full."

Pop was obviously angered, less by Funaro's appealing directly to me than at my taking three of his men as guards to Dorn's post without consulting him; learning that I let that liar off the detail by his phoney stripped rifle trick without consulting him. Reaching down without warning, he pulled the helmet from Funaro's head, slapping him three times across his face, whack, whack, whack, with the flat front and back of his hand, grabbed him by a shoulder and one-handed him up the road toward his place in line, bending down on the march, scooping up Funaro's helmet and bowling it after him.

"Pick that up, you sonofabitch and chogee! Hear me, *motor!*"

Bushed as I was, I could sympathize a little with Private Funaro, but Pop had his tough job to do.

After the long march was over I couldn't remember a single particular about a whole long stretch of that wild valley road. I do remember passing our march leader, company first sergeant, Sergeant Luther, almost forty-four, his back leaning on a large boulder, face buried in his hands. Sergeant Pater of King was thirty-six or thirty-seven, too damn old for a prize fighter or pro football lineman and what was Pater doing. I thought, "I'm thirty-one; he's much too old for this sort of thing," and, I asked Luther in passing, "Where's your field first, Sergeant Martin, old timer?"

He tossed me a hand. "Don't worry, sir, they're sending a weapons carrier for us old farts."

There must have been a squad of stragglers, one of whom, thanks to Pop, was not the city boy, Private Funaro.

100

I wondered where was the age cutoff. One did not have to serve overseas in WWII over thirty-eight. In the US Army prior to the Civil War officers could serve until they dropped, some seventy and even in the case of higher grade, in low eighties. They mounted a horse or walked, although General-in-Chief Winfield Scott, hero of the War of 1812 and the Mexican and Seminole Wars, eighty when he died at the end of the Civil War, was carried by four soldiers from place to place like some Roman potentate in a sedan chair. Although eased out of command, it was Scott's Anaconda Plan that won the Civil War.

We overtook and passed four guys miles behind their order of march, arguing bitterly.

"I told you for the last time, pick it up."

"I packed it the last five miles; it's his turn again, he knows damn well."

The man referred to whined, "But, sarge, I got an awful stitch in my side."

The sergeant roared, "I ain't fooling no more! One of you shoulder that goddamn machine gun or I'm personally kicking the shit out of you both!"

"Okay, sarge," the man with the stitch said, lifting the heavy metal load. "I've got a bad hernia. I know you're going to be sorry."

I could sympathize with that guy with the stitch in his side, though, of course, his sergeant had his job to do. I told the sergeant as I passed it was none of my business but our first sergeant had just fallen out and they'd radioed for a special weapons carrier.

I wondered could a draftee or someone like me, recalled Reservist, ever be a professional soldier? That is, could we be that impersonal and cold?

I could feel us grow more sullen in our hiking, 120 beat guys left of a rifle company of 400 strung out loosely along a winding hilly valley road; two files of wobbly guys. We marched, no, walked, no, slogged along through dark, daybreak and fifteen miles into sunlight, thoughts submerged in silence, as sweat stains under our straps and behind our belts grew larger and wetter.

"Where's them damn nigger trucks?" some loudmouth up front with a heavy southern accent demanded after an hour more of silence.

101

"Yeah," he was answered loudly in good humor by our self-proclaimed 'token nigger,' Sergeant Raymond Roundtree: "Where's niggers when you need 'em?"

Most everyone who knew Tree laughed sardonically.

"Tell 'em, Tree!"

I daydreamed I stood before the Division Provost Marshal threatening him, "Court-martial me, sir, but don't make me go back to that platoon. I'm not cut out for this sort of thing. I'm too old, I worry too much and I'm more sensitive than others. Most of them are kids who deserve better than me," and I tried to explain to the Army police chief how Sergeant Ulriche earned a field commission and Silver Star at Guadacanal and at Kunu-ri and how could I ever live up to that?

"That's well and good," the major sympathized, "but he won't be around to father them forever . . . he's four on the battalion rotation roster."

I switched off that daydream with nowhere to go, and when every bit of energy was gone, I had to make meanness do. "Old bastard sun, high over that mountain. Fuck old bastard sun! Hear? Fuck you, Chink sun!"

Finally, we arrived at the junction of a small road leading into what was our regimental assembly area. Red Battalion trucked by on its way out to reserve. I B Foney stood up in his jeep yelling at us, "Love over here. Let's shape up there; you act like you're going to a funeral. Get on the ball now, heads and eyes off the ground, shoulders back, chin in. Pick up the step. You're marching at attention now. Hup! Two! Three! . . . Hup! Two! Three! Let's show these people Love Company. Straighten your shoulders, Lieutenant Gould, get your men in step. Hup! Two! Three!"

"Sh-e-e-et!" I thought. "You wouldn't dare yell at Sergeant Ulriche like that. You bastard rode all the way; bury *you* in a Russian cunt and ain't nothin' permanently wrong with my shoulders."

We got relief from the old sun all right; it deserted us, darkened and without warning clouds swirled low to rain us hard. What harm had we ever done that jerk, Korean rain god? We milled about into the valley bowl, hunched over under ponchos, talking in low voices, wondering collectively what, if anything, we'd accomplished the last couple days.

102

Guys with sweaty blankets doubled around their shoulders covered with ponchos squatted around sputtering fires sitting on upturned helmets to keep their rears dry.

The sharp rims cut off circulation around our butts and standing to massage them was all that kept many of us from falling asleep. Every once in a while a GI on the outside of a fire went into nearby bushes and returned with an offering of wood. Having earned the privilege, he remained near the fickle heat until a new offering pushed through the circle. Stale wood smoke was our brand of perfume.

Some guys sitting on upturned helmets when the rain let up took off their boots and sticky socks to massage their aching, itching feet. Areas of the toes on my left foot were in bad shape, white from sweat and water, bloody from athletes' foot. I put a sock over a trigger finger and rubbed the area, so sensual I worked up fresh blood before forcing myself to stop. Damn, do I have to die to get rid of this burning, itchy bastard? It kept returning.

I sucked my infected thumb. It was coming along slowly except it cracked open as it tried to heal over. Later, our battalion surgeon lanced the thing and released some pus. I told him about my athlete's feet and piles and how tight my chest was, hawking globs up from a bad post nasal drip, especially right after I awoke.

"Nothing unusual for smokers," he warned, shooting me with penicillin. In WWII they'd have to handed you some APCs, Army aspirin cure-all with phenacetin and caffeine.

The guys murmured about all their troubles with the Chink Fourth Field Army. I still hesitated to butt right in and offer opinions, even though I was beginning to have a few. Generally speaking, we were two groups, those who talked of rotation and the rest of us. I was too tired anyway, so much so that I was way beyond even extraordinary tired feelings. My ears hummed like rural telephone wires I remembered as a kid and my eyes burned itching and intolerably sore, scratching like sandpaper when I blinked; all of me overly sensitive. My bladder burned to be relieved, but when I tried to go, not a drop would fall. I was unreasonably bugged by mumbled conversations fifty yards away and several times my overworked eyes saw Chinks moving through trees of a nearby murky skyline.

103

"Man," Sergeant Karl Eppler, fellow vet of WWII, sighed, seated cross-legged under a wide, black umbrella he'd latched onto in the ruins of one Korean farm house or another. "If this ain't the hardest war I ever fought."

It might have been humorous but I was too pooped to respond. Rain! Rain! Rain! Drifts of cutting rain started blowing again down the valley to make a complete mess of the slowly diminishing light. Thinking it much later than it really was, I was surprised when someone remarked how dark for five o'clock.

"Seventeen-hundred?" someone said unbelievingly. "We been here all day!"

Service Company trucks returned from hauling Red Battalion to shuttle us the rest of the way and carried us in the dark of an off-and-on rain over a rickety Bailey bridge at Upchon and south over a washboard road for another hour until we reached Hongsong directly north of Hoengsong where the guys found their packs, those the Chinks didn't have, lined up, pitched pup tents and were handed metal mess trays like in the field in the States as back in our kitchen trains we got a hot late supper of chicken pot pies almost like a stateside garrison A ration. Guys went back for thirds. All I could handle was sleep.

After breakfast most headed for a quartermaster shower point tent as hot as the meal. They put personal belongings in OD colored cloth bags, dropped handkerchiefs, underwear, socks and fatigues in piles, set boots down under the bags and ran en masse, dog tags swinging along with other things, under the hot showers naked as their mothers made them—oh, my God, that wonderful hot water, thanks to Quartermaster showering unit, toweling off with good, rough towels; receiving brand new handkerchiefs, underwear, socks and steam-sterilized fatigues and caps.

We stayed in that level valley of dried leveled rice paddies three and a half days and the first day I zipped my sleeping bag to my chin, curled up facing the wall of our officers' arctic tent and slept twelve straight hours while J J covered for me, explaining to Foney all we'd gone through on the outpost such a short time ago.

Replacements poured in by the dozens the second day and when I woke up, Sergeant Ulriche had ladled them out to squads, run skimpy too long. Dorn and his men were replaced by eight new guys and Pop Miller, who'd been acting squad leader, with Tree as assistant.

One replacement from Mississippi convinced Sergeant Ulriche he was so much better than 'niggers' he'd have to be reassigned. "That guy should have been drafted before he got so mixed up," Ulriche swore. "He's got one helluva' lot to learn," and proceeded to play him up for a swap to Lieutenant Hollingsworth where his platoon guide, Zigerfoose, in two weeks had him on charges for stealing a money belt, headed back to the division stockade for a fair trial and, after serving six months in the stockade at division, reassignment somewhere other than Love of the 38th. Word was the belt was a plant to nail the bigot.

Our PX rations arrived, free candy, lifesavers and lifesavers and lifesavers UTA, up the ass, candles, cigarettes, toothpaste, writing pads and envelopes. Being in an APO, Army Post Office, no postage stamps were needed any more than Federal income taxes. Along with paid-for items like pocket books, watches, shortwave, longrange overseas radios that could get San Francisco when high clouds were right and, of course, our own Armed Forces Radio Far East network, and cameras guys ordered and paid for in advance. Some ordered by guys since killed or evacuated disappeared mysteriously, making for furtively happy supply sergeants and other headquarters scums. The majority, however had been willed to buddies prior to going back on line.

Working on a fear course, Sergeant Eppler and I recorded our experiences, and worked out a system of our own for when the stuff hit the fan, particularly late at night. We'd stay in our holes near the center of the platoon and begin by getting control of ourselves, harness some of that wild energy ruling our bodies, shouting things such as "play it cool! . . . play it cool!" and with the guys, neutralizing their sudden fear reactions, shouting back as we scooted along to opposite ends of our positions: "Hey, Jerry, you guys all right? . . . Bud, how you and Ed? Get some talk going. Alert! Make sure there's one in the chamber, the safety's off."

Like a successful football team, quick thinking, working hard together, the more so, the greater morale. Could that be getting on the ball?

105

3
Task Force Joke

March orders disrupted our repose early on the morning of the fourth day of rest and we struck tents, made legionnaire rolls of blanket and pup tent halves to strap to our packs which contained private possessions, small cameras, radios, cherished letters, spare candy bars, toilet articles, pocket book or two; everything we owned tagged with our names by platoon in a mound behind the supply tent and filing over to the trucks, loaded in the silent aftermath of a well-enjoyed slumber – we all, we fierce warriors, condemned, all of us – guilty without evidence or proof, sentenced to die we knew not exactly when.

We left the dregs of a hot breakfast, coffee, cereal and reconstituted milk, bacon and powdered eggs, toast and jam to fall into a drizzly, low-hanging mist.

An hour later, winding up an old, unused oxen trail, we passed two fire-blackened hulks of tanks rusting there since January, displaying the heroic fatal acts of unsung Chinese peasants, two dead Sherman M24s, brightly painted tiger faces on the forward slopes, on the side of which holes burned neatly through eleven inches of armor steel by otherwise poorly-equipped big game hunters, individual champions of the Orient with captured 3.5-inch rocket launchers.

We didn't stop grinding and shifting gears, straining, revving, engine-snorting, diesel fuming: spewing gusts of energy being expelled in puffs of black diesel smoke until three in the afternoon. We dismounted (a term when horses were the mounts to come down from) as rain approached, destructive water, dissolving mud to make it slippery. We splashed slowly over until we circled into a perimeter on a valley floor and squatted under individual shelters of ponchos. Word passed

106

along for each platoon to send three men to the company CP to climb a nearby hill and set up a listening post, flank security for a newly organized battalion headquarters. J J and our soon-to-rotate hot-to-trot medic, Doc Lynch, dug our platoon CP hole on higher ground while I went with Sergeant Ulriche, checking squad leaders, helping settle new guys, trying to answer questions.

I was a bona fide oldtimer to all replacements, until they got baptized. With combat under my belt, having been shot at more times than could be counted, I tried to look silent and ugly, discouraging them from being familiar. I looked like I'd been there a year, that weather-beaten look. One had to be a real oldtimer to make it the other way around, shooting more than being shot at. Despite being in Korea less than two months, and all the off-and-on cloudy spring weather, I was tanned from being constantly outdoors, getting so thin my normally well-padded hip bones had little natural cushion, forcing me to be more fussy about working a hole to fit me just right, like that girl they tested for princess, sneaking a dried pea under her mattress.

I was by now not only a regulation dogface infantryman, digging like a dog, squirming my ass around in tight circles to fit a lie-down place just so, stopping to paw away stones, tree roots, peas, or whatever, before flopping to do some serious resting. Other less delicate guys I've witnessed just fell into their holes and slept. Since leaving Watertown in February, I'd lost twenty pounds, mostly my butt.

At 0530, dripping wet and chilly, we were lined up in tight formation to answer roll call. Released, we each scooped up a C6 box with three little tin can meals which J J handed to me, one can for each meal of the day, chopped fruit for desert, cigarettes and ass wipes, and saddled up again to continue motoring to the east, as near as I could tell, where Chinks had busted through the 7th ROK Infantry. We stopped four times for piss calls, although when a guy had to go bad, he'd stick it over the sides or, better yet, the tailgate. Pity him who let it go up wind to the guys.

At last the trucks zig-zagged slowly up a steep mountain road our engineers carved out, sinking two-foot thick logs into angled holes drilled for cribbing into a somehow hard rock cliff and cementing them in; such skillful road engineering no Army in history ever heard of.

Once we were held up half an hour while drivers up front ever-so-carefully winched the right rear wheel of a heavily loaded 2½-ton truck back onto the narrow road from a drop off of hundreds of feet. Coming down from one high pass, we watched in awe swirling vapors of cold mountain winds circling and twisting and, higher up, storming in earnest to clean themselves of cruddy clouds.

We descended the newly engineered road, covering a long wilderness track in third low gear, a narrow, treacherous trail over which nothing but engineer vehicles had rolled, cautiously; the outer wheels of six-wheeled 'six-by' heavy supply trucks skimming carefully, breathtakingly along the rim of one great drop off after another, passengers walking well behind, the driver, a demonstrating hero, riding with open door, ready to jump, moving slowly, concentrating his eyes for the life of him, fixed on the edge of the drainage ditch cliff side or on the forward edge of the drop off hidden by the body of his truck.

I'll never forget our mad, dangerous ride on those desolate manmade mountain wilderness trails. It was a long, dangerous struggle by itself which everyone talked about for days and like me still clearly recall; to us our engineers were real heroes. We pulled to the side after coming down to a valley and, it being dark early, again drew rations for the coming day from a jeep trailer and slept under or on the truck, drivers and officers, and, of course, Sergeant Ulriche, still an active platoon leader in a wide cab.

The next day we rested while our Second Engineers worked on a road into wilderness. Two days later was for me, the red letter, unforgettable, 23d of May, 1951. About five miles farther on we pulled into a large rice paddy, unflooded that year because of the war. As the sun came out to welcome us, officers and platoon sergeants walked to a briefing by the G3 operations officers of X Corps laying the groundwork for a coordinated drive to push back the overextended Chinks. It was given by a white-haired bird colonel, a crisp old Army pro who must have been in his late 50s.

Our acting battalion CO, Major Wilkes, had been sent down from X Corps staff to our battalion, not to benefit troops by his leadership for sure, but because he was a National Guard politico who needed a command following his staff job to be eased upstairs to light colonel.

He was older than me even with two political tours. As an assistant G3 of Almond's X Corps, he was being favored with a combat command he knew nothing about or apparently had a feeling for. Later his former boss, the G3 colonel in overall charge who briefed us, failed to mount the hill himself to see that the support part of his five-paragraph field order was implemented, and failed to see his protegee, Major Wilkes, in a hole back down the ridge sucking on a bottle.

The colonel stood before us and read off a classic five-paragraph field order, as taught, I understand, to ROTC college graduates at the Infantry School at Fort Benning, Columbus, Georgia. What we hardworking combat recalled Reservists with a two-week refresher course termed Benning School for Boys.

"Your battalion under Major Wallace W. Wilkes," he began, pointing to the guy who was presumed to be in charge, and went on almost tediously to point out where everything we needed would be — "Ammo supply at the dismount point; medical evac through the 15th Infantry's collecting station here," pointing to the 1:50,000 map, copies of which we all read from. No need was omitted but explained in detail how we would fulfill it.

According to the colonel, we had priority on Fifth Air Force Air support and an assortment of artillery that was, or soon would be, in position to give us battalions of preparatory fire, including the Wyoming National Guard's long-barrel eight-inchers on whose tractor bumpers were the unit's insignia, black silhouettes of cowboys riding bucking broncos.

At battalion level, Major Wilkes, we were told, could, in addition to artillery and Air, call for 4.2 chemical mortars from Heavy Mortar Company at regiment and Mike's weapons company, 81mms, and 75mm recoilless rifles, heavy, water-cooled machine guns and our own company mortars and light machine guns.

"Your battalion is the left flank attacking force of Task Force Yoke, with Eighth Army priority. A ROK regiment is already in position at your jumpoff ready to sweep up to your objective once it is taken and set up for counterattack. An entire tank battalion, the 72d of Second Division, will come down the valley in sight of your objective to work the target point blank. All fires are on call and all that stands between you

109

and victory is a battalion of demoralized, poorly equipped Chinks, short of ammo, at this minute ready to desert. "

All were elated, relieved from normal apprehensions. Man, this is class, I thought, the way we should be committed; a five-paragraph field order clear and as inclusive as you can get. Man, have we got fire-power and support! I pity those Chinks up there with all that artillery and Air. After all that shit, all we have to do is walk up and take it and let ROKs prepare the defense.

"Any questions?" the colonel demanded, giving a stern, challenging look around to preclude any. "All right, soldiers, move out!" We saluted, he returned with a high level hard salute, and pivoted around like I'd never seen before except in a movie.

Another thunder storm was brewing. Someone asked, "Is it like this every day?"

An oldtimer replied, "Wait for the monsoon."

"What in hell is *mon soon,* or whatever you call it?"

"You'll see."

According to the Blue Book—

While all units reported successes in their sectors, the 38th Infantry left Corps Reserve and moved north to Sokpyokkol on the Division right flank where it went into blocking positions. As it came onto line, its Third and Dutch battalions reverted to its control.

At 0800 hours on 23 May, the Second Division initiated its aggressive offensive, one of the most remarkable and spectacular of the war. For six days, the Division had fought a determined enemy, giving ground slowly while inflicting casualties estimated at 10,000 for each day of the Chinese offensive. Throughout the period, the Division had maintained its tactical unity and freedom of maneuver. Now it turned and drove against the desperately tired enemy who no longer had the numerical strength or supplies to continue the pressure. The heroic stand of the previous days and the sudden reversal of tactics embodied in the new offensive marked one of the most dramatic achievements of the Korean War.

110

The attack moved out on schedule against light resistance. Both the 9th and 38th Regiments secured their first-day objectives. The 187th A/B RCT, [airborne regimental combat team] making the main thrust, battled stiff resistance as it advanced along poor roads, ringed with enemy-dominated peaks.

A hastily-organized assault group, Task Force Yoke, commenced a limited northward drive to keep the enemy forces off-balance while the counter offensive was being racked up. Composed of the 3d Bn, 38th Inf; 72d Tk Bn (-)[minus a unit or more]; a platoon from the 38th Inf Tank Co; a battery of division field artillery and a tactical air control party, the mobile force moved northwest from Pungam-ni toward Habae-jae.

To the west, along the familiar Hongchon-Inje road, the 187th A/B RCT passed northward thru the lines of the 23rd picking up B Company of the 72d and securing the high ground around Hangye by nightfall thereby permitting the 23rd to fall back to an assembly area in the vicinity of Hongchon to prepare for its part in the coming counter-offensive.

And as Task Force Yoke and the 187th sent twin-pronged drives short distances northward, the 9th Infantry, operating between the two forces, jumped-off for two objectives—Hill 592 and Tappung-ni, former roadblock area. With the First Battalion on the left and the Third Battalion on the right, the Hill was secure by nightfall and the regiment buttoned up for the hours of darkness.

Love and King, with Item, the most beat up, still assigned to the 23d infantry, climbed a narrow trail for three hours without stopping longer than five minutes at a time. Despairing replacements wondered what they had gotten into and some fagged out, offering weak little smiles for consideration and consolation. After we hand-counted their loads, they were constantly ordered to go back and recover grenades and what-not. Losing Government property is a court martial offense they were reminded, to say nothing of weakening us all. We slept beside the mountain trail that night. Thinking only of dying from utter fatigue, we were astonished the following day to discover what grit we really had to

111

fall back on; this necessity for exercising your grit, a prime combat lesson learned.

Around noon we reached a high point on the ridge where lead scouts of King Company lay sprawled behind rocks, knobs of earth and small mountain trees. South Korean soldiers were there, helmets and shoulders covered with wilted grass and twigs, cutting fresh camouflage with bayonets so dull they were having a hard time. "Look, Kim," Sergeant Burris said, motioning them to come closer as he made a single swipe with his bayonet to cut off a twig the size of his finger, then thumbing the blade cautiously from one side, pointing to one of their bayonets, he said with exaggerated disgust, "ROKs no hucking good!" Like North American Indians once did, they had difficulty pronouncing the letters *f* and *l*.

Sighting Americans, many ROKs ran with enthusiasm to their emplacements and fired wildly hundreds of rounds at a bush-covered ridge to their immediate front. An angry KMAG sergeant tried to stop them, introducing them to some choice English. A few of our riflemen crawled up to peek at the enemy, picking out places where ROKS dug in and one show-off, new to combat, went walking back and forth exposing himself on a short section of ridge top. Guys gave him cat calls for his trouble: "My he-e-ero!" a sergeant imitated a woman's voice appealingly and then roared: "Get your fuzzy ass down!"

"I didn't mean nothing," the replacement pouted proudly, crawling down. "Just wanted to see what it's going to be like. They wasn't comin' anywhere near."

"Stand there another minute you'd find out."

As though to demonstrate, a high-powered Russian sniper rifle round, anticipating his reappearance, landed where the showoff had been.

The Chinks had excellent fire discipline and, aside from the almost playful sniper round, wasted no ammunition taking pot shots. After all, I thought, look at the thousands of miles and the way they have to carry it ultimately on their backs. Still, had they been at a greater distance I could have better understood their restraint but those aggravating Chinks were only 400 yards away as a crow might fly, straight across a saddle. I thought hopefully that maybe as the colonel said they

112

were short of ammo and not anxious to fan things up.

Pity things couldn't work out so there didn't have to be a fight. I wished I knew Chinese like Captain Brownell, old China hand from the Marines. I'd holler over and come to some kind of an agreement. I wished hard that Brownell was with us. I heard he talked friendly to Chink POWs. "Okay," I'd say, "when I count three we'll throw away our rifles and get the hell out of here."

Instead, the order was passed up for King Company to move out. "Tell King to haul ass!" was what we passed along for King to lead out on the attack, over to our right a bit. The lead squad of the first platoon of King took off right away but reaching the bottom of the saddle directly under the Chinks, ROKs, suddenly brave after facing the enemy overnight without assaulting, fired so closely the front men of King balked. From the ridge to our right in King Company came Sandy Opolous's replacement, Captain Toth, mad as hell, "What they trying to do, kill us!"

While the attacking squad dribbled back to the bottom of the saddle without orders, its aggressiveness gone, the acting battalion S3 (on loan from the 72d tanks) ran around in a tizzy hunting for the Korean military advisor and his interpreter. "Tell your people to cut that shit! Tell them to mask their fires! Where's KMAG? Where's KMAG?" he stewed.

"Dammit, Lee," the KMAG captain ordered his interpreter angrily, "Do you want to try again to take that hill? Been here since yesterday, want to have to go it alone again? Then tell them to cut out that shit!"

"That not shit, sore," the Korean officer answered gravely, not knowing about American idioms.

"Dammit, you know what I mean."

"Yes, sore!" he smiled with big teeth, saluting twice.

One or two artillery batteries slipped HE, high explosive, shells over the Chink hill on their way to another objective, directed by a little L-19 observation plane. From the height he was cruising, we surmised he was about to rotate. Loafing on the friendly side of the ridge, curious guys peeking over the top of the ROK positions started sniping at a cocky Chink believed to be an officer. Not over a football field away, he stood, arms folded, looking us over coolly, it seemed utterly disdainful. More and more guys crawled up to investigate, some old veterans. I wondered if he was their answer to the rookie exposing himself on our side. Answering a challenge, maybe?

"Hey, guys!" Sergeant Eppler yelled, waving his furled black umbrella. "We got a turkey shoot."

Lieutenant Hurtz and I left Foney with King Company commander and the assistant acting battalion S3 in the security of an overhanging rock ledge and climbed up cautiously to keep watch on it. This was the last I saw the acting S3. Soon half of Love was lying along the ridgetop firing at will. Once dirty smoke thrown up by a bursting ROK 57mm recoilless hid the solitary enemy. "Hot dog, they got him!" Ski yelled, jumping up and down. "Give him a Kewpie doll." Settling smoke disclosed the officer on the same spot, arms still calmly folded.

"Didn't hit him any!" Ski accused, imitating a woman's voice.

Word passed along to hold fire and after a moment of silence, when the Chink was sure we'd ceased our futile efforts, he knelt down and sneaked out of sight. Sonofabitch! Gave us the willies; were we all such lousy shots?

As the KMAG officer finished his pow-pow with the offending ROKs, King's field first sergeant, Master Sergeant John Pater, guided a very young-looking ROTC officer and his platoon reluctantly over the ridge down through the bushes of a faint path to the bottom of the saddle, stirring up a hornet's nest of enemy fire. Pater harangued the leader who seemed to be a teenager and returned. Twenty minutes later we could pick out individuals of that platoon coming briefly into sight between bushes, climbing cover-to-cover like animated puppets, one foolhardy rifleman a full twenty feet in the lead, an inspired hero or just ignorant of basic military science.

Chinks poked their heads up over their trenches behind brush camouflage, running back and forth, chattering like squirrels in strange sing-song. Now and then an arm came over the top to throw a tiny object down toward the guys of King Company crawling up from the saddle, followed by the weak-sounding ka-rumpt! of potato masher grenades, with a two-foot-high black dust cloud on the ground near the miniature soldiers crawling their way to the top.

Suddenly a rash of cheering broke out among King's men; then ceased as suddenly, and when it began again was sporadic and less confident. Twenty minutes later, word came filtering up with the first walking wounded that the platoon guide, an oldtimer and two of his men lay in their blood on the hill. Shocked, the remainder slipped and slid slowly down to the bottom of the saddle to crowd behind boulders with their young ROTC officer. Intermediate bugouts, I called them.

Another rifle platoon of King Company, led by an acting platoon leader, a sergeant first class, was immediately committed full front against the objective, but fired half-heartedly and only one squad managed to crawl up more than a quarter way, on level with the frightening dead of that platoon then sank down to join those among the large boulders. I listened to a thoroughly frightened shavetail over the 536 radio. "But, but . . . but, . . . sir, we can't, sir. . . . Can't go no farther, sir . . . pinned down, sir. Three guys dead; they must be dead, they're still lying there. No, no, sir. We can't."

Major Wilkes was nowhere to be found and it took about ten minutes to raise Lieutenant Foney. Some of us wondered aloud about the preparatory fire we were promised, but left it up to commanders, whose responsibility it was.

"Where are you?" I demanded.

"Never mind," he said, "get ready to relieve King Company."

"Where are you?" I asked again. "Can you see what's going on?"

Foney was described to me after it was over, moving slowly on the friendly side, ears cocked, ridiculous, hunched over beside men walking upright, eyes peering back and forth as though looking for someone, occasionally peeking over the ridge top to the enemy hill.

I discovered later that in his five months in Korea, by luck and good maneuvering this was the closest he'd been to enemy. While Foney and I talked, Lieutenant Dale Gordon Hollingsworth almost ran by me ahead of his faithful platoon sergeant, former Filipino scout, Master Sergeant Quaid (phonetic), and the rest of his platoon by about ten feet. I was surprised, yelled "Good luck." Looking straight ahead, a fixed stare on his face, his mind was too preoccupied to acknowledge.

I read about this heroic guy after returning from Korea, in Ma-

115

jor General S. L. A. Marshall's book, *The River and the Gauntlet*, whose book, *Men Against Fire*, was one of the required readings I enjoyed while in the Reserves. SLAM, as he asked me over the phone to call him, wrote about the heroic acts of three men I met after I got to Korea. He described our Holly "baby-face, thick-lens glasses, about twenty, smallish, talked quietly . . . a Guthrie, Iowa farm boy." After two days and nights at the Kunu-ri trap last November Holly was one of the few leaders left to the company, field commissioned when they got back to South Korea. The others Marshall was impressed by were Lieutenant John Fox, whose lecture helped save my life and who is now writing his own book, and Corporal Edsel Turner, of L Company, RA35545252, wounded quite badly and frostbitten at Hoengsong 12 Feb '51, who died hard of cancer several years ago at Kalamazoo. His wife and I deplored the fact that I didn't find their telephone number sooner. She was elated and proud, she told me, to learn from me of his exceptional heroism. No one else ever contacted her.

"I know he had that medal, that cross, but he was so quiet about Korea, he never told us things like that."

Holly was a very bright, brave young second lieutenant whom everyone liked. Three days before trucking out for Task Force Yoke, after mail call, Holly came into the officers' arctic tent, was quiet for a time and threw a one-page, two paragraph penciled letter and four color films on his cot, blurting: "Want to see something good?" He picked up the letter and forced it on Foney; giving the four photos to me. The letter was from the girl he married a week before embarking for Korea. She was doing a strip tease and named the neighbor who took the pictures. If Holly needed any more evidence, say so and she'd send it. She wanted a quickie divorce to marry the neighbor and if the pictures weren't enough, she'd send more. Did he think she was nobody, waiting patiently while he got all the glory? The last photo showed her naked on the couch, vulgar as a bitch could get, her legs apart. No words were said for a few minutes while we read and stared and Holly retrieved the pictures from Foney who spent too long studying them.

"Dirty bitch," Foney said.

I put my hand on Holly's shoulder and told him how sorry we were. He started to sob, then suddenly stopped and shook his head.

"Why'd she do it, Dud? What's wrong with this crazy world? Oh my god, it's all over."

Holly didn't say a word to anyone except his platoon sergeant during the days he had left. Like Kitty, his wife blamed his being away in Korea on a desire to be "a big heee-ro . . . didn't you think how lonely I'd be?"

The Third Division unit that finally took the hill found Holly and his faithful former Filipino scout a few feet apart, riddled with bullets from one of the Maxim machine guns.

I called General Marshall in June '52, at his editorial position with the *Detroit News*, because of the good things he had to say of Holly in his book and his first words were: "My god, what a terrible thing. I thought he was such an outstanding little man. My god, what a nasty thing." As an afterthought, "I hope she didn't get his $10,000 insurance." I learned that Foney called the division JAG officer to try to cancel it but never found out how it came out, presumably negatively.

Lieutenant Foney called on the walkie-talkie where we were huddled on the enemy side, asking for Sergeant Ulriche. "Why?" I interrupted. "I'm platoon leader; what you want with Ulriche? He's talking with a buddy in the second platoon."

"Okay, Gould. I'm used to dealing with Sergeant Ulriche."

"I understand," I replied, "but I've ordered him to stay back with Doc Lynch at the rear. Dammit, Sergeant Ulriche is number four in the whole battalion rotation roster, should be back at the Rotation Center with some of the guys he came over with. I've got to take over sooner or later."

"Well, okay," Foney answered. "If you're sure you can swing it, follow Holly and give him all the support you can." Lieutenant Hurtz and his second platoon were held in reserve.

My talking with the company commander seemed the signal for everyone to watch me—everyone of the Banzai Third watch me—disdainfully, I felt, certainly critically. I'll show 'em, but as I stood, I fumbled and dropped my carbine twice and when I called the platoon together, stammered and stuttered. I was embarrassed to show uncontrolled fear, not the fear Sergeant Eppler and I'd been training for that you can fight down by shouting, threatened by immediate action of an

117

enemy, but the purely mental kind, blood that didn't race around your body but stayed in your head to make you stutter and say strange things. Something like being at a podium under spotlights to give a speech you hadn't prepared for. Shouting wouldn't help a bit and would sound funny.

"Where's Sergeant Ulriche?" someone demanded.

"He's staying back; I'm in charge now; he's going to rotate."

I'd never done anything so crazy and dangerous, try to take a hill from someone who wanted desperately to keep it. Not many sane people do and tell about it. This for which I am named rifle platoon leader, fully trained, ready to lead on command, now compelled professionally to do without further preparation. No, my frightened friend, no more time for training, reading instructions or field manuals. None have ever been written anyway to cover this, only this threatening heroism on order that scares you so . . . Oh god, what a crazy thing to do.

Then, after a few full breaths, with everyone watching me, I sounded off tough as I could, "You're acting platoon sergeant now Sergeant Eppler. Sergeant Ulriche will stay to the rear with Doc, and Sergeant Roderiguez's squad is leading. I believe it's his turn, and then the second squad with Sergeant Miller. C'mon, Banzai Third, let's chogee!"

Talking firmly now, I'd prove I had the right to call Banzai myself.

"Sergeant Ulriche!" I yelled over my shoulder, catching sight of him returning from the second platoon. "And you, Specialist Lynch, I'm ordering you both to stay in the rear of the platoon." The first combat order I'd given.

I planned to work right behind Speedy Gonzales, assistant squad leader of the First Squad. I knew from old timers that Sergeant Ulriche always put a squad ahead of him as protection so he could lead without being pinned down. As we moved from the bottom of the saddle, I had already stopped shaking uncontrollably — just by moving — no longer felt helplessly frightened. Cautious now, in charge, studying the situation like any predator, hunched like a hunting lion in as low a profile as possible, ready to spring; completely in charge, on top of things, alert to what could happen to hurt us, I found it the best way to go into a fight

118

after controlling the fear pressure; be in charge of things; wade right in with eyes open; judging both the front and sides—front where the enemy is, sideways for my men. Scared, alert and determined to kill or be killed!

Suddenly, why was I physically leading? I turned and yelled for ez and explained to him where I intended to be. Rodriguez de- that I was in close proximity, not in safety far away. We'd er, like the gang at home in Laredo he used to run with to- always together. He'd be damned proud to lead out in front of lieutenant, long as the lieutenant kept pace. And right here and now want to say Mexican Americans have been the backbone of our infantry combat in every war since World War I.

Bullets from three old Maxim machine guns zipped overhead. All at once I realized how naked we were, we should have had all sorts of preparation the colonel promised—air strikes, heavy artillery, mortars of 60 and 81mm, light and heavy machine guns, recoilless rifles—everything that bird colonel promised—and here we were, a skinny rifle platoon full of replacements, a few days after being overrun, banzaiing with bare hands. Where were our vaunted leaders, Wilkes in charge of it all? Even one company commander?

Three rifle platoons preceded me—the college kid, the SFC from King Company and Holly's. I suddenly realized to take a hill like this we first of all needed heavy preparation and then, like we did so many times later, move fast, build a momentum and go right over the top yelling our lungs out.

I came fast to understand that close combat is never smooth, seldom beginning in an orderly surge of men side by side like in movies, and once it begins, always behind a spiritual leader of some sort, of whatever rank, it proceeds haphazardly from individual or small groups, twos and threes, well-trained fire teams formed around BARs darting now forward, inspired by natural leaders, inspiring others, now individually falling behind boulders or trees, out of breath, reloading, panting for air or demoralized and nearly overcome by fear reaction, then regaining control rushing upward again, encouraging, urging all to join the intoxicating melee.

There was no preparation, no Air, no artillery, no overhead ma-

119

chine gun of our own; no support at all and the absence and silence of Lieutenant Foney, supposedly our company commander, whose commitment the attack was by tradition, more than a mere rifle platoon leader's task.

There was no battalion OP, observation post, established from which to watch our progress and give orders, nor was there communication from Love or King Company commanders with the attackers. Those already committed, the two rifle platoons of King and Holly's men (where is Holly I wondered) were lying safe behind what cover they found at the bottom of the saddle, maybe one-fourth way up, the little momentum was what J C Rodriguez, Speedy Gonzales and I were able to whip up by screaming threats. I glanced back over my shoulder and was happy to find the second and third squads moving with Speedy and me. I like to think that Burris and Pop Miller were inspired to see me ahead of them. "C'mon," I shouted. "Get the bastards! Banzai! Banzai!"

I scurried, crouching, running like a crab or a crippled man from boulder to boulder sidewards or up, tree to tree, tuned to the jabbering of excited Chinks above. With energy I never had before, I pushed myself smack into the hottest center of the hill, without scouts, for we were now all of us front men, pushing up fast through thinning bushes, yelling over my shoulder, getting the guys to follow me without thinking. "C'mon, Banzai! Let's get them! C'mon, keep your ass down and chogee. Get 'em on the run."

Heavy, unaimed Chink fire cracked and zipped threateningly overhead. Pinned down in their trench by fear of our fire, heads down, Chinks held rifles and burp guns over the edge above their heads, trying to point the muzzles down at us. As long as we kept firing low, they'd be afraid of the zip-zip and crack-crack we were throwing at them. We crawled and pulled ourselves on our stomachs up to what I call the grenade line, until suddenly one of Speedy's best riflemen straightened up just a bit too much and was suddenly jerked upright to go reeling backward with a curse cut off abruptly, hit hard in the liver, heart or lungs or a heavy bone—"Oh g-a . . ." All he got off was the surprised, angry, "Oh g-a . . ." arms and legs out of control, flailing, wild arms and uncontrolled legs propelled by gravity as he fell with momentum down the steep slope, dropped with whirling extremities, crashing into a guy crouching below as his bright red blood sprayed away, reflecting red sunlight with every involuntary move. His body crashed through a clump of low bushes, grunting loudly as air was forced out his lungs, his chest banging heavily on boulders, slumping at last, a sickening sight finally lying still

For the first time my men and those of Holly's overtaken on the grenade line were aware of King Company's leaderless men cowering behind boulders and bushes behind us. With their organized fire we could've rumbled over the top.

"Get up here you sonsofbitches," Sergeant Eppler yelled at King's men and their ROTC officer. "This ain't no private war." Peering down the saddle out of the corner of one eye I saw Private Funaro and several others scurry behind cover back with the demoralized guys of King. I counted only eight of Love Company and two from King on the grenade line. Looking behind me, I yelled: "You heard the sergeant. Keep your ass down and get up here and fight. What're you afraid of?" They knew well what they were afraid of, our attack momentum, which we never really established, was gone.

We were caught in a dangerous stall. On my left Corporal Ichimura dropped his machine gun into a groove of a boulder, useless without the bipod carried by an assistant, and tried to charge it to no avail without the stability needed. As he yanked on the charging handle, the barrel skidded to the right across the flat top of the boulder he rested it on. He called angrily for his assistant down behind him, the only time I heard a Nisei use foul language.

As I continued to yell for guys to join us, a series of rapid single shots went off beside me, an M1 carbine fast as the guy could pull the trigger. It was our sixteen-year-old platoon medic, Doc Lynch. He paid me no attention until I reached over and tugged on the little canvas bag flung over his back. "Damn it, Doc, back where you belong. We might need you."

We were beginning to dodge potato masher grenades with wood handles. I tried to think what was best to do but could only shiver and stutter and smell a strange antiseptic odor I have smelled at several very dangerous times in my life. For example, once when I was almost clob-

121

bered by a taxi as I stepped off a curb in New York City. The Chinks jabbered in subdued voices as they did while we came caterwauling, up at them and now the most timid yelled loudly individually with inflections that could only be insults. Ski behind me answered, "Up your gigi with a rough wire brush!"

Karl, Pop, Edsel, and Burris all yelled, as we had in our little amateur fear course decided was best to do. "C'mon you yellow cunts! Eee-dee-waa [come here]! We got something for you! Come and get it!" and other strong curses.

"C'mon, you guys," I turned and shouted below me. "You heard 'em. Let's chogee. . . . Get the lead out; we got 'em on the run! Move! Move up! Damn it, get the fire going and they won't stick their heads up."

"Dunee! Dunee! Dunee!" a voice yelled, which I learned later was a Chinese dialect for 'fuck you,' certainly appropriate for the occasion but which never caught on nor replaced familiar English threats. I never found out who yelled it and by some strange fluke, although it must have originated above us, it seemed to come from behind; a Chink ventriloquist?

Eppler looked at me in amazement. I'd worked myself up to such a pitch of enthusiasm I was standing in plain sight, unmindful of bullets. The guys told me later they thought I'd lost my marbles.

"Get your fire up. On the move!" I yelled. The Chinese lowered their voices again, fearful of the sounds of rising morale. "Banzai!" I screamed. "Banzai the bastards!" Swinging my carbine with fixed bayonet over my head, I yelled, "Banzai the bastards!" I know banzai was a Jap yell in WWII (may we live ten thousand years) and there must have been at least one Chinese up there who recognized what meaning it once had for their fighters. Captain Brownell told me how Chinese feared Japanese more than us and have been known to use banzai themselves as an expletive, similar to a North China yell, *wan-sui*, a cry I remember but whose meaning escapes me.

The Chinks scooted back and forth above us, agitated pixies, busily firing three slow Maxim machine guns well over our heads, unable to depress down the steep slope. They were of pre-WWI vintage obtained as were burp guns from Russia, as captured Springfield rifles

122

were from America via Chinese Nationals. The heavy cast-iron wheels and armor plate were well dug in and with flash hiders and smokeless powder, difficult to spot. We picked them up one at a time by catching sight of the flutter of leaves and camouflage twigs and the slow, measured chug chug chug sound they made.

I yelled a warning to the guys and tried to spot them, and, out of ammo, four 30-round banana magazines emptied, I went so far as to stand again and heave a rock in the direction of the gun in the center. "Let 'em have it right back of where that rock landed. (only it landed far short) C'mon, guys, work your way up and toss a grenade." Chain reaction kept me going, but the majority, uninspired, feeling only guilt and fear, overpowered by their sense of vulnerability, were unimpressed and lost enthusiasm as they figured the odds.

J J handed me our 536 radio, Lieutenant Foney who, I realized, had to be on the enemy side of the ridge facing us for his radio to read. "C'mon, Gould, you're doin' good! That's it, right on up there! Atta' boy!"

"How about some of that stuff they promised," I demanded. "Where's Air and artillery, tanks and mortars? For Christ sake, Foney, where's our own weapons platoon?" I practically threw the radio back to J J. What did Foney know about taking a hill?

Soon I was all alone yelling. The morale had sunk so low it seemed time for someone to play the hero. Since no one in the platoon was shackled with the job, it dawned on me I must appoint myself. Damn, I thought, strangely pleased with the assignment, I'll have to show them. I been so very active the past half hour and my survival instinct was so refreshed in the persistent excitement another flash of adrenalin swept over me; all of a sudden it seemed onesided and I told myself, "after all, they're hiding, not us."

"Watch me!" I yelled, facing dramatically from left to right. "Keep your other eye on them Chinks and keep them pinned down." Pulling the pin from a fragmentation grenade, I scooted low uphill. Ten yards from the Chink trench, slapping myself against a sapling, I slid down to my knees and threw the heavy metal up with all my might. I had the terrible impression of it hitting a thin tree, bounced back, rolling, smoking and sizzling right at me.

123

"Crimus!" I yelled, standing up, back to the enemy, scampering down the hill, invisible bullets cutting the air above me with incredible cracking sounds. One could end it all.

Tripping over a rock, which fortunately lowered me as a target and probably saved me, I rolled over and over without losing speed until I reached the depression I started from. Instinctively tucked my head under my arm while the dangerous thing went off three feet above my helmet. Plowing into the ground, lying half submerged in loose mountain dirt, the grenade fragments sprayed up rather than down toward me. Because of many protuding places arranged to break away, the fragmentation grenade was named after Spanish *granada*, pomegranate; lit seedy apple.

Few soldiers listened to the fearful nearness of the high nervous whine of exploded metal fragments as I did for hours during my night of terror, one-night stand on the 15th of May, and lived to tell about it and I came suddenly to my senses. "Crimus!" I shuddered, raising the front of the heavy helmet from over my eyes. "Don't push your luck, you could have been killed. What a crazy thing to do." Crazy, yes, but not unlike a furious spontanious moment in a strenuous game—glorious, an aggressive act I'd succumb to several more times on my Korean tour.

Fortunately, the Chinks had few frag grenades, some Russian antitank grenades, short wooden-handle affairs about the size and appearance of toilet plungers, kraut panzerfusses captured by Russians that weren't made antipersonnel and wouldn't detonate unless hit on the fuse end squarely in a rock (or tank as they were designed to do). Mostly they used Chinese-made potato mashers, small imitations of kraut wooden-handled grenades with a small explosive charge in thin, metal containers, similar in size and thickness to six-ounce tomato juice cans.

Quiet and sober then, I watched Sergeant Eppler out of the corner of one eye handle a potato masher grenade like a hot potato, picking it up by its wooden handle and dropping it twice in a row, and, unbelievably, a third time, fumbling for it frantically as it exploded behind or beneath him in a small cloud of smoke and dust. Until then we had no idea how weak they were.

"Goddammit!" I thought. "There goes Karl."

His body cleared the ground by an inch and plopped back,

dropping his rifle. Seconds later, over the shock of it, he sat up, po-peyed, fingers scrambling around his back and sides, rummaging under his fatigue jacket for blood. Convinced at last that he was untouched, he exclaimed, "Shit!" One would give a lot for a legitimate stateside wound.

Seconds later it happened to me, making the left side of my chest black and blue and sore for days. The cans were thin and out de-signed to fragmatize and for the most part simply flared back to their junctions with the wood handle.

As our fire weakened, dirty tan sleeves popped into the air above us as the Chink' morale returned higher than before; heavy sal-voes of grenades got closer and closer as they rose from their knees for a better shot. We became contemptuous but watchful of this danger. There were two choices as a grenade landed nearby — pick it up by its handle and toss it downhill, or roll away and cover your head and chest. Within the time allotted by short fuses, throwing them back up was out of the question. In each case it had to be a snap judgement, either cover from it or toss it downhill. I was right ninety-five percent of the time to toss them away and it annoyed me to think one was ready to explode while I lay there facing away, cowering, shivering from fear.

Sergeant Eppler or I, one of us or maybe both, started yelling as we tossed Chink grenades down away from us, "Here's one from me, yellow bastards."

All too often, when they saw one landing close, so menacing, afraid they might miss and have no time to duck, soldiers flinched away from the confrontation and allowed the grenade to have its way.

"Shit," I fumed to myself. "If you'd the guts to pick it right up, you wouldn't be cringing like a damn fool." Once I turned away and covered my face with my hands, safe under my steel pot it seemed, it was too late to change my mind. Being delayed, most we tossed ex-ploded in the air.

About every twentieth grenade was a dangerous frag. A guy to my left caught a fragment and skidded downhill yelling, "Oh God, oh God!" a quivering layer of blood over the side of his face, fresh liquid sheen of scarlet. Doc Lynch dropped his carbine and like a frantic mother scooted after him over a low rock ledge. The wounded rifleman came back to us three weeks later with soft pink facial scars.

Impressions were how we decided whether we were dead or alive; impressions one after another in rapid succession, one an extremely accurate ROK machine gun sweeping back and forth from overhead behind us preventing Chinks from standing to lower fire to finish us off. One impression of two of King's men yelling, "Stick up your heads, you bastards." Someone, Pop Miller, I believe, urged a King Company rifleman to edge up closer to the enemy, get a fire going at any place he saw leaves fluttering, "they're all the same, all good targets," and one of my guys yanking desperately at the jammed cocking lever of his M1, making a strange whimpering sound being so scared to be defenseless.

After I ran out of ammo, I tried to raise either the company commander or battalion, on my 536 walkie-talkie, although seldom used by battalion. As head of the attack, Wilkes should have one turned on. "Anyone," I shouted, "send backup in a hurry; land some preparatory fire on the Chinks, bring us ammo, shoot some outfit through us, or give us permission to withdraw." From the growing silence at my sides, I realized other guys were running out of ammo and some were pushing with their hands on their stomachs down hill, as, with nothing with which to fire, well they should. I knew when there was no answer to my 536 Foney had gone back to the safe friendly side and must have taken his radio with him as had King's Captain Toth since we were all on the same channel. Where, I stewed to myself, was all that five-paragraph field order preparation, especially the third paragraph — supporting troops? Where was Fifth Air Force and Eighth Army artillery and all those tanks? And where was Love's 60mm mortar? Where was Wilkes . . . Foney?

Hearing our momentum falter, Chinks started lowering their fire. I sent J J, stunned by a grenade, back down to get permission to withdraw. "Hurry!" I ordered. "Hurry!" Meanwhile, out of contact with superiors was all the permission I needed to use my own judgement. Just as I was about to tell the guys in a normal voice to pull back carefully down the hill, a young loud mouth runner from battalion, charged with giving me the message in person, shouted from below,

"Hey, you guys. They want you off the hill; we're pulling back."

"Let's go-o-o!" a King Company man shouted hysterically. A badly frightened replacement of Holly's platoon faced around, dropped his rifle and started pell-mell down the hill. Breath stopped in my throat and my heart held its beat. Grabbing my empty carbine I chased after the panicked guy until close enough to prick him in the shoulder with my bayonet. He came to a skidding halt as I wheeled to face three more, insane with fear. I held my carbine bayonet up at them until they saw the look on my face and stopped, staring in surprise and disappointment at being held up.

Take any book on infantry tactics, Clausiwitz, Baron de Jomini, or Mao, you'll read retreat is the most difficult combat maneuver to control at any echelon. The men looked at me and then turned to look up where the Chinks were chattering.

"Okay, now," I told them calmly. "*You* reach up and get your rifle. Okay, you see, easy does it. See, you're all right. Now take your rifles and come down firing back if you can. Toss their grenades away. Let Ich's machine gun down first and that BAR. C'mon, steady does it."

We leapfrogged backward that way down to the bottom of the saddle, those with ammo fired to keep Chinks from lowering their fire on us. King Company's hideouts preceded us without instruction, in fact, they bugged like big birds, as two of Mike Company's heavy water-cooled machine guns finally got in the act, pouring red-hot shit on the Chink line overhead in unison with the gung ho ROK gun, keeping the Chinks down so they dared not aim at us. Eppler, a sergeant from King Company, Tony Burris, and I fanned out to inspect the hill. We confirmed that two of our five known dead were indeed dead and left there, three had been dragged earlier away by King Company's platoon medics, and Doc had done such a good job evacuating the wounded there was no one to haul and I was so occupied I completely forgot Holly. With the enemy menace so near and aggressive, we made no effort to bring off the two dead, nor, of course, had reason to inspect the hill left or right above the grenade line.

As Eppler and I walked carefully backwards watching the Chink position above, we came across a chubby, pale-face King replacement sitting head between his knees sobbing softly. I saw no medic tag and asked where he got hit.

"I can't move, sir. I can't move. I'm tired right out. Let them get me, sir. I can't go no further."

There was no reason for a medic's tag and Pop Miller taught me not to let guys fag out like that. Teach them to find their grit; force them to try. Instinctively, I jabbed at him hard with my bayonet not intending to actually stick him, as though I was just bawling him out: "Now get off your ass and chogee. I'm not leaving you here and I am sure as shit not staying with you. In a minute those bastards will push their machine guns forward, lower them and sweep the living shit out of this place. Now move! Hear me? Move!" The surprised replacement, frightened by the bayonet wounding, jumped to his feet and scrambled ahead of us over the ridge to the friendly side.

There was no officer on either side of the ridge, nor could I raise Lieutenant Foney or Captain Toth on the 536 nor was there any sign of a battalion observation post. Uncommitted guys from both companies were goofing off on the ridge trail in front of the ROKs, stretched out on the enemy side watching the show, Chink heads popping up and down, paying no heed to Maxim machine gun bullets cracking away, sniping like angry bees or cracking well over their heads.

I once asked Sergeant Eppler if, through all this activity we were engaged in, he recalled seeing any other officer. Negative except Holly and Hurtz; Totten and Foney one time each, and in getting together this journal, I asked Sergeant Eppler to jot down his impressions of that day —

Dud,

Let me write of my recollections of May 23. The first thing that comes to mind is how ill-prepared I felt our platoon was when it jumped off that morning. We had lost heavily since before the May 15 debacle and were now almost 50% replacements whose names we barely knew and whose knowledge and training were doubtful. I never felt any of our replacements had adequate training, especially those from reserve or guard units. Brave, maybe, but

128

trained? NO! I also recall we had little or no artillery preparation. We did succeed in closing within grenade range (theirs — one does not throw grenades uphill). But didn't have the firepower to go to the top. As I indicated, I got tossed around pretty good by a grenade and as my legs hurt, really thought I was wounded. I think I got the SOB that threw the grenade as I saw where it came from and drew a sight on the opening and waited. In a few seconds a face appeared for a moment and I fired. No more grenades were thrown from that position.

When the order came to pull back, I was much relieved to realize I could walk without difficulty as I was convinced I was wounded. When we pulled back and dug in, I was very disappointed when I couldn't find a wound.

I vividly remember your wound and seeing a very small amount of blood appear. Initially you made almost no reaction. It didn't appear to have caused much pain, but everyone, including yourself, was concerned as to the consequences of the wound. You initially moved very cautiously but once you realized you could move, assured us you could evacuate yourself and left for the aid station. I don't believe our unit saw any further action that day.

So much for May 23. It feels good to write it down for someone who understands.

> *Thanks,*
> *Karl*

No one but me and Eppler seemed aware of the great danger we still faced. "C'mon," I yelled. "Get off the ridge you guys. You're silhouetted. Get over to the friendly side."

W-a-opt! I was slammed by an axe, one ton per square inch, my head was shook forward and as my helmet and liner went flying, driven to my knees before managing to stumble several steps forward to get my balance and straighten up. Many years later seat belts were designed for less force. My neck and a streak across my back burned hot for a split second. I was furious, thinking I'd been accidentally hit by one of the guys. "Who did that? Who's the dumb bastard?" I yelled.

Sergeant Eppler, directly behind me a bit lower, heard the same sharp crack of the bullet headed straight at us and knew immediately what happened. "Medic! Medic! Doc, over here!" he yelled.

"See! See, what did we tell you!" I yelled. "See, you're sitting ducks! Now clear the ridgeline. Move!"

"Lieutenant Gould's got it!" Burris yelled, proudly it seemed, and an anonymous surgeon with buck sergeant stripes addressed himself confidentially to Doc Lynch: "Got it in the back, he'll be paralyzed!"

"Shut your face!" I told him. "I need a swig of water and someone light me a butt; can't you see I'm hit?" I remember thinking that's what they'd do for John Wayne. I kept hearing: "He'll be paralyzed," and worried the more that I could feel nothing from where I suspected the wound was. What was happening?

Doc studied two spots, the small, slowly spreading blood where the slug went in my neck and, lower down across my back, a slightly larger, faster-spreading blood stain on my fatigue jacket. He acted pleased and I called him on it. "No," he said. "I'm just happy to see that the damn bullet came out." He opened his little canvas aid kit and slipped off my fatigue top. J J offered me his remaining water and someone handed me a cigarette. "Gee, lieutenant, that's awful," he said, lighting me up.

I didn't agree it was so awful; after the initial shock and sudden flash of burning along the path of the bullet, I never felt a thing nor have I ever since. It was only the memory that bothered me from then on, a heavy speed slugging me; power of a sudden ax blow. Pain was an imagination; the reality feeling nothing to this day.

"My," Doc clucked like a hen, "sit on that boulder, sir."

"What's that mean?" I demanded. "My?"

"You're lucky, that's all; it could've got your spine."

"What's that like?"

"You'd never know, be dead or couldn't move some part of you, or all."

Crimus, I thought, hit my spine so bad I can't feel anything. I was ready to agree wholeheartedly with the guy who said I'd be paralyzed. He, alone, was honest enough to tell the truth. Whatever the lack of pain was in worst wounds, I had it good. But, hell, I was standing there feeling nothing; I didn't keel over, what about that fact?

At long last Doc reached his hands around my head from the front, snipped the top of my undershirt with surgical scissors and ripped the undershirt most of the remaining way, letting it fall below my armpits, placing a 4x4 Carlisle bandage over the bottom hole that was bleeding slowly. I started to move.

"Wait," Doc said, rummaging through his aid kit. "There's a littler hole on your neck there," and he put a large Band-Aid over the small, puckered entry hole.

Basically it was me and Doc Lynch, my sole caretaker, on-hand savior, entirely at his mercy, his to help me live or let me die.

For many years thereafter, I told people I was hit by a burp gun, but have recently been corrected by my platoon guide at the time, Clarence Karl Eppler, who has studied enemy weapons. Standing right behind me and listening to the cracking sound of it, he says that it was a sharp-pointed Russian 30.3 armor-piercing sniper bullet which, because of its sharp point and extreme speed, made a much cleaner wound than a burp gun. At the distance from which it must have been fired, Karl explained a burp gun would have made the sound of a lot of bullets rather than a single 'crack' and have torn a nasty hole, probably cutting the spinal cord. I shuddered to think of it.

Doc Lynch, with life or death in his hands, was about five nine, a little taller than me, ruddy cheeks, a Nebraska farm boy whose sharp city relative altered his birth certificate to seventeen and appeared as his father when enlisting. It was okay for his father or mother to sign for him to join the Army at seventeen but our gung-ho buddy, our sweetheart of a medic, fifteen then, was hot to trot. A man prematurely, he was a quiet, very modest young man, chock full of an urge for adventure, who rode bulls and broncos in local rodeos at fourteen.

With his little canvas aid kit and surprising tenderness submerged under his aggressive masculinity, Doc had plugged fifty dangerous bleedings and set a few bones in his very valuable year in Korea. And, yes, closed the lids on more than a few accusing eyes.

I suddenly felt beaten and terribly tired, yearning for another drink of water, entranced by the gentle medic's fussing over me, deluding myself for the time being that it was all a dream. Then as suddenly I was very important, very much as though I just paid my debt to the entire world, cleansed myself of all guilt and obligations forever. Having been sentenced to a long, dreary internment, at last I made the big sacrifice to spring me loose, free, free at last, free for good. I would never owe anyone, any institution, never be nagged and driven to prove myself ever again, anything ever again. I've had the bullet of self-importance through my back, fully delivering me from doubt; once carrying the clinging oppression of inborn debts to society, I freed myself in defense of our nation, paid my debt to society; don't call on me no more.

While Doc filled out the cardboard evacuation tag, DOD AGO, Department of Defense, Adjutant Generals Office, Form 8-26 Emergency Medical Tag, I tried cautiously to feel the extent of the wound, a definite pain or ache. "Crimus," I brooded, "I'll settle for an itch—anything."

"What's this place we're at?" Doc asked.

"Habae-chae," I said, "The nearest village anyway."

Doc wrote Habae-chae with his stub of a pencil and 1300 hours, 23 May 1951 for the time I was wounded. For the location of the wound he scribbled neck, even though the bullet had passed out lower down across the back, and signed his name and number, noting that I wasn't given morphine.

"Does it hurt, lieutenant?"

"I wouldn't say it hurt."

"Got plenty of morphine, say the word, one's yours."

"Wait till I feel something."

I began to worry, particularly because I couldn't feel anything except the outside of my left side and chest becoming quite sore. I thought, "maybe I should take a morphine for what the damn grenade did," but then I became anxious by the numbness, wondering if I had an important nerve shot up; better not numb it any more with morphine. I wished I could feel some little pain just to let me know I was all right back there. Doc tied the strings of the evacuation tag to the top button hole of my fatigue jacket and slipped the jacket back over my ripped undershirt carefully, although, I thought, there didn't seem to be

132

any need to be careful.

I suddenly realized how free I was. Damn it all, 'free as a bird' was to me more than a saying. Being wounded in the service of one's country the most beautiful fulfillment of responsibilities. Bled for your country—what a ring to it.

We Reserves were recalled to active duty for seventeen months, subject to extension, told to pass a year of that in Korea. With my MOS, 1542, infantry unit commander, we had but five choices of avoiding the terrors of combat: refuse to go, get too ill to fight, get a branch transfer to any other MOS, or be killed, missing, and, next to putting in a full tour, I had the best—being wounded; that dreaded category, one if not the easiest in my case, bullet through the flesh of the neck and back, hitting no major nerve, blood vessel or bone, not that I could feel.

In a random second, I'd paid my way honestly through all social levels the hard way, beyond question and on the immediate local level, no more fretting about right to lead the guys. Instantly, I became an undisputed hero authority on combat, no more worry about ammunition, chop chop, what's next, or anything. I was free now to go to an aid station and have others worry about me, little as it would be. As for Master Sergeant Ulriche, he can rest on his laurels now until he rotates. I'm in charge and don't nobody forget it.

I turned and yelled, "Sergeant Ulriche, take over."

There was no answer and I yelled once more. "Sergeant Ulriche, I'm leaving. You're it."

In retrospect, it never occurred to me that although I remember Holly's men on the extreme left, I have no memory of Holly pulling back or any recollection at all of Sergeant Ulriche.

I turned to Sergeant Eppler and asked about our platoon sergeant and Karl shook his head and told me he hadn't seen Sergeant Ulriche since we took off in attack. "Till Sergeant Ulriche shows up," I told him, "You're in charge."

Doc assured me two wounded were on their way down with an armed escort, one wounded in an arm, no bone, the other something like Perkins in the fat of the flesh of the ass went on a litter face down carried by two CTCs along with two ambulatory WIAs from King Company, and an armed King sergeant with a persistent stomach pain, like appendicitis. Down the long winding mountain trail to where litter jeeps were waiting to take them to the 15th Infantry collecting point aid station of the Third Division which made a wild 100-mile ride in less than twenty-four hours overnight from the Seoul front to block behind us.

I presented Doc with my M2 carbine with the scarce bell-shape muzzle flash hider and heavy pistol belt with first aid bandage, ammo pouch, two empty canteens and bayonet scabbard. The bayonet was still on my carbine in place of the flash hider. Suddenly, though wonderfully free, I was small and all alone, withdrawing within myself, no longer responsible for a thing, my worries all private, my only desire to get away to absolute safety as soon as possible. Escape, yes; escape forever from dangerous situations.

"Well," I said, "tell Sergeant Ulriche what happened to me. You guys did a terrific job and I'll be seeing you, I guess. I better be going now. Take care of each other."

"Take it easy, Lieutenant Gould."

There had been a short discussion before between myself, Doc Lynch and Sergeant Eppler about how every time a man got hit, three or four guys, some he knew only by sight, were more than eager to see that he got to the rear. Such solicitude was another way of bugging out. I waved two would-be companions away and started down, worrying only a little about the wound I could not feel or see which I wanted to know the extent of.

A few hundred yards down the ridge, I found a small party of officers and sergeants taking a break. Two CTC carriers had been toting a large radio which I recognized as an Angry-9, AN/PRC-9, long-range for aerial support. It was owned by X Corps and there were two Corps FOs, who should have gotten us Air and heavy artillery support, as promised by the colonel who briefed us so eloquently. Ranking man was a captain with a 'flash-bang' outfit from Eighth Army, able to triangulate incoming fire by calculating backward the inverted legs of a V in both sight and sound, not needed on our attack since rearguard Chink units left to fight us were not supported by artillery which they hustled north.

"Where the hell you guys been?" I demanded, facing the captain. "Where were you when we needed you?"

134

"It's all over?" he asked. "You got the hill?"

"No, the hill got us."

"We're damn sorry, lieutenant. Nobody told us you were pushing off so early. We understood the attack was slated for afternoon. We heard you'd laid on an Air strike first; you know how slow they are."

Seems the colonel hadn't waited for them to attend the briefing and I found out what the Blue Book meant by "a hastily organized task force." Thereafter, we referred bitterly to the operation as Task Force Joke. The damn colonel or somebody should have been cashiered. Good guys got killed because it broke down, despite his detailed briefing. The shadowy character Major Wilkes should've been court-martialed for not even showing.

Unbelievably, a hundred yards more down the hill I came upon the bastard, our new acting battalion commander, Major Wallace W. Wilkes and Captain Jones, his S2. I surprised myself at how authoritative and bold I became after wounding, which made me tower above all those not wounded. Further, I was a recalled Reserve who everyone knew had no intention of making a career of the Army, so to hell with ratings! Our tour by law was just long enough to fight the war for the Regulars while they worked at bettering their careers. It infuriated me, not so much because Wilkes was hiding out, but neither his SCR 536 or 300 radio was on nor had he any phone lines. How could they call for artillery or Air, or hear my plea for permission to withdraw?

I noticed a half full bottle of Jack Daniels Black Label beside Wilkes.

"You bastards!" I yelled. "Where the fuck's our fire? What're you doing hiding out? At least get up where you can see what's going on."

The captain jumped to his feet, leaning forward to read my name tag. "Who the hell you think you are, you sonofabitch, talking to a major that way. You the Gould the major tells me Lieutenant Foney told him bugged on his men at the outpost?"

"What do you know about an outpost? None of you were ever up there. Why didn't you inform the companies you were cutting your wire and turning off your radio?"

"Shut up, lieutenant!" Jones yelled. "We're going to bring you up on charges." I hoped they would.

Wilkes glared a little, content to leave it to the captain.

Court martial me for cursing a shirker? Go ahead; who of us closing with the enemy on those ridges was afraid of a court martial? She-e-e-it! That's a friendly game—way back, comfortable where everything's normal and nobody gets hurt—hot meals, compared to what we go through.

Wilkes noticed me eyeing his bottle and slid it behind him as his S2 continued to threaten. I stood glaring until, finally, as I took off, they began to gear up slowly so as not to seem in a hurry toward where the action had been.

Pushing my way around large rock outcroppings, rehashing my brief moment of glory—not the wounding but chastising those cowards—I kept my neck and back stiff, visualizing my spinal cord as white wrapping twine partially severed. If I was the least bit careless, it would fray against a splintered vertebrae and cut the rest of the way through. God, would anyone find me in time on this two-mile, lonesome mountain trail?

It grew very muggy as far away to the west, the sick, angry sky spit lightning toward us, coughing up heavy rolls of thunder.

I must hurry out of the mountain before the rains return; before it gets slippery; before night falls on me stumbling. I wished I let one of those volunteers run guard for me. Anxiously scanning the lowering sky for the first signs of trouble, I replayed with uncanny vividness memories of my playing dead on the outpost.

Crimus, I fretted. I was lucky Kitty visited me. Who'll believe it? Let a shrink figure that one out. It was her, no doubt it was Kitty, alive. Crimus, she could've got killed or do you suppose she was a ghost of some kind? Something I've never read about.

Back down the ridge I could still hear occasional bullets from the maxims firing at ROKs high above fanned wide apart, wailing lonesomely above me over the scrub oaks and twisted mountain pines and I worried that someone was engaging them again, or do you suppose the ROKs were giving it another try. No, I concluded, just a machine gun duel with those gung ho gunners of Mike Company.

A mile down the finger I stepped aside for ROKs bent over under large rice straw bags of rice on their backs and heads. They saw the lack of helmet or weapon on this American and the evacuation tag on his lapel and made toothy grins of approval, proud and respectful as combat men, especially, are of wounded. One ROK stopped, balanced his load on his bent-over shoulders, put the palms of his hands together on his forehead, and, facing me, bowed several times, saluted, then faced away and when his courtesies were finished, pointed first to the just visible bloody Band Aid and then to the enemy hill. Easing down his bag of rice, he grinned broadly, made zip-zip bullet noises, jabbing his right index finger through the air pointing imaginary bullets at my neck, smiling more broadly yet with two gold-capped front teeth.

"Numero uno," he giggled. "GIs number one, joto. Chinamen, number hucking ten."

The guttural way he said 'fucking' made me smile.

"Number one. Ichiban uno," the ROK reassured me. Encouraged by my smile, he laughed uproariously, shaking his head up and down vigorously, apparently telling himself one helluva' a joke.

I straightened and in doing so spread back my shoulders slowly, experimentally, carefully. At last I had something good strangers might relate to, a Purple Heart for all my troubles, true as a thousand dollar gold piece; take one look at it on my lapel they'll know automatically what for. I'm reminded of Senator Dole as I write this, another rifle platoon leader.

"Here, monkey," I told the ROK. "Have a cigarette."

There were treacherous slides where our battalion stomped steps with the edges of their boots into the mud of short, steep climbs. Great quantities of ammunition were scattered along the trail; must have been from the ROKs, mortar shells, metal boxes of machine gun ammunition, bandoliers of M1 clips, and especially frag grenades. An empty ten-man chogee train could have been sent up and loaded on the way. Hell, I thought, they didn't need them anyway.

King, Love and heavy machine gun crews of Mike had so ruined the trail I was forced at times to stumble uncertainly through the rocks and brush off the path holding my neck rigid as possible.

I left the low rounded foothill late in the afternoon and, peering anxiously back over my shoulder, saw the Chink hill half hidden under a mass of swirling black clouds centered where mountains meshed into a purple sky and man, it was raining up there bad.

I stumble-walked to the fork of the peaceful valley road where medics and drivers forward from battalion aid station of the 15th Infantry of the Third, Rock of the Marne Division, sat beside double-decker litter jeeps heating C's, looking up from time to time at the long winding mountain trail for their work to arrive—us dirty, dejected, weary, bloodied men coming like as not stumbling individually from that hill, smiling secretly, proud as peacocks. "I've got my wound! My ticket out," for a while, anyway.

"How they doing up there?" one asked. "Take it?"

"No," I answered, "it's all over. We got kicked off. Far as I know, I'm the last wounded."

"We seen ya' startin' down that last rise," a driver of an unlittered jeep remarked. "Gotta' wait for two more walking. Any right behind you, sir?"

"Didn't see any. We pulled off the objective, so I doubt it."
Boy, oh boy, I thought, wait 'til everyone in Watertown learns what I've been through. Nobody from there's been wounded way out here.

"You guys should've been up there," I told the driver. "Boy, were we ever close to those Chinks. Crimus, they must've had seven machine guns. I wouldn't wait for no more from this fight, I think I was the last to get it."

The driver was silent thinking, and then, anxious for shelter and a hot meal, waved me onto the front seat. "You say you're the last?"

"We've been out of it hours now," I told him.

"Let's chogee, sir."

Important, dramatic and novel as my verbal observations were to me, the driver appeared to listen only while he waited impatiently to change the subject. Wounding was normal, carrying wounded was what mattered.

"Awful lonely road," he mumbled. "Hope you guys didn't bypass no Chinks."

Him and me together spoke our minds to ourselves.

"They had a thousand grenades," I went on. "You should've seen us banzaiing up there."

138

"Listen to this old wreck," the driver replied. "They got new jeeps in Japan where they don't need them and we get old wrecks. I hear we're getting new ones, hope it's true."

Waiting for solace that never came, I ventured, "Funny, I can't feel a thing." I cautiously reached back and touched the Band Aid. "Wonder just how bad it is. Can you tell if it's still bleeding?" I asked the driver, trying to expose that side of my neck. "Suppose the nerves are dead and that's why it's so numb?"

Thinking I had his attention, I repeated myself.

"Can't see it's bleeding no more, lieutenant. . . . I'll shit you not, sir, one day the ass end's dropping clean out of this wreck and they'll have to give me a new one. You'd think with us fighting their war rear echelons would be more considerate."

Rear echelon?

The trip of the self-concerned was about five miles and, rounding the last bend, the driver pointed to the 15th Infantry Regimental Collection Station, a large squad tent. I hoped there would be a war correspondent and a photographer. I'd remind them that one of their heroes, Audie Murphy, went through this same 15th Infantry Collecting Station three times in World War II. It would make good copy to go along with my story. Where's that good-looking Maggie Higgins, correspondent you see in Stars and Stripes?

An evacuation helicopter, whirlybird H-13, circling blades around and around up noisily to whisk off head and chest wounds – at a distance, a large plastic bubble between two litters lifting itself. It was the first chopper I'd ever seen. In a few minutes another pushed itself into the air, two full covered baskets hanging on each side of the fuselage, aerial litters or coffins, depending sometimes on how fast they were. Slipping awkwardly sideways, tilted unnaturally to one side as it flew low above the valley road, it seemed that a fat man rode in one and a skinny guy in the other. Indeed. If an H-13 had one wounded only to haul, someone or a weight had to ride in the other basket to equalize the load.

We pulled over behind an ambulance from another battleground unloading and a captain-surgeon met us and made a quickie triage. "You there, you there, and, Sergeant Queen, this man *now*," and, sort-

139

ing the last litter case, turned to me, pulling up my jacket to check the bandage and Band Aid.

"How'd you get that bruise?" he asked, looking it over professionally, and when I told him Chink grenade, he asked, "One of our concussion ones?"

"No sir, one of their own; ours would have killed me."

"I don't understand, lieutenant, a frag would have done a lot of damage."

"No sir, a potato masher, a small can of explosive."

"How's it feel?" he demanded, glancing hurriedly at the ticket, poking near the exit point, taking a quick look before staring blankly into my eyes for reaction.

"Okay, I guess, okay."

"Guess?" the surgeon snapped. "Take off the jacket."

"Does this hurt?" he asked removing Band Aid and bandage, impatient to find something, while pushing along a line between the two holes from top to bottom and before I had time to answer, poked harder, on the spine.

"Ouch!"

With no further questions, he scribbled, 'missile in back,' on back of the evacuation tag, waved to one of the enlisted medics to re-bandage me and turned to survey ambulatory wounded who stood behind the tent smoking, talking quietly about their big battles and how, when and where they'd been hit. They were from about ten different companies, only me from Love.

I was among the least damaged ambulatory and was told, rather coolly, I thought, to wait outside for the next crackerbox ambulance. Four lay on blood-smeared litters outside the door, frightening, pasty-pain faces who no longer grimaced or were concerned. The last of time for those brave soldiers; shot full of morphine, forever avoided by working medics, slowly passing beyond all miseries without wasting anyone's time, waiting patiently for Graves Registration.

"Bring that head wound over here!" a blood-splattered surgeon ordered crisply.

Wounds were his job, not people.

Dusk spread rapidly through the muggy air. Lighting another

cigarette, I had to shit. Either I'd been too preoccupied or was constipated, but I hadn't shit in two days. I think it was two days, maybe three. Searching my way through the growing darkness, I found a long canvas screen strung near the collecting station to form an open box about 20x20 feet, open at the top, around six upright poles. Assuming it was a large latrine, I went to the entrance in the rear. Inside, about thirty bloody cadavers, many hurt bad or mangled, dead soldiers, including ROKs and a couple Chinks no longer enemy, line crossers clothed in white, piled three high, heads and feet alternating. Four Black soldiers lay together on one stack, beside ROKs, as though they died segregated from Whites. One, drained of blood was ashen, seemingly turning white. I wondered if they were segregated before or by some racist medic after death, or was it just an accident they ended up so tight together? There beside their stack of loneliness was a captain, perhaps to be the bottom of a new pile, officers only.

A sergeant from Graves Registration, 15th Infantry, supervised Korean laborers sliding board-stiff bodies into black human remains pouches. As I watched in horror, a large private's stiffened arm, outstretched as though signaling was dislocated at the shoulder and brought down to his side in order to fit into the rubber bag. As something broke, it made a hideous crack, not loud, just hideous. One little rifleman with a frozen smile, eyes protruding, body bent at the waist, sat up in a grotesque position of a puppet made up to be surprised as two Korean workers relaxed their grip on him for a moment to guide the opening over his legs. He was straightened at the waist without noise.

Another Korean behind the sergeant held a flashlight for a clerk filling out personal effects forms on a clipboard; identifying objects brought out of the dead men's pockets, Korean laborers placing them in individual tagged olive drab cloth property bags.

"Get this one here," the sergeant said, "and we'll call it a day."

"Hey, lieutenant, sir, strangers not allowed in the morgue."

I hardly heard him, so conscious was I of the grounded dead.

"Sergeant," I told him proudly, "I'm no stranger, I'm one of them."

I felt I was with them in a trance, a purgatory in which combat soldiers are held until they fall to a deeper hell underground. Night was falling heavy around us hiding our environment until us dead guys were united in that macabre scene silent voices telling me, "We're gone, gone off duty, lieutenant, want to join? Come, buddy, good bye; Kitty, I'm with my buddies forever. Gone, gone, gone far, far away, slid far under the Land of the Morning Calm."

I bent close to a gangly young master sergeant and saw that he and his new companions had been used hard, dead hard way; faces and fatigues caked with brown mud and blackened, dried blood; wide-open eyes of some staring unbelievingly at their ending. "Really it, sir?" they seemed to say, "We worn-out dead men gone now? This is how it ends, stacked here? This is it?" Pity, I thought, young men meet their Maker broken and dirty like this.

They died dropped like a rock or falling and stumbling forward or thrown backward by the force of a hard flung blow, on their faces facing enemy, or flipped up or down; left behind by their buddies forced to evacuate fast; spent shell casings, their lively substance emptied, dropped carelessly in bushes off the trail.

If you stared back at the dead you knew they were no longer them that breathed steadily, and sometimes yelled or laughed and joked and cursed or said hello; no, all those left for a very few others to see were frozen images. Here and there in stacks of the dead a guy more cared for, rolled carefully in an Army blanket, poncho or shelter half bound with commo wire like tall, thin Major Allen by his guys prior to sliding into their own black bags.

As I stepped aside for the Graves Registration party to leave the stacking place, the sergeant asked kindly, "Looking for anyone in particular, Lieutenant? I got a list here . . .turn out the bulb out when you leave"

"No thank you, I appreciate that."

Ten of us less seriously wounded were locked in a crackerbox (square-built Army ambulance with large red cross on its sides) from the outside by a young PFC medic who rode shotgun beside the driver with a puny little single-shot carbine – guarding a stage coach of invalids through Indian country with a BB gun. One of the less handicapped guys sidled back to the only exit, the rear door, and tried unsuccessfully to open it. "Dammit!" he said. "We're trapped."

Night found us zig-zagging up a steep mountain road on high

142

brights to light the way as far forward as possible, one wounded from a nearby artillery battery warned us that Chinks were everywhere. When he left the battery, their 105s were firing north, south, east and west and two MPs patrolling this same winding road two nights before were taken POW, or off to be killed, their burnt jeep found at one sharp turn behind a large log dropped across the way.

We wounded were too anxious to live to nap despite a string of hectic days and the monotony of winding slowly back and forth up the hill. That and the excitement of wounding. We were from different units; each related when questioned how, when and how bad his wound. We were the more important the worse it was. One guy's tag said 'missile in chest.' Another guy with a painfully shattered forearm in a tight sling groaned whenever the ambulance hit a bump, but broken arms were too stateside to hold interest. Another, a young pimple-faced rifleman, sick to his stomach from an unintended extra shot of morphine and utter fatigue, puked green slime between his legs on the floor, apologizing profusely as any drunk. The first medic to treat him forgot to place the empty morphine ampule in a buttonhole to let other medics know by his tag one had already been given.

When asked where I got it, I pointed to my neck and back, telling them the doctor said I was lucky it went all the way through. Seems everyone but the chest wound lit cigarettes and, despite a small ventilation fan up front, the air fouled and burned our eyes. At first everyone talked all at once and then all together grew quiet, reminiscing, each overcome by fatigues of several natures, screening thoughts of how thankful he was for getting this far, and the overall unique pride and excitement of being wounded, as though we were acquiring commercial value, joined an exclusive brotherhood, going so far as to feel sorry for those never wounded in combat.

As our crackerbox ground back and forth up the hill, we sat bent over or slumped right or left against buddies, which we wounded strangers were automatically, lost in thought and daydreams; blank, weary expressions on dirty, bewhiskered faces. Now and then, out of the corner of my eyes in the dim glow of two overhead dome lights, I watched a guy smile to himself and I knew just why; a combination of being full of pride and damn glad to be out of it for a while and the

143

thought, so important an accomplishment to a combat infantryman, I ain't dead or near to it yet and I'm in the Military Order of the Purple Heart.

Are there pretty nurses this far away? Oh yes, oh yes! one way or another they're all pretty, even in combat boots, above which it's all soft and warm and desirable, just to say hello to and look at and day-dream about screwing. Hear the beautiful melody of their laughter; a wonderful cure just being near and smelling them going by, watching them bend over.

As the ambulance settled in low gear up the grinding zig-zag mountain road, in between battle-tattle, we all noticed and pitied a young PFC staring straight ahead, wearing large Band Aids over small blood smears on each cheek. I, and others, I learned later, were convinced the poor guy had his teeth badly shattered and his tongue as well, and, for one, I figured he'd never be able to talk right again and would be on liquids the rest of his life. How'd you like to lose your tongue? Among all wounds he was number one in my book, above the sergeant with a missile in chest which, with proper equipment and technique, could easily be removed.

We reached the summit at last, worrying all the way that infiltrating Chinks would finish us off, and when the driver slammed into high and we began to roll freely downhill, the kid with the bad mouth we all thought must be so painful, unmoving as it was all the hour-long climb, shook his head and enunciated clearly, "Boy, am I glad that's over." I felt like choking him and a sergeant growled, "You sonofabitch!" I thought of all the pity wasted on him. When he saw our angry stares and heard nasty remarks, he quickly apologized for not having the troubles we feared. The bullet passed from one side to the other clean through his mouth, cheek to cheek, without hitting tongue or teeth as he yelled to a buddy.

This was the first of a number of close calls I saw or heard about. A corporal of King Company, for instance, whose case was well known and discussed among medics all over the regiment, was hit in the front of the throat, passed through and came out the neck, missing spine and everything vital. A replacement captain of the same company later, during the monsoon, on the Punchbowl in brand new fatigues and un-

144

tanned, was climbing to take over from Master Sergeant Pater. He carried $40,000 in South Korean currency, August pay for the troops, and was hit in the flesh of his right leg and helped back down by two CTC carriers. After the seven-hour descent in the cold monsoon rain he collapsed at the aid station and, despite all the battalion surgeon tried, could not be revived—dead, I learned, from irreversible shock. His musette bag with the money was never found.

We remounted our box on wheels after a piss stop and motored as fast as traffic and man-size potholes would allow down a much-traveled big valley road with one of the guys up front giving a play-by-play account of what he saw in the darkness peeking through the small window behind the driver. A steady stream of vehicle lights lit the twisting road all the way to Hoengsong. Big powerful trucks from ordnance ammo dumps, shifting gears, revving up, ten-ton trailers, huge rubber-tired bulldozers on lowboys in a hurry to level a supply road somewhere, and many six-bys full of white-faced, wide-eyed, superstitious, prayerful replacements speeding north, relating dire misinformation they'd heard from rear echelons; empty trucks returning for another load and several crackerboxes like ours speeding south toward serenity, full of wholesale but managable misery. Once our small world stopped abruptly, throwing us onto one another from front to rear as our driver tooted and set off a loud tank siren.

"Get that goddamn Mack to the side. Can't you see we're wounded?" our young shotgun hollered in a thin voice.

"Want to haul them youself?" boomed a large Black sergeant standing one foot on the running board to assess the situation ahead. Don't nobody tell him they don't cry up there for them big shells.

Pretty soon we felt ourselves turning onto a side road. Tired of my own desperate, somewhat enforced, therefore artificial and obviously unofficial opinion, I lapsed into a senseless series of frustrating semi-plan or loose daydreams, progressing haphazardly along between short periods of somewhat intelligent or rational worry. Proud as I was of my wound, I resented not having it worse, one of those million-dollar ones that got you stateside. Or did I really? Really? Wasn't I getting a little hooked like a gambler on the unpredictable thrills of infantry combat now that my survival chances seemed better? On the other hand,

"Crimus, some of those could cripple you for life and get worser and worser as you got older."

Come about midnight we corkscrewed into a broad valley with a partially illuminated air strip. We could hear diesel generators humming away. We slowed down and parked and our shotgun guard unlocked us and, stiff and somewhat sore from the long bumpy ride, we got out and pissed and were led into the receiving tent of a field hospital. Two chest wounds from another ambulance who hadn't been air evacuated from the 15th Infantry Collecting Station were well covered and belted down in litter baskets, one on each side of an H-13 big-bubble helicopter and flown to the Air Force evacuation field some twenty miles south over another mountain. The only chopper we had in the Army in Korea in 1951 was the H-13 and few there were. Meanwhile, Marines had the larger, lifting H-19s and were experimenting relieving men on listening posts and hauling heavy equipment.

We were experiencing what the Press labeled the May Massacre and triage selected a few more guys to go south immediately. We ambulatory, those able to walk, dozed on freshly washed litters until dawn to climb into an old Army C-47. Ten badly wounded Chinks were carried aboard and strapped down on litters in the aisle. We studied our adversaries, the first most of us had seen up close. About that time, my buddy Conley Clarke, *Journey Through Shadow*, who hadn't the opportunity to play dead, marching north nights with starved buddies dropped along the hidden ways, never seen again, was knowing Chinese better than one ever wanted to.

I thought what underfed, pathetic little buggers they were. I stared particularly hard at one little Chink under five feet who seemed chinless. "What a lousy deal," I thought, "to be killed by a jerk like that." As time went by on my tour in Korea, I saw many, many more Chinks, dead or POW, and remember many quite tall but never heavy and filled out, like too many were on our side. Six footers with large, high cheek bones, I learned, were likely to be Mongols or Manchurians.

We had a short flight over the mountains just barely visible in the early daylight below and on to an Air Force field where they loaded us into a white Constellation with large red crosses on its sides in case they met enemy Air this far south. Ambulatory sat in bucket seats facing the aisle; layers of litters slung above some of us. After takeoff, the guy immediately above bled all over my collar and shoulder, the side of my own little wound. I called for a nurse and stood out of the way while she worked frantically to stop his bleeding. Damn it, standing in the aisle behind her watching her work so efficiently only a foot away, I fell in love with the back side of that wonderful young Air Force nurse, her pants stretched tight over her lovely butt while reaching for the guy. Angel, that's what she was, flying in the air, a damn angel. How I'd like to get her between some sheets.

Landing at the K-9 airport outside Pusan at daybreak, the more serious were again whisked away, either to one of the several Army General hospitals in Japan, such as Tokyo or Osaka General. We with small bandages had a long wait for a large white school bus converted to run into Pusan on railroad tracks to avoid bumps and traffic to the Third and Tenth Station hospitals.

It was the height of the May Massacre and all medical facilities were working day and night until medics were forced to medicate one another for fatigue and lack of sleep. One MASH handled 700 wounded, including Chinks, in seventy-two hours.

POWs were counted by thousands and there must have been at least 600 litters of their seriously wounded lying near a hanger on the ground at the airport. They were being treated, for the most part, by Korean physicians and enlisted Air Force assistants, Air Force male nurses and master sergeants, who, for the immediate work they did were as skilled as any doctor, treating them every bit as well as we, if a little slower.

Lightly wounded POWs were cared for by the medical detachments of those that captured them at division stockades, often by Korean UN doctors. POW doctors were seldom seen since Chink physicians were never forward of division.

We ambulatory got out and formed rough ranks under the big Constellation; it seemed awfully big to a wounded man standing under its broad wings. We had a roll call and Air Force medics checked our evacuation tags to match them with our dog tags. We were then released to wait around for the railroad ambulance bus to take us into Pusan. Certain cases went to the large white Danish hospital ship, the

147

Jutlandia, docked in the harbor. The *Jutlandia* was later to be relieved by the big US Navy ship, *Hope,* painted white also with its own large red cross midway on both sides.

A bunch of sight-seeing airmen and a few officers apparently too diffident or embarrassed to look us face-to-face, drifted by gawking at Chink POWs. Most prominent was a tall, handsome, mustached Hollywood-type lieutenant colonel and two captains in leather flight jackets taking pictures. We assumed they were pilots off duty and resented the way they pushed into our infantry group, carefully ignoring us, looking right by to get closeups of the Chinks, not saying a thing or being friendly. They invited our hostility and one of our guys said, "Ain't we cute! Pin wings on me ma, I'm a bird."

The Air Force group pretended they didn't hear him and the colonel, face against a fluffy fur collar, with a voice calculated to sound macho, snapping his camera at a little bandaged Chink at my feet said, to impress his captain friends, "Don't look so tough now, do they?"

I could see the wounded dogfaces behind me didn't like it any better than I did and, although usually I don't think of the right thing to say until too long after, this time I was proud of myself.

"Where the fuck *you* seen them before?"

The wounded around me let out guffaws and the colonel glared at me but said nothing. I noticed that one of his captains covered his mouth to snicker quietly. Instinctively, I took the cigarette out of my mouth and put it into the mouth of a wounded Chink teenager. The gesture was obvious, even though the young Chink didn't seem to know what to do with it.

The colonel snapped, "Lieutenant, you can be court martialed for giving aid and comfort to an enemy."

"He's no enemy. He's a wounded dogface like us. Now get the fuck out of here, this is Army business."

The colonel did the only thing he could: demanded my name and unit.

"Lieutenant Gould," I told him proudly, "Second Infantry Division, Love Company, 38th. Come up and see me, we'll climb some mountains."

The GIs let out another big laugh which made me feel impor-

148

tant for having twice said the right thing at the right time.

Three ambulances backed up and picked up the more seriously wounded Chinks as we ambulatory sauntered on foot across the field, along with a growing crowd of curious off-duty airmen who made no bones that they were our fan club. We entered a temporary shelter, a bare Quonset hut. Outside, wounded POW prisoners, guarded by five armed air policemen, were parked unceremoniously in the sun which even so early in the morning this far south was becoming quite warm.

"How is it up there?" one of the guards asked politely.

"See for yourself," he was told from the doorway. "This ain't no private war."

The airman snickered self-consciously.

"Anyone bring a burp gun?" one asked. "Get you fifty bucks."

"Naw," a rifleman drawled. "They was hanging on 'em."

The Army guys laughed. Walking wounded, which most were, filed in out of the sun to flop on straw-filled mattresses lining the walls. I sat next to a grizzled master sergeant on a bench by the front door near the prisoners. He eyed my black, bloodied shoulder so long I think he wanted to ask about it. My sore thumb had cracked open again when I hit it on something and a little blood oozed out. In the excitement of my real wound, I'd forgotten it completely. My bullet wound didn't hurt at all but that darn thumb was sore as anything. I sucked on it brooding and my goddamn athlete's foot was itching bad and my bruised side hurt when I moved sideways or breathed too deeply or laughed.

From a gaily decorated Red Cross airmen's club next door came the plaintive strains of Patti Page singing the *Tennessee Waltz* played over and over by homesick youngsters. "I was waltzing with my darling to the Tennessee Waltz when an old friend I happened to meet." How I'd like to get my hands on her.

"Crimus," I thought. "That's sad." I never been to Tennessee but it made me wonder if anyone really cared what happened to the rest of us. God almighty, that's so sad it hurts; reminds me of songs in WWII that gripped us hard: 'Heard they crowded the floor . . . Don't get around much anymore' . . . 'I'll walk alone' . . . 'The last time I saw Paris' . . . that brought you closer to any girl you dated, as though

149

you were a potential combatant so long as you were in uniform; misery could happen to you and they better be nice when they have the chance. I used to daydream in WWII of all the women to lay, no damn Frank Sinatra bobby-sockers, big-breasted, sexy, mature women who had nipples that tightened when you sucked and knew how to fondle a cock.

One of the prisoners moaned. An older POW consoled him. The young Chink moaned again, louder, making a languid, supplication with one hand. The master sergeant, named Comifort, an ex-Marine, old China hand like our Captain Brownell, whom he'd heard tell of, talked softly to the Chink in his own dialect. The pitiful young man who'd been napalmed and had that smell made a weak smile and waved a limp forefinger of his right hand half an inch up and down above the heavy bandaging and God, how stunned I was, hating the pilot who did that, oozing tears in my eyes, wishing I too could say hello, good luck young fellow, I'm sorry.

"He says he's going to heaven soon and join his buddies who burned up," Comifort told me, and "an older wounded POW, a commissar, warned him against talking like that."

Commissars often allowed themselves to be captured so they could continue to lie to the POWs, proving to me that they didn't believe their own crap about us torturing and bayonetting Chink POWs as the damn Japs did as part of their training, and their charges were all made up. They would lead the mutinies at Koje-do prison island.

Sitting there quietly, plaintive music in the background, I was suddenly very, very tired and with all the excitement and danger and little rest in the past week, I fell soundly asleep and once again had to watch the ravaged refugee families at the big intersection fleeing gooks. God what a pitiful mess, tiny babies bound tightly to the breasts of thoroughly fatigued mothers and grandmothers with their own or other papooses strapped to their bent backs with huge loads on their heads, or, too often, scratched in shallow graves of the dry, hard roadsides, mangled remains of civilian bodies scattered promiscuously along mountain roads.

At 1100 a Red Cross woman entered with a couple of airmen

150

volunteers with more trays of doughnuts. We made sure to thank her.

"Any of you men would like to," she cooed, "come to the Club. We'd l-o-o-ve to have you."

Four or five privates accepted her invitation but the others were too conscious of the contrast; tanned brown by the weather, hard and thin, wearing prominent evacuation tags, blood-stained, filthy fatigues, OD stretch-bandage head dressings, arm slings, or hobbling on crutches, most of us sprayed with blackened blood — Spirit of '76 in olive drab multiplied, in dirty fatigues.

"Well," the Red Cross woman continued, "you boys are more than welcome, you know. We'd l-o-o-ve to have you, deserve it after what you've been through."

As she left, an Air Force major walked by, civilian type, fuzzy, fur-collared flying jacket casually draped over his arm.

"Hi, Joe," she waved.

"How's things?" he purred, carefully ignoring me and the sergeant.

For the rest of our stopover at K-9 airport, we wounded sat or laid on rice straw mattresses in the Nissen hut, listening through walls to the heart-rending *Tennessee Waltz*. Hear it a thousand times, you still sympathize. A substantial box lunch of sandwiches with oranges for dessert was served around noon and several Air Force doctors came out at 1300 with enlisted medics and several trays of supplies to check wounds, still triaging looking for head or chest bandages. The excitement and novelty had worn off. I wished that I hurt or the dandy flyboy would come back to give us a hard time.

"Jam it up your ass!" I'd tell him. "Got any friends, jam it up their's!" The guys would get a kick out of that.

At 1500 our turn in the steady influx of WIA came and the big white bus on train wheels took a load of us into Pusan and the Third Station Hospital.

When I got to the Third, the so-called May Massacre had been going on for about two weeks, beginning as Chinks overran the G800sters, our Second Division and the Fifth and Seventh ROKs. Doctors, nurses and attendants were practically out on their feet, as much as seventy-two straight hours without more than an occasional catnap, some,

151

eyes shut, sleeping leaning against a wall between cases.

The light colonel in charge of the receiving ward triage motioned to me out of ten or twelve ambulatories standing just inside the door. I hesitated, not believing it was me he wanted and he waved again harder, raised his voice across the large room: "Right here, lieutenant, don't be modest." It then dawned on me that what interested him was the great amount of blood splattered and turned black over one shoulder and in front by the guy hemorrhaging above me on the Constellation.

"No," I said soon as I reached him. "That's someone else's blood."

"Well, let me check while I've got you."

He had me remove my fatigue top and he slashed my torn undershirt away, raised my arms and twisted my torso in a number of awkward positions.

"That was fortunate," he told himself aloud.

"Why?" I asked suspiciously. "What happened? What is it?"

Ignoring me the colonel called over a captain and the two inspected my neck and back without Band Aid and bandage, using Latin words, pressing with their fingers, shaking their heads knowingly from time to time. The bullet curved somehow or torqued through the muscles of my neck and back to pass safely between the projections of two vertebrae.

"Hurt anything?" I wanted to know.

Looking at me the colonel answered, "Real close!"

"Crimus," I thought, "I could be dead."

According to my chart, which went with me to a large company grade officers' open ward, I was "white male, First Lieutenant Dudley C. Gould, 160 pounds, five feet eight inches, thirty-one, blood type O, agnostic, married, recalled Reservist. Aside from a minor gunshot wound, in good health. Temperature and heart rate normal."

My nurse scolded me when I insisted I was five feet, eight-and-a-half. She wouldn't change anything for half an inch, she told me. Nearly out on her feet from lack of sleep and fatigue, her speech was slurred and she looked at me with heavy eyelids, all of which I mistook for her being sexy, coming on to me.

"I can show you I got more than eight-and-a-half-inches," I told her, smiling.

"That so?" she told me, walking away.

The company grade officers' ward was full. One of the ward boys told me that every time a big push was made up north, officers with doctor friends came flocking in with all sorts of medical problems that, in most cases, had been pending for some time. Many were accepted, not through normal receiving channels, but by orders from the front office from other than practicing physicians, all determined to avoid being drafted to fill vacancies at the front.

The long process of evacuation and passing through echelons of medics dulled the original excitement of being wounded and for a day or two I was almost morose as hardly a sound was heard in the large open company-grade officers' ward except for an occasional suppressed cough or the pages of a paperback novel turning at intervals; now and then an easy-going conversation in low voices. Even those who rested all morning took long siestas after lunch. Sleep, beautiful comfort.

When my initial two day off-and-on recoup sleep was over, I lay on my sterile white metal hospital cot staring at the white ceiling, designed squares in stamped thin-gage metal repeated from one side to the other, thinking seriously of all the bullets that passed me by, I got thinking about all the comfortable safe living back home I was missing and I confess I was so occupied with my own problems and worries I seldom thought of Kitty or Dickie, our little boy. I was surprised later that Kitty had no such compelling diversions as beset me all the time. Afternoons, she'd tell me were worst; at night there were programs on the radio to give her unceasing worries a little rest.

I was ordered to soak my wounds with four-by-four gauze compresses of hot water three times a day. I was flexible enough to reach back there but even so I did it only three times. Potassium permanganate foot baths were prescribed for my athletes' foot, which afflicted me on and off since high school gym classes.

There was far more concern about that persistent fungus infection, whatever it was, than my unnoteworthy neck wound and nothing said or done about my black and blue side. Perhaps it was because the wound had, like John Wayne's wounds, healed overnight.

Once in mid-morning and again before supper, a tall, mannish woman nurse, a warhorse in Army boots clomped in carrying a wooden tray of assorted hypodermic needles, pill bottles, bandage materials, and miniature bottles of serums.

"Okay, buster, expose it!" she'd command, and I'd roll over on my stomach on the bed and modestly pull down the back of my pajama bottoms. She'd give me a hard slap on my pink upturned ass with her fingertips and simultaneously jab the needle in all the way.

"Ouch!" But I never felt a thing.

"Like that, honey?" she'd smile.

I became convinced she was out to get me and one time became so rattled I sneaked out of the ward before she arrived. That sadistic woman returned after lights out to give me a stab. I was told she always hunted down deserters.

"You men are babies."

The third day I was allowed out on pass in my hospital pajamas, bathrobe and slippers to call my wife from the Korean Overseas Telephone Center near the Pusan train station. I used the last money I had doing it and as it was they kindly stretched our time a little. The come-and-go static on our line was unnerving and frustrating. The Pacific overseas radio was having sunspot troubles so they let me talk only after promising not to blame the Korean Overseas Office. Our voices kept trailing off suddenly to nothing or into an eerie screech and we had to keep repeating ourselves, during which Kitty sobbed. I told her I had just a little nick and a telegram would arrive from the Department of Army and not to worry that I was wounded all over again.

I heard that some of our people were in the *Jutlandia*, the white Danish Hospital ship. Denmark, India, Italy, Norway, and Sweden had medical units to help our wounded. I walked up the gangplank and was welcomed aboard and, looking at a list, found in English what stateroom I would find a First Lieutenant Alexander (Sandy) Opoulus.

As Sandy and I joked around there on the *Jutlandia*, a corporal draftsman from the S3 section of battalion HQ looking for buddies saw me and, apologizing for intruding, came in to talk with us.

"Are you going back to battalion, lieutenant?" he asked me. "Sir, a couple of guys and I want someone to prefer charges against Major Wilkes and Captain Jones. While you guys were trying to take

154

the hill, they were drunk, arguing who was most worthy of rotating first. I was transferred down with Major Wilkes from X Corps where he and the captain was buddies. Both should be court martialed. I've seen them plastered more than once."

"Yeah," I told Sandy, "I passed them hiding out on the trail."

"I know, lieutenant," the corporal said. "I was there and heard you bawl them out and after you left they sobered up fast and moved up toward where the fighting had been. I left for rotation center next day."

"I don't know anything about Army law," I told the corporal, "but I can't do it alone. Are you and your friends willing to testify?"

"Sorry," he said, "we'll be boarding in two days."

Had I legal know-how, I might have gotten a sworn deposition.

When I finally got back to battalion, I found morale so bad under Wilkes that while we were trying to banzai those three machine guns, battalion headquarters and people at the kitchen trains rifled our personal packs, stole cameras and radios and drank up the beer ration which came in just after we left. Letters and other personal stuff were scattered over rifled packs.

Our Blue Book, page 136, says this of my wounding, 23 May —

A hastily organized assault group, Task Force Yoke, commenced a limited northward drive to keep the enemy forces off-balance while the counter offensive was being racked up. Composed of the 3d Bn. 38th Inf; a platoon from the 38th Inf Tank Co; a battery of Division Field Artillery and a tactical air control party, the mobile force moved northwest from Pungam-ni toward Habae-jae.

Nothing was said of two rifle companies weakened and overrun on an outpost, further debilitated with green replacements to care for. Evidently no one in our history section at division rear knew about the abortion our so-called attack, Task Force Joke, was, or about the failure of leadership at every echelon higher than platoon. What burned me most was, in skipping over this futile effort, no mention had to be made of the good, courageous men we left there.

4
Return of the Wounded

I quote again from the Blue Book—

This latest flurry brought to a close the most notable period of the Second Division's actions in the campaign. It brought forth, for the first time, a powerful counterattack which followed on the heels of one of the most spectacular defensive stands of the war. It was a counterattack which not only killed thousands of enemy troops, caught completely off-balance, but proved that the Second Division could absorb the pounding of overwhelming numbers of enemy forces only to turn and cut them to ribbons. In the 20-day period preceding the conclusion of the final attack the Indianhead Division had killed more than 65,000 enemy soldiers, the cream of the armies of Red China.

Judging from Love, King, Item and other companies I knew of in our vicinity, to make such a great slaughter, the rest of the division must have gone off like a million-dollar fireworks. Me and my guys? Busy as we were on the outpost-patrol base and Task Force Joke, I never saw a wild Chink or gook close up dead or alive in the wild except while peeking over a parapet until I returned from the Third Station and joined the guys working for the Dutch battalion near Inje, where plenty of the poor, hard-working little rice farmer draftees were caught by our state-of-the-art, million dollar fighter bombers, on the roads in broad daylight and the cruel, unChristian one-sided technology napalm.

Again from the official Blue Book—

*It was a major defeat for Chinese and North Korean forces.
Their ranks were decimated, entire divisions rendered useless.
They had flung themselves in an all-out attempt to annihilate the
Second Division and had failed under the merciless pounding
of hundreds of thousands of rounds of artillery, tons of bombs
and millions of rounds of small arms ammunition thrown at
them by the determined, steadfast and victorious men of the
Second Division.*

*On 5 June, the Division began its movement into reserve in
the vicinity of Hongchon and by 11 June the move was complete. The relief from combat was utilized for the needed training and reorganization accompanied by corps command inspections of all the units. It was to be the longest non-combat
period enjoyed by the Division since its arrival in Korea and it
was the unanimous opinion of all that no division deserved it
more.*

*As the first year of the Korean conflict came to an end, the
United Nations could look back on their accomplishments with
considerable satisfaction. South Korea had been cleared of the
invading enemy, and the UN forces, after receiving and delivering severe batterings, had pushed north of the 38th parallel and
successfully executed the missions that were within their power
to accomplish. Thus, when on Sunday evening, 23 June 1951,
in New York City, Jacob Malik, Deputy Foreign Commissar of
the Union of Soviet Socialist Republics and his country's dele-
gate to the United Nations, proposed cease-fire discussions between the participants in the Korean conflict, his proposal,
while it may have been made for the convenience of the Chinese, came at a fortunate time for the Eighth Army.*

*Enemy casualties for the last half of May, Eighth Army head-
quarters reported, included 17,000 counted dead and 17,000
prisoners of war. Its own casualties for the entire month num-
bered 33,770. South Koreans lost the most; American losses
totaled 743 dead, 4218 wounded, 572 missing, and 6738 nonbattle casualties, most of which were caused by disease.*

Time Magazine reported 28 May 1951 —

The Second Division historian wrote that the second Division alone had "killed more than 65,000 enemy soldiers, the cream of the Armies of Red China . . . the 23rd Infantry claimed inflicting over 13,000 casualties of which 2200 were counted. . . ." There was little evidence to support these claims. General Ridgway asked for an end to such guesses ordering that claims henceforth be limited to counting enemy dead and prisoners.

Early in the afternoon of the fourth day at the Third Station I reported downstairs to supply to trade in pajamas, slippers and maroon robe for new socks, underwear, fatigues, fatigue jacket with my Indian-head patch sewed on, and cap, and checked out my boots with a property tag. Freshly laundered fatigues and jacket felt good again. I couldn't wait to get in harness, resupplied with hunting paraphernalia at company; field pack with entrenching tool in canvas case, poncho and blanket, area map, and on my web belt two canteens, first aid pouch, bayonet, carbine ammo; binoculars around my neck and on my left wrist with my Army watch an issue wrist compass, and secreted about my pack or upper body pockets, at least one box of C rations.

At the blasted, bombed-out Hoengsong station, I was directed to Second Division's replacement center where I learned my platoon was on duty with the Dutch battalion and got a ride in a 2½-ton truck to division forward where I grabbed a ride with a captain in an artillery jeep to cannon sites in the middle of the vast Inje Valley, just south of where X Corps was heavily engaged with NKPA (North Korean People's Army) gooks.

There were big guns dug in all over the place in circles of batteries and from my distance, little figures fussing with them, whatever artillerymen do to their pieces. A couple, maybe half a battery, of 155 long toms four miles north in the valley were registering impact actions for FOs, otherwise it was peaceful.

A sergeant at the battery I chowed down with that night told me of a young replacement getting down from the tailgate of a six-by, caught a stray round in the leg, hitting a major nerve and, with less than a day in the war zone, earned a combat infantry badge, Purple Heart, and trip home. I should be so lucky.

No sooner did darkness fall than demonical fire broke loose in the wide valley full of battalions of artillery pieces, assembled to do the most damage to enemies. As it darkened, the valley became dotted with frightening flames, thunders and separate storms of fires, burping gases, flaring rumbling fires and burning vapors, a battleground of heroes from Hades struggling with smokey giants of blazing cannon all around me in the early dark for miles of valley bottom, released from the snouts of short-barrel howitzers and big long barrel toms which made the sky about them glow red.

Simultaneously, huge blasts of flame, bursting points of fire like spark-spewing, tipped and pouring openhearth crucibles booming, lighting the dry river bottoms and empty rice paddies more spectacularly than Public Square at Watertown on Saturday night. Hell, no, Times Square, New York City.

Shells had been stock-piled for days for this powerful event driving hordes of enemy north, this blowout supporting a regiment of the Third Division and the 187th Airborne charging out of Inje on the ground, headed at dusk north on a rare night attack for Americans, pushing, not Chinks anymore, North Korean gooks, hated especially since they treated our prisoners so badly.

Piled away from the guns were hundreds of brightly-burning, partly used nylon powder bags. A full charge of powder, capable of throwing a shell maximum range, came in nylon bags with each shell and the unused had to be destroyed. At Inje range was minimal, the enemy so near when the attack began cannon barrels fired almost straight down the level a few miles northward toward foothills less than a mile away. Ka-pow! Ka-pow! Ka-pow! Ka-pow! went our cannon fast as could be loaded. Flash! Flash! Flash! of hell-fire burning unused powder bags.

I borrowed a blanket and found a spot under a small tree and, working softer room for my lean hips, curled around on dry grasses to bed down, as familiar with the bosom of mother earth as any Indian fighter out West. It was hours, however, before I could sleep, harkening to our powerful artillery firing, each boom of the 155 battery near me bouncing me on the ground as they let loose, further and further north, indicating the success of the Third Division dogfaces and the 187th Airborne Regiment night attack. Gooks at this range also fired occasionally into the wild circle around us.

My platoon was attached to Second Company, Captain Jan van Rusbroec, on a high ridge, both we and the Dutch patrolling for security behind lines for the French battalion of our sister regiment, the 23rd on the right flank. Before I joined them, the guys had two minor fracases with trapped gooks, the first since I was in the outfit, and a few Chink stragglers. As long as they didn't stay to fight, we were content to hurry them along with artillery and Air.

According to Holly's platoon sergeant, a former Filipino scout, gook was from native dialect *gugu*, slang for westernized Filipinos, for people like Americans, considered inferior.

At dawn the mountain finger I should climb was pointed out and, well wishes made, I was off to join my platoon. On the way, about daylight, I witnessed a spectacle that sickened me for several days. Three twin tail Flying Boxcar C-119 cargo planes, killing time, flying 360s, waiting for clearance to drop heavy equipment for the 187th, got caught too low into time-on-target artillery firing proximity fuses, hitting one cargo plane which crashed into another. I heard the awful noise, saw the huge black puffs and felt it in my bones. Ten men in each plane; the last plane hitting debris from the second, fought the stick frantically, pulled up too short and stalled. Field stoves, to be dropped, slid out the rear before the pilot lost all control and the last plane smashed into the side of a ravine. At least thirty sturdy, intelligent, honorable, fearless, well-above national average young men wiped off the face of the earth because some son-of-a-bitch at Air Fire Control Center back by the guns allowed the big planes to circle too low. Who needs enemy with 'friends' like this?

"Hi, lieutenant," Doc Lynch greeted casually as though I'd never been gone.

"Back so soon?" Sergeant Eppler complained.

"Disappointed?" I asked. "You saw it, a scratch. Wouldn't have got as far as Pusan unless they thought something still in my back."

Karl helped me remove my new fatigue jacket while Doc lifted my undershirt to examine the two little pink scars with professional interest.

"Beauties," he decided. "In a few years you'll have trouble finding them," remembering how his dad's scars disappeared after World War II.

Ulriche rotate? I asked.

Doc and Karl looked down.

"My god!" I said. "Not Sergeant Ulriche! How'd he get it? He was hot-to-trot, number four on battalion rotation. After all he'd been through. Damn it! Goddammit!"

I was several years older than Sergeant Ulriche, still over here he was my father, teacher, role model, guide, and more. He was my inspiration, my protector. Damn it, God, Sergeant Ulriche's our leader. He came from the mountains of Kentucky to save his buddies one crucial day at Guadalcanal and then scores more after Chinks entered the fight at Kunu-ri and then the Banzai Third; brightening my learning days in teaching me to stay alive.

"Didn't you hear?" J J butted in. "Found him right below one of them machine guns on the left out of sight—Lieutenant Hollingsworth and that Filipino scout, his platoon sergeant, out of our sight to the right under another gun they tried to outflank. All three got it bad."

"He didn't have to die, was supposed to stay back with you, remember? Goddammit! He wouldn't listen to Dud Gould. Where was Lieutenant Gould at Guadalcanal and Kunu-ri?" Tears started to come and I slammed a fist into the palm of my hand, shaking my head, facing away. Goddammit! I gave him an order, stay back with our medic . . . with you, Doc, and you wouldn't obey either."

"After you left, Lieutenant," Eppler told me, "the whole battalion was called off the hill by our battalion CO, Major Wilkes. Remember how muggy it was? That night we had the worst thunderstorm I ever saw with lightning all over. The next day, the 15th Infantry, Third Division, pushed through took that hill without a fight and found Ulriche, one of our platoon riflemen, Lieutenant Holly and his sergeant. This other guy, a kid named Alvarez, a PFC replacement I don't think you knew, followed Sergeant Ulriche all the way, evidently blown up by

161

a frag grenade. His guts were bad off and he bled a lot and I heard he quivered a little and gulped trying to talk, but died on a litter at the doorway to the 15th Aid Station."

Damn, they must have crawled up the far left flank where I couldn't see them. I was too damn self-centered, busy with Burris and Corporal Turner and those daredevils on the right. Memories haunted me for years, not really memories, silent, accusations of neglecting my men. I should have seen Sergeant Ulriche passing by on the left and stopped him—just how I don't know. Had I been a halfway efficient platoon leader, I'd of made Ulriche stay way back as I ordered him. But, no, I wasn't man enough for that and the Sergeant didn't respect me enough to obey.

As time went by, however, I was able to convince myself that it was Ulriche's fault too, he should have respected my goddamn rank, if not me, personally, and recognized me with the bars as his leader.

The longer in combat, the more quietly you expressed regrets; sometimes a mere shrug of the shoulders; sometimes it seemed you didn't care. You found yourself looking forward more and more for the last attack or defense or patrol and there was always more pressing work to do than sit around a campfire and grieve; one more hill—another unknown place to pencil a goose egg for artillery and mortar on our 1:50,000 scale maps, just as hard to find, where you had to leave a good man or two.

Beginning June 1951, Communist propaganda in Korea began to show signs of failure. Short of manpower, gooks selected ROK POWs and captured southern Korean civilians they thought could be brainwashed, gave them a two-week dose of it and integrated them into the ranks of their soldiers. The gooks were naturally curious about the foreign devils invading the South and asked little Kims if it was true about wholesale raping and general pillaging their commissars told them went on. Just how bad was the situation in the South? They were amazed to learn the truth and chalked up one more against their lying leaders.

Every few days an Army C-47 flew low over enemy territory within hiking distance from our line working a loudspeaker featuring trained former NK soldiers urging their buddies to give up. Safe con-

162

duct surrender pass leaflets were dropped for their convenience.

Early one drizzly morning at Inje a trembling, wide-eyed teen-age gook soldier came crawling up on hands and knees, clutching a surrender leaflet. Like a begging dog he flattened his body, all but wagging his tail, desperately showing friendliness and with a big, toothy grin, pleaded with his eyes from one GI to another for acceptance as a POW. For all he'd been told, he'd be shot outright or used as Japs did for bayonet practice.

The Korean interpreter for the Dutch Battalion discovered he'd sneaked away from an enemy patrol. Thirty more were trapped in the deep valley over the ridge opposite Inje, starving and without water, waiting for the last of their two badly wounded company officers to die. The Dutch told him to return and lead the rest up when the time came. For three days we were kept posted on the wounded officers' health by escaping gook privates and then on the morning of the fourth day, twenty-six dirty, half-starved very young North Korean men came trembling up on hands and knees through the early morning fog to our barbed wire. Once through, the interpreter talked to them and soon they began laughing and gesticulating as if there was no war at all, looking around at one another from time-to-time self-consciously for assurance, then at each American in turn, smiling broadly in case someone might think they were even a little unfriendly.

Noncoms had their hands full dispersing the crowd of curious.

"Look," a Dutch soldier spoke up in good English. "These youngsters' hair it's turning gray."

"Not gray," Doc, who'd been looking them over, said. "They're lousy. Take a good look; those are dead or living lice covering their hair." Body lice were allies in other wars, spreading typhus as they did, the plagues of Xerxes and typhus that along with zero weather stopped Napoleon in Russia, to prevent which all UN troops were inoculated.

One of the worst trials at the tragic Valley Forge in the winter of 1778-79 was not only lice, to kill which they smeared themselves with sulfur in neat's foot oil (from boiled cattle feet), and heated their clothes in farmers' ovens, but dreaded scabies, a form of mange caused by mites smaller than lice, that burrow under the skin to bite and drive you almost crazy with itching. Scabies are rare in the United States now.

Our new company commander, Captain Shallow made an appearance on the Dutch ridge puffing and panting, bringing up our overdue May pay in a musette bag less than half full, for combat men were encouraged to make large allotments. After signing three copies of the pay form, the majority turned around to the company mail clerk and made out money orders to send home. Some young bachelors simply signed that they refused pay and let it accrue without interest while they were in Korea.

There were quite a few foreign nationals in the Eighth Army, some drafted, some few true warriors by nature who looked forward to combat and being decorated and advanced in rank, which was, I suppose, to many Europeans, an honor worth achieving and many joined the US Army to get their citizenship after a three rather than a five-year wait. I once had two immigrants, Sergeant E-5 Frank Smith of Hamilton, Ontario, a machine gunner, and Poly, Corporal Jerome Polychromus from Cypress, who refused pay and let it accumulate in Finance. Why didn't he sock it into a bank to draw interest? Nobody 'back there' to trust.

John R Folmer, fellow member of the Korean War Veteran Alliance, heavy weapons sergeant in the Dutch Battalion, an American citizen since 1958, international systems consultant, Salem, South Carolina, watched as did I the C-119 Flying Boxcars in late morning 3 June knocked out of the sky by our own artillery. He and two other Netherlanders were part of an investigation team to comb the wreckage. His first battalion commander Lieutenant Colonel Eric Van Oden, was killed at Massacre Valley and his replacement, Lieutenant Colonel Christen, like our first battalion commander, Lieutenant Colonel James Skelden, retired a lieutenant general.

Late on the last night with the Dutch battalion through a storm I heard an harassing and interdictory round land down the ridge in the first squad area and, hustling in the rain to see if anyone was hurt found the body of J C Rodriguez on the trail above his position. What he was doing outside his hole we never knew. Speedy Gonzales, murmured in Spanish, which he translated for me, that J C's superstition was typical of immigrants from Mexico, complaining his time was approaching, he was getting tired of it all; Death had bypassed him too often and he felt in his bones it was time to join his buddies on the other side.

Lieutenant Hurtz once told me that Buddha didn't believe in a god, and one of his nuns taught that man himself created God because his mind is too puny to stretch to the absolute. We saw that plainly from our mountain that terrible night of storming when I myself became a rain-soaked God creator, standing brutishly astride my fallen squad leader cursing: "Jesus! Jesus! God! God!" glaring angrily, jabbing my trigger finger accusingly Godward, beyond the height of rain, way past silver-rimmed thunder clouds. I yelled, why I don't know, and repeated over and over, "J C talk to me, tell me hello; say hello, J C." Bloody Jesus, half his face gone, had nothing to say it with.

I thought hard for an answer until it hurt to think, and in deep despair, utter resignation, offered him the consolation, "Never mind, Jesus, when God finds time to see you crumpled there. . . ." Then I blubbered out of control; lowered my head, shaking side to side: "Shit, Jesus, I can't help you, you knew we're on our own. Nobody can help us, we're on our own."

Oh carrion thou art no longer man.

I learned unquestionably from J C Rodriguez that night this is how worship and prayers got started, cries of hurt from a mountaintop, and that night Jesus got it so savagely I learned for a fact that fear of death is the fundamental cause of all religious activity, no matter how diverting bingo and other colorful rites and ceremonies. This also accounts for our hard yearning for and belief in immortality and as Lucretius the Roman philosopher noted, fear of death is the mother of all gods.

Sergeant First Class Jesus Carlos Rodriguez, furious foe to foes of Anglos, a buddy, a nice quiet guy who did a good job running the first squad of the Banzai Third; scion of immigrant working Mestizos; at the tender age of nineteen, blue-green-sickly-yellow, all color drained from his half face; blue-black glistening Indian hair, one pale, unwhiskered, smooth, light-olive-brown Aztec cheek, lightning etched, waxen, bloody, already hardening.

Jesus Nobody now dead, one eye wide open upward, forever beseeching empty Catholic promises, staring through impenetrable

165

storm clouds, playing out his utterly insignificant role in the hidden scheme of the vast universe, dead as immediately his life's blood sloughed back to his true home, the earth.

Poor, lonely soldier-boy, dying without absolution, no snow-white Mexican angels in attendance, no sister to recite prayers for the dying, no elevation of the Host; without a woman's tears; no mother nursing nightly, no friends of before to raise a drink to; no relatives sobbing at his bier. No bier lonely guy. Jesus, our good buddy, on whom south Texas suns once shown so brightly—J C no longer anywhere.

Goddamn shitty death made Jesus lose control to crap on what dignity was left, returned to the past, a barefoot, skinny waif on dusty lanes of Laredo, son of migrant workers; missed all the fun of being twenty-one; messed his pants the wild, hunted-animal way he died; naughty little Indian boy, what will mama say?

Come on, big-mouth, professional patriots under ivory domes, stand up for Jesus! Make like believers! Believe in our Jesus for a change! Face Korea fat-ass, pork-barreling bastards and scream stars-and-stripes forever 'till Jesus comes marchin' home. Long may Jesuses wave and wave and wave o'er the land of the brave, brave, brave and brave, who are not home anymore, slumped lumps of sod in an Asian charnel in The Forgotten War.

Jesus was KIA'd by a fragment of a 76 self-propelled high velocity harassing and interdictory artillery on one of the ridges of the mountains of the east-central front in Korea, ten miles south of the 38th Parallel in enemy land west of the Sea of Japan.

We can't all be Agnostic or serve a quantum god and in the spirit of ecumenism, let me offer to the memory of our warrior amigo, quiet teen hero Sergeant E-6 Jesus Rodriguez, died in Catholicism unattended—alone—

Requiem aeternam dona eis, Domine, et lux perpetua luiceat eis.

Give him eternal rest, O Lord, and let a perpetual light shine upon him.

The bloody body of Jesus our beloved squad leader, an inert lump, was taken away by Dutch morticians in a body bag and life went on and nobody ever saw him again, an E-5, Zigerfoose with grade over

166

Gonzales was sent by company to try to take J C's place as we were detached from the Dutch battalion and returned to Love.

No firefight was heard or seen for three more days and our kitchens convoyed cautiously out to meet us in the Inje Valley. The guys, well rested, plucked wild, short-stemmed blue irises and wore them protruding jauntily from the upturned bores of their rifles. Not that they were your run-of-the-mill ostrich-plumed dandy musketeers of the Court of Louis XIV, low-bowing, sweeping hats, and obsequious - soldiers of times gone by, but they'd seen a movie or two and obeyed pleasant impulses. Time to sport a posy, buddy, Death is looking the other way.

Good byes are short in the infantry, bitterly final but life does go on as Buddha's vital changes are better known by the Queen of Battles. Here today and. . . . One good thing about an army at war, if you don't like someone, wait a while and either he or you'll depart one way or another. No one can wrong you forever and Lieutenant I B Foney, the strong, silent, stupid type with his ill-gotten DSC, made captain and was transferred to X Corps, a junior on Lieutenant General Almond's staff, sure indication he'd make Regular. The publicity-conscious general got another pretty boy John Wayne, tall, decorated, college graduate, inarticulate.

From *The forgotten War* by Clay Blair, Anchor Books, 1981 —

The battered Second Division withdrew from the Inje area into X Corps reserve, in accordance with Ridgway's orders. By that time the division was shattered; it was to remain in reserve for forty days, rebuilding and reorganizing and rotating those who had been in combat longest. During that period three regimental commanders, the 9th's Ed Messinger, the 23d's Jack Chiles and the 38th's John Coughlin were rotated. Coughlin retired as a Colonel in 1954.

The new commanders of the 9th, 23d, and 38th regiments were all young West Pointers. Command of the 38th went to the youngest of three, Almond's G-3, Frank Mildren (West Point, 1939).

167

Frank Mildren's nickname was Fearless Frank, with a DSC in World War II, he was a thirty-seven-year-old officer with long ties to the Second Division. Upon graduating from the academy, he joined the 38th Infantry where he commanded the 1/38, First Battalion, 38th Infantry, at Omaha Beach, D Day two, and in six years rose to be regimental executive.

By 1951 good aggressive combat company and battalion leaders were not plentiful. Class of 1950 West Point was hit hard the year they graduated and with few exceptions, rifle platoons and companies in the Second Division, were led and would be led in the forseeable future often by recalled Reserve lieutenants, rarely captains. Some few were even ROTC officers who aged and learned fast, earning infantry master degrees in fierce combat; rapidly promoted by attrition, and in a few cases, master sergeants, like John Pater, later to receive a field commission with a limited duty waiver on age.

After Lieutenant Foney left, Love was supplied with a captain, I M Shallow. Both Captains, Ted Toth of King, already in Korea six months, the recipient of a Bronze Star, and I M Shallow of Love, were to leave their commands within a month in disgrace. Coincidently, both were somewhat overweight, wore dark-rimmed glasses and had considerable experience in the supply field, which in the peacetime Army isn't such a bad field to be in. Expertise in requisitioning, inventory and supply is a plus in any branch at any time, in any business for that matter. That those particular captains ended up commanding rifle companies speaks of the shortage of that grade. Neither Toth nor Shallow would be seen in a rifle outfit during better times.

Major David Duncan shipped over from the 101st Airborne Fort Campbell, Kentucky to become Third Battalion commander. His kind lived for infantry combat; it's what they did, with strong willpower and years of training he strained hard to sustain it.

He once told me bluntly: "We like war and we're tooled for it." And reminded us at an officers' call when some reference was made of the powerful CCF: "Don't ever forget America's powerful secret weapon, the SAM-51, Soldier American Model-1951."

Duncan, battlefield commissioned early in the fighting in Europe, was about as short as they allow in the Army, hawk nose, perhaps appropriately having been a veteran of 'screaming eagles' in World War II and afterward, which patch he proudly wore on his left shoulder when he arrived in Korea.

In a few days, a Sergeant Bill Hanson, E-5 from Fred Hurtz's platoon with the longest time in that grade in the company transferred to take Sergeant Eppler's slot as guide and make SFC, E-6. Eppler stepped into Sergeant Ulriche's position to make master sergeant.

We learned that the Fifth Phase of the Communist Spring Offensive was over when one soldier, leading up a CTC chogee train of supplies, was stopped by a fat, pale-face rear echelon captain and threatened with the standard $50 fine for not wearing his helmet forward of regimental headquarters. I'd like to know what brought fatty so far forward.

"Why them damn piss pots all the time?"

I sympathized, my steel helmet sometimes gave me a dull headache and the leather sweatband engraved a red mark across my forehead; besides, it strained my neck. You had to have the neck of a pro football lineman to get used to one and you notice even pro football players go off the field helmets in hand.

Tables were suddenly turned on the over-extended CCF. Their little Mongolian horses streamed north dragging their tails behind them, our tired Blue Battalion in close pursuit. The weather heated up and the far north of that broad Inje valley was soon littered with musty gray cotton batten pulled from quilted Chinese winter uniforms. As the Chinese drove their many captured vehicles north, Air Force Operation Tacks scattered 5,706,000 long roofing nails from low level along the road to puncture tires. Changing tires, when they had them, was major mechanics to those rice farmers.

We had a ring seat at the beginning of a grim harvest as a team of four Saber jets skimmed in over our backs out of the sun down into the mouth of a long narrow valley to our right front On the dusty road ahead within sight was a rag-tag column of fleeing yellow men, the first seen from our mountain perches on the roads in daylight, or heard tell of so near in daylight. Some pushed bicycle-wheeled ammunition carts, others had huge bundles of sundry supplies on their backs, while yet others bullied along weary, mangy, overloaded Mongolian ponies. Ten or twelve captured Korean bullocks pulled creaky, ancient, Korean farmer's two-wheeled wagons, drivers walking beside frantically cracking long, black whips. Some of our animal-loving fighter pilots seemed to avoid this helpless prey, even though they could assume that, because of the obvious heavy weight, the wagons were full of ammunition.

So preoccupied were the Chinks that the only warning to many was the insane fury of 50-caliber machine gun bullets tearing through them. Others were alerted by screams and groans, for the jets were beyond their targets almost before the sound of their guns were heard. Some country guys remarked how it broke them up to hear the heart-rending screams of the little horses from the distance, above hysterical shouted curses in Chinese.

Korean civilian forced-labor recovery squads, struggling hopelessly with wounded Chink soldiers, panicked and dropped their crude bamboo litters, running headlong into the squirming mass of men caught along the narrow ledge road of a defile between a cliff that towered up on their right and a drop-off 100 feet into a swollen river into which Chink and laborers were continually falling.

The road was cut by a twenty-foot deep 500-pound aerial bomb, craters impassable to wheel vehicles and by the time the airplanes zoomed back for their napalm pass, two companies and more of Chinks were bottle-necked at the lip of the crater. Some made half-hearted efforts to raise their rifles but all ended the same, a clawing, screaming, blackened mess as napalm tanks end-over-ended through the air p-u-u-u-W-OOFT! charring flesh, sucking air from lungs; a black puff of greasy smoke rolling skyward after each strike. Was there ever a greater terror weapon? Ancients hurled fire and brimstone (crude mined sulfur) catapults, but burning balls were petty compared to large metal containers of blazing jellied gasoline hurtling through the air at three hundred miles an hour, sometimes spreading and spilling forward flaming even before impact, burning ten feet wide and forty long. The mere thought sickened us hardened infantrymen.

Later, we walked among cooked meat, some roasted without a

mark of violence. Those in the center of every burst well done, bloated orange and black skin bags, yellowed teeth grinning sickeningly from burned black charcoal skulls. The odor was especially repulsive because, with eyes closed, it might seem almost edible.

One Chink's uniform was burned off except for what he was lying on, his taunt skin a weird bloated dark orange, cooked brown, glistening like a well-roasted Christmas turkey — not a puncture wound anywhere. Four metal buttons surviving the burned cloth rested on his bare chest, around his waist the blackened remnants of a leather belt held pieces of charred cloth. Even the tops of his cheap tennis shoes were flash-burned away. His little dinky stood up, baked stiff between his legs, ridiculously small to be so rigid.

"One Chink died happy," Funero observed.

The most unpleasant work came when battalion commander Wilkes ordered Love company on a burial detail with Graves Registration back up the valley. I took the dirty job personally, like he took all of Love just to get at me. My Third Platoon alone covered over sixty-two Chink corpses with the aid of a tank with a bulldozer blade, altogether an estimated 3,000 were buried in the Inje Valley. Dead horses, bullocks, and Chinks were all the same. All dead flesh smells alike, man or beast. More tragic to me were poor innocent dead horses on their backs, bloated, four feet straight in the air.

The ground was too hard along the road and it was inconvenient to drag cadavers to rice paddies. A few had been rotting a week. Bending over to push them with the short-handled entrenching tools, we disturbed clouds of large angry buzzing purple blow flies, maggots dropping squirming and wriggling and black carrion beetles darting swiftly away when their rotting banquets were disturbed. Guys announced unusual wounds.

"Hey, look, blew half his ass off."

One little Chink wore a cheap pair of wire-rim glasses tumbling into his grave. I, for one, was resentful that his Army hadn't provided a better-looking pair. He was pathetic enough.

"Yeah? Wanna' see something, look at this."

"Here's a sight for you, lieutenant."

When they grabbed wrists instead of sleeves to move a body,

171

flesh slipped off greasy bones which, of course, without gloves they did only if absolutely necessary.

Rains came during the night and sunk loose dirt and by morning withered yellow-brown feet, hands and heads popped up pleading with us living for another chance, one more chance to live, exposed rotting flesh that shriveled dry and hard in two days under the baking sun. Under dust and under dust to lie—left exposed wasn't enough dust, not in that rocky ground.

The quilted uniforms of the Chinese were tan and uninteresting, the only distinguishing mark of any kind being an occasional small, dull, half-inch, red enameled star centered on the front of a cap. Some intermediate bugouts went ghoulishly into pockets for souvenirs. Rumor had it that an 81 mortar gunner in Mike Company recovered over $500 in American money that way. I wouldn't have touched it for a thousand.

For the two days we were kept in that stinking valley of death, poorly buried, over-ripe corpses literally sprang up from their insufficient coverings, sickening, slimy black fluid exuded from uniforms stained around the wounds. Bodies moved with maggots and blow flies. Guys soaked handkerchiefs in water and tied them as masks over their noses, but as they were forced to bend close, scraping with short handle entrenching shovels, panting, stench precipitating on our tongues; in that disgusting way we tasted death.

Why was it, I pondered, the Banzai Third gets all the shitty assignments? It seemed we got hit with every crappy detail that came along. Still, somehow, we seemed also to have too much time to kill—easy to kill enemy, hard to kill time; too damn long to worry about if and when we'd ever make it back. I'd rather keep busy than die so many times of worry.

On the 5th of June, one hectic month after the last Chink assault, our company collected legionnaire rolls wrapped like inverted horseshoes over our packs and, following kitchen trains in their trucks, made a long bumpy drive into X Corps reserve to the valley at Hongchan just north of Hoengsong, of such bitter winter memory of so many of our old timers. Here regiment gathered its own and battalion its own and rifle companies sought small private valleys radiating from a wide former rice-growing drained flatland. Erecting a neat, straight-line pup tent village, we slipped into garrison, as armies do, and into the training routine which in the uncertainties of combat we forgot was so boring.

The company fell in and spread out by platoons and squads to lay lines as enlisted men in formation took so many paces along his line away from the man behind and, facing right or left, side stepped to their sides marking out streets into pup tent homes away from homes. Once in place, unrolling half a pup tent, the outside of the legionnaire roll, to set up a full tent, two men button together the tops of their overlapping halves, each half with reinforced button holes, and zinc alloy buttons labeled US. Each puts the spike, the top of his tent pole that folds in three sections, into the metal eye at one end of the tent half and runs a white cotton rope down to stake into the ground. The tent is stretched and steadied sideways with five wooden pegs on each side. A foot-deep trench is dug all around to run off rain water. Rice straw or heavy grasses are hunted down to soften the earth under bed rolls, fart sacks not named for nothing, especially when beans were on the menu, and when lucky, an air mattress that held air.

Businesses were quickly reestablished, supply, a pyramid tent, combination clothing store, gun shop, boots and Army surplus store; our large squad tent messhall a thriving restaurant, popularity depending on the ingenuity of the cooks and mess sergeant, or mess steward.

Some among us worried aimlessly or brooded unnecessarily, as did untested replacements living outdoors for the first time even this far from danger. For them a few nights were almost as sleepless as those of their platoon leader trying to readjust to the opposite, peace and quiet, a subtle uneasiness not having someone on guard.

J J Jenkins, runner, radioman and along with Doc my holemate in a tactical situation, was one of those worrywart guys who always had to check things. J J, by the way, stood for, of all things, Jack Jerry, what was probably the basic reason for his nervousness; afraid someone would find out. He blurted it once resentfully and was later wary of my power, even though I swore on my mother's memory not to tell.

Mostly it was body chemistry he worried about. He worried about his blood, cerebral and spinal fluids, glands and metabolism which he had read up on a couple times. Also, he warned, never neglect the color of your urine and excrement, "that's, your shit," he explained.

173

"Especially when your urine, number one or piss, seems unusually brown, or gold. All is not gold that glitters said the pirate as he peed in the sea," he joked.

"I always turn around and look over what I did," he once explained, "whether it's okay or not. If I'm ever cut, check to see if my blood's too dark or too thick, or maybe too thin or something, and once last year it was sort of bluish but I didn't get to a doctor and never found out why. Of course, you need a powerful microscope to see what kind of bugs you got.

"Sometimes I get tired too easy and wonder what's wrong with my metabolism. Usually if there's trouble, it's got to be me for us guys eat the same all the time. Everything you eat has to go somewhere, you know. Sometimes I have an awful craving for candy and I know that's wrong; you don't have to tell me, too much sweets makes your teeth rot and you get sugar diabetes from too much too often.

"I wonder a lot about what happens when you die. Does your soul actually go anywhere, like the Bible says, heaven or hell? And what is a soul, how does it live anyway? And Catholics, they also worry about that Purgatory place in between.

"I'm almost on the verge of discovering something real big, but then every time I start getting close, I get tired or something, my mind wanders, and somehow can't seem to follow my thinking through and my thinking just runs out of steam or goes off on a tangent. Lieutenant, suppose I could have a tumor or something in my head and that's why my thoughts seem to just melt away right when I'm on the verge of something big?"

"I know what you're talking about, it happens to me, but I honestly don't know, J J. I honestly don't."

We trained two nights a week until 2200 hours. I was beginning to answer a letter from Kitty and it took about three days, in between training, to finish it. Nights were the worst time for loneliness. I began to dream almost as bad as when very young when I'd walk and talk in my sleep. I'd give almost anything to avoid that type of sad, sometimes miserable and always frightening dreaming. My mother, not Kitty, appeared more and more frequently, always a losing battle to keep her alive like she appeared to me for so short a time; sickening thoughts that

174

sneaked up on me. And coughing. Oh, God, spare me those rags of blood she couldn't hide.

It seemed that only me and a couple lonesome privates were absent from the anxious mob at daily mail calls by the company water supply, a hanging Lister bag. Kitty and I were having a little misunderstanding over the claim she kept harping on that I didn't love her anymore; according to her, all I really wanted was to be off in the Infantry to be a hero.

Real estate was rough in Watertown with no building during World War II, shortage of materials and labor, and the apartment Kitty finally found, she complained, turned out to be a rat's nest. She wrote that I had no idea how hard it was to bring up Dickie in a lousy apartment where you froze in the winter and now in summer was sweltering with no central air-conditioning and her old secondhand Maytag danced all over the kitchen floor, had a leaky hose making a swamp of the linoleum floor, the boards of which were rotting.

I got an especially insulting letter describing her "garden apartment, they have the nerve to call it," she wrote. "It's a pigpen Someone is always taking the parking spot for my apartment and a couple crazy young men moved in next door that wrestle and pound on the wall and get Dickie crying. And sometimes I think they make indecent remarks as I pass by. If you were home, they wouldn't dare. The old Maytag wringer-washer is broken again and they have to send to Syracuse for parts and where will I get the money? And the truck's down again— won't even start."

"Should have bought a new washing machine. We had almost a thousand bucks left, where'd it all go?" I wrote back. "What did you spend it all on, plus what I borrowed on my pay?" What did it all go on, I'd like to know.?"

When first in army reserve I was claustrophobic and for four nights took my cot out of the officers' arctic tent to sleep under the open sky. Hurtz and I really missed Holly but we didn't have much to say to our new company commander, Captain Shallow. For a week I woke regularly as I did on line, hand on an imaginary carbine; sometimes at reveille it was as though I didn't lie down at all. Fighting alone hope-

175

lessly, rolled in a ball in my canvas cot in my corner of the arctic tent trying to hide from melancholy paranoia, doubting my ability to meet yet nameless fears. And Kitty, she had turned against me.

Reserve was one big make-believe. Just what were we doing now, fooling around? Training? There's no better training than combat where you learn hard in a hurry. Death is the real teacher; waiting to explain, explain good just once before failing you. Death doesn't have to yell like a drill sergeant. Training was a farce, 'position of a soldier at attention,' a one-hour bore; 'interior guard,' three hours in one week. 'Drill and ceremonies' and stupid preparation for parades. Up your ass Benning School for Boys, there's a war to fight!

"Don't they know we got twelve new guys to get ready?" Eppler complained. "What good's all this crap, this goddamn division training schedule? I had this shit in basic training."

One afternoon we had off, personal time, it was called, and Sergeant Eppler was a roaring bull all over the company area. "All right, who's the wise guy tired of livin'? C'mon, make it easy on yourself. Who stole my umbrella? Kee-rist! Nobody can have nothing of his own around here."

After the roar subsided, Pop Miller cornered Funaro and demanded the umbrella.

"Why to hell you do that? You know Sergeant Eppler's got no patience."

"I know, Pop. Muggsy dared me and things been pretty dull around here. I was going to slide it in his tent tonight and run."

Pop, being no child psychiatrist, couldn't decide whether Funaro was more malevolent, mischievous or malicious, but warned the pain-in-the-ass not to bug Karl anymore. "There's better ways of dying."

We got to debating about Funaro in a rather heated way and Pop blurted out, "Leave me alone, lieutenant. I ain't had kids of my own."

"Well," I told him, "I got a boy, not very old yet, so there's not much to understand. You just have to slap his fingers and say 'no.' One thing you and I know, Pop, your Funaro will never make a soldier."

"Yeah," Pop confessed, "that's what he keeps telling me."

Sometimes, unmindful of the policy not to fraternize with enlisted men, I'd sit with Sergeant Eppler on the fringe of bull sessions at which they amused themselves shooting the breeze, what shrinks call ventilation and charge outlandish fees; old timers wishing mightily for rotation to hurry up and save them; young ones bragging about broads they'd had or women they wished they'd had, very prestigious jobs they held or high-paying jobs they wanted to have, which were more believable among draftees, some few of whom were sons of wealthy men patriotic enough to avoid fixing the draft, and college graduates waiting for their real lives to start.

Despite the goodly percentage of conscripted men in the services, the percentage in dangerous infantry positions was proportionately very small, sixteen rear echelons to back every rifleman. Millionaire sons, to begin with, managed, with help of their fathers' attorneys to keep out of uniform or at least be assigned safe in the States. Sons of honest, hard-working fathers, the greatest percentage of our RA, Regular Army enlistees, 'RA all the way,' many of whose dads were proud to have fought in the infantry in World War I, disclosed the obvious wide gap between them and sons of the wealthy and influential. Being a real man among men is of high value and not once did I hear one of my dogfaces wish he was a millionaire's son to dodge the draft. Without saying so, very probably without even knowing so, they accepted manhood's hard-to-obtain value as life's biggest prize; where else could he brag, "I was right there packing a rifle," and be known automatically as a fullgrown man, a real patriot, a dangerous man to an enemy?

They were attracted to campfires at night like Indians, the center of night life, except that American Indians, like Asians, squatted, which whites can't do very long, and, like wild warriors of our past, they bragged about what they did or thought they did in the fury of combat, coups, they were called, sometimes inadvertently attributing to themselves the exploits of others, never dishonestly. "No you didn't, Hank. That was me." It continued to amaze me how many true versions there could be about what went on during the hysteria of battle. Even in as small a unit as a rifle platoon, no one could hope to encompass the entire panorama of its fire fights every minute of every guy.

"Why you was way over by that big rock all the time. How could they be peppering you so bad?"

"Insinuating I'm a liar? That was Johnson over there."

"Didn't say that. Maybe you was getting it bad, too. I don't know, I had them up the ass, myself."

"You should have some of the fire we got. How about it, Red? Know he was in it, right?"

"Sh-e-e-it! You guys back there was rear echelon, practically back at company. Ask Smitty where we was when them 82's started droppin'."

"Like so much fun! You won't believe me, ask Pop how about it?"

Pop, slowly sipping cold coffee from his canteen, was slow to give his version. "We-ell, now, I don't know . . ." so slow they went on bragging without an answer.

Guys talked about anything and a lot of nothing worth remembering or repeating during breaks in training classes or short rests during work details, or just lying in warm, wild Korean mountain valley grasses heated by the sun. The main themes were evaluating their future, rumors and wishes. Can I survive? Will I live to rotate? What rotation number do I have? What about peace talks? How far they gone? Will it save us? Why don't they get the lead out?

Draftees vs Regular Army—RA all the way! and 'them stupid bastards' the US serial numbers who had to be dragged in. Regardless, everyone felt he could be promoted given ordinary breaks and enough combat, if he survived, for ranks turned into second lieutenants after many battles, if they survived. Like Napoleon told his men: "There's a marshal's baton in every knapsack."

And then came weather and women, silly arguments about the latter in which some of the very young men without sisters showed surprising ignorance. One corporal, a self-proclaimed lover tried to wear his hair longer than regulation rear echelon brushcut and was always getting nailed for it when we were in reserve long enough to get a GI cut by one of our dozen or so Korean houseboys, each company with a barber kit.

"C'mon, no woman's like that. You saying she didn't have no thing!"

"Cross my heart; must've grown together."

178

"Come on!"

"Sure she didn't have even a little hole?"

"No, damn it, you couldn't get your finger in beyond your knuckle. Hell, I've been around; I've had a few all right."

He then appealed to Sergeant Roundtree who gave one of those deep, gurgling, infectious laughs no whitey whose laugh was from his mouth, could ever imitate.

"Ha ha ha ha, he he he, ho ho ho, dummy, you got hold one of them whatcha' call 'ems, of them transtights or something, guys made up like women."

"Oh yeah, smartass, then where'd the prick go? I tell you I got my finger in about two inches and the rest was solid."

"Maybe the way she was sitting."

"Or got it sewed or something."

"Hate to change the subject guys," Sergeant Eppler butted in, "I heard we're pulling all the way back to Pusan."

"That again!"

"Forty-eight ... forty-nine ... fifty, s-o-o-me shit!"

"Laugh, you bastards. We're getting amphibious training so we can land way up to the Yalu and blow bridges to shut off Chinks."

"What's wrong with the Air Force, out of bombs?"

"Air Force, shit, they overshoot everything."

Another chimed in, "Yah, I heard that one about special training, returning to Fort Lewis for some top secret training that'll can the war for sure."

"Atom bombs?"

"Maybe yes, maybe no. It's classified. I ain't saying."

"You got a clearance?"

"Maybe yes, maybe no. That's classified."

"Sh-e-e-e-it!"

"They changed their minds now about that amphibious deal and we ain't going to the States just yet."

"Sh-e-e-it! They're always screwin' us outa' somethin'."

"First we get to go south of Pusan and guard that Koje-do prison camp we been reading about. Stars and Stripes guesses each regiment will spend two weeks. Anyway, it's better than back on line;

179

look at all the lead you dodge."

"May be true what you say, but I'll bet fifty bucks it'll all be over in a week or two anyway. According to a guy I met who works in division headquarters and has a top secret clearance, they've decided to drop the old A bomb."

"That's what Pete says."

"Makes sense," his friend reflected. "Won't take many."

No sweat anyway, there were other ways the war could end. Pop Miller went around telling everyone the Ruskies were trying to get all Chinks killed so Mao wouldn't be too big for his boots. "What else makes them Chinks stick their necks out? Look how the little bastards'll run right at a machine gun. Don't think Mao's no fool, do you? He knows well as we do Stalin's planning to take over China and pull out and let the war fizzle. The Chinks are going to revolt anyway. A guy was telling me he was talking to an interpreter back at the prisoner cage that Chink POWs are sicker of this war than us. Wait and see."

Peace talks began at a nonoriental appearing place named Kaesong, above the 38th parallel, ancient capital of all Korea. The positioning of the place itself gave prestige points to the Asian mind. Despite bitter memories of the false negotiation promises with Soviet Communists in 1946, resulting in the necessity for the Berlin Airlift, our gullible State Department and United Nations started out in good faith not knowing, or more probably, we thought, not caring, that the enemy was using the occasion to secure objectives in lieu of using their weakened military.

Right or wrong, there was order again in one's mind and strict regulation of time as the majority tried smiling and relaxing, content to be ordered about from one menial housekeeping or training task to another. Putting in our time, we were. Suddenly one night, end of the third week in reserve, Private Ethan Youngs, one of the first squad's new men, became delirious. His tentmate, PFC Quick, guided him stumbling to the aid station where the duty CQ, charge of quarters, asked what Youngs was complaining of.

"I don't know. Just started talking funny, slurring his words, and finally got like this, almost out on his feet. When we hit the sack tonight he did say he had a bad headache and his chest hurt some. He

180

took three APCs but he wasn't complaining enough to worry me, nothing real bad until he started mumbling in his sleep. What is it, sarge, suppose it's catchin'?"

The medical sergeant didn't answer but told Quick to put a thermometer in Youngs' mouth, pinch his lips over it but don't touch the thermometer, while he took his blood pressure. Obviously, out of it, Youngs was not resisting. Once done, the medic turned quickly to his assistant and told him to run, not walk, and wake a litter jeep driver. "On the right going in the aid squad tent. Hurry, understand. Now!"

Youngs died at Regimental Collecting without awakening just minutes before the arrival of an evacuation helicopter. Choppers didn't usually fly at night in Korea. The surgeon said he wasn't sure what Youngs died from but a medic, a Spec-5, told our Doc that it looked suspiciously like a new sickness called Manchurian fever, the sudden way it came on, brushed over in medical training.

Tears gather in my eyes today, fifty years later, thinking of the great sacrifice Ethan made, not that I remember the kid personally, for I have no memory of anything physical about him.

"That thin guy Doc Lynch always talked to on breaks," Speedy Gonzales would tell others. "They'd get out of the way and talk serious for hours, great friends in short order like guys often do in the field. . . . Youngs spent a lot of time talking to the guys in the aid station, remember? Maybe he caught something up there."

"Poor Youngs," he worried. "One year to go in college, then med school. All he was planning to do for everyone, having to die for nothing way over in this damn hole."

"He what?" I asked.

"Didn't you know, sir? He was halfway to being a doctor and got reading about what was going on over here and talked himself into enlisting. His dad, he told us, used to be a medical missionary somewhere in South America when he was a kid. He learned Spanish from his friends, could talk it better than me."

Speedy was silent for a minute, a kind, sorrowful stare on his face rare for an infantry sergeant before suddenly exploding with a hateful glare. "God damn fucking world! Don't make guys like Ethan! Take them goddamn draft dodgers in Canada. My uncle died a volun-

181

teer with them Princess Pats, fighting for draft-dodging bastards. He'd turn over in his grave to know Canadians are harboring our cowards."

The 2d Princess Patricia's Canadian Light Infantry was fighting a little west of us in the Canadian Brigade of the Commonwealth Division.

I was told Youngs joined 23 May, the day I got it, which explained why I didn't know him so well He was with us the three weeks I was back but I couldn't recall his training with us. He was not a medic; medics don't train with us except in certain reserve classes. They have their own special classes training at division medical company, but they really belong to us infantrymen; they're with us during combat to save lives.

"No, sir, Youngs wasn't a medic," Doc agreed. "He joined us the day you got hit and heaven knows, rather, hell knows, how busy you've been ever since you returned."

"Shitty-ass war!" Pop agreed. "Nothing here worth fighting for in the first place."

"Look," Funaro said, pointing expansively to the barren, eroded Korean mountainsides. "One dogface is worth more than this whole goddamn country put together."

Turned out it was Manchurian or hemorrhagic fever, the first any of our enlisted medics had heard of the dread disease. PFC Quick was quarantined, whisked to the 11th Evacuation field hospital behind division, checked over ten days. An epidemic was rumored and their tent was buttoned up without moving anything and fumigated.

"Makes your eyes bulge and turn red," one man said.

"Eyes turn red?" a medic corrected. "Hell, I heard blood leaks out all over, anywhere. Got all the doctors licked; it's a virus, you know, no medicine for it. All we can do is what they call support him, see he gets lots of rest and liquids and hope his insides can hack it out alone.

"I heard from a guy at division, it's powerful stuff to fool with. That's probably why they got so many new replacements in graves registration."

"Not exactly unknown," the medical sergeant told us, "and there's more than one group of viruses cause hemorrhagic fever; it's an arena virus so far confined to Manchuria, eastern China, and the Soviet

Union and the north central mountains in Korea. They think its carried by vectors, something that conveys, like humans, insects or rodents, but primarily chiggers living on mice. Aren, by the way, as in arenavirus, is for RNA granules which they find in this particular virus."

"Oh."

Colonel F L Wergeland, surgeon of the Eighth Army Forward, recalled that the disease, precisely *virion*, the infectious form of a virus, wasn't isolated until war's end. It was often confused with atypical scarlet fever, war nephritia, songo fever, kokku disease and korin disease, none of which can be found in the average dictionary. In its first year, 1951, eighteen of every thousand soldiers were stricken, ten percent of whom died quickly. Lucky for us the disease was most prevalent in the Chorwon Valley miles to our left.

"More graves registration guys than ever before, know why?" someone asked. "The general was going cross country in his chopper and spotted two GIs, one thrown on top the other, somewhere in the wilds where one of our outfits was fighting a month ago and he landed and found them rotted."

A new job called vector control, with special training classes, suddenly became more important than preparing to kill Chinks and gooks. And there were Japanese B influenza (Italian, under the influence of a bad star) and soft chancres that Korean men are immune to which rot off your prick, and water flukes from snails whose eggs or whatever get through the skin between your fingers and down to your liver, which blows up and hardens, with no cure, all they could do was ship you home. And there were rumored to be a couple other beauties, such as a sleeping sickness like no other in the world, different from African sleeping sickness.

Normally, unless there's a large attack, on a daily basis nonbattle casualties in a division are double, even triple battle casualties. The actual killed in action, KIA, in the Second Division in Korea 1950-53 was 27,700. With 77,596 WIA and 2542 nonbattle deaths.

Someone has figured out that early September, 1951, an anonymous soldier killed in Korea was the millionth American man to die in combat since eight minuteman got it on Lexington Common, Massachusetts on the morning of 19 April 1775.

183

A division's like a city, with all its jobs and hazards. There were many sicknesses, even among such healthy guys, and jeep accidents, drownings, stepping on by-passed mines, accidental shootings, and even a few suicides. A careless jerk in King Company killed his best friend while cleaning a forty-five.

I was summoned to Graves Registration's morgue back at regiment the day after Youngs died.

"Have a seat, sir," a private told me. "Sergeant's on his way."

"What's he want?"

"Some mix-up on one of your men, sir."

"Must be Youngs. Someone find out what happened?"

"We're not supposed to tell anyone, but there's more of that Manchurian Fever, Hemorrhagic Fever they call it, and some bad Jap flu."

"Want to see something good?" the private went on self-importantly. "See what we do back here?"

I didn't say anything so he went all the way.

"Some guys think all we do is sit on our ass and ship bodies to the mortuary. That ain't no picnic. Anyone told me I'd be an assistant to an undertaker, I'd say was nuts. But that's what I do."

He handed me a form, a copy of an Army coroner's Preparation Room Report. "Go on, sir, read it, and this is only half what we do back here."

"This for Youngs?" I asked, glancing at the title.

"Not this one; it'll give you an idea. This is a lieutenant crashed in an L-19. We just got this copy back from the mortuary in Japan."

The private then retrieved the report immediately when he heard the sergeant bid someone hello outside the tent. I was thankful I didn't have to read it.

"Lieutenant Gould? Sir," the sergeant said. "Sorry to bother you but some tags were switched and we needed his officer to identify these things we think belong to Private Youngs. Would you know of anything that might be missing?"

"Sorry to say, I didn't know him that well. I'll sign it blank and send his buddy, PFC Quick up to check it out. Right now he's quarantined. What happened to Youngs?"

184

"Well, Special Regulation 600-400-5 states: 'When remains are recovered and individually identified, they will be buried in an overseas cemetery.'"

"In them black bags?"

"No, they're just to handle the remains until they can be placed in Army transfer cannisters or caskets. The SR states that in case of death, a letter of sympathy written by the unit commander or chaplain will be addressed to the emergency address. It will contain condolence, cause and place of death, any religious services administered to the individual before death, an appropriate expression of appreciation of the services rendered to the nation by the deceased, and other information of a personal or sentimental nature which may be comforting. No one but his company commander or the chaplain is authorized to write. No reference will be made to the recovery or identification of remains, date or place of burial."

This visit made me more morbid than I wanted to be. Back home you don't give these guys a thought but in Korea every regiment has to have a Graves Registration officer with assistants.

You could run a small town with the talent and trades in every division.

Fred Hurtz of our regiment was an exception, what could Freddy do aside from fight? Philosophize? At least I might do some landscaping or pour a casting. He majored in psychology and minored in Asian philosophy, which I'd kid him about.

"What you going to do with it, Freddy? Open a Chinese laundry?"

I got to know Lieutenant Frederick Hurtz in those June reserve evenings when there wasn't a good movie on or night training, although Fred did a lot more letter writing than me. I'll never forget when he told me he majored in abnormal psychology.

"I thought all psychology was abnormal," I said, tongue in cheek. "I suppose you minored in strange birds."

"Why sure, Dud, didn't I recognize you?"

"Plan on owning a Chinese restaurant with educated fortune cookies?"

"That's not funny, any more than ending up here in the center

185

of the Orient just because I minored in it. I do have a little more insight than the average; know how these people lived before Communism. The 38th has always been a line of demarcation. Mongols stopped along this imaginary line in the 12th Century and natives we find in these mountains live pretty much as they did in those days. They have the world's oldest religion, Animism."

"What's that?"

"They believe that everything has a soul, even rocks if they display a characteristic different from other rocks. One's spirit can exist without his body."

We talked more about death and the hereafter than most guys, even in the middle of Frozen Chosen, so-called Land of the Morning Calm where a hell of a lot of it was around—death, I mean. You don't have to pretend, it's all around. We agreed there's a big difference between a dead civilian and a dead soldier. When I look down at them, it isn't all in their face. I can look at one boot and know how awful dead.

A dead civilian looks like he's resting just home from work resting; like my mother freshly rouged, proper care, a decent sendoff. The only dead Hurtz and I saw were those who met it like hunted animals. Over here you don't have to be lonely and sick to go and you don't lie down for death, it grabs *you* on the move. Civilians look so peaceful in their caskets; we never see soldiers in caskets decorated and perfumed; soldiers look so terribly wasted and outraged and hurt and somehow noble in spite of the grim, hateful atmosphere.

Christ was my age when he got his. Dead GIs remind me of statues of Christ, a cross right there telling you his occupational hazard, whereas our guys carry rifles to drop beside them. Spikes through his feet and hands to hang from, to die slowly from loss of blood and traumatic shock, or whambo, a hunk of shrapnel through the hearts of GIs dead in bloody mud.

They both died hard for what a lot of people say are good causes. As with Jesus, many were hurt bad before they died but some never knew what hit them or that they were hit. Some were familiar old dogfaces, hurting you bad to look down at them. Many pained for only the split second they're hit; lying there on that whole belt of pain along the 38th Parallel across Korea.

5
Relieve Marines

At 2200 hours on the 8th of July, 1951, Korean time, company commanders were paged by loudspeaker at the hillside battalion movie. Men peered knowingly at one another. The movie was about a mixed-up drunken playboy in New York City who wore a tux all the time and threatened to jump from a building. The fire department strung nets while a daring priest crawled along the ledge pleading with him to consider how his dear father would feel.

"It's no use; nobody loves me."

"Get your ass back in the room, Father," someone commanded from back on the hill.

"Let the sonofabitch jump!" another sneered.

"Think he's got troubles?"

"Push him!"

Then a chorus of voices began the chant: "Draft him! Draft him! Draft him! . . . Forty-eight . . . Forty-nine . . . Fifty.

The film stopped abruptly and flood lights went on.

"Up and at 'em! Roll up! Roll up, you he-e-e-roes!"

"This is it!" guys shouted at one another. "Strike those pup tents, this is it! Let's go! Let's go everyone, let's go!"

Me? I could never discover why the big hurry, concluding it must be mainly because of being excited by the very idea of what we were slated to do. From our Blue Book—

The Second Division had made good use of the well-earned period in reserve when, on 8 July, it received notice to prepare for relief of the First Marine Division between 15 and 17 July.

187

All units had been reorganized and resupplied. Rotation had gotten into high gear and, as a result, training was speeded up to prepare incoming replacements for the days which lay ahead. Special service shows had been sandwiched in between training problems and the other activities of the period. Many of the officers and men had the opportunity to see Jack Benny for the first time in person when he brought his troupe to the Division Command Post for a show. [Men and officers of division rear ten miles south of any combat unit bivouac.]

But with the alert order in the proper hands, all efforts were turned to put the finishing touches on the training program. Reconnaissance parties went out to view the Kansas Line where the active defense would be undertaken. Division engineers, who had been devoting their efforts to improving the roads to the reserve sector, shifted northward on 13 July and began extensive surveys and work on the roads in the new sector.

Onset of the peace talks had, of course, raised the possibility that an armistice might be reached at any hour. No one in Eighth Army wanted to take chances and be the last man killed. Rotation changed the face of the infantry, old hands replaced by thousands of newcomers green to combat. Signs went up along the main roads: "DRIVE CAREFULLY. THE MAN YOU HIT MIGHT BE YOUR RE-PLACEMENT."

Some tankers nearby, bivouacking like a carnival come to town, not alerted like us, pissed off to have the movie unplugged no matter how bad, baited our guys: "You're going to Koje-do! Chinks and gooks down there are rioting again. You guys get to change their diapers."

"Shit!" someone yelled back. "Forty-eight! . . . Forty-nine . . . Some shit!"

"C'mon, we got hiker boots for you tankers. Earn your living! Can't hide in them cans *all* the time!"

Hum of short conversations; guys running around giving and taking orders, trying to give away things they couldn't carry into battle, unloading on fortunate ones who remained in the kitchen trains. Certain

188

highly nonmilitary objects were pulled out, checked and kissed; silver crosses suspended on more delicate chains than dog tags; a rabbit foot tucked safely in an inner pocket; a creased photograph; very particular letters from mothers ordering 'boys' to take good care; and a souvenir copper good luck coin originally obtained way over value after a few beers at a county fair.

Down came neat rows of pup tents and fires blazed with absolutely nonessential letters from home and knickknacks the guys picked up here and there since early June. One GI tried to stuff down an entire can of peanuts in a few minutes. "Futsin damn louthy lut!" he sputtered. After push came to shove, all that was shoved in our packs was topped by a three-meal, thin cardboard box of C rations which had to be disassembled, a can in one pocket, a can there, cigarettes and the remainder under your T shirt, ass wipe in your helmet liner.

While I was checking my platoon in the dark, heavy-duty six-bys arrived from division trucking company, fussing and arguing, machines revving up and down and leveling off, shifting into a long line across the battalion bivouac like a string of high-strung heavy-muscled dragoon horses stomping and snorting, roped on a picket line ready for battle.

"Okay, you guys," officers and noncoms ordered, "Off with them patches and mount up."

The proud Indianhead shoulder insignia were ripped off and slipped into pockets until the next reserve—if you were that lucky. Doc Carlson and other medics made beelines to the aid station to sign for morphine ampules, kept under lock and key by the medical service corps officer.

Young, prayerful replacements who came on line that reserve time with blue battalion would be dirty, tired old veterans, shaving what whiskers they had when they returned—or they were bagged—and mister, how they'd all like to make their own choice.

It rained lightly, the annual monsoon.

"'Bout time," Funaro said, pretending to be happy. "For a whole fuckin' minute there I thought we'd make one fuckin' move without getting' fuckin' soaked."

We stood away from the trucks to piss and while I checked

with squad leaders each man's harness, pack and equipment, a replacement motor officer, Lieutenant Von Holtz Werner, strode along the line shouting authoritatively, "Mount your vehicles. Make it snappy now, mount up."

When he reached our Banzai Third with his authoritative 'mount up,' I told him, "Stick to the motor pool. I'll take care of *my* men."

The guys snickered as the motor officer tried briefly to stare me down. "Lieutenant Gould," he said petulantly, "Colonel Duncan was the one who wanted it, not me."

At the next platoon, "Okay, fellows," he said, "the colonel wants us to move out in five minutes."

"You heard him," I ordered, "load up. On the double."

The guys jammed in, twenty-four to a truck, with all their personal fighting paraphernalia and cartridge belts unhooked to be able to sit comfortably. I crawled into one cab beside the driver. Before I could sit, I had to unbuckle my cartridge belt. Hooked to it were two canteens of water, a first aid bandage in a small web case, a carbine bayonet so short we called them knives, in scabbard, two pouches of thirty-round magazines for my carbine, two thirty round curved banana magazines joined upside down by adhesive tape in my carbine and a 38 caliber revolver I was given by a rotating sergeant in an issue 45 caliber revolver holster stuffed with rags to keep it from falling out.

On my left wrist was my issue luminous dial watch and a luminous dial lensatic compass, which, not having much occasion to use, I normally kept in my pack. On my body, strapped over my shoulder, across my lap or in my hands, always inches from me every minute once we left the kitchen trains, was my sweetheart, my faithful M2 carbine which Doc Lynch returned to me. Hanging from a strap around my neck was a pair of 10X binoculars.

The heavy six-by troop trucks rolled away slowly, while the four jeeps per company with trailers loaded with boxes of chop-chop, jerry cans of water, ammunition and what not, pranced by impatiently on the left shoulder of the road, led by Captain Shallow's number one jeep—flaunting high on an eight-foot varnished oak staff the blue pennant forked guidon with the large white L for Love Company. Captain

Shallow, on the front seat, arms folded across his chest, stared grimly ahead, reminded me for a moment of pictures I'd seen of Hitler's storm troopers parading in the early years. Following were weapon carriers with ammo and the real bulky crew-served stuff.

I was actually looking forward to going back to combat. Maybe excited like a high-stakes gambler would fit better. I was becoming hooked on combat; the excitement of anticipation as to which cards you will be dealt next, you never knew what would happen. We had a whole new batch of guys to add to those who joined us at Honchon, replacing those wiped out KIA, WIA or my nine MIAs.

Slow rain kept the air cool even in mid-July in the valleys and the guys in open trucks, helmets and cartridge belts between their feet, undid their blankets from their packs, unfolded them and covered their heads and shoulders before replacing ponchos over them, leaning heavily on the man next in line, heads bobbing with the bumps of the hilly, winding valley road.

Moving north into and along the combat line in darkness we passed other battalions on the move. It didn't matter, Dutchmen, Frenchmen, Canadian, Turk, ROK or American, we were samo-samo in this bloody business and we waved generously at one another, emphasizing we were on the same team.

Leaving the MSR, trucks crept along a narrow mountain road up to the wilderness country of Pia-ri and Satae-ri, using cat-eye, down-shining slit, blackout headlight covers in pitch darkness, lighting no more than a few feet of the road. Rain came and went and returned and for a time eerie fog formed and rolled in mysterious dense clouds silently through blackness of night glimmering reflected starlight on top across drained highland rice paddies as the enemy's harassing and interdictory artillery fire, H and I, came searching for us awakening those sleeping. One shrill menacing whimper way over to the left, s-s-s-s-wampt! A quick blink of bright yellowish-orange flash against the side of a gully. A quarter of a mile closer, e-e-e-umpt! CRASH! Then, back only a hundred yards on the road we had traveled, S-s-s-s-swampt! on a visible bit of road selected and zeroed in in daylight by gook forward observers for just such an occasion. After five, long worrisome minutes, another, and this time well ahead of us. They were reaching, searching, questing relentlessly, feeling, wanting us badly. We were being bracketed.

Where would the next one land?

The guys who up to now were dozing mumbled low, peering around nervously. I leaned under the dashboard to light a cigarette and smoked it hiding the glow carefully in the cup of my hand. It was stimulating to be in action again, to be important and useful once more; if it did make you shiver a little.

"Yes, sir, 1179, here we come!"

We knew that no matter where we went tonight, H1179 was in our offing, a little nearer, more real to our fate than the final enemy OP (observation post) 1243 which we couldn't consider seriously yet.

We unloaded before the hill mass of the Taeusan mountains lining the Pia-ri valley on one side and the Punchbowl and while the trucks gunned out fast as cat-eyes would permit, back to the safety and hot meals of trucking company. Everyone found his place in the dark and organized with whispered confusion into a long single file for cho-geeing, or if you prefer, motoring or stomping. Those of us in charge spread the word for each guy to take a five-yard interval between himself and the man ahead. But it was cool and wet, dark, lonely and mysterious in our fearful wilderness and the guys naturally bunched up and stuck close to buddies despite threats — humble, very suspicious and apprehensive of what was concealed up ahead in the dripping darkness. "Dammit, one round will get you all!"

In leaving sea level passing by one of Love company's jeep trailers, each picked up another cardboard three-meal box of C6s with a grumble as we tried to find places for it. *"Find* room," Field First Sergeant Martin hissed loudly. "Can't tell when you'll get more."

A commo guy handed out four-foot pieces of wire for us to tie the box onto our packs.

"Kee-rist," Ski complained, "some sneak's grabbed our fruit again." He held up everyone pawing through the boxes in an effort to find one.

Captain Shallow hissed loudly, "Let's not hold up the line. What you want, sirloin steak?" He chuckled at what he took for humor and was then suddenly peevish. "Dammit, soldier, I said *move!* Don't

192

be so damn fussy. Grab any box and move along."

Ski lifted his leg and farted.

"Period," someone added.

I never heard of anyone on C rations make so many farts.

"There's another kiss for you!" Ski added.

The rain poured on us as we slipped, slid and crawled, cursing and panting, up the steep zig-zag path that led to our ridge 900 meters (2827 feet) above the valley road. Gloomy, yes, but there was humor to be sure, laughing at some poor guy losing his footing and sliding in wet mountain clay, six to ten feet back down, guys stepping gingerly out of his way. Geezus, that was funny, or did we find humor in his bad luck because laughs were so far behind?

Many veterans dug out olive drab army face towels from their packs and wore them tightly around their necks to sponge water dripping from their helmets.

Seven hours after we began to climb half the guys were still trying to make the greasy slides. Sounds in the rain were sharp curses and equipment being dropped or thrown away by fatigued men.

Great lumps of sticky yet slippery clay clung to my boots. I needed superhuman strength to lift them and plant them forward time after time after time again. The rain that dripped on me until broad daylight, just enough to make sticky mud slippery, turned the mountain trail into an escalator of churned-up mud moving the wrong way.

Guys on more level places rested for what turned out to be shorter and shorter efforts. One bunch, huddled figures from K company covered with shiny wet black ponchos, blocked the path where it leveled off a few feet, dozing there in the mud like shrouded dead men under rain-slick, rubberized, dark olive-drab sheets. I was cold and miserable and mad; when I was mad, I plugged along steadily putting my head down near my knees as they upped and downed under the steady load of me, resigned to slavery as any bridled ass.

The lead element reached the top ridgeline about 0830 and found Marines sullen and unfriendly. It was customary when transferring positions for the officer in charge of the relieved unit to run the line with the reliever. I sought out the Marine platoon leader, a bright, young twenty-three-year old Naval Academy graduate. I was a recalled

Reservist in his early thirties, quasi-civilian compared to this guy with four years of expensive military schooling."

"Hear there's gooks, been tough?"

No answer. No frivolity, friendliness or even common courtesy as bright eyes snapped, "Where in hell you been?" The Annapolis graduate, almost with tears in his eyes, accused, "You were supposed to be here last night."

"Made it soon as possible."

"Why doesn't nobody relieve on time?" the young man whimpered. "My men got all they can take."

"We was takin' in a movie!" Funaro offered out of order.

Death tainted the air while maggoty eyes of two bloated enemy blinked unceasingly near where we stood.

"I should think so," I chided. "Why haven't you hauled this mess away?"

"Never cleaned up their mess," Sergeant Eppler repeated bitterly. "Get some heavy sticks," he ordered. "Roll them gas bags out of here."

I found out that one of our replacements was night blind, a nice little draftee from Long Island. He had to be helped find things even though when rain clouds spread open for stars one could read a newspaper. After two nights of complaining by Sergeant Olsen, the draftee's squad leader, his hole mate came scurrying into my CP bitching at two in the morning.

"Lieutenant, lieutenant, get rid of that guy. Can't see dick in front of him and I ain't had a bit of sleep last two nights, not when he's supposed to be on guard."

I carried the poor guy to battalion the next day in a borrowed jeep. He humbly apologized to me over and over for his shortcoming, telling me several times how he appreciated my saving his life and he was sorry it was such a hell of a long heavy climb returning. Duncan, without advising Shallow, whom I gathered he didn't trust, sympathized with me.

"Life's too short to worry," he told me.

"Yeah," I told him. "That's what's worrying us."

I learned later that the night blind kid was dropped from our morning report and ended up a member of X Corps Honor Guard, his spot in our defense not filled for a week.

Colonel Duncan surveyed the line and ordered us to destroy the Marine bunkers and build a new defense down from the skyline ten feet on the enemy side instead of smack on top where they were silhouetted targets for artillery. Later that day, after the first chogee train brought us heavy leather gloves and big cutting pliers, we strung barbed wire down the hill in tangled or concertina rolls, using some of the little laid by the Marines.

That first day I examined old artillery shell holes closely. By the hardness or looseness of the soil, the size and shape of the craters, the direction the spray took leaving the impact spot, the smell of the dirt, and the age or freshness of powder burns, I gauged the extent, direction, approximate time, and effectiveness of enemy artillery even though it happened earlier to Marines.

We watched in awe our first night as darkness was challenged by an eerie light of the mist-screened Chinese moon, mountain glows like weak, shapeless florescent lights, signaling the peak of another moon month of turmoil, lighting the country around except where occasional dim outs occurred from puffs of low clouds drifting northward. Machine gun tracers, straight line, red-orange jewels traveled directed paths across our world and further than that came the distant underworld rumble of artillery contesting peels of thunder.

We slaved on our bunkers the next few days, Doc Carlson and I helped by J J, who lamented as usual: "Over thee mountains! W-a-ah-ay o-ver the seea a-see mah bonnie come back to me-e-e-."

As darkness covered us the first night, I appointed myself first guard. With the three of us, we had two hours longer sleep in between than did the normal two-man holes. It continued to rain lightly when J J relieved me at 2100. An electrical storm moved through the steady monsoon above us delivering separate cloudbursts that filled an inch of our CP hole with ice water. Seated on our hard-rim helmets above the mud, none of us got sleep until it let up, fizzling out about 0200 as puddles sank away.

We dug communications trenches between bunkers so resupply could reach each safely during a prolonged attack, and our medic could slip from hole to hole without being clipped. Bugout ditches, they're called

We had just settled into the earth as darkness overcame twilight over the mountain world on the second night when a series of sharp single whistles came over the inner-platoon sound-powered telephone circuit—someone raising first squad. Sergeant Eppler held the receiver to his ear, eavesdropping. We did that, whispered and kibitzed on the phone to help pass hours of darkness.

"Wh-e-e-et w-e-e-e-t, wh-e-e-t!" came the whistle. "Eppler here, who you calling?"

"Wh-e-e-e-t! Wh-e-e-e-t. Third squad, did I give three whistles? Get off the line, Karl. I'm calling first squad."

Gossiping with other platoons and with company made our perimeter tighter and stronger. It was good to know that in the dark other guys were awake and nervous and, hopefully, as watchful as you. Hero of riflemen, General George Patton, once warned his Third Army men to be on guard always, "or some kraut's going to sneak up and hit you over the head with a sockful of shit."

The first night passed without incident except complaints about the night blind guy, and for the next few days we made parapets, walls of sand bags heavy with wet spoil from our diggings. The platoon sergeant and I made the guys string barbed wire until they complained it was coming out their ears. One chronic goof-off bitched that Tree, Pop Miller's assistant, by-passed the squad leader and was chicken for riding him so hard. Only in such ways could one take a cheap shot at Tree for being black. Not that it bothered Tree any. Those were the few eight-balls in the platoon who ate our rations, gave us a hard time, and then bawled bloody murder for somebody, white, purple or black, to save their lives.

"Just nice you don't like me," Tree told him. "Don't want nobody liking me; liking leads to love; love leads to fuckin' and ain't no one fuckin' *me*."

We were paranoid, clinical cases, suffering persecution in varying degrees; doomed men who only occasionally found temporary release from some great anxiety or another. None of us liked it. It was a very unlikable place. We were sent there against our will to die and would not do it cheerfully. No soldier since the Christian Crusades ever *gave* his life for any damn political 'cause.' For a buddy, certainly, whenever necessary, for a stinking politician preacher or weird poet who lies about our so-called willingness to die, never. Aside from a fierce combat loyalty to one another as with any group of condemned ones, most work was accomplished under threat. We moved north against the enemy under constant threat of death at the hands of that enemy and to turn our backs without competent orders, military imprisonment and disgrace. The few who did give up resigned themselves immediately to Leavenworth, even though some, like Captains Shallow and Toth, lucked out. This motivation, dire civilian law threat, noncombatants fail to consider when they attribute a certain amount of bravery to us.

Not to run the Marines down, they're good, average, untidy infantry, but under Mighty Mouse Airborne Duncan we toiled without breaks to clear fields of fire, cutting down every concealment for forty yards downhill, chopping and hacking with bayonets and entrenching tools so a gook would stand out. Less appreciative of camouflage than the enemy, we put off replacing tell-tale wilted leaves covering the spoil around our holes, thus pointed to our positions rather than conceal them.

We hung empty C ration cans Marines littered the hill with on barbed wire with small stones to rattle, and heaved empty cans way downhill so enemy, moving at night, might accidentally kick them. We made brush piles over three 155mm cardboard shell canisters filled with napalm—planting a white phosphorous hand grenade in each after replacing its friction fuse with an electric percussion cap and manhandled fifty-five gallon steel drums in front of two very likely avenues of approach by attackers, up prominent fingers, one downhill from our machine gun. They contained napalm triggered by a remote controlled electric detonator or a white phosphorus hand grenade with an electric detonator set off by a crank of the magneto of an E-8 phone, in place of the ordinary pull fuse. They were otherwise known as *fougasse*, a French military term, originally a mine (explosives) so placed as to hurl stones in a desired direction. We hadn't enjoyed such security since I

197

joined for we hadn't been on a regular defense, always on the move, attacking, flanking, patrolling or on outpost.

Each squad dug a small slit trench latrine on the friendly side of the ridgeline opposite its bunkers leveled off so it could be straddled. An entrenching tool was stuck in the loose spoil and one shoveled in dirt after going. "And you . . . yes, you, Funaro," Pop Miller warned, "No more pissing outside your hole."

One night gooks took over our band on a spare 300 I'd scrounged. I'd just called Item company commander to let him know I read his trouble with fading batteries; he should call me on a 536 and I'd relay his messages on a 300 until he got new ones.

"Buzzard Five leader . . . Buzzard Five leader, this is Seven, save your batteries. We'll relay."

As soon as I released the butterfly switch on my 300, a North Korean monitor took over the classified channel picked for us that day, one of fifty channels on the SCR 300 each normally good for an unobstructed range of three miles.

"Buzzard Buzzard Buzzard," he mimicked in his high, oriental voice. "Want me reway?" Then a long series of meaningless "Audi-audi-audi-audi-audi," followed by an even higher pitch, certainly higher than the ordinary GI would reach. A senseless "Ondong-ondong-ondong-ondong-ondong," whatever that meant, if anything. It kind of frightened you, as if, by taking over our communications, they knew all our intentions.

Two could play this jamming game and after waiting intently for a break, as a gook voice momentarily stopped while handing a receiver to another, or to listen if we would try to talk, I pushed the switch fast and yelled: "Ee-dee-waa fuckface, I'll jam that radio up your keister meester; Audi-audi-audi, ondong-ondong-ondong and audi-audi yourself." After that it wasn't so scary worrying that they were there all the time listening.

Mighty Mouse Duncan, regiment's sarcastic sobriquet for his exceptional aggressiveness and small size, put out an order for every bunker to dig a firing well, unencumbered by a roof, from which we could toss grenades and do individual firing; every other bunker to have on hand half a wooden box of forty-eight fragmentation grenades.

Replacements long before they were committed became well acquainted with their weapons and in the combat zone all the way back to regimental forward went nowhere without them. Like Pilgrim forefathers facing the threat of hostile Indians. "This baby here," they affectionately referred to M1s and carbines. Some were seen kissing them in the small of the stock, hugging them, purring lovingly, "Old sweetheart, don't let me down." The closer to combat, the more they realized rifles were all that separated them from graves registration.

My carbine and civilian Smith and Wesson .38 caliber revolver were my constant companions. I oiled my weapons and rubbed them and polished and sharpened my bayonet knife, patted my carbine, always in my hands or on my right hip or slung over my right shoulder. With nothing else to do, I'd remove rounds from the magazines, wipe them and put them back. The creases of my hands were dark with particles of dirt dissolved in gun oil like carbon during my foundry days and my guys and I smelled of gun oil blended with stale wood smoke and sweat.

Korean laborers were assigned to help construct an elaborate sand-bagged company command post half way down the long winding trail to the jeep dismount point. On Shallow's first inspection trip of our positions, he complained, "Lieutenant, the colonel's order was very clear. There'll be roofs of three feet to withstand a direct hit by 120mm mortars."

"Yeah," I answered, "and we're supposed to have carriers get the stuff up here; you've got them tied up."

We cut what necessary-size logs we could with our little hatchets, and small axes, the few trees in Korea that recovered from Jap excesses during their thirty-five-year exploitation but no one in our battalion had formal instruction in bunker building. While we were exposed on the bare May Massacre outpost patrol base in open holes, the other outfits on the main line had been instructed by Second Division engineers and greatly aided by Korean carriers to build mortar proof bunkers.

Engineers sent up by General Ruffner after a fatal bunker cave-in to inspect ours in our new location were appalled by the mistakes we made in supporting and laying bunkers. They told us how hydrostatic pressure works in those mountains and we were also able to thank the engineers for their primer cords, putty-like shape charges of C4, ignition caps, pickets and fugasse to prepare us for the first time since I'd been in Korea for attacks on the several plausible approaches in front of our zone of responsibility. We were so confident we wished gooks would step into our fields of fire. We'd blow the hill down on them.

Beginning with our third night on line, we would hardly know a quiet one for weeks. Gooks were aggressive, so much more harassing than Chinks. Battalion established an all-out alert at 0400 every morning just prior to false dawn, favorite hour of attack by both Chinks and gooks. False dawn is generally known only by sailors on watch at sea, outdoor night watchmen, others who work late at night in the open and soldiers in trouble and they thrill silently to that strange, weak zodiacal glow, that faint nebulous effusion in the sky seen as a promise in the east before true dawn. Both men in every hole had to stand guard together and catch what sleep they could during the day. No hardships for Sergeant Eppler or I for even before the general alert order, either of us was up taking turns roving the 400-yard front.

Come what may, guys did sleep on guard. Eppler and I tried to keep our platoon reasonably honest and woe unto the jerks like Privates Funaro and Sizemore, his buddy, if we caught the two sleeping. Once I beaned Funaro on the noggin with a golfball-size rock. I hadn't intended to hit him quite so hard or hit him for that matter. I guess I'd been waiting too long to catch someone at it, but it didn't do Funaro a bit of good to complain to our battalion surgeon. He refused to believe PFC Funaro that his platoon leader beaned him on purpose, "Not Lieutenant Gould; he'd never do that," and warned Funaro about horsing around so roughly with his buddies. One thing about a known goof-off, his word is worse than anyone's.

Hardest job for Sergeant Eppler and me and the squad leaders, was the first week on line keeping guys from tossing grenades promiscuously. After the first probe the third night, jittery guys tossed grenades off and on for several hours, as guys up and down the line thought they heard something. We analyzed the night sounds. Stuff thrown by nervous GIs was hesitant and widely spaced.

200

Even old timers were skittish for a few nights back on line and gave jumpy nerves benefit of the doubt. In their case, it was rotationitis. Invariably, when I demanded to know what was going on, they'd say, "Lieutenant, we heard something down there," or "something moved." I don't care how sharp you think you are, you stare at any bush in the weak light of a starlit night at a distance and you're facing enemy that moves. Many times a bunch of them move. Not stand up and move fast, but sort of slide stealthily along like a gook sneaking or something.

One night Freddy Hurtz caught a small grenade fragment in the shoulder, thrown by his own men—just barely broke the skin. A field grade officer or general would've gotten a Purple Heart. Believe it or not, like a baseball in the bleachers I once caught a hot piece of artillery shrapnel in my right hand holding it up to wave back a guy prone to spend too much time out of his hole after dark gossiping. It didn't burn me, having cooled off cutting small tree limbs. That happened often, shrapnel and bullets zinging overhead snipping off leaves and small branches.

Because of the threat of infiltrators probing behind our line at night, the wounded not considered dangerously so were set down by the company CP to sleep if they could until there would be light to evacuate them with Korean carriers.

Two or three times every night, quiet or not, at different hours platoon Sergeant Eppler and I split, taking separate flanks to check. On the worst night we got a real probe, they tried to penetrate your defenses with no intention of following through. Doc Carlson took three slightly wounded down to company. Sometimes, when there was heavier activity one way or the other, we went together to investigate, but most times sat outside our bunkers listening, keen to hear what, if anything, would develop. I thanked my experience in reading with my ears. Twice during the third night I called for mortar fire in front of our hill; concentration number seven for the eighty-ones of Mike, Heavy Weapons Company.

"What you think, J J?" I asked, listening intently. "Any more?"

We were scared a good many times and made awkward jokes

to cover our anxiety and embarrassment, but only after broad daylight did guys laugh outright at their fidgety nerves, kidding one another with catcalls back and forth from hole to hole.

"Who's the brave guy threw a grenade without pulling the pin? One landed—no explosion."

"Sh-e-e-it!" Tree answered, "Never seed such a bunch of women."

No one came out immediately to admit his fear, but each accused others jokingly of being scared and kidded any guy known to have done something foolish; forget to pull the pin from his grenade, or yelled that the enemy were right on top of us.

"Say I didn't toss one? Stay right here, I'll find out."

"Wouldn't do that if I was you."

"Oh yeah, why?"

"Pulled the pin, it had to be a dud. Tired of living? Pin stuck, got to be a dud; wouldn't step four feet of it."

Sometimes in early morning, we'd warm C rations over tiny smokeless fires, a civilian type camp stove run with canned heat guys ordered from the PX, or a rare sometimes issued squad burner on gasoline you pumped like a Coleman camper's stove, or if you had a buddy in the engineers, lighting marble-size composition C4 plastic explosive, like balls of putty pinched off from a larger, soft brick, that burned fiercely for a short while.

Tensions of the night were released inadvertently by a man too honest, or too naive, to carry on a pretense. Ski was like that—couldn't disguise his true feelings. He was comic relief for us and if he wasn't there, he'd have had to be issued by Special Services for morale.

"Yeah, for a whole minute there I didn't know whether to wipe my ass or wind a watch."

"You mean shit or wind my watch," Pop corrected.

"That, too."

Immediately the tension was relieved, everyone blabbed excitedly how scary it was, as though each discovered it independently. Light humor without tension was lacking as was literate expression or serious discussion of any length. The laughs came not from healthy fun or playfulness but sudden releases of animal anxiety and wisecracks they snickered at went with bitter expressions as "Fuck 'em!" . . . "Trigger-happy bastards!" . . . "Scared? Man, I was shittin' and gittin'." "Sh-e-e-eit!"

The Korean monsoon was on and around us night and day, days that usually were free of fear. Gooks liked night. Early one evening before rounds J J, Doc and I sat in our mildewed tomb, our command post bunker, the most secure position I enjoyed in all my days on the line on any objective, listening to erratic gunfire move slowly in our direction. Awfully slow, I fretted, coming at us too damn awfully slow. I lit one cigarette from another.

"How many you figure?" I asked.

But they backed off their probe about 2000 and firing faded. After listening intently, Sergeant Eppler scurried from his hole.

"You guys hear anything suspicious out there?" he bellowed.

"Loud mouth!" I swore under my breath. "Yelling away our position; every gook within five miles knows exactly where we're at."

Then I recalled my stupid, seemingly cowardly silence the night of the outpost and I yelled, "Yeah, you guys, get on the ball." Shit, they know exactly where we are all the time so don't be bashful.

"Lieutenant," Sergeant Eppler asked, crawling head first into the CP firing well, "you really think them peace talks are on the level?"

"Think they're going to hit us?" I asked.

"S-h-h-h!" he said anxiously. "King's tangling with them."

"Yeah, listen, they're at King. Listen to those Russian 120s."

We donned our helmets. Was it night already or a very dark monsoon afternoon? Little difference. We lay in our hole watching lightning silhouette the far away northern mountain tops well into gook land with uncanny, startling blue light against a deep purple sky, and heard random rifles—a hundred angry dogs barking up and down a line across the low mountain ridge. Ski slid in, splashing muddy water from the grenade pit, whispering excitedly that four white-clothed men walked slowly past his bunker almost floating across the path that led to King Company.

"Regular zombies."

"Let them get away with it?" J. J. Jenkins scoffed.

"Took me by surprise, I was stunned."

"That's buck fever, where's your rifle?" I demanded.

"Goddamn!" Ski swore. "In my hole."

"Get back, tell Pop and the guys," I told him, as Sergeant Eppler and I left in opposite directions to alert the other squads. Gooks were very professional at line crossing; seldom seen and less often shot at. They wanted no trouble crossing through us, usually in Korean peasant white one at a time, to rendezvous in the rear to kill higher ranks if possible, prepare maps for future actions, or whatever mischief they could find.

Brilliant heat lightning flashed three or four times beyond where the most monsoon rain was falling, then stopped without apparent reason as though by a celestial signal; or went away fast angrily chasing black clouds scudding off to the Sea of Japan. A faint, frightened voice cried out pathetically way back on the trail, maybe from King.

"They're comin' all fours."

No one heard from the mysterious zombies in front of King until my midnight tour when something rustled bushes a hundred yards downhill. A hideous sound made hair rise on the nape of my neck. Coming from several directions at the same time, at first I was convinced it was inhuman, bringing to mind zombies—living dead.

"J-o-o-e!" it whimpered, a very sick woman pleading in a soft, but loud, wavering lament. "You g-o-o-o-o n-o-o-o-ow!"

Few of these gook demons followed easy-going, marked and possibly mined trails, but made their athletic way up through bushes, scrub trees, steep fingers leading from western valleys. They'd sit behind a boulder a hundred yards down a finger and whistle or taunt us with a smattering of expressions they'd overheard. "Hi, Joe, Ko ka mo. You go Kokamo, Joe. Go now, Joe," and map our fire plan from jittery guys throwing fear at them. They were especially after machine guns and BARs and mapping artillery and mortar concentrations.

They never got artillery or heavy mortar merely by calling for it unless they were field grade. They quizzed you at battalion, those who had to relay to Fire Direction Center, the S3 wanting to know how many you thought there were out there and what you thought their intentions were. Back in the valley they asked how much incoming artillery and/or mortar you were getting and could you locate their positions. They were much more detached back at battalion than we were and they were right, most of the time gooks were fooling with you simply to waste our mortar and artillery ammo. How many are there?

"Keep asking and you can count them going by."

While an apprehensive dawn spread light slowly throughout the scene on my last watch, it was whispered in awe over the platoon phones to be alert for a powerful gook capture team that dragged off two from their holes on a Charlie Company listening post. Like probably happened to Dorn and his men. You were terrified by the cold nerve of the enemy and at the same time shuddered at the fate of those men. It was known from escapees that they were interrogated without letup less than a mile away and sent north to starve to death for failing to give them choice information. Gooks were usually merciless like Japs or kraut SSers, whereas Chinks were more on our scale of humanity. I was thankful many times that Chinks took Sergeant Dorn and his guys rather than treacherous gooks.

The following night, frightened by a silly giggling downhill, I made the mistake of throwing a grenade. Guys along the ridge tossed grenades sporadically for an hour, encouraging the probing gooks to increase their harassment, and on my last tour when they whistled disconnected bits of what I imagined were popular Asiatic tunes to attract fire, our platoon machine gun disclosed its position.

"Doesn't sound like Ich," J J grumbled. "Should know better." But then, so should I.

Item struggled on the far side of King from us and the main pressure of gook's probe was strung out generally in a long column along the ridge. Our regiment, weakened by untested men from civilization who had to be taken by the hand, stretched out along our defenses until, even during fair weather, its elements were lost to view.

Occasionally, from his lofty observation post on the MLR, Colonel Mildren was able to point out to a visiting congressman, a news photographer, or war correspondent, the tiny spectacle of a bent-

205

over figure hurrying point to point. The lieutenant or a platoon sergeant would drop away from time to time, and Colonel Mildren would explain to his visitor, "Now he's briefing his men one hole at a time; or maybe distributing food. They're hard to supply."

A civilian photographer peered into his view finder and cursed the distance.

Settling down for a long grind, it wasn't enough that our enemy came to test us, we had to take turns patrolling from the main battle line to test him and platoons were dispatched piecemeal to assist Red Battalion in maintaining a precarious toehold on the steep approaches to H 1100 across the Pia-ri valley.

Love Company's command post alone was impregnable, a sand-bag fortress located as it was at the end of a short path backed by a cave. Company runners armed with tanker's grease guns stood twenty-four-hour guard over the entrance and a squad leader of weapons platoon was briefed to allow no one to pass without signaling the company commander, especially Colonels Mildren and Duncan.

Reconnaissance patrols worked nightly from both sides to ensure contact and grab prisoners if possible for Intelligence, to keep tab on gook outfits facing us, and so limited were traversable pathways of the wild terrain that on one of our patrols we lay flat to the ground off to one side, almost suffocating as a larger enemy patrol passed dangerously near. We heard gooks argue in low voices, strange, oriental voices growing steadily louder and more excited as the argument deteriorated. I thought sadly of Dorn and his guys. It was funny the following day—we were starved for humor.

Insomnia overcame me again. "What you have to do for shuteye?" a voice in me demanded. My brain raced against nothing full speed without arriving anywhere as I went down a familiar road over and over and, as each succeeding fear and its peculiar threat arrived, multiplied by the deaths I in some way participated, reviewed and closely examined by my conscience, the sum total a gnawing guilt which, in the best of nights pressed me awake, shaking my ears like any startled wild animal. I indicted myself:

"Go after them!" voices urged. "Help them, help them! . . . Never mind now, they're dead. Oh my God, all dead! . . . Why did you let them down?"

"Damn," a voice nagged, "why did you have to be so military? Why let Foney send those wiremen to certain death? Why didn't you keep them safe with your platoon on the ridge for just those few hours and make up a story to Foney?" That would have been the right thing to do and none would have been the wiser. Discipline, it's called, wouldn't allow it; damn obedience killed them. Learn again how to think free like a civilian.

I catnapped as I could and the following night enemy sneaked up in the stealthy manner of wild Indians from Satan Valley to hit us with vicious probing, a series of short, rugged jabs starting a mile or two to the right and bouncing along four miles of front. I was terribly nervous over a three-hour period, waiting, listening and wondering when they'd get to testing our platoon, and what was their strength.

Our artillery flares came over every ten minutes. We avoided looking at the flare itself and placed our hands over our eyes to shield them from the intense glare as we carefully followed the powerful light down, scrutinizing dense shrubbery at the bottom of the hill, full of 'enemy' movements caused by swinging flares. "Crimus, look at them bushes move!"

My nerves were highly pitched, waiting and listening, when suddenly b-r-r-r-r-rupt! 900 bullets a minute from several guns poured at us. A deliberate action of my own was necessary to counteract the stunning effects of the flood tide of blood and adrenalin surging all through my being and it was a whole minute before I was able to snap control over my thinking and yell, "Up and at 'em!," crawling from the bunker.

I had to shit, no avoiding it. My asshole muscles didn't have patience or strength to stay shut. I stumbled to our latrine and squatted there fearfully, pants down around my knees, carbine across my lap, paper between my lips, peeking around nervously, both ears strained to the utmost for incoming mortar. No time for wiping, I dropped the folded paper, yanked up my pants and ran stumbling bent over to the rear of a large boulder on the ridge top, holding my unhooked belt together with one hand, carbine in the other.

"All together, men!" I yelled, setting down my carbine, zipping my fly with my left hand, anxiously threading the end of my belt through the buckle. "Play it cool! Check and make sure safety's off."

The guys liked my yelling. It was as important to them as our flares and the powerful searchlights which our engineers on several occasions lit the ridgeline. They wanted to be led and liked to hear from their platoon leader and sergeants during a fight and know we were up working for them. Soon as I yelled down my own fear, I visited replacements in bunkers near the CP and found one new man cringing, lying sideways on the bunker floor, legs pulled underneath him in the passive pose of a fetus, as though fated to leave the world in the position in which he entered.

"Please, Mister Gook, shoot at anyone but don't hurt me."

When I spoke to some replacements, two in particular, they ignored me completely or motioned anxiously for me to be quiet and hunker down, afraid I'd attract attention. Man, did I understand the fear that numbed them. They wished to play possum, those badly frightened guys, whispering and begging me to get down in the safe, dark hole so the horrible monsters wouldn't know where we were.

"If we're awfully quiet," they'd think (as I did on the outpost) "and don't make no noise, or threatening moves, the gooks will go for someone bothering them."

"That's wrong! Wrong!" I scolded. "You can't cringe like that and lose initiative." Damn it, hadn't Sergeant Eppler and I drummed that into you?

"Listen to me!" I shouted. "Stand up, face 'em, and sound big, or you'll wish you had only gooks to put up with."

"Yes, sir," they promised, relieved and bolstered by my aggressiveness.

I slipped back into the CP bunker, put on my wrinkled fatigue cap and pulled my civilian revolver. It gave me more confidence at night than the unwieldy carbine, and out checking the line the steel hat was an amplifier, making false echoes of each warning sound, lying about where it came from. You needed something soft that wouldn't make or reflect noises.

I ran at a half crouch to the assistant weapon squad leader's hole from where shots had just come.

"Brown?" I called out. No answer. "Brown? Brown?" I questioned, louder and louder as I approached, thoroughly apprehensive. "Goddammit, boy, it's me, Lieutenant Gould."

Something clicked. I went flat as wet paper.

"Who's there?" a voice hissed.

"Lieutenant Gould," I answered, relieved and at the same time angry, slithering head first into his grenade pit. "You deaf or something?"

"Why? What's the matter, lieutenant?"

"Matter? Who fired the shots? You scared the hell out of me. Gooks are somewhere downhill from your squad, now clean out your ears and shape up."

Poking my head slowly over Sergeant E-5 Brown's parapet, I turned my face toward him. "Hear anything?"

"Me and Wheeler heard some funny jabbering before you came along," Brown said. "Just now we thought you might be gooks."

Suddenly a burp gun tattooed the darkness, a 220-volt shock! Thump! Thump! Thump! Thump! grenades showered from nearby bunkers to the sharp staccato bark of rifles and there was a fierce one-sided firefight for five minutes. Firing slackened and Brown started to talk. I slipped my hand over his mouth and pulled him forward. Cocking our heads over the sandbag wall of his firing pit, we listened to noises quiet as raindrops; faint rustle-rustle of cloth downhill rubbing branches and the indistinct snapping as they returned to place. When a tin can rattled, I pulled the cotter pin from an illuminating grenade, holding the handle down.

"Take off your helmet," I whispered. "Watch carefully where I heave this grenade and get ready to blast them."

The grenade sailed far downhill, the handle landing ten feet from the bunker with a thin, tin noise. The fuse popped in flight and we heard the snakelike sizz of its fuse and soft tennis shoes running for cover. Two shadows scurried as the grenade blossomed, a sputtering magnesium flower spraying shards of light on the wet branches.

Sergeant Brown and I blasted our frustration with an Army forty-five pistol and my civilian thirty-eight revolver throwing bullets into the bushes where the enemy had been.

The probers moved left hoping to draw fire and map fire plans and defenses. Our company continued to fire sporadically and toss grenades every half an hour.

Enemy 76mm, SP, self-propelled, high velocity artillery paid a screaming visit, landing greedily back and forth along the ridge top.

"Where you, Gould?" Death shouting for me in that heavy traffic of shells. Avowing my complete innocence, I crouched against the enemy side of my hole and explained that I really wasn't harmful. I cringed waiting for heavy broken hunks of metal to come crashing down, thankful they were weak at making air bursts.

"Why, me?" I whispered. "What've I done to you?"

We knew from the peculiar loud screech when a shell would be especially close. Immediately afterward we were speechless. Looking across the hole to one another, we could express only sickish smiles of relief until someone said, "Wow! That was close!" Or, simply, "My Gawd!" Anyone attempting a conversation was hushed so we could track everything incoming. None of us could carry a thought further than a short sentence; and if we were very quiet, sometimes we heard the initial warning sounds of mortar shells leaving the tubes—pw-w-oooop! On their way, their range very short compared to artillery.

There is no accurate way to describe that rushing-at-you, howling, death-on-the-way sound of incoming artillery, except perhaps that of a heavy express train bearing down with you tied to the tracks, or slightly less than a tornado although I've never heard either first hand. Quietly and carefully, oh so carefully, we breathed our last, never knowing so satisfying a delicacy as what might be a final draught, that wonderful, clean taste of mountain air. We treasured this great luxury, the air we breathed, particularly the ability to breathe in succession, and, gazing quickly along the small perimeter, experiencing a deep feeling of brotherly love, as danger molded us tight; all of us there that night felt the same, at the same moment—fear.

"Now I lay me down. . . ." I began unconsciously, interrupted then by another sudden scream of hell fire.

"Medic! Doc!" came from the left in the Second Platoon and I had to order Doc Carlson to Stay put.

"Cisco'll patch his own; he'll yell if he needs help."

In the First Platoon, one burst opened the ground and flung shattered rock over and into two riflemen in their hole. Neither knew it.

We preferred a dirt hole, for shards of rocks could finish the job the shell set out to do. First and Second Platoons were hit. A Second Platoon man, Hurtz's, had a leg blown off and as the fifty-round barrage lifted, I watched the sad spectacle of two guys struggling awkwardly, slipping and sliding back down the ridge past our CP with their buddy, a little man on a litter, his neatly severed leg beside him tied on with commo wire.

"Hurry!" they urged one another. "He's bleeding bad."

"Put him down," I yelled after them. "Stop the bleeding; press something on the wound, feel for an artery . . . Medic! Medic! Myles!"

Myles scampered over too late to save the guy as his head dropped beside his shoulder on the litter. If only Cisco'd tried first to stop the blood, but Cisco couldn't, he was patching a head wound when the guy was rushed away by fellow riflemen replacements who should have known better. First, stop the bleeding.

When he discovered that one of the dead of the First Platoon was an old-timer, J. J. swore under his breath. Had he been a new man, he would've said politely, "That's too bad." Learning a familiar old-timer was killed was like hearing prematurely of your own death; you lived in violence so long your memories are the same. Time was closing in. If we live too long, are hit too hard by too many attacks, we get the fixation that since all our buddies have died, we must go soon, it's only a matter of time, and watch out for guys carelessly standing straight up; one might be you.

"Hey," I asked, "who'd they say?"

"Lederman. Remember Lederman? Came with us at Inje."

"Lederman? Must've been a pretty quiet guy. I can't remember his face. Tough, but that's the way it goes."

Working on our hole later, busily discarding rock loosened by hacking or picking at it with my locked down entrenching tool, Lederman returned to mind and I suddenly remembered exactly what he looked like. I could see the guy standing before me.

"Oh, sure, Lederman, Indiana farm boy; blond kid about eighteen. Always in the front row at battalion movies. . . . Sonofabitch! Dirty, lousy luck! Now Lederman."

We were moody and silent, each paying his last farewell to PFC Leo Lederman, another of us nobodies gone forever from his mother who bore him, gone into a cold military grave in a foreign boneyard.

"Remember?" I said. "Always first at the movies; he'd go sit there to get the best seat an hour before dark reading a pocket book while we were still at chow, having another coffee and a smoke."

"I don't know 'bout that so much," J J said, "but man, sure had a good-looking sister."

"Goofed up on parade, remember?"

"I know one thing, he was dicked out of a Bronze Star once; they went and lost the paperwork at regiment. . . . He wasn't the only one."

"Lost it, yeah. They write 'em for their own that never get lost."

One of our most cherished surprises in combat was after dreading death all the dark hours, finding yourself at first light alive again, an infantryman's Easter Sunday. You've risen again, revived, allowed to hope for another day.

Late the next night there was more H and I than usual for so late and promiscuous rifle fire on our part as though someone actually saw a gook, until machine guns opened up almost playfully, each signing off his own way. B-r-r------upt. Lewis of the Second Platoon, Love. A long, drawn-out burst ending with a sharp tap! tap! tap!, a showoff gunner from King Company down the way, heard from other nights when he shouldn't be. It took finesse to knock off separate rounds from a machine gun, tap and tap. You have to acquire a light touch, snap your thumb down and off the trigger fast for rounds to be separate and individual. Gunners would brag with it.

One night after I returned from checking the bunkers about 3:30 as a light rain all evening became quite heavy, more typical monsoon, I heard low voices approaching commiserating and crawled out to find two men carrying a litter. Another walked slowly behind with

212

bowed head.

"Look where you're going," one complained.

"Won't hurt him none."

Seeing me, they set down their load.

Him, I discovered, was a little man on a mud slimy litter, soaking wet, covered with mud-thickened rags, jet black hair under slurpy mud. Bending closer, I recognized Corporal, soon-to-have-been sergeant E-5, Tommy Ichimura, ears and eye sockets packed with mud, right hand dragging limply along the trail over a side of the litter.

"What happened?"

"Bunker cave-in," Doc Carlson said, shaking his head sadly. "Roof crushed him on his machine gun."

"No!" I blurted, overcome by a compelling urge to make Ich live again. First J C, now Ich. I couldn't understand our guys going their lonely ways, especially little Ich; not pleasant, alert little Ich. Damn!

"You," I snarled at our new medic, uncontrollably savaged by the tragic event, "Used artificial respiration—everything? Can't let him go like that."

Carlson was silent as I impatiently rolled Ich on his stomach and pulled out his tongue, a long, unresisting, dead man's tongue. "Out goes the bad air," I said aloud, pushing in on Ich's rib cage, the old-fashioned resuscitation way. "In comes the good air. Out goes the bad air. In comes the good air."

"I wouldn't," Doc advised humbly.

"That's the difference," I snapped. "Doc Lynch would've tried everything. Out goes the bad air . . . God's sake, try it all!"

A crackling, juicy, popping noise came from Ich's mouth, followed by a bloody froth slowly bubbling from his nostrils. I stopped, motioning for Carlson to look at what I heard and saw in the predawn glow and turned to look up at him.

"I know," he said without moving. "Broken ribs; pushed them into his lungs."

"Oh God! God!" was all I could say and stood up glaring at the hands that mutilated Ich. No blood glistening as storm clouds opened to let stars out on his small muddy body and to me where there might have been some little hope, now these hands of mine, which continued to feel the smallness of our Neisi's broken chest, the soft, still warm, damp limpness of his body, had killed him. I should have known how dead he was after seeing the awkward angle of his head.

"You pushed in Ich's ribs," one of the litter bearers accused.

"I know! I know it!" I snapped.

Tears fell from my eyes as Myles placed his hand on my sleeve. "Sir, Ich's neck was broken anyway."

I yanked my arm away. "Shit! Shit!" I cried. "I hurt him bad. . . . Oh, shit! Shit! What've I done!"

I ordered them to leave Ich's remains and crawled into my bunker for my blanket.

"Nobody can help him now," Doc said.

"Shut up!" I shouted. "Shut up!" He was right, of course, but I thought the least we can do is see he's covered. You always see that in the movies. Much later I pondered the meaning of covering the dead, especially their faces. You can't stand their stares accusing you? Even with their eyes closed they haunt us and we cover their faces to hide our guilt, our mistakes and omissions.

Picking up Ich's litter, the bearers, buddies of his from the weapons squad, moved with their light load. To think he'll always be light now, hidden, embalmed skeleton, never a potbelly Neisi, esteemed member of his Japanese-American community. Tommy Ichimura, tough little guy's gone, feisty little boxer never use fat gloves again on any opponent. Ich is gone. Goddammit, Ich too.

Crawling into our bunker, our platoon command post, J J asked, "What's up, lieutenant? Where's Doc?" When I told him, he hung his head and said softly, "Oh God, Oh my God," and he really meant it for he was a devout Christian. With us there were more "my Gods" than in a church on Sunday. When I said 'Oh God,' it was purely a handy, violent expletive, an automatic expression hardened in me many years ago, what any Agnostic would say in lieu of knowing anything as powerful. A very sick old man, I fell into a fitful sleep where a scolding nightmare lay in wait.

Passing Tree's position on my way home from my 0400 tour, I paused to listen to him after coming off guard promise softly to himself, singing himself to sleep in a musing, slave jargon retrogressive talk-song—

Swing low sweet chair-e-et, come for to carry me home. Hear de man say he be resurrection and de life. Believe in him, man, you'se all right. Sweet chair-e-e-t, you'se ain't ever goin' to die. Man, I believes in Jesus. I'se comin' Lord! I'll be there! I'se comin' with ole black Joe. We's ready.

Early that July morning it steamed. While I slept the sleep of tormented, our guide, Bill Hansen, carrying the 536 walkie-talkie, worked carefully down the enemy side of the hill in front of our positions, setting out four additional flares with almost invisible steel trip wires, checking the wet ground closely for broken weed stalks and footprints. Our hard rubber heel combat boot footprints were obvious but those little guys with their soft tennis shoes left no prints in the soil. We found trip flares hadn't gone off because gooks bent cotter pins back on the pull fuses and stuck cotter pins they must have brought with them in the release ones and safely cut the wire, feeling for the tautness or slackness of the wire and tracing it down. From the signs of broken weeds, Bill concluded there'd been a reinforced squad; half a platoon at the most.

That day the sun came clean and dry two hours. Back home rain clouds were occasional, in the Korean monsoon the sun was. No one but us goof-offs, no-good dogfaces, flop and snore almost before hitting the ground. But then no one but us and insomniacs are up half every night. Others lolled about relaxing, puttering infantrywise — noses buried in pocket books. I was too tired and grieved to sleep, a quiet gentle man, albeit combat aggressive, gone in another nightmarish night.

J J carefully cleaned the glasses of our binoculars, using ass wipe, stopping every once in a while to focus on distant objects, never quite satisfied with the adjustment. Sergeant Brown took over, recovered Ich's machine gun from the mud and sent it to company for a trade. Everyone spread his equipment on his blanket to dry in the hot air. What a filthy lot; greasy, flat, matted hair; dirty beards and worn-down black fingernails; dirt-caked, horny cracked hands. Our soggy rags and blankets steamed as we scraped mud and removed boots from dirt wet socks. Fatigue uniforms were stiff from a mixture of dust, mud, rain and sweat and occasionally blood— someone you tried to help.

We poured rainwater collected in staked out ponchos into the steel hull of our helmets and in rare sunshine used face soap to shave, wash our dirty underwear, socks and handkerchiefs. Water was lugged up the torturous trail in five-gallon jerry cans, forty-pounds each, two cans per Korean carrier on shoulder yokes, so we dabbed at our faces and shaved, when bullied into it, with a single cup for a rinse without trying to really clean anything well.

Without rain it rose to eighty-five in the shade. Through the clear mountain air of our high land, we watched a peaceful convoy crawling slowly along the MSR (main supply route) behind the MLR. A truck brake screeched, handing up a little piece of America to our lofty wilderness. Some smart guy offered to bet the truck was thirty-five straight air miles away.

"Sure?"

"Simple mathematics."

College boy draftee we got in the last batch.

Monsoon rains held off two days in a row, midsummer Korea, sixteen hours of light from 0500 to 2100 and the damp earth stewed. A pretty little mountain bird warbled rippling stanzas, starting low, climbing up over ten complicated music scales ending in shrill beauty. What a little sweetheart. I'd love to take him home with me. Home? Home?

Six riflemen worked in relays to fell the largest of the knotty pines up to five inches in girth for bunker roofs with sharp engineer saws delivered at noon by Korean laborers. Chain saws? Not invented. All afternoon Ski lay under Sergeant Eppler's large black umbrella in undershorts and unlaced boots, reading a lurid pocket book, *Machine Guns Through Hell.*

"Where'd you get that?" Pop demanded.

"Traded with Funaro for *Sex in the Alley.*"

"Damn it," Sergeant Eppler demanded from behind, "he

216

means my umbrella. Ought to beat the shit out of you."

"Funaro told me you wouldn't mind," Ski said. "No one asked for it, he just handed it over."

"Hold up a sec, Karl," Pop interceded. "You have Funaro to thank for this."

"Sh-e-e-it!" Ski said, and, finishing the page, laid the pocket book down hard, his bookmark a dirty finger. "The lying bastard."

Sergeant Eppler, realizing there was no bad blood, retrieved his umbrella and left toward a heated argument taking place down the ridgeline.

"You promised me the fruit cocktail this time, you know you did."

"Think I'm crazy? That's all that's good."

"You did so! Ask anybody."

"You're full of shit!"

"I ought to kick the shit out of you!"

"Want to try?"

"Keep it up and I'll kick the shit out of both of you," Sergeant Eppler threatened.

Way off to the left someone fired a lazy old machine gun in short bursts; sounded like a housewife on a sunny morning beating a rug. From where I was up the trail I heard Sergeant O'Neill, weapons squad leader, yell angrily to the distant gunner, "Check your head-space!" knowing from the sound it was loose.

Becoming irritably tired, avoiding our damp hole for the rare sunlight, I tried dozing against a tree, back to a large rock, and then propped up against the same tree again. Lying nearby on their sides, facing each other, Sergeant Olsen and Sergeant Tree were playing whiskey poker, neither much ahead.

"How're the squads?" I asked, tired right out, mean- spirited, lighting another cigarette.

"All right, lieutenant, we just this minute checked. Pop's with them."

When I remained silent, feeling threatened, Sergeant Avery Ol-sen looked up from his cards. "Lieutenant, what if something bad should happen to me? I should get it, or rotate, or something? My assistant's got to learn, doesn't he?"

"I just asked how's your squad, Olsen. I know you guys are tired, but someone has to finish the bunker roofs."

"There aren't logs enough, sir," Olsen said, working up an indignation. "And the guys are picking them up fast as they're ready." A pause. "Those guys better get on the ball or I'm going to start turning them in."

Laying down his hand, he added, "Hold these cards down, Tree; don't cheat. Lieutenant's watching you. I'll be right back."

While Sergeant Olsen was satisfying his conscience, heavy artillery opened suddenly against the hill we knew as 1179, swishing close above us. Usually we listened to our artillery only when we wanted to, but on this day the big eight-inchers jarred my nerves. Proximity fused, so sensitive a drop of dew or a fleck of dust in the air could set them off. Sure enough, black cotton smoke puffed suddenly high overhead and showered the ground widely with jagged fragments. We pretended not to worry, but when falling shrapnel thudded and crashed especially close in the bushes, we buried our heads in our helmets. Friendly fire premature? Sh-e-e-eit! "Set them damn fuses right," someone yelled. "Elevate them big bastards!"

Each infantry division in 1951 was authorized three 105mm artillery battalions of about 500 men each, one per regiment, manning eighteen 105mm howitzers in batteries A, B and C, which included the Dutch. Each division had two battalions of heavies in support, 155mm tractor-drawn or self-propelled, also batteries A, B and C. The relatively few 8-inchers belonged to Corps or Eighth Army. Two years later 240mm and 280mm 'atomic cannons' were sent over by President Eisenhower and an armistice was quickly signed.

Ideally, each infantry battalion had a train of fifty semi-military KSC, Korean Service Corps, formerly CTC (Civilian Transportation Corps) carriers issued like pack mules, signed for, fed, handled roughly as property, and given such unpleasant nicknames as 'Old Fuzzballs,' 'Charlie the Creep,' and 'Greasy-Ass' by surly, goof-off soldier handler guards happy to stay out of combat.

The first train before daylight left daily in a strung-out column of climbers from the new company forward supply point with food, ammo, water, and if the riflemen shot up their basic load the night before, the chogee train was instructed by radio to pack nothing but ammunition and water. Up where we operated water was hard to come by.

KSCs wore brilliant blue uniforms easily detected from the top of 1179 and when a chogee train arrived late in the afternoon gooks greeted them with self-propelled seventy-six shells. Somewhere across the valley and up on that ominous mountain a particularly personal enemy, a gook forward observer, was trying his best to wipe them out. Later, at 1179, climbing the more difficult protected route, we lost two to precipitous falls.

The usually accurate grapevine had it that Marines would have to take Death Valley and we would cross the Pia-ri Valley to capture the western rim of the Punchbowl, remains of an ancient, long-extinct volcano. Everyone buzzed about a place called Taeusan, which the gooks referred to, according to prisoners, as the Gateway to the Orient. To us it was plain Hill 1179, the fourth highest knob on the rim, what the Press nicknamed from many miles in the rear Fools Mountain, and tabulating the tons of aerial bombs and artillery shells expended softening it up, Five Million Dollar Hill. We were fools to risk our lives on so dangerous a hill with the Peace Talks going on.

6
Hill 1100

From the Blue Book—

Later in July Van Fleet ordered a northward advance in the X Corps zone to shorten the line, prevent the enemy from freely observing the Kansas Line, and force the enemy to pull back his mortars and artillery. The specific objective was a 3878-foot mountain, Hill 1179 designated Taeusan, Gateway to the Orient, at the southwest edge of the Punchbowl, known to the American press as Fools Mountain, which ROK marines had unsuccessfully attacked. It was defended by an estimated two regiments (3400 men) of North Koreans. Elements of the US Second Division were directed against the objectives. Air and artillery pounded enemy positions on the 25th in preparation for the assault; 7000 rounds of artillery hurled into the well-bunkered positions and H and I on the approach behind it.

The attack was scheduled for 26 July and the 38th Infantry named as the attacking element. The 23rd infantry was to launch diversionary attacks to seize three objectives on the Punchbowl from which it could cut off escape of enemy elements from 1179 and also provide fire support for the 38th.

At 0415 hours, 26 July, I Co of the 38th Infantry moved out in a dense fog to take Hill 1100 forward position of the elements defending 1179. Although hampered by poor visibility, supporting fire were all the weapons of the 38th Regiment plus the Heavy Mortar Company of the 9th Infantry. Attacking through the haze and streams of tracers, I Company became

220

*exhausted by 1245 hours, with its forward elements giving
ground. K and L Company immediately inched upward. Suddenly the sun broke through clouds giving artillery and mortar
observers a clear view of the enemy and immediately crashing
salvos of exploding shells were called on the defenders. The
infantry surged forward, following the artillery bursts within 75
yards, firing every available weapon. By night fall the inspired
foot soldiers had battled to within 50 yards of the crest of Hill
1100 and there they halted, digging in to wait until daylight for
the final assault.*

Five days earlier, our Third Battalion, 38th, was relieved in
place by elements of the 13th ROKs and we bivouacked back where we
dismounted trucks several weeks earlier. At 0400 hours on the drizzly,
misty morning of 25 July 1951, 30 km north of the mountain wilderness of that 38th parallel border between North and South Korea, the
order went out to blue battalion's rifle companies K and L to move out:
"Off your cocks, on your socks! Hands where we can see 'em! Move
dogfaces! Let's go-o-o! This is it! Chogee!"

By the time blankets and pup tent halves were rolled tightly together into legionnaire rolls and strapped to knapsacks it was pouring
rain and sitting under little pyramid tents of ponchos bloused over our
knees and weapons—hurry up and wait—a half-hour wait for the
trucks. No doubt at all something big was up but as yet none of us were
in the know. The most prevalent rumor, introduced by a corporal who
worked for battalion operations and was sworn to secrecy, was that we
were going after 1179 all right to whip two crack regiments, 'Hero'
and 'Tiger,' toughest outfits in North Korea. First however, 1100.

We trucked over in dripping blackness to the Pia-ri Valley using cateye headlight covers and dismounted, falling in our accustomed
company groups, answering roll call in low voices. I remember roll
calls well from World War II, roll calls and long queues and every time
ordinary GIs, sergeants excluded, when transferred from one unit to
another one place to another, they underwent short arm inspections for
venereal diseases, pausing before a seated doctor, taking it out, our

221

short arm, skinning it back for a look-see, what British Land Army girls called the monthly flip the lip.

By companies we turned our faces toward the always-inhospitable north and marched away in the normal column of twos from the retreating trucks up the road for several miles until we turned right, broke ranks into a single file and started to struggle up a steep, wandering finger of land, zig-zagging back and forth in the dark, slipping and sliding as usual on mountain mud trails.

Just before daybreak we were told to rest in place; the low-voiced order, "Rest! Keep it down! Don't light up!" traveled, a ghostly voice from the rear, upward. I dozed off and awoke abruptly a number of times sliding slowly downhill. All that was kept dry that memorable monsoon morning were what we wrapped double in plastic C ration accessory bags—wallets, handkerchiefs and cigarettes tucked inside our fatigue jackets. Many of us that long gray morning caught sniffles, noses that ran, as the palms of our hands got blue-white and wrinkled from stabilizing upward movement, pawing under heavy packs at the steep, wet trail.

At 1100 hours we reached the top juncture of our trail and a wider mountain path leading down another steep finger into the huge Punchbowl where Captain Shallow ordered Ich's replacement, our new machine gunner, to set up; Sergeant E-5 Frank Smith, Hamilton, Ontario. I was pissed off and knew then how much Pop Miller must have felt; the next time he took one of my guys without my permission, I'd complain to Colonel Duncan.

I laid down the rest of the platoon up the high trail atop the Punchbowl running northward toward H 1100, 1179, 1180 and 1243. Fools Mountain, 1179, heavily fought over by ROK Marines and, more recently, the First Battalion, somehow was the only one that avoided the name-labeling Press. No correspondent ever made the difficult climbs to find out what went on up there and we were above and beyond long-range photographs.

We were a mixture of hundreds of disgusted, cursing draftees, reserves, Guardsmen, and Regular Army facing their first trial, Hill 1100, many wishing they'd never enlisted, discouraged recalled Reservists and federalized National Guardsmen under a few career officers and sergeants, painstakingly crawling, often on all fours, still standing at an angle, grabbing at finger holds, holding the rifle or carbine or helmet straps with one hand while edging slightly off the trail for traction, one long torturous mudslide. Damn this! Damn that! Why can't we bypass this bastard?

Someone leaked out the big picture that King Company would man the rear ridge of the Punchbowl behind us while Item and then Love pushed through to take H 1100. H and I fire from several 76mm SPs and old US Army 75mm mountain pack howitzers captured from Chiang Kai-shek's Nationals rustled low above, overshooting but, I worried, dangerously near Smitty's dominate trail-crossing position, apparently zeroed in.

Captain Theodore 'Teddy' Toth who, one day out of the blue, refused to go any further, there being no other experienced officer in King Company, was replaced summarily by first sergeant, Master Sergeant John Pater, who one day was called on the SCR 300 from battalion headquarters in the Pia-ri Valley. John related to me that Toth, like so many sensitive ones in that godforsaken war had enough— reached his limit. He earned a Bronze Star during the winter at the Twin Tunnels which proved he could be courageous. Now he was through.

Duncan told Pater that he was now in command of King Company permanently, noting that Pater was a real pro; his leadership and example common knowledge on at least four occasions. Sergeant Pater was too old for a commission, but Duncan didn't think it would be very long before an officer would be assigned.

"What's wrong with the captain?" Pater asked.

The colonel, on the defensive, told Sergeant Pater not to worry, the Captain was being transferred to regiment.

"I don't understand," Pater said.

"You'll know some time, Sergeant, right now I'm not at liberty to say."

"We got two ROTC lieutenants."

"I know, sarge, and despite you being thirty-six, I'm putting you in for bars with an age waiver."

The next time Pater or I had dealings with Captain Toth was while he was Regimental Graves Registration Officer. Both Pater and I had occasions to raise our voices to him, the careless job being done. One never did see or hear of him climbing up on the Punchbowl checking his work, looking for bodies and his assistants were equally incompetent. After all, it was the least choice job in the infantry, cleaning up after battles.

Master Sergeant Pater and myself received Silver Stars for taking two high objectives in a row, both decorations initiated by Awards and Decorations section Lieutenant Colonel Rowny, regimental exec, at the request, I was to find, of X Corps, generous giver of pretty ribbons, one for every objective taken.

The Blue Book—

Meanwhile, on 26 July the Third Battalion of the 38th began moving forward to join the First Battalion. Eastward, I Company was Struggling to take Hill 1100 and by nightfall its every attempt had been repulsed for the enemy, hanging onto it to keep open his supply route to Hill 1179, was determined to stay. Item pulled back for a renewed attempt the following day.

Throughout the night, the big guns laid a protective screen of steel around the weary infantry clinging to their slim foothold just short of the crest of H 1100. At first light on 27 Jul the Third Battalion, L Company of the 38th moved forward toward the peak guarding the natural, south approach to 1179. Braving a rage of machine gun, mortar and small arms fire, they were repulsed and K Co pushed through L Co, returning to the attack and by evening the hill was secure.

Item pushed past Love on through the mist but was soon hit with a strong counterattack and knocked back, taking six casualties, two from our own fighter-bombers. Because of this, Item fell back twice the very day it attacked and because of its additional weakened effort along that ridge and finger, gooks didn't slow their protective fire, keeping Item's men properly frightened. By the sounds we knew much of the fire was from captured guns.

Driven off the enemy saddle by heavy fire, Item was forced to leave dead where they fell as we side-stepped the trail to let the parade of wounded hobble back down, ambulatory slowly, those on litters, usually bounced up and down hauled tied down by worried buddies or carriers when available, on a hunched over run and down steep descents backing slowly with great care of those wounded who couldn't hold on, down to where Korean carriers took over.

The mountain breezes exhaled on us as Item, engaging in its third effort, fought valiantly upward, replacements climbing up white-faced at the end of the supply train, bound for the open trail of a dangerous kangaroo court; hell of a bad time to be tested. Pure pandemonium, presided over the continuous fighting, a ruthless judge exonerating only dead and wounded. One GI, big smirk on his face, fatigues scissor-slashed in a jagged line across his chest, flapping over large Vaseline Carlisle bandages, with yards of heavy gauze, under strips of adhesive tape, on the left shoulder to under the armpit, that arm in a sling, came triumphantly down the bloody hill from the firing where two platoons of Item were still exposed to the bluntest of human cruelties.

While we were supposedly resting in place, Sergeant Eppler and my gang carried ammo to Item, cloth bandoleers of M1 clips and 1000-round metal cans, four belts of 250 each, of 30 caliber machine gun ammo, either web belts or newer metal links. Crossing a beaten zone exposed saddle path, they crouched low and made dashes, zigzagging to reach Item digging in desperately under the noses of gooks. Sergeant Eppler was asked by Item's commander if he minded taking the ammo around to the men. Minded? Anyone preferred being pinned down to visiting guys who are, but being a warrior, my platoon sergeant complied.

One of Item's reluctant replacement riflemen coming past us up the trail kept spinning his wheels, falling down twice trying to crawl back to the top of the short, slippery incline. While we all were laughing, I heard powerful hissing and saw white smoke coming out from under the poncho that covered him and his rifle slung upside down.

"Grenade! Grenade!" I yelled, scrambling sideways as far away as the brushy terrain would allow, burying myself under my helmet. As I scrambled, from the corner of my eye I saw the man's poncho blow into the air like a lady's skirt over an air register. My God, I thought, the guy's had it for sure and immediately rummaged about my own body for a possible wound.

An Item Company medic was over him in a flash and, hard to believe though it is, the guy was the only one hurt, a nasty blood-gushing gash on the inside of his right thigh. The medic scissored off his trouser leg and applied a tourniquet above the gash and sterile Carlisle 4x4-inch bandage over the wound, tying as tightly as he could. I understand that the man, a replacement, survived and with large damage to a nerve was returned to the states. So much for attaching grenades to one's shoulder straps by their pull rings, al la General Ridgway, which were dummies with their handles taped down.

Colonel Duncan caught me on my 536, pissed off for not being able to contact Shallow on either the 536 or the company 300. It's unheard of for an infantry unit to be out of contact, usually indicative of a tragedy, as with Sergeant Dorn's listening post.

"Gould, I can't raise Captain Shallow; take Love Company through Item. King will back you. Toth's no longer with them; a Sergeant Pater is in command. Don't bother telling me they have two second lieutenants; Sergeant Pater's the man for the job. I want you to work with him and when he gets bogged down, work your men through his."

"Okay," I replied, "Don't know all the guys in Love Company, all I can say is I'll try."

"All anyone can do."

Banzai Third was already first in line and we chogeed along almost within touching distance of the last engaged platoon of Item. Our guide talked up the spirits from the rear, telling the guys how tough they were, threatening any man wanting to give in to the boy within him, checking on everything. In wars with horses, the job was performed by hussars, dragoons, who, foot soldiers knew, were ordered to shoot anyone skulking, hiding or sneaking away.

Behind us, Captain Shallow, paleface and reluctant to move, cowered snug to a big rock formation as all three rifle platoons passed

226

by obediently to meet fate head on. As I prepared to lead Love through the rear of Item, I came to a particularly advantageous hole for safe observation off the open trail to my left. I hand-waved a halt, needing its protection to have time to study the immediate dangers but it was occupied by a wounded guy of Item, his pants undone, a tag tied through a belt loop and a large blood-stained bandage on an inner thigh.

"Hit any other place?" I demanded, lying flat on the open trail. When he failed to respond, edging closer I saw he was going into shock, black pupils dilated wide open, staring straight ahead, sweat over his face of a pale greenish-yellow pallor. My God! I got an ugly sinking feeling in my stomach like I always had as with the sight of Ich; what a terrible, useless way to go. I'd seen guys go off the deep end this dreamy damn way and knew it as a failure of blood to circulate, either because of excessive loss and therefore no pump pressure to get what's left to the brain, or an overall contraction of small blood vessels pulled taunt from fear, also preventing free flow of blood and instinctively I reached impulsively down and gave his face a hard back-and-forth slap to force his blood to move, whereupon he shook his head, color returning immediately, his eyes focusing as he grunted "Huh? Huh? What?"

Sticks in my craw to watch a poor bastard slip away as he was doing and nobody do anything to help him. I simply reacted to a strong instinctive need to express my anger at what was killing him and slap the fatal shock out of him — the crazy idea they have to die of their own fear. No! Man, how I hated them sliding away like that! No! That's what happened to the King Company replacement captain, dead on arrival at battalion aid station from an overdose of self-concern and pity, mere flesh wound on a leg.

I was told later it sounded like the reasoning behind giving newborn babies a soft upside-down whack to jump-start their circulation and breathing. The same general principle, maybe? I'm no doctor.

"Not hurt bad!" I yelled at the wounded man then recirculating his blood. "Stop selling yourself a bill of goods and get the fuck out of here!"

I had no thought he was a coward, except that it was weak to give in like that. I couldn't see how he'd lost any great amount of blood. I grabbed his sleeve, guiding him to slide sideways out of the hole and as he started to stand I brought him down fast and warned him to keep his ass and head low or he'd get it again. The wounded man went clawing with his hands, dragging his leg, kicking with the good one, bent over up the red-hot trail toward safety.

After we got moving up 1100, PFC Funaro slipped and fell in front of Pop Miller and remained on the protected side of the trail complaining of a broken ankle. Pop took him by an elbow and pulled him up. Funaro slipped again, obviously on purpose. Pop yanked him roughly to his feet.

"Like I said, Philip," pretending concern, "nothing beats exercise for a broken ankle. Now exercise!"

The line dragged even more slowly than forced to on that slippery trail until word passed from the rear for the lead man to move out smartly and Captain Shallow came rudely elbowing his way up, sliding on his feet, turning all the way around two or three times as he skied back down the slick mud, hanging to bushes.

"Sonofabitch, Gould," he hissed fearfully. "Battalion's on my ass. Why don't you keep it moving?"

"Who's on your ass?" I quizzed. "Duncan tell you that?"

"Not exactly, but I know he'd want to."

"Duncan's trying to get hold of you."

No answer and Shallow settled into a safe hollow as I took off pushing the men.

Master Sergeant Juan Maldanado was my Love Company point man that morning physically leading his First Platoon smoothly with as proven expertise as any efficient tradesman on any job. Juan earned his first two stripes as a rifleman in B Company of the Second Division's 23rd Infantry at the Battle of the Bulge in WWII, helping in the cruel cold and snow to relieve the 101st Airborne at Bastogne, Belgium.

We approached the violent staccato of machine guns dueling in close as, stooping, I motioned overhead with my carbine to deliver the guys with momentum into the forward-moving column and was sucked into Item's fracas without being technically committed by our company commander, who didn't realize until it was over that I was in command. By then it was obvious to the observations of those who passed him that Captain Shallow was no longer combative; in fact, in spirit no longer with us.

To have enough men up to bolster the attack, I had Fred Hurtz's platoon, Master Sergeant Red Rose leading, pushed on either side through thin brush off the trail and my platoon along the broken, rough Taeusan, dangerous, side of the ridge trail.

We finished chogeeing through Item half way up H 1100 from the depths of the saddle where Corporal Edsel Turner took over the right flank. I knew by then by his reputation that Turner was a damn good man when shit was hitting the fan. No surviving officer knew he had successfully protested being evacuated to the states. He was a maverick, a rebel who, like me, wasn't overwhelmed by authority. In reserve, like Funaro, he went looking for trouble and excitement and having been out of sight, out of mind in hospitals for months, had not been promoted since the past November, nor had anyone behaved generously toward him since the whole regiment had all but turned over, with no mention of his heroic exploits at Kunu-ri. Fact was, the Banzai Third platoon got hit good at Kunu-ri and aside from close-mouthed Sergeant Ulriche in a different platoon at the time, there were not more than three originals left. Tony Burris was one, the strong, silent cowboy type, half-breed from Oklahoma. Edsel was in Korea longer than anyone in the regiment except for rear echelon Regulars reupping to further their safe careers.

I worked my way, urging guys from my platoon especially, up through the brush from large rock to large rock, yelling my lungs out, as Sergeant Eppler and I taught each other to do, when, checking the extreme right flank about fifty yards toward the Punchbowl drop-off, I saw, not Eppler nor any sergeant, but little tornado Corporal Turner. Right away I found what a beauty of a terrorist Turner could be shouting orders like a combat veteran rifle platoon leader, bossing sergeants around who hopped to at the sound of him.

"Come on! Get firing! . . . FIRE! Dammit, fire! Get your asses up and chogee! C'mon, you bastards! Let's go! Get up there! Nobody lives forever. Chogee!"

With his strong loud-mouth inspiration, the guys moved and

229

after that day I found myself paying attention to the little guy. I say little for at 5'7" he was an inch and a half shorter than me.

I never mentioned rotation to Turner, but I'll bet anything he would've insinuated for me to go pound salt, he'd rather stay with his buddies. Or maybe it was the outfit he loved, like street kids loyal to gangs, the nameless thing with deep mysterious spiritual continuity some willingly sacrifice for; in this cruel world, a home away from home. He wasn't happy to leave the area of combat even for a DSC but the regimental powers there allowed him no alternative.

"I'll be seeing you guys," he waved in our general direction, but none of us ever did for he was handed his hard-earned DSC in its blue box and rotated to civilization, which he distained. His days of bullying gooks and Chinks were over.

I had read Slam (S. L. A.) Marshall's article in the April 1953 *Saturday Evening Post* about his personal experiences in the massacre at Kunu-ri, North Korea in November 1950, which mentioned Corporal Turner. Slam had been cut off with the Second Division as the CCF entered the war.

As remnants of two shattered battalions of the frostbitten 38th sought to escape to the south that late November, Corporal Edsel Turner volunteered to take a BAR with as much extra ammo and grenades as he could handle and hold back the Chinks on a defile road as long as he could. His company commander, killed in an ensuing action, saluted him and enthused that he would write Edsel up, possibly for a Medal of Honor—at least a DSC. Everyone present said good bye to Edsel, what a selfless, brave little guy, never expecting to see him again. From about five miles away, as they reached safety and daylight failed, they heard his BAR peppering from way up the valley, music to their ears.

Turner was dropped MIA two days later on the morning report, but he came in several days later, yelling for food and water, dragging a foot through the lines of the 23d Infantry shouldering an empty BAR, having survived, wounded and a little frostbitten. Flying Edsel to a general hospital, the surgeon told him he was lucky it had been so cold or he would have bled to death.

With far less resistance, I reached the trail above on the left ahead of Turner that day where I shot the first of two men I personally know of—a young gook so busily tossing potato mashers down toward where Turner and his guys were yelling up a storm he didn't know what hit him. I watched him falter and fall with one hand outstretched to break his fall, and in the hot flush of the occasion I pumped several more rounds into where I thought he ended up in the low bushes. We had heard tales of guys killed by enemy wounded after they hit the ground.

Finding what cover we could along the trail the guys and I crouched expectantly, blocking behind a loaded King Company which pushed off through us in a discouraging mist to consolidate the attack. Master Sergeant John Pater climbed behind his first platoon up toward the bunker-studded top of Hill 1100, against emplacements that covered each other with automatic weapon fire against approach from the south. The steep sides of all but the north-south trail precluded us attacking from any other direction, unless, most unlikely, air-dropped to the north. We called them suicide bunkers because the only way to get in or out was through firing apertures facing us.

"Follow me you bastards! Let's get 'em!" roared Pater as he held his carbine high to the sky for emphasis facing the final objective. "Big Time, we're going over. E-e-e-e d-e-e-wa-wa. You yellow cunts, here we come. King Company! King Company! Show 'em who's King!"

The way Pater said bastards was a compliment as well as a curse.

There wasn't time to repeat himself, for the enemy stopped his spirited attack on the grenade line; one arm in particular lobbing many from behind a dead tree in the very middle of the trench. King Company was able to heave its heavy frag grenades half as far. I worked up on elbows and knees to survey the threat.

"What now?" a King rifleman asked, turning on his side, smiling nervously. "What do we do now, Lieutenant?"

It was a fierce battle, a noisy hot bloody engagement as Item

231

buttoned up in place and Love and King, or King and Love, got mired in a series of hot firefights, but the only explanation anywhere in the world in writing for the deadly period from one minute after midnight on 27 July 1951, Korean time, was a terse mimeographed paragraph of the activities in the Division's periodic operations report, seen only by a handful of business-as-usual professional Army staff officers and their unemotional sergeants.

The firing up ahead was anxious, at times frightening to hear. Wounded stumbled by dull eyed, scurried down past us holding to the bandaged red marks made in them, ran past hunkered down, white faced, slipped or limped by us waiting our turn, silent; staggered along half blind with hands out thrust dripping blood through fresh bandages, feeling bushes going by, led by less wounded ambulatory; and undulating passively on litters.

"Good going man," we murmured to brave men passing.

First one and then another fired along the stalled line of King. There were no fusillades. Everyone else was a sightseer, lying on his belly or his side watching the battle ebbing away, yelling occasionally to correct another's aim, a few detached and careless enough to light up. The longer they stayed cringing in that awkward position, the more brave the enemy became. Suddenly a terrified bunch of five GIs turned, stood up, and ran pell-mell, slipping, sliding and stumbling down the hill from the left flank, their backs to the enemy.

"Here they come! . . . They're coming down!" they cried.

I scrambled sideways like a crab across the ground, yelling, "What're you doin'?"

"Orders to withdraw," one of them yelled.

"Whose orders?" I demanded, working into them. "Who are you guys?"

I threatened them with my mounted carbine bayonet, stopping them with the help of two sergeants. They were some of Item's people—what I called intermediate bugouts—who, remaining hidden behind boulders, mixed somehow with Pater's holdbacks, not knowing of their company's silent withdrawal.

"Somebody said better withdraw."

"Get back before my men let loose on you goddamn cowards!"

I yelled.

"Yes, sir!" they said, ashamed, realizing their panic; Item men along with King as though they belonged now to King.

The silent rains, lifting, hung poised in a heavy gray sky in what seemed the most pitiless day of the war. Apertures of enemy bunkers staring coldly from the very top of 1179, unblinking reptile eyes fixed upon us, winking death, 'seeing' us dead, with outgoing flashes of aimed rifle fire. As our demoralized men returned the stare with nervous upward glances, someone near me observed sadly, "Our last go-round."

Leaving the stymied protected riflemen, I crawled into an abandoned gook hole, mind and body, every bit of me, aching so it seemed I had to squeeze my chest with my hands to breathe. I needed at least a half hour rest. "Take over. Give me a few minutes," I stuttered to Sergeant Eppler.

"King'll get livin' shit kicked out for sure," J J said, glancing anxiously over his shoulder. "Nobody, brother, I mean *nobody* getting over that hill alive."

Little Kims are anxious to get off the ridge and every once in a while they'd hear a cry in Korean and dart from cover in two-man teams to hurry back with a ticketed wounded man on a litter—their ticket to safety. Sometimes they'd be so rattled and scared they'd put a corpse on a litter and head down the valley for safety, kimchee and a big black pot of rice.

Four KSC came down past me hauling a litter high on their shoulders, bouncing a large man strapped on with commo wire. Sergeant Eppler saw at a glance that the man was dead and ordered the carriers to set him down, indicating for them to take him off the litter. He called Smiley, our company interpreter, and told him to give the carriers hell and even though they belonged to King, remind them that they were not to pick up soldiers on their own; the decision whom and when to evacuate being left to medics, certainly not to take dead until all wounded were off. Smiley jabbered away, as was their custom, it seemed five minutes, and by his weak inflections and volume, we knew he didn't have the guts to bawl anyone out.

"What they say, Smiley?"

"They say they make mistake. Man look living."

Another litter came by carried hip high and I could see that the man still lived. I motioned the two carriers to set him down to check his tag and make certain bleeding was stopped and he was properly bandaged and given a morphine shot, if necessary. He was what gun-fighters out West called gut shot, his fly hastily ripped open, exposing olive drab undershorts soaked through with coagulating gore oozing slowly from above. The man, a rugged, dark-bearded sergeant from King Company, opened his eyes slowly with a dreamy, morphined, far-away look, half focusing as I bent over him. I had noticed him leading his platoon in King Company on our June parade, passing by so proud, handsome and virile – a recruiting poster to entice our Nation's manhood to do something patriotic.

"Lieutenant?" he asked feebly, catching sight of my silver bar, almost begging, it seemed but he had not the energy to pursue his thought and ended with a feeble, "Good luck . . . sir," closing his eyes to return to a dream.

"Good luck, sarge," I said, patting the man's shoulder. "You did a number one job."

We cherish praise from our own kind, and half unconscious, the wounded man smiled as a reaction to my valuable praise, or perhaps because he was returning to his fantasy world of morphine, hopefully kidding around with his girlfriend. A true warrior, RA all the way, he'd die proud to have it said by one he respected that he did his job well. Save your pity rear echelons, it's his chosen profession, the job only a real man can do.

"He don't look so good, do he?" Tree commented.

We resumed crouching behind a large boulder splitting my can of lima beans and ham chunks.

"Knows somethin'?" Tree said awkwardly, clearing his throat. "Lieutenant's changed."

Still mindful of that brave sergeant, I was taken off guard.

"What's that?"

"Sir, we knows you changed."

"Soldier," I countered irritably, "we all have."

"Never tole a guy he done a good job 'cause he's dying."

Having spent the day standing back of King, we passed through

234

to take our brief turn again and then after two hours on the stalled grenade line, Pater led a rejuvenated King through us, amid the clamors,
cheers, clashes, shouting, explosions, screaming, swearing and plain
battle noises wherein it became obvious to us that neither side was
having it easy. We curled up in the most protective positions we could
manage under our ponchos.

As darkness fell that violent night, the battle subsided. A temporary cease fire took place not over twenty climbing yards from one
another. I begged the average American's God's pardon for leading
that wire patrol to oblivion, an entire squad made into dead unsung heroes, gone, especially the young wire man whose blood-full goiter I
remembered too easily, and my sacrificing three of Pop Miller's men
without clearing with him. While in that God-beseeching mood, I asked
Him respectfully to try to take better care of my guys. Should be Your
guys first, and pardon me for being Agnostic.

We dozed on the battlefield. I was knocked out by fatigue,
leaving one ear open, not so much tired muscles but nerves; tension
that terrible afternoon and evening sweeping softly over me, lulled
again by our amateur gospel singer, Sergeant E-5 Raymond Roundtree,
mouthing a muffled musical deep-throated litany —

Is I blue? Is I blue? Tell everyone around de' place I is
blue. De' angels tole me dey's comin'. Hear what, man, dey's
comin'. Man, angels dark as me, you see, as this night's
gonna' be. Hear me . . . how dark this night's gonna' be. De'
angels tole me. Is gonna' be dark as me. . . . Is I blue? . . .
Tell everyone I'se blue.

"Crimus, Tree," I pleaded to myself as its touching tenderness
put me under, "It's bad enough without mooning like that."

Rifle shots landing nearby like heavy bees shook me fully
awake and Tree went silent as a hooty owl. Mooning like that was no
way to lick the problem; it was just another temporary escape. Better
we sing *Battle Hymn of the Republic* sad but angry tune, loud as we
could and get furious and angry and mad. I began mumbling uncertainly, off-key: "Mine *eyes* has *seen* the *glory* of the *comin'* of the

Lord," and broke off weakly when I sensed Tree's change of pace, wistfully louder than his usual, from two holes away of the upper class white man's *Whiffenpoff* song, the few introductory words he knew from what little he'd heard me trying to sing.

"From tables down at Duffy's. . . ." large, white eyes staring through the dark fixed in fatigue as he improvised pathetically: "From young squads that were Love, to 'de fresh graves outside Seoul, good men come and go . . . down 'de dark ground of 'de soul."

Tree was right, *Battle Hymn* wouldn't work. It was theatrical and out of pace with our miserably low life.

"I'm sorry I interrupted you, Tree," I apologized silently to myself. "Go ahead, talk to anyone who'll listen."

Later, as it darkened more, gook terror teams behind cover below on the steep Punchbowl side banged C ration cans and yelled taunts in broken English to draw our fire. "GI, you die." My men were restless and Eppler and I crouched, scooting sideways cheeking positions.

It would be hard to prove if any of our three rifle companies should get full credit for taking H 1100 midway up the Punchbowl rim from the south, but Master Sergeant Pater got his Silver Star, as I would later for 1179. One can always tell who was in on the final assault for they have trouble breathing. Pater and his field first sergeant were rubber-legged, gasping desperately for breath, bent over, gagging, close to vomiting on the smallest area of the very top of the objective. We let loose with unbottled tension, wild Indian warwhoops, yelling cheers hoarsely, laughing and choking, and he was yelling when able for his sergeants to get the rest of the men up fast when sergeant Eppler and I arrived out of breath.

While Pater and his men gasped for wind, men of both companies dug in around the top where King's sergeants pointed, taking sporadic plunging fire from 1179; despite which, everyone was deliriously happy. What a pumped-up happy feeling; proud, teeming up there in the tight, proud ball with your guys.

"Christ's sake, dig defense, they'll counterattack within the hour soon's they turn their men around," "dammit, man, get your ma-

236

chine gun facing north and charge one in . . . move!"

Combat noises were partially muffled by the thick air as Mike Company's 81mm mortar men set up their own effort in a small gully behind 1100 to chase back enemy sliding down from 1179 to muster a counterattack, dropping shells into tubes so fast they ran out of all but the few rounds kept for self-defense. The tubes steamed in the slow, cold fog-rain while strong-smelling, thin, bluish smoke from propellent charges and oil burning from the tubes mingled with mist into a heavy swirling haze over the gully in which they planted their heavy base plates.

Mortar observers made sure bursts stayed well ahead as they called out to their gun crews over 300 radios to correct azimuths and ranges of new targets on the trail just north of 1100. "Drop two-zero," they instructed Double-Bubbles, nickname for their gunner. "Right five-zero. Check your bubbles again." After two more adjustments for range. "Okay? FIRE FOR EFFECT! . . . Let them bastards have it! On the way! On the w-a-a-y! On the way!" mortar forward observers yelled to everyone within earshot.

Everyone ducked just in case the rounds were short which I never saw happen with mortars, and listened intently for the air fluting whisper of indropping enemy mortar rounds, much more apparent and threatening at the receiving end.

"You guys and King better be damn much on your toes tonight, we're out of ammo. More on its way, but you know how few a man can carry, only six front and back of in those canvas mortar vests. From the valley a good eight miles at a 30-degree climb. . . . Poor monkeys, most older'n my dad."

Our platoon casualty report reached me through PFC Wheeler from Sergeant Roundtree. "Thompson and DuBonney got it, sir."

Since both were new men, I concentrated on PFC Bob Cartwright from Farmingdale, Long Island, who took a shell splinter in his thigh. Doc Carlson worked on him.

"Get a bone?" I asked. "You bleed bad there."

"Hell," Doc said, "you bleed bad anywhere."

Company runner, PFC Blum, came all excited looking for me. Private Funaro, Private Sizemore and two privates from King were

237

threatening to finish off a gook. Pooped as I was, I went up the trail to a tight group of about ten Johnny-come-latelies gathered around a wounded gook unmindful of the world around him, trying to crawl away, pulling himself over the ground ever so slowly with outstretched fingers, like an old abandoned dog trying to pull himself off a busy highway by his front paws.

"Let the cocksucker have it," bigmouth Funaro ordered.

"Yeah," another intermediate bugout agreed. "Put him out of his misery!"

Yet another, "Finish him off!"

They dared each other like naughty boys.

"Get the fuck out of here, you yellow bastards!" I yelled, firing a burst of my M2 carbine close over them.

It was hard to imagine being that cold-blooded, or even so anti-social. Much later, when I had time, I figured maybe down deep in their beetle brains they were trying to do the guy a favor for he was shot up bad and did die of his own accord before one of our medics got to him. At the time, I hated their guts for not contributing to our banzai and then talking so damn tough to an honorably wounded man when fighting was over. In the real old days an officer could shoot the pol-troons on the spot for skulking—turning their backs on an enemy and threatening a wounded prisoner.

"Get to your squads, punks!" I yelled.

On the subject of cowardice, I used to have an unsanitized copy of General George Patton's speech to the men of his Third Army on the eve of crossing the channel—

". . . And if there are any cowards out there, I hope you get it the first day. We don't want cowards going back to the States breeding more cowards!"

Subconsciously, I've thought since, PFC Funaro and his bud-dies must have pitied that poor gook, maybe felt so deeply the pathetic sight of the courageous dying man striving for safety and they not suf-fering at all by comparison made them angry or they needed to put him out of his misery like any painfully wounded, incurably sick animal;

actually to ease their own conscience because they were helpless to aid them. Or do you suppose they were just hardened, brutal guys like Genghis Khan, who so despised an enemy? I don't know.

The few of King and Love who did the dangerous in-fighting were dehydrated and could do little more than cough and spit sticky saliva. Johnny-come-latelies were busy souvenir hunters, running about searching enemy pockets, poking through dank supply bunkers for loot, shouting impractical threats toward the top of 1179.

"Had your chance," Eppler yelled. "Next time keep up with us."

King Company men, first to overrun the very top and the bunkers, passed around bright red North Korean paper currency and inspected rusted pieces of our own heavy artillery shells and 500 pound aerial bomb shells, jagged hunks of steel several inches thick. Abandoned by the fleeing enemy were twenty or thirty Russian-made carbines with unstained, unvarnished, poorly finished pine wood stocks and, in one supply bunker, open rice straw bags half full of millet and barley crawling with white grubs.

Pop Miller explained to Ski that gooks fattened the grubs to eat rather than the millet which they hated.

"You're kiddin'."

Captain Shallow, arriving cautiously about an hour later, talked the battalion S3, Detweiler, out of Love remaining on the scene; that Item and King could hold without trouble. I didn't give the captain a hard time even though, technically, until Duncan said otherwise, I believed I was still in command. Pater declared it plain crazy "expecting a half-strength company to out-fight burp guns at night." And, indeed, at night one Communist with a burp gun was worth ten GIs confused and fearful of the dark.

"Let me clear with Captain Shallow," I told Pater.

"What's the matter?" Shallow, already halfway back down the finger, stammered in his 536 radio. "Afraid to run his own company?"

"He's in a jam, morale's sinking; they lost *takusan* guys."

"We all got troubles."

"You don't understand, Captain; we shouldn't leave a beatup company like King without a backup."

"Duncan's in charge, not me, and how about Item?"

"I was only asking."

Colonel Duncan *was* in charge and after I radioed him of the situation he made arrangements for Item to set up on the western side of the newly captured hill and for us, Love, to marry with them at the center to the north running east and north where King Company, facing 1179, the greatest threat, closed the tight defense circle.

Lieutenant Rawn, artillery observer attached to Love, came up to register defensive fires, relaying through the artillery liaison officer at battalion CP. From Fire Direction Center he would order a marker round of willie peter safely away from us on a preregistered map coordinate so many range clicks up from existing goose eggs (concentration or circled impact areas drawn on map overlays) and from visible willie peter smoke markers make quick corrections—typically, say, 50 meters north, further out, or 60 south, nearer to us, or left or right, further away or west so many increments. When he had the burst exactly where he knew or thought gooks were or might be later, he radioed back, "Give us that one." Fire Direction Center in the friendly valley five miles to the south radioed back through battalion what number to label the new concentration. Lieutenant Rawn and I, acting company commander on the spot, made ovals on our maps where each concentration landed or should land and wrote the number given to it in the middle. Concentration number 15, for instance, which we never asked for, put fire below and behind us smack on what the Press would label Bloody Ridge.

Not until Love was settling in after the battle, digging new holes facing north, did we learn that Ski was missing again. For some reason, his boss, Pop Miller, had a feeling that this time he was killed, asking members of his squad when they last saw the wanderer.

"Feeling?" I accused. "Where'd *you* last see him?"

"You know Ski."

"Damn right I know Ski. You and your assistant, Tree, were supposed to keep an eye on him."

"Christ, we got our war to fight."

"Too busy? I've known you a long time now, Pop, and you've never been too busy to watch after any of your men, much less Ski.

What's the matter?"

"Lieutenant, he volunteered to help distribute ammo to Item Company. I told him I'd rather he didn't, but he went anyway. I'll bet he decided to get into the fight himself. You know how mad Ski can get seeing just one man hurt. . . . I've had to tell that guy when to shit and how to wipe his ass. He gives me a worse time than everyone put together; expects me to be his father."

"He's also a damn good fighter once you point things out."

"Geezus, Dud, none of us live forever. . . ." He paused and then, choking up a little, "I'm going to miss that kid. God, wasn't he funny, and nobody didn't like him, even if it was pity." Then, glaring at me, he practically shouted, "You accusing me of something?"

"I'm not accusing nobody of nothing, and don't yell at *me*."

"Who you think I am, everybody's old man?" Pop shouted.

"Who *you* yellin' at?" I shouted back.

"*You*, lieutenant, dammit! You should've taken my request to send Ski to the rear, like that kid who was night blind. Ski was every bit as bad off."

We stood toe-to-toe, both of us flushed with dread at losing Ski. A second later, confused and ashamed, we looked away from each other. I doubt if either of us thirty-one-year-olds was aware at the time of Pop calling me Dud. When I did recall it, it made me even closer to Pop. He was one guy, he and Sergeant Eppler, I couldn't get along without. They inspired me to stay alive, like I used to depend on Sergeant Ulriche.

As Pop armed himself at dawn to go look for Ski's remains, the object of the upcoming search came wandering in with two heavy boxes of machine gun ammo, stewing and fretting.

"Fine buddies, where'd you guys get to? One of these days you'll want something from me. Fat chance! I won't give you the sweat off my balls. . . . Fine buddies, sneak off and leave a guy alone."

"You for real?" Pop demanded, feigning anger, wrapping his arms around the big befuddled Pole. "I'll shit you not, Ski, you're too ignorant to get yourself killed."

He pulled Ski tight to himself, causing Ski to lose his footing and Pop held him steady for a minute, as his voice cracked with emotion, blurting, "Goddamn you, you homely bastard, you damn Polock, you! Next time you gotta' shit, let someone else wipe your ass." He reached out and gave Ski a couple slugs on his arm.

Late the next afternoon Captain Shallow called on the 536 from down the saddle ordering me to report. When I arrived, I was told I'd have to spread my men to back up Master Sergeant 'Red' Rose and his Second Platoon in the hottest part of the perimeter.

"Give him a hand, Gould. I don't know about Hurtz anymore. I'm thinking of taking a little rest myself back in the kitchen trains or maybe R&R and I need someone I can trust. I'll see you get a Commendation Ribbon and maybe another Bronze Star Meritorious."

Green hornet? I thought, commendation ribbons are for rear echelons, and who wants another Bronze Star? Colored ribbons mean so much to careerists like the captain.

"And if you write it up for Sergeant Dorn again, Bronze Star for Valor, and Soldier's Medal for Kiezlowski, I'll sign them this time and push them through, only you got to know your Sergeant Dorn's dead as a doornail. He's MIA and can't qualify for posthumous for a year. By the way, would you mind taking some ammo up to King Company?"

"Captain, we were the last to do that yesterday afternoon to Item and even took it around to the positions, which is more than others do. You know it's someone else's turn."

"Yes, that's the point. It's Hurtz's turn and I don't know about him anymore."

"What do you mean?"

"He's been acting strange."

"Strange?"

"Various things. Made an ass of himself yesterday with those bodies, risking snipers, going around pulling their fatigue tops over their faces, bothered the hell out of me to get up a burial detail. You know we haven't authority to make even a temporary burial and with short rations and everything, the guys are too pooped to do extra digging. Besides, it's all rocks up there and I can't have people moving around the ridge attracting fire."

242

"What's wrong with Lieutenant Hurtz?"

Captain Shallow laughed uncomfortably. "I never knew Hebs were so religious; said we were sinning, leaving dead unburied. Sergeant Luther stopped him from ordering chogee bearers to haul bodies down. He knows them King carriers don't take orders from us and are due back fast as they can to grab a wink and bring up more critical supplies. Hurtz knows well as any one how used up they are. I can't put my finger on the trouble, but he acts like he's nursing a yellow streak." He stopped abruptly to correct himself. "I mean, he's getting timid and too concerned about guys getting hurt. . . . I can't do everything. I need officers I can trust."

"He's got a number one sergeant in Rose."

"Would you mind awfully taking up ammo again?"

"Don't ask me to volunteer for my men, sir."

"Then I guess it's an order, if you don't mind," he laughed nervously and went on angrily. "It's not our responsibility anyway. Jesus H Christ, I tried my best to talk Mighty Mouse out of it but battalion is way short of carriers. And we're not supposed to expose them like that. Well, I guess you better get at it."

I thought Major Duncan must have reinstated Shallow without relieving me and planned to give him a hunk of my mind next time I talked with him. Or was I good only for combat?

Sergeant Rose himself was worried that something was very wrong. "I got a damn good officer there," he told me. "Wasn't a cooler guy in the Army back there in January on 755 at Hoengsong and everyone freezing their asses off. Lately, however, I think Lieutenant Hurtz has had the course. Simply had enough. Jesus, can't any of us just have our fill all the time and not too much? Couldn't we be relieved sooner?"

Lieutenant Hurtz went about with a bewildered expression. One of the few who reckoned time with any accuracy, he made a point to remind the men when Sabbath came, only it was Jewish Sabbath, Saturday. Even more religious guys never called Sunday Sabbath, that was old fashioned like the Bible.

"Today's Sabbath," he told them enthusiastically. "Let's clean up around here."

The men smiled secretly, looking nervously at one another.

"Our Heavenly Father," I stumbled over the words and broke off to begin anew. "Please, dear Lord, protect us." Man, that Ski thing opened me up. My eyes moistened and I blew my nose hard. Why I said, 'Our Heavenly Father,' I didn't know myself. Hell, I'm not religious.

Later, while visiting Pater on the enemy side of 1100, I overheard a heated argument. Men of King grumbling that a lieutenant of Love Company held up their fire to allow a squad of gooks to escape.

"He's bugs!" one exclaimed. "Instead of shooting, stood right in our line of fire, hands in air, yelling us down."

"Gave me willies," another said.

"Christ!" a squad leader remarked angrily. "Aside from letting those bastards go, somebody could've clipped him."

"What was he yelling?" I asked.

The sergeant and the riflemen hesitated.

"Well?" I insisted, "what was it?"

"I might've heard wrong, sir, it sounded like 'forgive them,' some screwy thing like that and 'put down your guns.'" He laughed uneasily.

"Yeah," the squad leader agreed. "I heard him plain as day. 'Forgive them, Lord.' He's plain ordinarily had it."

When there was a lot of firing on the ridge, Captain Shallow stayed in his cave, hole, bunker or anywhere he could seat his ass and lower his profile at the moment it began, rousing himself only when it quieted down, or when a carrying party arrived with mail and news and other supplies from the forward ammo supply point behind the MLR.

When Colonel Duncan arrived at my platoon on an inspection, he asked if there was anything we needed and I told him bluntly we needed food. We were down to two twelve-ounce cans of C rations a day and on heavily rainy days the trail was unusable for the little men in sneakers with heavy loads. Although Army field rations were supposed to contain extra calories and vitamins, judging from awareness of our weakness, it wasn't enough. I told him the dead lying around were a bad morale problem, not only a few guys we used to know, but gooks and ROK Marines from earlier days felled by artillery and Air

244

who, in some cases one had to breathe, others turned halfway to skeletons with blades of grass grown through their rotting fatigues.

"We're well aware of that, lieutenant. We were confident that if anyone told us the truth, it would be you," he said smiling. The colonel continued to explain as curious sergeants gathered around, that so many things were popping all over the Corps area—Marines on line pushing across Death Valley, Saber Ridge starting up, along with Bloody Ridge and the Second Battalion, all to put pressure on the so-called peace talks—so busy hauling men and ammo and water, supply trucks for soft stuff like food were in short supply.

"How about commo, reconnaissance, P&A and your shotgun guard; how many Cs they getting?" I suggested to the colonel's obvious displeasure.

"Lieutenant," he sounded off sharply, "I appreciate your concern for your men, but suppose you leave headquarters for me to run." He paused then, mulling over just what he was going to say. "That so-called shotgun guard went to the companies two days after I took over and don't think for a minute I'm Major Wilkes."

"No, sir, I'll give you that. He was somewhat bigger."

"Lieutenant!" he barked.

"Yes, sir."

"I apologize for not telling you were relieved of command of Love, but I told you how damn busy we've been."

Miles to the rear, Colonel Mildren reflected on the situation of his beleaguered blue battalion—being mildly reprimanded by the new X Corp commander, Lieutenant General Clovis E. Byers, going over division commander Major General Young's head asking for relief. Our foreign battalion, the Dutch, had left for Pusan to rotate and exchange time-expired men. Another Second Division Regiment, the 23d, was heavily committed on the right flank in the open Punchbowl and it was rumored that a massive Chinese buildup and movement was crossing in our direction over the North Korean front.

"They [meaning us] must maintain positions at all costs," Fearless Frank told Mighty Mouse Duncan. "While essentially a holding force, bad off as they are the NKs are not only hurting for food and ammunition, POWs and dead are found with empty pockets, whereas they were in the habit of carrying rice balls, cooked rice patted into softball-size lumps wrapped tightly in seaweed.

"Two gook divisions facing the 38th were cannibalized to fill one on line. Intelligence tells us that gook soldiers, who hate millet, are down to half a pound per man per day and, as always, no medical attention forward of division."

As early as his May 30 inspection of forces in Korea, Ridgway cabled the Joint Chiefs of Staff from his headquarters in Tokyo of an unusually large bag of POWs and a large stock of abandoned enemy weapons. All three corps commanders reported a noticeable deterioration in the fighting spirit of CCF. In many cases their units were so desperately short of rations the men had to eat grass and roots and the withdrawing CCF abandoned ammo dumps, mortars, machine guns, burp guns and rifles, indicating that disorganization existed among both CCF and NKPA forces.

"The results are already being felt at Kaesong but to complete the pressure we have to take H 1179 and the most important objective, H 1243 at the north end of the Punchbowl. 1179 may be indefensible afterward, too difficult to supply, but we must show Nam Il and Kim Il Sung, political officer and dictator, supreme CO of the North Korean People's Army, we're capable."

Just as negotiations seemed to be pacifying Kim Il Sung, a misguided plane of the Third Bomber Wing on 10 September 1951 bombed a North Korean camp at Kaesong. Ridgway was compelled to apologize. The error did, however, succeed in getting the enemy to move to a more neutral position, Panmunjom on the border, a tiny unoccupied hamlet just over the 38th parallel of four abandoned huts with mud walls and thatched rice straw roofs, which area the United Nations preferred. Its name translates 'Shop Within the Wooden Gates.' Not shown on the most detailed maps, it was the most neutral spot in Korea, six miles south of the communist-occupied Kaesong.

Three days after we got 1100, I happened to be at Captain Shallow's new fortress when Colonel Duncan called. The captain huddled in a corner of his cave, staring at the section on his mapboard featuring 1179.

"Captain, Lieutenant Colonel Duncan calling, sir," Tony

Zurlo, Shallow's radioman said, extending the receiver toward him. Captain Shallow remained in an apparent trance, staring at the map.

"Captain Shallow!" First Sergeant Luther said loudly, "Captain Shallow, the colonel wants you."

Finally Captain Shallow reached for the receiver and pulled it into a corner, facing away from us and the cave opening. He answered in a low voice and when ordered to speak up, began to stutter.

"But, but, sir, that's impossible . . . ask Lieutenant Morris . . . Yes. . . . Yes, sir, I mean . . . I know, but, but, sir we can't. . . . But, but, but, sir, there's more than a division up there. . . . I know, sir, but, but, please, sir, we'll all be killed. . . . Maybe in a couple days with reinforcements. . . . It's 1630, do you roger? . . . What? . . . Oh, no, sir, what I mean is there isn't time anymore today . . . . Maybe we could get the Air Force to work it over with bombs a couple more days. . . . But, sir, I. . . ."

Shallow turned, holding his hand over the mouthpiece and smiled sickeningly into the air. Then, turning his wrist, he studied his watch.

"Yes, sir! Sir? . . . But, sir, they won't go for me. No, sir! I mean, yes I will, sir!. . . What? . . . Yes, *sir*! . . . No, sir, I didn't say I refuse, sir, its just that I. . . . I just can't make them go for me, sir. . . . They've had too long to think it over. Yes, sir! . . . Alright, sir. . . . Yes sir, Gould's right here. . . . Here, Gould, he wants you."

"Lieutenant Gould, you're it now. I'm, placing you in command of Love with Item in support for the assault on 1179. Hear me?"

"I hear, Colonel."

"Well, okay, Gould, say something. Give me your ideas on how you'll do it. Might have time to get a little air-ground support."

"We don't want Air now, sir, too much time lag. We can make it tomorrow . . . bombers today. We'll work better with artillery. But, sir, tell them to lift it when I say to and I'd like to have eight-incher on concentration 11 until we're fifty feet from the very top." I paused to catch my breath. "If it's all right with you, Colonel, I'd like to work two platoons forward and one not less than 100 yards in support followed closely by Item Company. I'll have our observer, Lieutenant Rawn, take charge of supporting overhead fire. Sir, I never studied

247

planning. Don't see what's to plan, looks like a clean, nasty, one-way shot, sir. Any ideas on that, sir?"

"You can estimate the situation better where you are, Gould, but I should think it would be better to try to flank them if at all possible. I'll call back to confirm your attack plans. Put Shallow on."

Listening for a moment, the captain's face turned blank. "I'm sorry, sir," he said in a low voice. "I'll have to take my chances. Here, Dud, he wants you again."

"I've informed Shallow he's under arrest for refusing to go," Duncan said in disgust. "I want you to take his pistol and see he gets back here soon as possible. Over and out."

Shallow busied himself cleaning his glasses with a dirty handkerchief, holding the lenses to the sky examining them and then covered his eyes and sobbed softly.

"Sorry, Captain Shallow, sir," I apologized, "I have to take your pistol."

"But, Dud, might be infiltrators along the trail."

"I can't help it, sir, orders. If you want, you can wait for the next chogee train with guards. Sorry, Captain, I'll have to take your forty-five."

"I know you don't think much of me, lieutenant," Captain Shallow said, drying his eyes and becoming suddenly as if he was in full control, unhooking his pistol belt, removing a canteen and handing the belt with forty-five and holster over to me, "I'll be alive."

"In what prison?"

"It won't be so awful bad; one way or another, I'll be alive and soon it'll all be over for all of us. How about Captain Toth, what did he get? A dirty job at regiment, at least he's alive."

"And maybe Sergeant Pater won't be for long."

The captain had the bad habit when excited of holding on to his subordinate's sleeve. I used to think I had to put up with it, but now I yanked it away abruptly.

"Dud, I'm giving you a good efficiency. I'm not going to stay in the Army after this is over. I wouldn't stay in the Army now if they got down on their knees and begged. Maybe they should beg me anyway after all I've done for them. They should write me up for at least the Legion of Merit after what I've done. I have a commendation ribbon from my last job in civilian clothes.

"I think I'm losing Shirley. You think Shirley will get a divorce without letting me know? Gould, think her father would let her do that? Why else would she stop writing and go back to Boston with him? . . . I'd resign my commission right here and now but they need good supply experts and maybe won't let me resign. I know too much; never should have been here in the first place, what with my two clearances. You have no idea how I worry about us up there. . . . no idea what it's like commanding a company in combat."

"Sorry, Captain," preparing to tell him I'm *Lieutenant* Gould should he use just my last name again, and I'd never heard of Shirley.

I was excited as hell. I'd probably never make captain out of it, and didn't really want to anyway, anymore than I ever wanted a commission. With the acute company grade officer shortage in the 38th, I could understand why me. Shit, they wouldn't think of it otherwise. Still, I was excited; I was going to lead an infantry company, in the assault. Maybe I'd get stuck with it longer; look at Sergeant Pater, in charge for a couple weeks now, and him with two second lieutenants, one of whom was acting exec, while the other was about to get a promotion. Sergeant Pater led his men up 1100 all right and he, like me, no college graduate, we didn't know diddly-dick about supply, running a messhall, administration or military justice. We learned to hand out military justice—to the gooks. We didn't study banzaiing, it's obvious; we just did it our way. I was fortunate to have Roy Carse to take care of the rear, as he did with Shallow, and Duncan promised me I'd soon be relieved by a Regular Army captain.

Peace talks remained in hopeless impasse. Our small, worried, worn end of the Army, unleashed temporarily by the United Nations Command through corps, division and regiment prodded Lieutenant Colonel Duncan and he, in turn, let it be known to Item and Love Companies that we, me in charge, must get together on an attack against the main defenses of 1179, Fools Mountain, Taeusan, or whatever. Here we are; miseries, here we come!

I tried to think what a company commander was supposed to do preparing to lead a major assault on one of the best defended positions on the eastern edge of the Hays Line. First, I had to take over the company. Master Sergeant First Sergeant Luther had gone to the rear to rotate and field first sergeant, newly-made Master Sergeant Ray Martin was now first sergeant in charge of headquarters forward in lieu of an officer. Ray Carse technically commanded the rear CP, appointed to that position. I turned the platoon over to Hanson and took Sergeant Eppler with me as a sort of unofficial enlisted aide de camp. At the company CP, Tony Zurlo raised Captain Arthur Detweiler, battalion S3 operations officer, for me, well back down the ridge at battalion forward.

"Buzzard One Three. Buzzard One Three. Buzzard One Three, come in. This is Buzzard Seven."

I took the mouthpiece and announced myself: "Lieutenant Gould; I'm sending a written battle order for our attack tomorrow. Be on a C ration box, got no paper."

No sooner had I released the butterfly switch than Captain Detweiler radioed angrily, "Buzzard Seven leader, don't transmit in the clear. I repeat, do not send messages in the clear. If there are serious questions, Buzzard One says to report in person ASAP [as soon as possible]."

Tony Zurlo expressed amazement at my ignorance of such matters. Evidently I had a lot to learn about communications and procedures.

"Buzzard Seven," he said, "first you jeopardized yourself by giving your name in the clear. They have captured equipment that allows them to sweep all channels until they identify units facing them so they can listen in. Now they know that Buzzard Seven, leader of Love of the Third Battalion, 38th Infantry, Second Infantry Division is commanded by a Lieutenant Gould rather than an anonymous Buzzard Seven. What they'll do with it, I don't know. Worst of all, you gave away our biggest secret, we're going to attack tomorrow."

Later, face-to-face, Colonel Duncan expressed his disappointment with my lack of communications discipline and marveled at how I got commissioned until I told him that I wasn't even a Ninety-day Wonder; I got my gold bars after sixty days of madness, a special

250

rough and tough combat indoctrination course in Napoleon's old Artillery School at Fontainbleau in the Barbizon Forest, France. All emphasis was on the purely physical aspect of leading a rifle platoon, and testing to see that we candidates could take it, such cute tricks as blowing the whistle at three in the morning after a day of strenuous physical training, making up our cots so tightly a centime could be bounced six inches from a two-foot drop; making one's pack immaculate, subject to close inspection and within five minutes out into formation, marching. March in pitch blackness a mile in cold rain to a swamp, halt, sidestep left and right off the road and sit, pack and all, in fifteen inches of cold water holding carbines over our heads until four more guys complained and were returned to their units. One officer marveled openly that I, an Army Air Force, could take it so well.

"Buzzard One," I radioed, "when you told me over the radio I was to take over and what support we could get, were we using a scrambler?"

There was a long pause and Duncan said, "Dammit, you're right, that was in the clear, wasn't it? Sometimes one gets so wrapped up with what he's doing he forgets proper procedure."

When it came to tactics, the colonel agreed with me there wasn't any choice for there was no room to flank but to go straight up to hit fortifications head on on top up a long finger with dropoffs on either side. All we could do was stick to the old SOP, standard operating procedure, plaster the objective with artillery and Air and work right under it with accurate heavy machine guns and 105 and 155 HE ahead of us as we banzaied. Like a football game, you planned on what major maneuver to make and take alternatives as indicated, and made them on the run fast as possible. Like no game, however, it's all up steep hills, moving individually over the terrain, maneuvering from cover to cover with a heavy load of ammo.

Should your yelling lessen or stop and you lose momentum in upward movement, get permission to get the hell off that hill. Attacking in Korea was always up a steep incline loaded with combat gear, hot, thirsty, sticky mouth, sucked dry even, packing two canteens. Oh for an attack on the level, but that's tank country where they get to ride to their death.

251

Very important, as Sergeant Eppler and I discovered by ourselves, yell like demons, get it going loud from man to man to build a momentum of high spirits to motivate your men and yourself and overawe the enemy. Old-fashion battle cries, man! Eppler and I didn't discover it, we uncovered it. Hell, lions come on snarling and roaring, as did savages all over the world. Shout your lungs out! Battle cry; just what words no manual recommends. In fact, no manual in the American Army says a thing about charging a hill; at least not when I was in uniform. Probably because no real infantry combat veteran was ever in charge of training. It was left to rear echelon generals with their phoney, unearned combat infantrymen's badges, Purple Hearts and DSCs.

Maybe as a result of my booboo over the radio, we were hit by three widely spaced probes that night as I tried to sleep in a hole outside the command post Captain Shallow had built in a cave; as far as I was concerned, a trap. If I got overrun again, I wanted to be able to get up and go, not pinned down from the start.

Twice after I dozed off, PFC Sidney Blum, company runner, woke me.

"Lieutenant, you awake? There's something out in the Punchbowl. Something going on in that big valley."

From our lofty perch we sat in the dark watching the surrealistic firefights of a tank infantry team outpost of the hotly engaged 23d dug in the center of the Punchbowl. Many minutes after watching long lines of slowly moving machine gun tracers lobed gracefully through the air, we heard the reports, individual shots mingling into a continuous gentle eruption many minutes later. Putputputputputputputput, a small motorboat far away; maybe thirty miles as the crow flies.

When Blum awakened me the first time, I thought he must have something, then, seeing what a stupid thing it was, I snapped irritably, "Crimus, I told you a thousand times, that's our tanks down there clobbering gooks. Now listen carefully, you woke me enough for one night; between gook banzais and you, I'm not sleeping at all. We've got a busy day tomorrow."

Blum was paying no attention. "They say some poor guy from King was taken prisoner tonight. Could hear him yelling."

252

"I heard him, now shut up and let me sleep."

I was a bit worried at being a company commander with so little military background as far as combat was concerned. I was a veteran who paid enough attention to be a West Pointer, so I was grateful for being handed such a prize, as if I passed an important test that seemed easy and natural for me. Now I'll have to show them.

I raised Lieutenant Hurtz on the EE-8 and the Weapon's Platoon sergeant and told them I was in charge and I couldn't say what over the phone but get ready for something big. I asked Hurtz if he was okay and he said "affirmative, he'd be with me soon." I called the sergeant platoon leaders and told them what little I could. After all, what was there to know? Later I found that everyone knew anyway.

Even before leaving the valley our target had been obvious; only a matter of time and who would be the unlucky guys to try it? Certainly there was no flanking available, straight up about four hundred meters, to the ridgeline and a left turn over a saddle and straight up to it. Our only shield would be artillery rounds, machine gun bullets going into the apertures of their bunkers and recoilless rifles keeping them from leaning over their ramparts aiming directly at us and, of course, what firepower we carried with us, rifles, automatic carbines, BARs and one light 30 caliber machine gun per platoon.

Fortunately, division called off the attack, postponing it a day; most probably because of my blabbing our attack time over the open radio. Sorry, I told myself, but we can use a better workover with several flights of fighter-bombers, and maneuver several batteries of my favorite, eight-inchers, for a few minutes from direct support of the Marines. Even with such additional support, I heard odds at division were ten-to-one we'd fail.

7
Fools Mountain

Fools Mountain, the smart ass American press called H 1179, never nearer to an angry shot than thirty miles, shepherded by rear-echelon division information officers and other starched fatigues who explained grease-pencil marks on a huge plastic overlay in the G-3 operation tent War Room. Commenting knowingly—noncombat rear-echelon officers talking to protected civilians authoritatively—for transmission to State-side customers about us getting rubbed into it.

Fools Mountain they labeled it from afar. Those dogfaces are fools, they opined, dying for ground returnable in upcoming peace talks. Fools themselves! The talks were used by our enemy to tie up our tactics in protecting painfully paid-for advantages. Talks began in the first place only because nobodies with scruffy beards and muddy faces were simple, brave, trusting of one another and obedient enough to be on the top of Hill 1100 looking down a long tank-country valley straight to the commie seaport of Wonson.

Gooks called this 2878-foot roost Taeusan, Gateway to the Orient, overseeing vast valleys from three sides. Before we took it away from their bravest, it was ordered held at all cost. Our good soldiers, last name, first name, serial numbers, blood type, year of tetanus shot, and first letter of their religion stamped in stainless steel tags held on chains around their necks, paid their share of the high price so fat, bald-headed old men in Congress and the United Nations could prevail in their petty piques against other peevish bastards.

We took H 1179, Fools Mountain, a week ahead of X Corps schedule, before the leadership failures of our sister regiments, the 9th and the 23d Infantry and its attached battalion of French Foreign Legionnaires dribbled platoons up their objectives one at a time with no backup—on what the press named Bloody Ridge. Their artillery forward observers had climbed to our position on 1179 to mark targets southward on their maps, lower and behind us.

As always in war, efficiency attracts no media. Our casualties were not overly tragic nor exotic enough to interest the jaded press; not extraordinary even to us considering the importance of the objective, although steady and painful. So much for reporters' views of our misery, Fools Mountain, by itself the deaths of soldiers fighting to take it are of no importance, even expected, prepaid by your taxes. Technically, you paid us to die.

Captain Shallow placed Fred Hurtz on the northern, hottest spot of the perimeter of 1100 where a lone sniper wounded one of his men and was terrorizing the rest, shooting the entrenching tool out of the hands of one man tossing spoil from his hole. When I called Fred over the EE-8, there was no answer and when I couldn't get him on the 536 radio either, I sent Blum to see what the trouble was. Soon thereafter company First Sergeant Ray Martin came down the trail.

"Think I know where the sniper is," he told me.

I followed Martin up the trail to within firing distance and followed his finger down to a solitary mountain pine. There was no movement but I planned on dropping a WP grenade over the most likely spot. Kneeling, I placed the butt of my carbine on the ground with a grenade can held by a spring in the grenade adapter, lined up my carbine, estimated elevation for distance, and fired it off. To my dismay it repeated the disastrous grenade the day I was wounded, hitting a sapling down the trail to bounce in front of PFC Blum returning from hunting for Lieutenant Hurtz.

"Oh Geezus," I thought. "You've killed one of your own."

The thing did explode on line with Blum but, fortunately, far enough in front to no more than scare the shit out of us both. As the puff of stark white smoke of burning white phosphorus was cleared by a breeze, Blum, eyes wipe open, stunned by the unexpected threat, was running toward us off the trail to avoid the burning phosphorus, pawing himself all over for a wound.

"Medic! Medic!" he cried unnecessarily since E-5 Doc Lopez

was already in plain sight running toward him. "I'm hit. Doc, I'm hit."
He came to us running, holding up an inch-wide hole in his sleeve that, with frayed, bleached threads, obviously had been laundered more than once. Although he tried his damnedest to be evacuated, I'll give it to Blum, he stuck it out to his end.

Giving him a good look over, Doc said scornfully, "C'mon, Blum, quit acting. You aren't hit any."

I went back working the company's SCR 300 trying to catch the French Battalion, a bunch of chattering women off air line, the second they ceased hogging our wavelength. The French, given our working channel for the day, had evidently not been taught radio discipline. I had a list of things, particularly machine gun ammo and water, which we would badly need to get and keep 1179. My French was very poor, a year in high school, but it seemed plain in the pace of their blabbing I'd catch the word *mange*, which I recalled was food or eat.

Sitting on my left talking across me to our company medic, Blum moaned how a terrible headache was going to kill him. Nervous little city boy from the Bronx, PFC Blum was blown to pieces like any brave soldier the following day in a 120mm barrage in the saddle before 1179. Later, Sergeant Eppler and I wrote him up for a posthumous Bronze with V for valor for his folks' sake. Like no damn rear echelon ever could, we appreciated what an extra hell Blum suffered being scared practically all the time with no confidence in his own ability. To have resisted the urge to flee was courageous in itself. Compare him with bugouts Captains Toth and Shallow.

Later, I discovered that the reason I hadn't heard from Fred or his platoon guide Collins was that as the sergeant awakened Fred and drew him close to peer over the rim within their CP foxhole, his face lined up almost touching Fred's, pointing out where he'd seen the sniper, Collins was zapped in the forehead by the sniper's bullet, blood and brains exploding over Fred's face and neck, the sergeant's head slumped on Fred's shoulder. Shit, it can't get worse than that!

Meanwhile, knowing nothing of this, I sent another runner to find Red Rose and have him report but in a little while, Fred Hurtz himself came sliding down to where Blum and I were sitting on the friendly Punchbowl side off the trail. He pulled up unusually close and sat down. Concentrating on slipping in a call to battalion on my 300, I gave him a brief, impersonal 'hi.' Hurtz said nothing that I recall but made a faint baby-like whimper, a pathetic appeal, I thought later. I was too occupied trying to cut off the French to learn what everyone else seemed to know, the lieutenant was in serious trouble.

I began to sense Fred's presence uncomfortably and looking sideways saw him staring into space, sniffling, a strange, hurt look on his face.

"Shit!" he mumbled, "shit." I stifled a nervous laugh; Blum and Doc stared at him in disbelief and snickered. Lieutenant Hurtz wouldn't say shit if he had a mouthful.

"Look Beth, shit," Hurtz went on, almost inaudibly, picking up a handful of loose earth and opening his fist to let it sift through his fingers to the ground, like a good farmer inspecting soil. Crimus, I thought, Fred would be the last to talk crazy like that.

Blum stared incredulously at Lieutenant Hurtz and watched Lopez out of the corner of his eye, obviously working up nerve to say something. Very shortly he addressed Doc loudly enough that I would be sure to hear, "Doc, got any APCs, a thermometer or something?"

"Thermometer?" I asked. "What you want with a thermometer?"

"Oh, sir," Blum whined. "My head aches. I got an awful feelin' I'm sick. I tell you, I think I'm coming down with something."

His whining and complaining continued until I raised my voice, "We're all coming down with something. Have your damn headache *after* we take 1179."

Lopez and Eppler snickered.

There was something pretty wrong with Fred. Instinctively, although I had the reputation for being hard ass, a quick flash of Kitty protecting me that night in May swept over me and I reached my arm around Fred's shoulder and hugged him to me, telling him, "Buddy, don't worry, everything's all right." This was the worst I could have done for instead of soothing him it was like bursting a boil; he put his head in his hands on his knees and bawled like a baby, convulsively, desperately, shaking, sobbing loudly, trying to catch his breath as though he'd gotten rid of everything, even his breath. I didn't know what to do. Doc did; he started writing a tag.

"Crimus, Fred," I said gently as Lieutenant Hurtz continued to shake, sob and gasp for breath. "You've got it bad, man. Hit the trail."

Controlling deep sobs, gulping, Fred shook his head violently back and forth, at the same time incongruously making crude attempts to clean his fingernails as though nothing was wrong and he was only sitting there passing time. Seems his mind was in two places at once. I was beginning to get mad at what was wrong with him.

"C'mon, now," I said coldly, inching away from him. "Quit feeling sorry for yourself."

"No!" Lieutenant Hurtz shouted petulantly, closing a nostril with a finger and blowing loose, watery mucus from his other nostril on to the back of a hand, wiping it on his pants and motioned me to move further away.

"Honestly, Dud, I'm all right. Let me rest a while; I'll get hold of myself."

His bloodshot eyes were so steady then and he spoke so calmly, so matter of factly, I was ready to agree. I wanted to; I couldn't understand what was going on with Fred. Maybe he'd be all right after a little rest. No one was exactly normal anymore.

With a vacant stare, Fred began again to brush at the dirt by his side, pushing it into small piles away from himself and again addressed a specter, "You see, Beth, shit!", looking knowingly about the dirt, poking certain loose clumps with his fingernail file. "Nothing all over but shit! Shit! Shit!" He snickered uneasily. "But you know it's ordinary shit." His forced artificial laugh grew louder. "Scout's honor, it's plain, ordinary shit."

It was somewhat funny, a veteran platoon leader acting that silly. I was on the verge of laughing again. Blum chuckled uncomfortably to himself, laughing low from embarrassment with no enjoyment. Fred stopped and stared slyly at him, then spoke loudly facing him, but addressing an unseen audience. "You should be ashamed. You aren't so darn smart either, or you could tell it's shit."

"Get hold of yourself," I ordered. I'd never heard tell of anything like it. "Doc's writing you a tag to get out of here."

"But, Beth, I can't," Fred mumbled in a monotone, studying

Doc. "I can't, honey." He whimpered again, turning to face me and implore: "I can't leave my boys up here alone tonight."

"Fred," I shouted, standing up. "Let Doc tag you. I'm not fussin' any more. Get hold of yourself and that's an order."

Lieutenant Hurtz, momentarily hurt by my sudden anger, sat silent for a second, slyly studying my face. I was tired and irritable, dirty face under whiskers as were all of us. Fred must have seen that I meant it. All of us were weary. Nobody really let loose last night and slept, tight as we were, knowing what an impossible task we faced,

"C'mon, now," I told him, trying to sound normal and pleasant. "Let's chogee out of here."

His face was calm. "I can't. I can't. Dud, I can't leave my boys alone up here tonight."

Boys? Crimus, what're you, all of twenty-four?

A chogee train came around a bend on the friendly side of the mountain trail, loaded with bandoleers, 60mm mortar ammo, radio batteries, and mail but no water. We'd been having trouble with batteries with short lives made in Japan. Those under sixty today have no idea how junky everything manufactured in Japan was before and after World War II and up until the 1960s.

"Letter from Catherine," the guard said, anticipating my interest, reading the return address before handing it over. "She your daughter? Say, lieutenant, when you see Ski, he's made corporal."

Corporal? For a minute I'd forgot why, although he was a little smarter than Woody, our mailman, I thought, that's the furthest from my mind right now. Somehow I never got to open that letter and in the ensuing confusion and material madness of Fools Mountain, lost it.

In my several months in Korea and in all WorldWar II, I never heard of a guy cracking up like this. I mean in his own world of make believe, going back and forth with phony names even, like Beth. I'd never heard him mention that name. First he'd be nuts, then tired and acting almost normal. I guess it's to each his own, the way we flip. I wondered how, if it happened to me, perish the thought, I'd act and talk. I felt bad losing my buddy like that, although it beat dying.

Sergeant Eppler and I soaked up what gossip was to be had from the chogee guard; what was going on in the trains. "Lieutenant what's his name was killed the other day."

"Infiltrators? Long-range H and I? No, they don't have any-thing would reach that far south. Step on a mine? No. Well, how? Who did you say he was? Rear echelon, battalion headquarters? Motor pool?" He repeated names of headquarters officers until he came to Werner. "Von something or other Werner. Lieutenant Werner, that new officer. Right?"

"Yeah, that's him. Lieutenant Werner. Motor pool jeep went off a bank and busted his neck like a carrot stick," the chogee guard said, snapping his fingers.

"$50 fine for officers driving jeeps in the division anyway un-less on special assignment as I was."

"He wasn't driving; got thrown. His driver didn't get a scratch. Them jeeps aren't made for over forty and sharp turns—they're top heavy."

Borrowing the filled out evacuation tag and the stub of Doc's pencil, I turned it over and jotted down a list of what we badly needed—grenades, BAR ammo, machine gun ammo, C rations and water, more water. I underlined machine gun and water and scribbled 'very urgent' in large letters. Must have machine gun ammo and water!

"Fred," I said, "if we don't get this stuff, it's curtains. Under-stand? I'm sending you because we have to have a good officer on it." As I talked, I stood up and pressed the tag into Fred's limp hand, giv-ing him a friendly slap on the shoulder.

Fred, eyes glazing over, absently-mindedly dropped the tag and I picked it up and as he watched me closely like a curious little boy, I tied it around a button on his upper fatigue jacket pocket.

"See that the lieutenant gets this back okay," I said, winking at the chogee guard behind Fred's back, indicating the evacuation tag tied to him. "The lieutenant has a list," I went on in a theatrical voice. "See it stays on; he's got to get it back, understand? Make sure he gets back with that *list*."

Holding the palms of his grimy hands over his eyes, Fred stood up slowly behind the guard. He'd done his mortal best and now had to admit he was through. He couldn't be forced any more to go on killing men week after week, so conflicting was it with his religious upbring-

260

ing; his own men he was responsible for, buddies he'd lived among so long. Sobbing softly, Fred mumbled, shaking his head slowly, "Terrible, terrible," and followed the chogee guard back down the ridge like a programed zombie. Fred was gone, really gone.

C Company, in a diversionary attack up a finger down to the left of 1179, encountered unexpectedly savage resistance and was forced to withdraw. The following morning, according to our official history Blue Book, Love, my company, backed by Item in position behind, set out in the attack—

The first day's action sketched the picture of the enemy defenses. He was determined to stay on 1179 at all costs. His elaborate preparations, plentiful supply of ammunition and determined resistance in face of terrific concentrations from all the supporting fire weapons, including nine battalions of artillery, indicated the fight for Taeusan would be more difficult than first anticipated.

The night before, the skies were kept a flaming red as the artillery fire was intensified. Dust from the roads swirled hundreds of feet into the air as trucks rolled around the clock to provide ammunition for the barrage.

At first correspondents gave it the name Five-million Dollar Hill, after someone supposedly figured out the cost of artillery and Air laid on the preparations for four different artillery battalions one after another. It was estimated that more than 115 tons of bombs had supported the attacks on Taeusan. A total of 74,823 rounds of artillery had been hurled onto the hill and added to that were 49,000 mortar rounds fired in the assaults.

The 38th spent the morning and early afternoon of 28 July in preparation for an attack on 1179. Murderous artillery concentrations were laid on the slopes and at 0600 hours 29 July L and I Companies struck out in face of enemy cross fire. The assault was carried out with such vigor that the crest was reached and Hill 1179 was in the possession of the Second Division by evening. The enemy fortress fell after some of the most intense offensive fighting the Division had undergone in months. The

261

fanatic defenders had to be dug out of their deep entrenchments and it was a slow, bloody, body-tiring job. The enemy was pushed off suffering more than 2000 casualties with the annihilation of one complete regiment and the crushing of another. The decimated North Korean 27th Tiger Division withdrew its thin ranks in disorder after the onslaught of the Second Division.

In a terse military manner that follows, our work in the field was described in the S3 and G3 operations sections of regimental and division staffs for record and historical purposes. As this stylized division operations report indicates, Love Company of the 38th Infantry shoved off in the morning of 29 July 1951, Korean time. Not written, what I would like made a matter of record, was that the brave (maybe stupid) asshole, First Lieutenant Dudley C. Gould, laborer, college dropout, amateur soldier, was acting commander of the whole shebang—

Period 29 0001K Jul to 29 2400K Jul. L Co relieved K CO at 29 0100K Jul and I Co relieved C Co. One platoon of I Co occupied location DT 204363 at 29 0600K Jul to secure trail junction. I Co placed one plt in vic DT 193346 to observe left flank Third Bn moved to DT 204381 arriving at 29 0500K Jul. From the position at 29 0600K Jul at 0800K the battalion launched an attack to secure hill 1179. Enemy was immediately contacted. L Co was lead Co. At 29 1630K Jul L Co and the Bn secured Hill 1179. Enemy broke contact at 29 1850K Jul.

As soon as Fred departed with the chogee train, I got busy with the upcoming attack for the following morning at 0600 and called SFC Sigmund Zigerfoose on the EE-8. Ranking Speedy Gonzales, he became leader of the first squad after J C died and made sergeant first class. Master Sergeant Robert Red Rose, ER enlisted reserve, led the Second Platoon, and Master Sergeant Karl Eppler, another recalled Reserve, was then in the position of acting platoon leader of the Banzai Third but was physically with me as an aide. Ziggy would lead the assault with his squad of the Banzai Third. Later on I had to review my conscience as to whether I favored or condemned my own platoon in placing it first in line, but it really was Ziggy's turn.

In our pell-mell scramble up the steep slopes of 1179, Zig led his first squad ahead of me by about 40 feet and with five of his men threw grenades into the bunkers of the fanatics defending the top of Fools Mountain, then turned left and ran footloose, screaming wild turkey calls, like General Davies' Kentuckians charging Little Turtle's Miami Indians at the Battle of Fallen Timbers, just before he, Davies, in his fancy white coat, was killed by 'friendly' musket fire.

Ziggy, a lanky blond of German descent in his early twenties, would not harken to my cries not to overrun the objective and for him and his men to return to the crest— always dangerous to overrun an objective, overextend, until a single short 'friendly' 105mm round came barreling in in front of him on the trail leading south. Fortunately, it hit a high rock formation and the spray went up. Who to hell's big idea was it to throw that one?

Too many are the true tales of guys killed wholesale by our own artillery or Air; so-called friendly fire. Name one thing friendly about it. Such 'accidents' occurred during some air strikes when Air Force liaison jerks at Army/Air Force forward air control centers were lousy at correlating actual landscape azimuth with their maps and in the confusion many Korean names looked alike. I was surprised once to learn that one young fighter-bomber pilot diverting with extra ammo after an attack learned the hard way that our enemies never wore helmets, which of course we always did forward of regiment.

Before we shoved off, Colonel Duncan in his OP an eighth of a mile south on the ridgeline at the newly acquired 1100, kept raising his voice over the 300. I have reconstructed his harangue like this—

"Gould, get up there, Gould, they're running. Air reports them bugging out the Pia-ri side! Keep 'em moving, Gould, you'll miss the opportunity!"

"Yeah!" I hollered back over the radio. "Opportunity to be clobbered. Did you say the air strike was called off?"

"Dammit, it is, now move!"

263

"My guys won't move so long as Mosquito is up there waiting to direct an air strike."

"They'll see your air panel and if they do come in, they'll avoid you."

"Avoid, shit, colonel; there's no air panel where we've got to go!"

That gave me a great idea. I folded and wrapped one section of our two-by-five-foot bright red air panel, code of the day, which we carried with us to lay out atop 1179, around my helmet and had it tied with commo wire.

"C'mon," I waved, yelling back at Love Company. "They'll know it's us up there."

"Make it snappy, Gould. Air spots gooks bugging off the objective toward the Pia-ri Valley."

The Air he mentioned was a US Air Force circling AT6, an air target identification plane, code name Mosquito Air. An air strike had been laid on by division for early in the morning, but called off at the last minute due to urgent priority assisting an attack by the Marines in Death Valley. Apparently Mosquito had not been called off as well.

None of my sergeants was born yesterday, so they balked, yelling or radioing me on 536s to suggest that we either wait up for the air strike or call off the attack.

The colonel kept telling me to get moving, they're bugging off the enemy side.

"Good," I radioed back, "less we'll have to deal with."

"C'mon, Gould, get crackin'."

"I can't convince my sergeants the strike's called off. Who wants to get hit by that?"

If only that damn AT6 Mosquito would clear the hell out of the picture.

"Gould, get on up there! Air says they're bugging down the Pia-ri side."

"Damn it, colonel, call off Mosquito Air."

"Never mind that, get up there!"

"Fuck you, sir. Not with an air strike pending."

"Never mind, it's being called off."

"Yeah? Mosquito's still flying."

"He's observing for us now. Goddamn it, Gould, get up there while they're still bugging."

"I'd rather do it *after* they're through, but okay colonel can you see the red air panel around my helmet?"

"No. We can just make out a bunch of you guys moving up the finger. Where are you?"

"You blind, colonel? Look up ahead, I'm at the front behind just one bunch of guys, under that red air panel moving up from the saddle."

"Okay, Gould, we see the red. Chogee! Will relay to Mosquito."

NOTE: Two of my guys on the scene at the time have vivid memories of the air panel on my helmet: Kenneth D. McConnell of Philipsburg, Kansas and Thomas M. Miller, Silver Star, of Oakmont, Pennsylvania.

Fred Hurtz's platoon went up rapidly with him on their minds, Sergeant Red Rose in charge with SFC Phil Overton, their new acting guide, pushing from the rear.

"C'mon, guys, let's go over. At 'em, c'mon!"

Most of Hurtz's platoon had been in a deep slump, as infantrymen do when losing a good leader. They needed strong, immediate revenge. Forget Lieutenant Hurtz? Remember other attacks, him always up there — yelling dire threats — leading fighting fools!

Our attack on H 1179 started as they usually do, walking slowly, carefully, self-consciously. Everyone beginning at the same increasingly dangerous level, as the long file widened to skirmishers for the assault, skirmishing about ten guys wide, as wide as footing on the finger of land permitted before it dropped off, looking sideways each way at who's there and back to see who's coming, assessing one's position in relation to such critical strong points as the BARs and moving machine guns which might set up or engage one or two a few times in the assault but was along mainly to set up a defense. Overhead covering machine guns were the heavy water-cooled guns of Mike heavy weapons company, laying down a steady protective fire. Everyone sought to see who else was coming, wanting them to come hurriedly to their aid when need be. They must keep pace with those who inspired them, else the attack would falter. It was usually one man who inspired and maintained upward movement — not always designated leaders, often changing to one born leader or another as Corporal Edsel Turner.

"Why us?" was the first question as Love's rifle platoons kept careful tab of what, where and who, and we platoon leaders were never shy to remind one another that they were the first at such-and-such a place, and how badly they'd been hurt. Pick someone else this time. There was no question, however, about who should lead in assaulting 1179, for I knew well it was Love Company's turn and Item had been hit as hard as Charley as a flanker back on 1100.

Half way up, Tony Zurlo dropped behind with his 300 but, driven by the banzai spirit, I kept on stumbling, running behind Sergeant Zigerfoose's Banzai First squad, Third platoon of Love, all cursing and the courage that cursing aroused, spreading up the trail like a mountain wildfire with an updraft. Nobody but Zurlo was hit among us up front doing banzaiing, but Item and some stragglers of Love Company suddenly lost twelve, killed in seconds in the saddle behind from a well-directed mortar barrage that had been zeroed in long before. PFC Blum got his bad there for not keeping up with me. I glanced back to see Ed Lopez go down holding a dead medic in his arms, and impressions so terribly, terribly vivid. Combat veterans I have talked with who think they were on 1179 should have been up with us; no way they could ever forget.

Gook heavy Russian-made 120mm mortars came crashing down upon the saddle bottom without warning, dragging up and throwing tons of rock, shrapnel, wood splinters and parts of soldiers whizzing through choking clouds of gun powder smoke and dust, well zeroed in, blowing up a hundred square feet of the path, with sharp shards of steel. Men behind us, including two stragglers of my Banzai Third, lurched, suspended three feet in midair like high, wavering dancers, slammed to the ground, or scrambling madly through choking dust, men screaming like wounded horses, falling, hitting ground, wind knocked out in horrible grunting. Demanding God, as customary, they came face-to-face with Satan.

Others entered an endless reality, scared white, left this world forever, quietly toppling over. Enemy 120s continued to land in fast salvoes of three, an awful cutting, smashing machine of widely scattered, razor-sharp shrapnel.

"God!" a helpless dying man ordered and then humbly, no longer giving orders, "Please?"

"Get up out of it!" I shouted loud as I could, facing behind toward the barrage. "Get on the move! Git up here!"

"Where are they?" a man sobbed in the storm of dust. "Nothing to shoot at. Where are they? Somebody, where are they?"

There was barely time between mortar salvos for the guys to hear our yells (and add their own), for them to reopen their eyelids and stumble upward, climbing hands and knees up the steep hill. How those gook FOs on 1179 must have jumped with joy.

Ziggy and other sergeants in the squads above me turned looking back down toward them momentarily in their concern facing away from the enemy, yelling for them to get out and up fast through the barrage for that was all could save them. There, in the pandemonium of exploding shells was the most contained, destructive barrage I've ever seen or heard of.

As youngsters swept by me assaulting 1179 in their pumped-up enthusiasm, I heard a polite voice, "I'm sorry, sir, I'm hit." Slumping under his own weight, Tony Zurlo, who had caught up to me, repeated, "Sorry, sir," as he stumbled down to stay.

Yelling, "Doc! Doc! Here, doc!" I retrieved the radio, handed it to the first private I could reach and hurried to catch up. Weeks later, Tony wrote to a buddy from the Army Osaka Hospital they were letting him go home minus his left arm to his wife and new baby.

Moving up to where a fellow rifleman ended his life, a leader would decide that he's had it without listening or feeling for a heart beat, just by observing how he lay impossibly contorted and staring hard at you. "Get his ammo and rifle. Let's keep moving." And to young replacements, "Quit rubber-necking and get goin', there's guys paid to take care of him."

"Why don't they? Aren't you going to take his dog tags, or wallet or anything to identify him?"

"That's Grave Registration; we're not allowed to touch them, even write their women. "

Past the grenade line we took little fire due to the accuracy of our artillery, recoilless rifles, heavy machine guns, mounting light machine guns, stopping occasionally to sight on particular targets to keep the defenders under cover. Climbing was a full-time occupation, especially tough when bent under a load, firing our pea shooters was secondary. It was critical that once begun we must not stop at the grenade line but pour on more energy somehow and shout curses and scream battle cries to display a superior morale. We must make them know we know we're going over until suddenly they agree that it sounds like its true.

Try this at home, run as fast as your legs can travel with forty pounds around your waist, plus five four-pound hand grenades in your deep fatigue jacket pockets; heavy cartridge belt flapping with aid kit, two canteens of precious water; bayonet scabbard, ammunition pouches and, in my case, a thirty-eight caliber revolver in a forty-five caliber holster stuffed with rags to keep it from flopping out; up an uneven, sometimes mined, thirty-degree slope, stopping from time to time to get off a round or two and straighten your helmet that's almost jiggled off its liner, shouting and screaming, keeping your ass as low as possible and still breathe, move forward and up, and always prepared mentally to meet your Maker.

Faces I remembered in the screaming inferno—Tony's and First Sergeant Ray Martin, a kid from Fred Hurtz's platoon—even Private Funaro yelling and laughing like someone intoxicated, at home in our crazed banzai as incapable of reasoning as in any of his street-rioting affrays. With all that furious yelling and explosion, it's possible, as one swept along in a street riot, to be taken out of himself, incited to do things he wouldn't normally do, like any riot, mass hysteria gone amuck, people welded into a moving monster, led on by those shouting the loudest violence.

We climbed together, side-by-side, sometimes crawling, stumbling through a downpour of sporadic, usually overhead, small arms fire, using rifles and carbines for crutches, careful to keep muzzles up out of the dirt, stopping only to get off a choice shot until we closed ready to duel hand-to-hand with the enemy, the majority of whom gave way to sudden panic and fleeing as we crossed the grenade line. Gooks fled their bunkers. A few, cowering, hiding with the badly wounded, were grenaded through their firing ports, and we drove the panicked survivors from 1179 by yelling our lungs out and with the appearance of shiny bayonets.

"Kill the bastards! . . . stick 'em! Let the sonsofbitches have it, they're getting away."

Wanting them to leave us alone, I never saw anyone chase after them.

"Let's go! Get over it!" I yelled, and the classic combat observation, "Nobody lives forever!"

Mass combat hysteria. Love Company to the front and Item hot behind, guys crawling, stumbling uphill fast, Item belatedly fastening bayonets on the move, Love fanning out to cover the ridge top. Ziggy and I waving more and more action into them until we were a machine devoid of sensation with momentum carrying it forward and up. We were aware of how essential to low casualties was our smooth, unwavering upward momentum for it is a fact that in any war, many fewer infantrymen are killed in an aggressive attack than a passive defense. More and more and more on their feet firing from the hip, screaming insults, frolicking among demons of death shaking them like dice, striking fatally here and there. "Dirty bastards!"

What crazy yells and wild war whoops! We were madmen. Love was unlovely to the extreme, waving weapons, trying to out race ourselves, little yellow sonsofbitches couldn't understand a word we said, but how they comprehended barking rifles and insane babble of fury yelling up at them.

Some of our attackers, inconspicuous dogfaces, were suddenly wild, rioting Indians, darting cover to cover, berserk screamers, suddenly flamboyant actors, photogenic, reckless young heroes aspiring to conquer or die on center stage, playing lead rolls in the greatest drama of all ages, foe against foe, yelling away their dread—"E dee waah! Cuda-cuda! Bali-bali." Come here! Quickly! Hurry! "Come and get it, yellow cunts."

We stopped once before the grenade line to get our breath

without which we never could have finished the job, thanking the god of war there were no mines, barbed wire or frag grenades. A strange silence above told me that Mosquito Air reported well to Duncan, panic overcame the gooks and most bugged down the steep trail west to the Pia-ri Valley where pass after pass of triumphant, greedy fighter bombers greeted them without resistance other than popping of puny rifle fire. Being unsure of total victory, as soon as we got half our wind, we climbed quickly, still short of breath, wobbly-legged over the parapet, thrusting our bayonets into bunkers and trenches.

Behind Zigerfoose's second squad I was among the first to reach the summit. No last-ditch fighting as our history Blue Book says, for the gooks panicked and ran off downhill toward the Pia-ri Valley or, wounded one way or another, cringed in the dark recesses of bunkers, one calling out to us pathetically, "No, no" over and over. Most were so terrified of us "devils" they were motionless. An interpreter might have convinced some of them to come out safely to us, but the only interpreters we had were our weapons. We couldn't trust them to be left behind so we tossed in grenades. It was necessary to do this because desperados were known to play dead and shoot well-meaning dogfaces in the back rather than try to escape or surrender. It takes only one treacherous gook to spoil it for all. None of our guys was stupid enough to crawl in to coax them out and our Korean combat interpreter wasn't up with us yet.

"Goddamn it, Gould!" Duncan radioed. "Goddammit! We did it . . . licked the bastards. Buzzard Seven, old man, a terrific job. I'm making you honorary airborne."

"Airborne, shit!" I radioed back. "We're Love of the 38th on top of Fools Mountain."

We found the positions empty from which showers of potato-masher grenades had stopped falling but in one bunker ten gooks huddled together, some badly wounded the night before by artillery. They didn't subscribe to the Geneva Convention and I put two men to guard them, alert and watching for tricks. Two of our medics got to them before night fell and the five faces that lived occupied spare litters early the next morning.

Withered, blasted, twisted, tortured trees, hanging forth loose

270

torn branches with brown-paper leaves stuck on; earth crumpled and thrown up, artillery-quaked disaster land.

"Blown-up cemetery," one man observed, gazing into a 500-pound bomb crater with shredded remains of gook soldiers. Three heads, I saw.

I'll never forget Zigerfoose leading the platoon ahead of me, beating me to the top of 1179 and the big bunkers there; skirting bomb and heavy artillery craters, some of which still smoked, burning willie peter all night. In truth, I can't tell you how proud and excited my men made me, and being in charge of Love they were now all my men, such disregard for their lives and bodies, derring-do, the proud wild banzai up 1100 and 1179 against the best the gook Hero Regiment had to offer. We all screamed and cursed in unison, and, relieved suddenly of all that strain, with energy we no longer needed for survival, laughed and cheered even choking on sticky saliva, some laughing, hysterically, coughing, a few with tears of emotion in their eyes, in all that wild hysteria of victory.

A high point well below and south of us was to be referred to as Bloody Ridge; north down the valley would soon be known as Heartbreak Ridge, a favorite of war correspondents, made notorious to people back home and in France solely because of cruel repeated tragedies brought on by incompetent colonels who, rather than form and push along a smoothly resupplied juggernaut as did Duncan of the 38th, committed individual rifle platoons of the 9th and 23rd, piecemeal without close backup and without resupply, using officer-less ROKs spooked by the night.

We used a headlong attack so shocking as to weaken the resolves of our foe. By speed and battle cries alone, we saved a lot of American lives, while at Bloody and Heartbreak Ridges they died weekly and into months attacking piecemeal.

Our avenue of attack in taking 1179 had been relatively simple but dangerously exposed to 1180 and 1243 and long distance sniper fire from Bloody Ridge. We were often at least partially surrounded, easily watched from the gook OP on 1243 north of us, the highest ground on the Punchbowl.

The unnecessarily violent, unsuccessful escapades of our sister

271

regiments made our men worried—our fellow Indianheaders going down so needlessly isolated and unsupplied. The in-house, combined services, *Far East Stars and Stripes* newspaper, and no others worldwide, mentioned our smooth success in taking and holding Fools Mountain, to that date the highest, most valuable point on the enemy side of the Punchbowl. How quiet it became early on all over our battlefield, as our noisy sister regiments bled daily and every night for pitiful weeks on Bloody and later Heartbreak Ridges.

Sleeping in my open-top dirt grave atop 1179, I expanded with my riflemen in a great primordial force, knowing that all things live forever if in some perhaps forgotten or unknown way as electrons move within atoms within molecules; a secret life ever changing, where all is one and one all, as is the massive mountain we clung to, whose flanks we profaned with flesh, scarred with high explosives.

Physically and mentally exhausted, after voting to nominate Edsel for a DSC, ordered by 10 Corps for taking Fools Mountain, I slept soundly the night of our great accomplishment. White phosphorus smoked lazily among the artillery-plowed ruins of the enemy fortification. Somehow in the mysterious realm of make-believe, in the swift passage of great fantasies, and, of course, fatigue of a bruised brain, I dreamed I saw bloody waters flow downward from 1179's crumbling granite slopes on Nature's way over the ample bosom of our protector, mother earth.

I dreamed of green, unharmed trees giving sweet breath to cool mountain night winds; live rustling leaves taking on sinister meanings at night to worried riflemen in some country somewhere, in safe, hastily dug holes in the ground everywhere; stars glittered down among clouds of heavens sent awry, scudding the vast mountain darkness seeking to brush us off; empyrean clouds grazing our mountain tops, black clouds formed again and again and reforming, cast away by the breath of giants, racing along with the urgent whisperings of fleeting lives lost in the ground, souls of warriors; rain and shafts of lightning, pale, blue-purple to brilliant yellow-white.

Standing on Fools Mountain that first night after midnight, a break in overcast exposed a trillion twinkling stars and I felt belonging, a follower of setting suns behind angry, tossing, distant clouds; some puffing up cliffs to greet me, atoms of all Nature enfolding me with atoms of my mother and Love's many dead, and I was one of and among them. Having lived months intimately with Nature with only fatigue clothes between us, breathing open air on and off 1179, in her when shells arrived, in Korean wilderness as, sleeping coiled within mother earth, hugging her passionately under fire, cowering among tree roots, watching the blood of buddies disappear fast into loose earth, running away on flat rocks, deeply embroiled in symbolic cohesion in dark, damp earth, jagged mountain outcroppings and silvery-gray, brooding skies capping the setting sun, I was home.

In the distance were muffled rumbles of thunder challenged by heavy artillery, that world over there by the faint blue-purple mountains going to sleep snoring now, echoing further and further away; then, suddenly, without warning, wild storming from behind, blazing blades of blue lightning flashes flying by an optical illusion straight toward us from a terrible tempest and furious skyquakes.

You live whole lifetimes in half an hour's shelling, turn yourself recklessly over to blind fate, forgetting petty worries that beset you stateside — material things, picky personality differences and money worries. Uncommon love, or call it companionship under fatal pressures if you will; mutual, complete trust involving the very soul, unselfishness, camaraderie or single-mindedness facing imminent demise, as people link together their thoughts, objectives and fears facing prolonged tragedy and senseless destruction.

Not in all the United States of America, in all the world in all military establishments thereof, are there such straightforward, humble, hard-run heroes as those who shoulder rifles in Infantry combat.

Death dealt with us bitterly in unpleasant ways day after solemn, joyless day, without the mitigating aid of tolling bells or black trappings. Still I dreaded it more than gave it hate, for it seemed I was always fated to ask, "Just how bad is it?"

Item pulled up on a hill tight under us the following morning just in time to be greeted by a furious counterattack from H 1181. I hustled down with my radioman to see how it was going when two sergeants, a corporal, and a private from Item's weapons platoon came stumbling along with a heavily loaded litter, bent over on the run. The way the litter occupant bounced freely on the canvas, not strapped down, made me assume he was dead, at least too far gone for carriers to feel the need for gentleness. His eyes were shut tight—eyeballs puffed terribly, swollen round ping-pong balls of stretched purple skin from the sudden air shock of a nearby exploding shell. His face was a grotesque mask, pale yellow-green, sweaty, cold-looking skin, irreversible death shock.

"Take him off!" I ordered impatiently. "Save the litter for someone can make it."

The taller sergeant, master sergeant stripes proudly stenciled in black on the front of his helmet, glared fiercely. "Shut your fuckin' face, that's our lieutenant."

"Lieutenant Murray," the corporal said with enormous pride.

It was Murray of Item all right, his face so bloated, bruised and bloodied I hadn't recognized him. He was a big man, too much to fit comfortably in our rocky holes, white matter mixed with the thickening blood where the back of his head rested on the olive-drab canvas. I couldn't understand why they thought him still alive until Murray's mouth gaped slowly wide open and then slowly, very slowly, closed like a tired goldfish.

The corporal supporting the left rear handle had a brilliant florescent chartreuse air panel strapped to his back.

"Anyway," I told him, "take off that panel. It's a good target."

I praise the dead among whom I scooped C rations and as my admiration grew individual by individual, it dawned on me that the earth is full of soldiers in such numbers as stars in all galaxies; young soldiers gone under the earth to uphold the living, losing their lives that others might prosper unthreatened; quitting life far from home, slipping unthanked, unknown, unhonored into the deep river of time flowing darkly along.

On Fools Mountain on the Punchbowl, most days after the first hectic weeks of shelling and intermittent close combat counterattacks, I goofed off with the guys of Love Company's forward headquarters, under an Arab tent of ponchos buttoned together. On quiet days that August, on the friendly side of the ridge where it was safe from all but mortar and where it wasn't so steep, we sat on our piss pots to keep our tails dry, huddled together under cold mountain rains around small fires of waterproof, 'fire-resistant' cardboard C ration boxes and splintered wood from grenade boxes; knees-to-knees, soggy, muddy, olive-drab army blankets doubled, wrapped around damp shoulders; straight-legged, bewhiskered dogfaces, black crack lines in dirt-packed skin, smelling of stale smoke of many campfires; foot-slogging infantry, kept outdoors like smelly dogs with poor manners, dogfaces chatting idly; fussing aloud about the totally discouraging, cool, gray-black, always disagreeable weather.

Sometimes we snickered at bitter remarks, punctuated with sharp hissing sh-e-e-e-it!, our carefully protected inner selves secretly nourished by fond memories of sweet, feminine wives, girlfriends and mothers who blossomed into dainty, delicate angels in our absence. Attempts at Hollywood humor stuck in our throats.

Tired by short rations and guarding nights, mostly uncommit-ted, we curled like the dogs we were and slept on dirt, face sideways on our paws for pillows, indifferent to light and dark, night and day.

We fortified rocky 1179 as best we could, skyland of grief and great peril, sacred to Korean mountain dwellers not known to American fighting men until early in July when daring L-19 reconnaissance pilots, skimming low above the quiet, secret land in their little tin-covered kites to scan for us, drew occasional angry flecks of fire. What lurked in those dark ravines we would climb up and over, behind jag-ged rocks and slides of crumbled, decomposing granite over small bodies of Korean Marines? We did not know until we reached taunting, high-pitched voices head-on.

We were very difficult to supply. The relatively safe, round-about way took nine hours of tough climbing, in some places, espe-cially when wet, only hand-over-hand steadied by heavy, knotted ropes, for battalion supply trains of KTC to reach us by the only route possible unobserved from 1243. Slippery, sloping slides of mud-slime and loose rock, some beside drop-offs hundreds of feet to oblivion.

Can you imagine packing an A-frame loaded with a hundred pounds of supplies up and wounded or dead down those steep slippery trails when you're over 40 and they call you papasan, or you're young Koreans who can hardly understand orders, transferred as misfits from

ROK infantry units.

We hadn't been able to bring up litters for some time now; the few we have are held for badly wounded. After that ballbreaking zig-zag climb up here by the protected trail, you can't expect them to haul down a 200 pound rotting body. Besides, they were terrified of unburied soldiers.

By the time fatigued carriers reached our aerie the first two weeks, unloading 100-pound rice-straw bags of loose supplies, cardboard boxes of C rations and green-painted wooden boxes of grenades, OD-colored cans of machine gun ammo, OD cloth bandoliers of eight-round M1 rifle clips and five-gallon jerry cans of water from yokes or A frames, they were too pooped to haul down the dead—only the strongest able to assist our few walking wounded, stumbling, hanging to empty A frames from the rear; others hauling crippled or weakened wounded strapped down with empty machine gun web belts or commo wire, when we had litters.

After a day's rest, those carriers who hadn't deserted or been removed for medical reasons, were sent up again with ammo, water, grenades and Cs, but there were times, as many as three days in a row, when the rains were too heavy for them to use the mud-slide trail, and we lost two of those little guys and their precious loads to falls from which they were never seen again, and one to sniping infiltrators.

Other than the flight from Japan, the Air Force tried several times during short breaks in the overcast sky to supply us from above at low level. They dropped cardboard boxes of C's, jerry cans of water, precious water, pickets (triangular steel stakes six feet high for stringing barbed wire), barbed wire, flame throwers, axes, picks. Each time only nine parachute packs in twenty hit the ridgeline high enough to retrieve. What gooks were unable to reach hung in bright, multicolored nylon chutes from scrubby trees down the steep slopes—each color a type of supply. Soon, the gooks wore jaunty red, blue, green or yellow nylon scarves. To us, chutes were returnable and we were warned of a $100 fine for tearing one.

For a month and a half we lived on short C rations, two cans a day instead of three each of wet ration (that is, containing 'meat'); one twelve-ounce can of beef (gristle), spaghetti and meat balls (gristle in thin tomato sauce), sausage, lima beans and ham, hash (too salty, gristle), which at one time our starving prisoners refused, and an anemic pasty chicken something-or-other. Killers of little girls enjoyed wide news coverage, years of appeals and favorite hot meals before execution (the few that occur), while the last suppers of us professionals out to kill strangers on sight were cold, paltry, picky picnics in the rain with little clear plastic spoons.

We ate as-is, never dressed for dinner, only occasionally built a small, ration cardboard or wooden grenade box fire, or were lucky enough to have a so-called squad stove, one for canned heat or heat the tiny cans over pinches of burning composition C4 plastic explosive we bartered for with engineer buddies making a solemn ritual of scooping out the unsatisfying rations, holding cat-food-size cans over the lower lip carefully so as not to lose any—stingy *fêtes des fous.*

After meals, we lit smokes, 'em that got 'em,' an old Army saying, harkening to the Great Depression when it had meaning.

There was a greatly reduced need for pre-folded C-ration asswipe, and to our surprise we thrived, growing alert and lean as hunting hounds; napping any hour night or day when not on watch or being fired upon, snarling when rudely awakened; fatigues rotted in the slime we wallowed in during the monsoon rain which ended 15 September.

Reason floundered on those mountains and hills in the unpredictability of random and frequent killings gone amok, a deadly game of madman's bluff, sorry scheme of unbridled hate, rotten tales gasped by vicious idiots, mouths oozing blood.

As days came to nights, often blended in that monsoon malaise, the hostile atmosphere gave rise to an equally universal fear. Who among so many dangers is ever safe from snipers and H and I night and day as that which killed J C Rodriguez, and several men in King Company along the ridge, by unpredictable, random rounds? We learned that fear is as accumulative as carbon monoxide—sensing full well that the longer threatened, the more remote our chances of surviving for very long.

The heavy Korean monsoon wetted us sporadically for August and half of September almost into the first thin mountain snow flurries of fall. We slowly sagged in sadness as damp as the air of our earthen holes, reduced to bones pushed outward at the filthy skin that bound our blood and tissues; hunting and hunted animals; stark, eyes sore of thousand-yard stares, black balls of grime rolled by sweat.

But who of us carried mirrors; as we grew to complain less, fatigued, some from mild malnutrition, others from constant attention to nagging worry; knowing that the ultimate price of relaxation was death. Our hiding in dampness of our holes was also unsatisfying, constantly alert for H and I and snipers, in muddy slime so close to an ever-menacing enemy. We were as tame animals gone wild quivering nervously, when exposed rapid glances around, crouched alert, peeking over the rims of our holes like prairie dogs, catching naps whenever rather than a good nights sleep. We grew short-answered, snapping, ugly men, childishly resentful of one another's real or imagined comforts, eyes wilted sadly when unstimulated by fear, earning well our name dogface.

Time passed unregulated, escaping our attention for days, knowing dark and light only, one after the other, yearning for something until someone, seeking order in chaos, might ask, "Hey, what day is it?" and likely as not receive a wrong answer.

Some few were felled by shrapnel from exploding shells; hot, jagged sirens, sharp chunks of steel whirring every way from point of impact or worse yet from an airburst, Soviet-tracked SPs (self-propelled) artillery dug in and hulled up for high trajectory, and hollow whooompt!, deep-throated 120mm mortars. Others, replacements, as they prepared to leave the floor of the valley to climb and greet us old warriors, died crossing an abandoned rice paddy, where they were forced to run splashing, hunched over, from unseeable zip-zips of snipers, and we had to leave our buddies floating and bloating and in short time noisily blowing out their gas before sinking from sight. We seldom returned to land we fought over and there were many places in those wild landscapes of death for MIAs, the obscure dead, to hide from the living, where no American ever climbed again, where sense-deadened soldiers of graves registration preferred not to be; ground unvisited even by curious Korean woodsmen or rice farmers for another planting season as our dogfaces sank slowly, flesh bloating, worm eaten, cloth and webbing rotting.

278

I sat in my hole gasping for air, a cigarette between my lips constantly, at night carefully covering the glow. Something was awfully wrong with me. I'd never been this terribly run down and utterly fatigued before. My heart seemed sometimes to flutter and leave me vibrating weak. If I ever find safety, I'll sob myself to sleep and see a cardiologist.

In the quiet periods between probing, we picked at ourselves, joked miserably about bushy hair, and with Doc Singleton's surgical scissors snipped and hacked out clumsy haircuts for each other. You could tell those most recently returned from Japan R and R, relatively clean smelling like women and could smile some.

We scraped mud and worked out rocks and made what improvements we could to our homes. Alternating with my 'aide,' Sergeant Eppler, I checked the platoons of Love. Creeping along between widely-spaced holes at night, I stopped frequently to listen, startled at a twig seeming to snap or when wind scraped together the few dry, brown leaves of shrapnel-shattered branches of a maimed tree. As routine wore us down, I found myself longer and longer at each hole, crouching, talking to guys of their home and families, keeping it low so as not to waken their buddies; studying snapshots by hand-covered flashlight of love at home of one form or another, kids, wives and often dogs, which occupied their minds so much of the painfully wasted time away from them. Within weeks I knew nicknames of their friends back home — "This one's Jesse."

"I know . . . sister's boyfriend."

While we clung to our North Korean gateway to the Far East, Peking radio broadcast that the 38th Infantry had been completely surrounded and all officers killed or surrendered. Hard hit by the Chink breakthrough in November 1950 at Kunu-ri and bearing the brunt of another in February at Hoengsong, the May Massacre and elsewhere from February to June 1951, the Chinks already held 1252 POWs from the Indianhead Division.

Several magazines printed the false boast verbatim without an effort to qualify or even to state that it was a boast, cruelly giving wives, mothers and girlfriends the belief that the Chink lie was true. It made exciting copy, the bastards that kept it going. In a week or so guys came to me with letters beginning with such Statements as "This letter probably won't reach you . . ." or "I pray God you have escaped" or "I hope you were not up there with the 38th Regiment when it was captured." Somehow, I guess Kitty didn't read that yellow journalism; she never mentioned it.

Like 'friendly' artillery and Air, greedy sales-hungry editors did more damage to our morale and efficiency than a division of Chinks or gooks, just to sell their damn papers and magazines or draw listeners to their radios.

A new rumor circulated every day. We are going to be relieved soon, look how beat-up we are. We broke an all-time US Army record for time on line without relief and every rumor made sense because we wanted relief from the Punchbowl and considered each unit in the corps, which conceivably could be used to effect our relief.

Later we learned of poor guys in the western sector down the Pia-ri valley on what the Press called Heartbreak Ridge, also badly clobbered almost nightly, committed piecemeal and overrun. Our King and Item companies were to be involved on Heartbreak before it was taken, as was Love on Mundung-ri even further into North Korea. Those regimental commanders of the 9th and 23rd should have taken lessons from our paratrooper Lieutenant Colonel Duncan who ran his companies steady ahead, bolstered, and well-supplied from behind. Hit, take a few casualties, run low on ammo, fall back, let another company through, as we juggernauted up 1100 and 1179 like an obstinate rhinoceros, head down and heavy, ready to gore, being continually resupplied and reassured of direct support and relief as Love and Item were on 1179.

Those poor guys were slaughtered by the dozens almost daily on Bloody, hundreds of meters below, behind us, and Heartbreak north and below us. We could have pulled up a chair and watched the one-sided firefights as gooks ran them off piecemeal at night from the top of Bloody, platoon after platoon.

Of the proud White and Blue Battalions, including the Korean Marine regiment, in two months on 1100 and 1179, 200 were killed and 500 wounded of 9400 engaged,. On Bloody and Heartbreak, the 9th and

280

23d infantries with the French battalion lost that many in a week, very embarrassing to generals and politicians, what with bold talk of peace. It took 103 days and savage nights to take Heartbreak. It might have been so with us on 1179 if Item and us, not mere platoons, weren't close behind King to play musical chairs. Knowing you got all that more power backing you up close by makes for morale and a damn powerful machine.

Our Blue Book—

In due course X Corps succeeded in slaughtering uncounted thousands of the NKPA and advancing to its 'limited objective,' a new line north of the Punchbowl. But the cost to make these minor improvements in the X Corps line was shocking. The Second Division and attached ROKs incurred 2700 casualties in capturing Bloody Ridge and 3700 American casualties in capturing Heartbreak Ridge. Concluding it was "unprofitable to continue the bitter operation," Van Fleet told corps commander Clovis Byers to "firm up his line" and "plan no further offensives."

Fighting bogged down across the front at about thirty kilometers above the 38th parallel where we were dug in, positional warfare in which neither side could force a military or diplomatic decision. Nevertheless, hours and days and weeks passed in killings at or around us. We followed the long, tedious, peace talks from the first word, with every new issue of the *Stars and Stripes* delivered by our chogee train, one copy per ten men, read on the friendly side of the ridge or down in our holes out of sight.

You can't depend on peace talks. Gooks and Chinks used peace talks to stall while they restocked their caches of ammo and stuff. Our generals knew this and that's why in the May Massacre we fell back for five days and went after them on the sixth.

Peace talks, shut down since 23 August, began anew in November. Especially applauded by the guys was the Communists' insistence that all foreign troops be withdrawn from the peninsula.

Weeks passed reckoned by failed negotiations and as the blood of our men sank into Korean soil through July, August and September of the year 1951, from short, jabbing, probing enemy attacks and our combat and reconnaissance patrols went deep into no-man's lands without letup, I caught myself sighing often, complaining to myself I died too slowly. I knew then how fatalistic Gonzales felt about J C. "Come get me, you bastards, get it over with!" It was a monotony that was not dull because it was always threatening, quiet, a violent, threatening sameness. Time was oppressive while the monsoon hung low upon us; yet, because time now was all there was to our lives, we looked forward sadly to our own sudden death, or, less certain, that healthy day when we rotated.

When not engaging a persistent enemy, who wanted very badly to regain Taeusan, the men rested and worked on their rocky holes and went, hunched over, calling on buddies up and down the line. Unfortunately, being an officer I had no kindred spirit now that Fred Hurtz was safe in Tokyo General Hospital, now an artilleryman no longer wearing idiot sticks. Sergeant Eppler? College man, yes, all business.

I heard promises from battalion via Lieutenant Carse, who I knew was pulling for me, that a replacement captain was on his way. It was a scandal for the high and mighty West-Point-owned Regular Army to depend so much on a poorly trained recalled-reserve lieutenant and, I might add, Master Sergeant Pater also doing a regular captain's job? Me? Sunday soldier, they called us, didn't know how to play the Regular Army game. I was a sometimes rather nasty, outspoken thirty-one-year-old, questioning one at that. Fortunately, the act of commanding a rifle company in combat was itself direct and earthy, rather exhilarating to this warrior's psyche to remain in combat, weary though I was.

At Lieutenant Carse's suggestion, Sergeant Eppler was moved to a platoon leader's slot pending my return from company, so he could more easily be field commissioned even though he turned it down twice. Master Sergeant Warren Milligan became the Third's active platoon sergeant. He was a Regular, vet of the mountains of Italy in WWII, a real pro. We went inspecting the Banzai Third together and when not checking firing positions, ammo reserves, and equipment (I was especially fussy about cleaning gas ports on BARs), weather permitting, we lolled about the CP gabbing. Carbon builds up after a lot of firing in the BAR port hole for escape of gases not needed to eject the bullet, slows the rate of fire of the weapon and in the midst of a fatal battle freezing solid so the BAR won't fire at all. I've seen this happen and heard about it in other cases.

There was constant sniping from 1181 as well as 1243 for weeks after taking 1179, and both sides took cover, then seemingly by tacit understanding allowed a certain amount of untroubled daytime housekeeping. But there was no written agreement and at least one notable exception was enough to keep us from ever relaxing. On cold days of light blowing rain, normal for those mountains, the new first sergeant, Martin, and I often sat huddled together in the Company CP hole, olive-drab blankets around our shoulders, playing cards, of necessity close to the vest, squirming for warmth on the Korean mountainside as summer fled south from crazy Manchurian winds.

We scratched ourselves nervously like caged monkeys; bunker sores with serum leakage on our thighs and asses. Some picked up a maddening fungus crotch itch appropriately called Chinese crud by our sister regiment, the Ninth Infantry, following the Boxer Rebellion in 1900 in China. Unbrushed teeth contaminated our mouths; the excuse, hard-to-get water after the monsoon, not toothpaste. When it rained solidly, we rigged spare ponchos to collect water and store it in empty five-gallon jerry cans. Steadily, relentlessly it dripped on us and when there was a dry hour, me of the bloody toes ordered the guys to remove their boots and socks to massage their feet while the platoon sergeants, after checking their own, inspected them for potentially dangerous sores.

Rosters turned over, replacements grew old in a few days, and veterans lucky enough became ancient and rotated. I'll swear some died up there whose names had never been mentioned, most likely replacements.

Because of the greater area exposed as we moved through space, most wounds occurred to extremities, arms and legs, being mingled with the flow of legitimately wounded from the battalion, a few SIWs, self-inflicted wounds, most always in a foot, rarely a hand.

Most of us combat veterans were so rubbed into it we probably considered it once or twice but not seriously. We old timers didn't despise them, they'd been brought up with less self-respect, less stick-to-it-ness than we who would, we told one another, rather die than flinch this way. I've never seen statistics but I doubt if ever a Mexican-American or native Indian was SIW. Ones I saw were city boys of soft lives from well-to-do families.

At times I could've given it all up, slump to the ground and sob. It was no longer a secret dependency, their making it so obvious I was there for them to lean on and talk to and it was a long tedious wait for peace, interrupted negotiations from 8 July 1951 to the cease fire on 27 July 1953. The only sure things were death and rotation; at least you knew where you stood. In our time on 1179 we waited for the peace talks to reconvene, as Love passed an Army-wide record line time, 50 days on line facing enemy, exposure to every type of fire except Russian MiGs; especially snipers and unpredictable H and I.

Supplies were haphazard, depending on monsoon rain that washed out footholds on the mountain trails. Our physical conditions grew sorry waiting to be relieved so we could attend to bunker sores and exchange rotting fatigues, and me, the bloody mess of athletes foot, skin sloughing off when I tried to itch it. Damn lucky it didn't get infected.

We missed our secure, mortar-proof roofed bunkers on the Marine hill, for 1179 was very difficult and dangerous to supply with building materials, no light soil to fill sandbags, carriers so few the best we could do was build deeper holes in rocks and depend on good crossed fields of fire.

Having waited nearly two weeks for Graves Registration, both Pater back on 1100 and I got Colonel Duncan on the horn about Captain Toth and after explaining to us that the other two battalions were also committed, he had body bags sent up to zip in all but two of our dead to get them down from 1179. The two landed in inaccessible places over drop offs too dangerous for retrieval.

We had to blast rock to make high-priority machine gun emplacements and the mountain ground elsewhere with our little folding entrenching shovels was too rocky for graves, the ridge too narrow and burial being contrary to Army regulations anyway, no one suggested we lay bare hands on our buddies while we waited vainly for Graves Registration from regiment to do its job or disturb them in any way as guys we kidded around with and exchanged short biographies with and gave orders to receded into soggy lumps of rotting fatigues beside ridge paths, exposing their sunken eye sockets and triangular nose holes. Teeth minus shrunken gums and lips grew longer, like snarling dogs, protruding ominously, faces no longer with simple death smiles, one's last sign of a humanity, now macabre and threatening.

We had not wanted this terrible thing to happen. By our brotherly love, I swear we had not intended it. We felt very bad about it but could do nothing.

Although not as harassed as during the first two weeks on Fools Mountain, more rested, the bearers balked with well-demonstrated anguish at handling our decaying buddies, cadavers, carrion; grotesque fetid monstermen; bloated until exploding; stinking, rotting liquid protein; black fluids draining from injuries, oozing stinking blackness that once was the pulsating blood of a young man's life; swarming, squirming maggots, black carrion beetles and sickening mephitic stench of putrefying flesh.

Our Korean interpreter, Smiley, explained apologetically, patiently, yet obviously perturbed, that little Kims (our sobriquet for all South Korean males) were afraid that darkness would overtake them going down 1179 with unburied dead on their backs, and being devout Animists, they were far more frightened than any American could ever be of evil spirits hovering over those who have not been buried early enough with proper rites. Spirits of men who die violently, especially warriors, not properly buried, are condemned to wander forever, harassing and terrifying the living as they seek expiation, he explained. Oh how sensitively we knew our unburied were disgraced; what a prolonged, dirty, pitiful association, the crying out from diminishing, flesh-dissolving heaps for decent burial in consecrated earth.

"Men who do not bury their dead suffer eternal damnation," Smiley warned—as if our consciences didn't nag us.

I shuddered at the corpses lying about in various stinking stages of decay and occasionally, with unsteady fingertips, carefully traced the outline of my own skull, fingering around the outer rims of my eye sockets the short-lived flesh, reluctantly addressing the physical me it's just a matter of time, assuming my features weren't smashed as poor J C's, I'd be left smiling like other guys, teeth protruding, shrinking lips, matted hair.

They didn't die clean, white-sheeted deaths and come to rest in flower-covered, pink-satin-lined, polished mahogany caskets; they went twisting into the ground where they got it, some dead before landing, and there was no hushed, hallowed viewing of their cleverly waxed replacement flesh and rouged remains in well-staged funeral parlor dramas; no church-ordained solemnity or respectful calm, but rather the bedlam of hell erupting as they left us, an occasional curse or choked-off plea to save his life, surprise, half angry reaction to pain and terrible power of the hit, a sudden final, pathetic sinking, meeting Death lying down on bare ground.

Dogface soldiers and sad-eyed deer get slammed in their tracks by hunks of hot lead at a ton per square inch, dropped where they stand. Deer get gutted right away and trussed over the right front fender of four-wheelers, proud signs of macho depravity. Hopefully dogfaces are found in a few days, depending on the nearness of the enemy and, already stinking, covered with vicious flies, slid into airtight black body bags, zipped tightly and shoved into the back of cracker-box ambulances or swung unceremoniously onto the beds of six-by supply trucks that are in wait below as far as trucks can climb.

Dropped KIA by company clerks on the daily morning report to higher headquarters, pathetic little piles of personal belongings mailed home, if mothers were lucky enough, in a cloth bag in a box, a cheap wrist watch, mildewed leather wallet with cracked, worn photos of females and young children — good luck charms that failed.

Death can meet you early in combat in some guise but those who get to know him never tell what it's all about — indescribable in terms of the life we know so well. They dropped pawing at death wounds, bled short whiles, died without a word to buddies, stiffened in a few hours, bloated, and in two days erupted swarms of squirming maggots — bright, living young men suddenly very disgusting, spoiled meat rotting fast, sinking to disjointed pieces of flesh held in place by rotting fatigues or tendons.

In lighted hours we observed their deterioration and smelled them between rains throughout dark nights, much more closely than we liked; sadly, but without expressed sympathy, knowing that sentimentality has no place in infantry combat and is a feeling untrue to that most profound subject; replaced by an indescribably terrible feeling utter hopelessness.

The real drama finished when the bullet or shrapnel slammed into them with finality, THUD!, a long-handled sledge hammer well-muscled into a bag of wet sand. Since society already passed judgement on their relative worthlessness, determined by draftability, of what count was the final act in the short, tragic tale of the young condemned ones? Rather than display sympathy for our pathetic dead, in mute ways we died with them, in modes of respectful solicitude.

I spent too many times for the well-being of my mind meditating on the weird disappearance of Sergeant Chuck Dorn and his entire squad, the deaths of Youngs, who I never got to know, J C Rodriguez, the silent one, and Smitty, my short-term Canadian buddy, Ich and Holly and Sergeant Ulriche and, goddamn it anyway, all the others, some like Lieutenant Werner who I spoke crossly to and hadn't even met. I was being relentlessly crushed under a load of compounded guilt. I wasn't exactly to blame for the death of Werner what's-his-name, but I was inexcusably unkind—I didn't have to embarrass him.

Although I was becoming every day, experience after experience, a more capable a combat leader, I was also a weakened guilty old man with no future to contemplate. At thirty-one, believe me, I was old, old, worrying from thirty-one to sixty-one in a few months.

The greatest crime was that I let myself down, considering me too often a victim out of control neglecting the positive. How does that song go? Accentuate the positive? Worry was ruling and ruining me. My death was made certain, as with all guilty ones. One day on the ridge H and I artillery would land on me in the open and I'd go down like Jesus did at my age or his namesake, J C, a decade younger, 1951 years later, a professional assassin would focus on me all the way from Bloody Ridge in a moment of my carelessness. No one lives forever in this business

8
Hills 1181 and 1243

From the Blue Book—

Plans were drawn up on 29 September at X Corps for a new limited offensive. Scheduled for 0600 hours, 3 October, it called for an attack to the newly designated 'Hays Line.' The principle objective of the Second Division was a north-south hill mass extending 3000 meters in length in the eastern portion of the Division zone, dominated by a rocky crag-covered peak, honeycombed with enemy bunkers, one of the most rugged, inaccessible peaks it had encountered in Korea. Towering high in the distance, its top shrouded in clouds and mist, the objective was the northernmost crest of a string of hills jutting northeast from Taeusan. Like an arrow, it penetrated into the heart of the enemy defenses, 1243, Kach'il-Bong, Magpie Mountain it was called.

Between H 1179 and H 1243 was a well-dug-in outpost on H 1181, command responsibility for taking it was rumored split between myself and Master Sergeant John Pater. Three officers were with Love, myself, leader of the Third Platoon on duty as temporary commander of Love Company, Roy Carse, and newly-commissioned Second Lieutenant Robert 'Red' Rose.

Blue Book—

Supporting fires, including eight-inchers, directed from Battalion OP, were registered and effected into known positions on

1181. At the same time, a lieutenant from Mike's Heavy Weapons company would aim rounds from a 75mm recoilless along with a 57mm recoilless of L Company's weapons platoon with excellent results at ragged North Koreans seen many times in and about the bunkers, bobbing up and down along the trenches.

Pater was still acting CO with one ROTC lieutenant up with him to support the attack. Because of the acute officer shortage, Colonel Duncan ordered company commanders, me and Morris of Item Company and Pater, to direct our attacks "from maximum protective positions," which made Pater and me sneer, "She-e-it, man, move troops against fire that far behind? Never; that's not leading."

On the morning of 3 October, Third Battalion was five days ahead of X Corps schedule. The First Marine Division, 5th Infantry, was that day still in general attack two-thirds of the way along the northeastern rim of the Punchbowl, their registering phosphorus clearly visible from the towering real estate of 1243.

Following is the S 3 Third battalion's official operations report from 0101, 03K to 2400 04 K, Korean time, October, in other words, from one minute after one Korean time on 3 October, to midnight the next day—

1st Bn remained in previously reported positions providing fire support for 3rd Bn attack on Hill 1181, two platoons of L Company, forward elements of 3rd Bn in vicinity DT 199380 at 0100 03K Oct engaged by an estimated two (2) enemy companies. At 0155 03K Oct the 3rd plat of L Co was dispatched to reinforce the 1St and 2d plats at the forward positions. K Co was dispatched from its positions to join L Co for the assault on Hill 1181 and the objective was secured by 1600 03K Oct. Battalion (-) broke contact with the enemy at 1930 04K Oct and consolidated its position vic DT200340T by 2400 04K Oct.

I went around 1179 to brief the attacking rifle and weapons platoon leaders of Love and on the following morning, minus an artillery forward observer who failed to show on time, I proceeded with the assistance of King's acting commander, Sergeant Pater, to call in and adjust preparatory artillery fire. We used my SCR 300 to battalion, who relayed to Fire Direction Center on an Angry Nine's SCR 609, who then fired the batteries. The summit of 1181 was defended from long irregular ditches and several heavily constructed log bunkers.

Initially, two light machine guns positioned by Pater give overhead support fire and I added two light thirties from Love Company which continued to maintain in short bursts a good accurate fire; then, with minimum delay, replaced light thirties one at a time with the sustained fires of heavies from Mike, Heavy Weapons Company. These 30-calibers, whose barrels are water-cooled, maintained direct, almost continuous overhead fire on all targets known, raking the rims of the ditch tops, correcting by tracer sighting plunging streams of bullets into bunker apertures.

I worked from a rock hole facing enemy down the northern forward slope of 1179 about ten feet from the silhouetting crest. The communications between Colonel Duncan, Pater and myself were at all times excellent. Nevertheless, there were occasions when the situation became confusing to the man in charge, for Duncan had poor visibility of the forward, enemy-facing portion of 1179 and the saddle leading up to 1181. From his OP on 1179 he couldn't see concealed elements of Love Company for his OP was slightly to the left of the line of sight along the north-south ridge mass.

Machine guns attempted to conserve ammunition by lifting whenever salvoes of artillery hit the objective. Once they were slow in starting again and during the lull when neither artillery nor machine gun fire landed on 1181 we observed five enemy slip out of the apertures of suicide bunkers in panic and disappear over the hill behind them. Germ of an idea, turning to the heavy machine gun sergeants: "When artillery lifts next time, button up your guns; give them a chance to bug. Remember 1179 how much easier we made it? Let's synchronize."

An estimated twenty to thirty enemy vacated in this manner, reducing our occupational hazards considerably. Our FO, an artillery lieutenant independent of our command, was supposed to join us sometime in the night well before our attack but failed to show in time and I called Pater to tell him how we were synchronizing with the machine guns only to discover that his ROTC officer was acting CO. Pater was hit and evacuated.

The young lieutenant, then automatically acting company commander of King, was pleased when I relieved him. What a thrill dishing out so much HE (high explosive), what power! I never realized FOs had so much fun. I almost didn't know when to stop; imagine throwing whole batteries of three-gun salvos at them. The regular FO then appeared and took over.

As we watched enemy chogee between bursts, a little bareheaded gook, about fourteen, in a dirty, sloppy uniform, slid through a bunker aperture near the top of the objective and came running hellbent on surrendering down the open saddle path. When some of my men fired at him, I yelled: "Can it! Let the kid surrender!" By the time he started up from the bottom of the saddle, a gook was whittling away at him with a burp gun. The kid finally made it, running sixty miles an hour right up over the rocks and onto my lap. The machine gunners and riflemen within sight laughed, clapped and cheered. "Who's your girl friend?" someone yelled. Still on my lap, the visitor wiped sweat from his forehead with a sweeping movement of his hand and, face-to-face, went: "Whew!" saying in North Korean what I imagined was 'what a relief,' then beamed like any happy little boy and grabbed my left hand to shake it, an uncommon gesture for a gook.

Remembering my training, I opened a ham and lima bean C ration can and, setting him up in full view on my lap, gave him a plastic spoon. There, in front of everyone, he sniffed the can suspiciously while cringing as much as he could and, though our intelligence told us that they were starving, made a face and handed it back. No reflection on Army dietitians, and we couldn't interest the hungry little gook in a C ration hash either.

I stood him up in the hole to let gooks see us good from 1181 and stuck a cigarette in his mouth. The kid was impossible to light up, refusing to suck in, turning for frightened looks at 1181, trying to crouch. I wanted his buddies to see how well he was treated. Then the youngster and I nearly got our fuckin' heads blown off by a sniping elephant gun. You can't mistake that big bastard. Evidently the lad never smoked, for Corporal Alverez saw him throw the unlit butt away with a look of disgust when I wasn't looking.

Meanwhile, Colonel Duncan kept pestering me like on H 1179. "C'mon, Gould, get up there. We can see them crawling out of their bunkers and bugging."

"I know, I got one. Who do you think's giving them that opportunity? The fewer we have to fight."

He called every five minutes asking what in hell we were up to and for us to get the lead out of our pants.

"What makes you think it's lead?" I asked.

There came a time, however, when no gook crawled out during the lulls and I had to move. I figured out the fields of fire of enemy bunkers and two separate machine guns and then checked with the lieutenant in charge of Mike's heavies, also noting the opposition was the greatest threat. We agreed that most faced the Punchbowl side of the enemy hill and the finger that led down into the bowl, most likely avenue of approach from where they had the greatest fear of attack.

Love's platoon leaders and a few eager sergeants of King were in a ten-foot-deep ravine to left rear.

"Lieutenant Rose," I yelled, "lead your men on the trail along those supply bunkers on the left. Keep well off the saddle trail. I'll be behind you. Third Platoon, follow in right behind Rose. Ziggy, good luck, again. Weapons platoon, give us all the machine gun and mortars you can. Don't forget to keep it high when we near the top."

"Ready, everyone . . . let's banzai!"

It's not necessary to tell each and every soldier exactly where to go and what to do; that's where hours of training went teaching him, his squad leader's job. As a lieutenant rifle platoon leader, theoretically the only ones I order are my platoon guide and platoon sergeant, who in turn has four squad leaders and they, each with an assistant take care of directing each individual soldier, eleven when up to TO&E, table of organization and equipment. That's why any major general who's been in the infantry will tell you a rifle squad leader has the toughest job in the Army, more men to command directly than a four-star general.

I called the colonel to remind him to lift all preparatory fire when I asked; we were finally shoving off and for him to tell Fire Direction Center I'd personally call off artillery when we were ready and to make sure battalion relayed immediately and correctly. King Company and its machine gun sergeants would support us with their own fire from the northern ridge of 1179 to keep gooks above us from poking their heads up and lowering rifles.

I turned to my new radioman, Corporal Andy Hill. "C'mon, we're taking off."

"I can't," he pleaded, pointing to the stripped-down carbine lying beside him. "It won't fire right. I have to clean it."

No one could pull a Funaro on me again. "Damn it, come along with the 300, you'll find someone's soon enough."

Several replacement riflemen who needed to be broken in thought the trail on the saddle looked easier going but Lieutenant Rose hustled them off just before a swarm of bullets drilled in. I took up toward the end of Rose's platoon. The men stopped near the bottom of the saddle, going through a thick clump of tangled bushes.

I worked my way forward, yelling, "What's the matter? What's the holdup?"

Their lead man was getting high fire from unexpected enemy on a finger leading east-west toward Heartbreak. We directed our combined machine guns to take them out and before we got out of the bushes just off the deep saddle path, King Company's water-cooled guns and two 57mm recoilless rifles were on to the unexpecting enemy. King's overhead made it so hot gooks abandoned their machine guns and bugged.

When they heard me hard by them, Lieutenant Rose, Pop Miller, and two or three other noncoms got the men to scream war whoops and "E-e-e-e D-e-e-e W-a-a-a-a! Cuda, cuda!" Corporal Boggs, a Louisiana swamp boy, let out a stream of ear-piercing wild-turkey calls, that in an early American war were 'rebel' yells. We moved right along then and I got hoarse keeping the yelling up to pitch. Scattered along one section of the vague supply bunker path we passed a dismembered 75mm mountain pack howitzer, ten pieces or carries altogether; two spoked wheels here, the heavy breech there, and so on for about fifty yards. The only thing missing was the hard-working mules that packed them up mountain trails under Colonel Bull Boatner's Chinks. By one supply bunker there was a neat pile of what must have been about 500 rounds of 82mm Russian mortar ammo — 82 so they could use our 81 ammo but its ammo is too large to fit 81mm.

A rifleman behind me let off a round by my ear. I whipped around: "Goddamn sonofabitch! Watch where you're shooting. I know you can't *see* gooks, but fire up where they *might* be."

Guys whammed into the ground a few yards ahead, subconsciously not wanting to offend gooks and make them retaliate.

I ducked behind large rocks to answer Duncan on the radio. Friendly fire was tight over our heads. I felt so safe where I was I had to work up willpower to make myself move again. About ten riflemen bunched up behind the rock formation with me and I had to move out first before I could expect the guys to chogee. I was stopped a couple more times when the battalion commander called. It burned me up every time I was handed the radio receiver; the guys thought I was quitting them and lagged and stopped yelling. Finally, half way up, I told Duncan my radioman would continue to receive but I was too busy to reply. As I handed back the receiver, I heard him say something about a direct order. "Fuck you," I muttered, "want to run things get your ass up here."

After a while, when we started over the bald, dangerous top of 1181 through the grenade line, I shoved Ziggy's and Pop Miller's squads through Lieutenant Rose's platoon. They balked just as the tail end cleared Rose's men. "Lift the damn artillery," Pop yelled back. I had planned to work in about twenty-five yards closer to it, but it worked out just as well. I learned not to argue with fate.

"This is Buzzard Seven. Lift the artillery, it's holding us up." Then I yelled to the men ahead of me, "Okay, it's lifted."

Unfortunately, one three-gun salvo, in flight as I talked, ban-sheed in close above. The men stopped, dropped to their knees, turned and glared at me. One shook his fist.

"See," I yelled, hoping to calm their fears. "Just one salvo already loaded. They're through until I call for more."

A few minutes later, as the first half of the lead platoon and I were in an irregular circle, panting and puffing, stumbling through artillery-plowed earth just below the enemy position without warning a single red-hot 105, as had threatened Ziggy on 1179, tore the air apart, crashing like a meteor into the middle of our group. When the black smoke and dust settled, all I saw were white-eyed Tree and white faces, stunned, questioning, angry.

"Where the fuck that come from?" someone yelled.

I bellowed into the radio, disregarding procedure. "You dirty cocksuckers, have them lift that fuckin' stuff or we're gettin' the fuck off here, hunt you bastards down." Hopefully the right guy heard it.

As with Ziggy on 1179, we were lucky the round hit a huge rock formation above us and the spray went up. No one was nicked and it was observed from 1179 that it helped to break up a ten-man counter attack beginning to form near the summit.

By 1400, when we reached the very top by the large OP bunker, one old Maxim gun to a flank was still chuggin'. It took a few grenades. We rousted out altogether twenty unarmed and pretty tame-looking gooks, one of whom kowtowed to me when riflemen brought them over. I figured he was a *honcho* (Jap, important person), so I told the sergeant in charge of a guard detail to tell S2, intelligence, about his kowtowing. He was older than me — festering, draining burns on his right forearm and shoulder. It had been about three weeks since Marine Corsairs worked this ridge with napalm for the ROK Marine Regiment attack.

The Johnny-come-latelies scrambled over the rocks and into bunkers looking for loot, checking everything carefully for booby traps and throwing around what loose junk there was. They found about eight Russian carbines, several long rifles, two elephant guns, beauty of a well-machined WWII kraut machine pistol with a skeleton stock and a brown Bakelite hand grip.

It was a job getting the men back to their squads and calmed down after that exciting victory. The NCOs and I were so pooped and hoarse we could hardly talk. I had to stumble around, gasping, to get us into a perimeter defense and then drank dry the last of my two canteens of water.

Half an hour later, as Sergeant Martin, the ROK interpreter, and the late-arriving artillery FO were moving up the saddle path to join us, we got a very aggressive counterattack; it sounded like a hundred jabbering monkeys firing and throwing grenades. Hashing it over, however, we agreed it was only about a reinforced squad, nevertheless, athletic, armed with burp guns.

A private named Miller was killed in this attack (no relation to Pop or Tom). To our rear, Corporal Robert Davis, Love Company's 57mm recoilless gunner, did a terrific job until killed by a sniper. Sergeant Richard 'Nick' Nicholson of Beaver Falls, Pennsylvania, his squad leader, told me on the phone what a terrific young man Bob was and what a good shot. Also KIA was Corporal Salvador Bourbon, National Guardsman. Bourbon had just returned from the 10th Station two days before with a draining head wound and was ordered by the battalion surgeon to remain near the aid station to have his dressing changed. King Company found him the next day off in the bushes on the right of the trail, apparently trying to outflank one of the gook guns by himself, how Master Sergeant Ulriche died. Bourbon was one more heroic Mexican-American, as I knew them all to be potentially.

The taking of 1181 was nothing like grand conscript armies of Napoleon sweeping across the plains of Europe, flags thrust aloft by mounted noblemen cornets, or George Patton's snarling, clod-throwing Sherman tanks, guidons and antennas fluttering aloft, sweeping across open fields of France with truck-speeding infantry regiments of flankers outmaneuvering the enemy; the static mass tragedy of muddy WWI trench warfare or the horrible mass suicide stumbling up twice to die on Cemetery Ridge in our Civil War. After all, we were engaged in a Police Action never accounted for. Forgotten, unworthy of American civilian concern.

What we had to do on mountain hopping (loaded with equipment) was crawl up wooded fingers to ridgelines and slip-slide up or down narrow trails and footpaths, sometimes with scary drop offs on both sides. And we lost three good men who turned wrong in the dark or misjudged foot- or handholds and the enemy had a pretty good idea of where we were at all times.

By far the worst casualty to Third Battalion in that assault was the loss of Master Sergeant John Pater. I particularly felt terrible and worried since his company medic told me he got it in the back, the vertebrae with their important conduit of nerves. I came as close to prayer as an Agnostic is permitted. Instead I hoped hard, conscious of how much important scientific work was being done in the spine field. He did return several weeks later but was wounded worse on his way back to King.

We spent the rest of the day and most of that night on 1181 digging emplacements facing enemy, with overlapping fields of fire, registering mortar and artillery impact zones, watching beautiful greenish-blue lace lightning (St. Elmo's fire) play up and down our commo wires in an electric storm.

About seven the next day, I was awakened and ordered by Duncan to report back to 1179. What the hell now? I thought, poor radio procedure? I turned the company over to Lieutenant Rose. Knowing the great odds against field commissioned guys, before leaving, I went over everything I could think of bad that might happen to him until he stopped me. "Don't try to prove anything," I told him.

"Geezus, Gould, who you talking to? I've been over here a few more months than you, right?"

"It's just I'm superstitious."

Lieutenant Colonel Duncan returned my salute, took me aside and without beating around the bush told me point blank I was picked to lead an assault on 1243, which didn't surprise me; I was on a roll. What got me, was there wouldn't be a lot of time to get ready, it would take place on the morrow, hardly time to get resupplied. Seems it was the bright idea of our newly arrived division exec, General Boatner and I was cautioned that he would question me to check out my self assurance and how I'd take the emplacements. "No secret about it," I told my colonel. "The same with the others; you approach it up a finger, the only way, get as much preparatory fire and Air as you can, move up as close to the artillery as you dare, lift it, and banzai the sonsofbitches."

With Lieutenant Colonel Duncan was Fearless Frank Mildren, and to my surprise the new assistant division commander, Brigadier General 'Bull' Haydon L. Boatner, chief of staff of the Chinese Army in India in WWII. After brief introductions, I told him in short order my simple plan. He was not enthusiastic, as I heard generals generally aren't, but had nothing to say against it: get as much preparatory fire as possible, a good air strike that afternoon if possible before dark, and charge up there as close behind our artillery as we did at 1179 and 1181.

"Stick to those plans; you ought to come out all right, lieutenant," the general said as a benediction of the highest order.

"I'm *sure* I will," I said and was handed an angry glance from Duncan. Later, at my request, he told me why.

"Getting in the last word, as you do, Gould, you appeared trying to up the general."

By this time, Lieutenant Colonel Duncan, paratrooper, and I had been through a couple battles, and so long as no one else was listening, I knew, if I felt it important, I could say what I pleased. After Mildren left with Boatner and his aide, I let Duncan know how tired I was becoming. I told him I was very proud of what I found like a game, natural to me if dangerous, but it's gotta' stop sometime. Exposure, it's called. I was fatigued and weary and as he well knew, no one lives forever and why push my luck. Besides, it's not my job, not at my rank; it belongs to a Regular Army captain.

"Colonel, I don't give a shit anymore, if I ever did. I'm getting tired of sticking my neck out for your Regular Army. I'd like a crack at my own career; instead, on every hill I get further and further away, closer and closer to getting knocked off; I'm tired of doing some Regular Army captain's work, wherever he is."

"Gould," Duncan said, seriously. "Right now your career is leading men in combat for your country. I don't have to tell you what patriotism is and nobody has said anything to you, but ever since you took over from Captain Shallow, you've exhibited those magic qualities that cannot be learned; not taught at the Academy. Some things can't be taught and you've got the men with you. There's something about you that makes the men want to follow and please you. Maybe it's because you're not professional, a relief worker like so many in this war; one with more enlisted time than officer. They seem to realize that you have a naturally aggressive attitude and are generally disrespectful and it's a good thing you're in a rough and tough rifle outfit in the field, you'd been court martialed long ago in a quiet unit in the rear. Apparently you've become a soldier's Jesse James.

"I'm talking out of turn and could get my ass in a sling if you tell anyone, but personally I'm trying to say I wouldn't want you around in a peaceful situation junking the division training schedule, for instance, made up by Army pros, but for your valuable service at 1100, 1179 and now 1181, General Boatner and General Young are putting you in for a DSC and a captaincy and as soon as he prepares a suitable slot transferring you to division. Boatner said he was thankful for a few leaders like you in WWII."

The few times someone is kind or speaks well of me, I tend to get belligerent.

"Shit," I blurted, "I wouldn't last back there a day. I'd be calling them rear echelons to their faces. I worked back there with Regulars for a week when I landed in Korea and its prissy-prissy military careerists who hang together and have their own jokes and do things their way and look down their noses on Sunday soldiers like me. I made the mistake once of pissing down the wrong tube."

Colonel Duncan, who wouldn't know about that one, probably took it as an idiom; pissed down the wrong tube?

"Well, the general could make other arrangements for you as a captain. Damn it, man, you certainly earned it, but don't push your luck."

"Thanks, Colonel, I'll believe it when I see it. I'm proud though that it comes from an old combat man like 'Bull' Boatner."

Man oh man, I told myself, after quieting down some; that's the best compliment I ever had; shit, that's the only compliment aside from Colonel Rowney's Silver Star. Captain? DSC?

Division called in a good FEAF (Far East Air Force) four-plane rocketing, strafing and napalm attack on 1243 that afternoon and that night an extensive bombardment by ten batteries of 105s and 155s, FO'd by a captain from division.

I returned to where they were still digging in a defense facing the gooks and called in Lieutenant Morris and the ROTC officer of King named Wadsworth as acting commander, telling him here was his big chance and the platoon leaders and I all agreed it was too bad losing

Master Sergeant Pater and after reminding them all to move fast from cover-to-cover and keep together and get their machine gunners and mortarmen to give us good cover and for Christ sake, stop when they see us taking the hill, and, damn it all, good luck. Nothing fancy about it, here we are and there's the friggin' hill and each has his job. Let's do it again. Love, King and Item in that order. We'll shove off in the attack at 0600. Oh, yeah, let's synchronize watches.

"Sh-e-e-it!" someone complained in good infantry style. "Here we go again."

At 0530, before the sun was up, I worked through King to a safe hole on the enemy side of 1181 where I could observe, I radioed for two of Mike Company's heavy machine guns and as preparations began with our FO registering rounds on 1243, soon to be in better view, I noticed a tall blond guy just off the trail behind me, Pater's company radioman, Ken Johnson, I learned, lying on his side, radio beside him, rubbernecking, watching the stuff land on 1243. King was well behind and Johnson came forward for the sideshow. When he first came over to the enemy side I told him to take cover. "Dammit," I yelled. "Get off the trail, it's zeroed in!" I had thrown myself off that trail after a bee's nest of bullets came zinging in on either side of me. "Get your ass out of here!"

Instantly, SWAAP! smack in his heart. I'd never witnessed so direct a shot before so closely. I was yelling right at the guy. He died as blood poured freely out of his chest through his undershirt and fatigues over his tight belt collecting in a puddle down by his feet, his face turning rapidly yellowish, pale and blank, like pulling down a shade.

Someone behind him yelled, "Medic!" and I turned and yelled back, "Get away, zeroed in! He's gone!"

So strong was his instinct to save guys, Love Company's second platoon medic disregarded my warning, and as he continued to slide low down the ridge, I yelled again to get back over the hill and fired a burst of automatic carbine over his head into the trail behind him. He stopped, wide-eyed, finally got the gist of what I was yelling and crawled his way back over the ridge top. Plain luck he wasn't hit.

Pater remembers the dead radioman well to this day. "A real

beaut, Dud, one hell of a nice kid. I was evacuated by then, I never knew it until you just told me."

It's my belief, although I have no proof, a fifth to a fourth of men killed or wounded in rifle platoon combat become casualties because of their own carelessness, curiosity, laziness, or utter stupidity. They somehow detach themselves from the action to be neutral observers. I'd warned Johnson twice that he wasn't needed on the forward slope and to get back to the friendly side where it was safe.

The new first sergeant brought Love up about 0600and we began to move down to the saddle. I was the only officer aside from Lieutenant Rose along the ridge from the enemy side of 1181 to the approaches to 1243. Our new FO, a young captain named Blackwell, wasn't aggressive, but there was one heroic 57mm recoilless rifle gunner back down the trail from us, Corporal Davis's replacement, who fired canister on his own, doing a terrific job.

Swatches of morning clouds brushed the tops of mountain trees at daybreak on the southern side of 1243, exposing holes through which threatened the guarded top as forbidding as Count Dracula's castle in a thunder- storm.

"Good day for murder," Sergeant Milligan told us.

"We will!" he was promised.

Shoving off that cheerless dark morning, Love Company was relieved in starting positions by Item so we could pass through King's defense of 1181 over a line of departure in the fog and drizzle. As we moved out for 1243, guys bitched, demanding to know how come Love did it all.

"Because we're Love," I told them proudly.

But then, I brooded, who gets really hip to this job?

Since H 1100, we were indeed the preferred point company, which I took as a big compliment, especially to the guys. Shit, no company, no goddamn rifle company in the world was more aggressive, worked so smoothly together. But, as I explained to Sergeant Milligan, much credit goes to Mighty Mouse committing companies like steam rollers in train. We hit, got hit, passed our wounded back, stepped to the sides of the trail for resupply, and let King through. King was hit, and stepped aside for Item, and just as important to the juggernaut was

supply, back down the trail near enough for all of us, resupply of everything we needed, ammo to an armament specialist and extra weapons, to chop-chop and, particularly important in those dry mountains
now the monsoon was over, water. Above all was our terrific morale.
We'd been through things together and trusted one another and like the
colonel said, I was at heart one of them. I never really wanted to be an
officer.

The first peek of the rising sun was enough to run off mists and
low clouds as I hissed back from the front to be relayed to the rear to
be sure bayonets were fixed. "One in the chamber, safeties off." Our
column moved slowly as delays up front became longer.

Group intuition told us it had to be about time for something to
pop. It did; someone accidentally tripped a taunt wire stretched by King
Company across the trail about six inches above the ground, pulling a
cotter pin from a flare fuse that released a striker to ignite an explosion
that popped up a flare to ignite 500 feet above — colorless, brilliantly
burning in the weak daylight, swaying back and forth, splattering
burning, spitting magnesium dripping fire streaking toward earth,
blown slowly along by an early morning high-flying breeze as it descended slowly on parachute, sizzling and crackling. It was strange, no,
ridiculous, to see a flare in daylight. Our mountain world knew someone goofed.

"Damn fool!" a sergeant hissed, "watch your step, pass that
back."

Each man said goodbye to the world as he passed King's hasty,
scanty barbed wire. That damn flare was more than a bad omen; certainly destroyed any surprise we might have had. Or, I hoped, might
actually reassure the gooks that it must have been one of their returning
night patrols; no enemy on the attack was dumb enough to throw up
a flare over himself in daylight.

Slipping and sliding on wet ground leading down the saddle
and up toward 1243 in the light of early morning in that strangely luminous environment, Private Funaro landed on his ass the third time,
no record for that miserable morning, but a good average. He remained
down, refusing to budge.

"Damn sonofabitchin' Army!" he swore out loud. Always

damn Army; never dirty statesmen or even bad enemy; always a hard-on for the US Army.

"The Army ain't ours, it belongs to taxpayers; blame them," someone hissed nearby. "Keep it down!" another hissed more loudly than Funaro.

"You keep it down," his sergeant said in a higher voice.

Pop waited patiently until Funaro, sensing him standing above, looked up.

"Can't make it sarge," he whined. "Ankle's broken."

Pop reached under Funaro's arms and yanked him up face-to-face talking softly as a trainer to a recalcitrant animal.

"Damn it all, boy, we'd be mighty lonesome without your old M1. Step along best you can, all our ankles are broken."

"I ain't no RA," Funaro shot back. "I didn't sign up for this shit."

"Shut your fuckin' mouth," someone ordered.

Funaro was lucky to have been permitted to join, to find square meals after his stepfather or one of the men he sometimes called that, ran him off. Lucky he'd not been convicted of a felony for then he could never be accepted in the US Army, and felonies were just where Funaro and his street corner gang were headed.

Who *is* hep to this job each man brooded? Looking back, I realize I was becoming pretty much on the shaky side again. My right trigger and middle finger were dark mahogany from cigarette tar, smoking up to three and a half packages a day depending on the supply. I was once put in my place by the platoon sergeant of the Second Platoon (who took Red Rose's place) for snapping at him over the EE-8 and warned by Colonel Duncan on the radio to watch the way I talked to my superiors.

I could hold out my hand and stretch my fingers and they'd quiver. I mean move up and down by themselves. Nights I was often wide awake reminiscing, talking in the middle of the night imagining I was about to be awakened for my two-hour tour, and sometimes when I did get to sleep, I'd be awakened by a violent dream. "God! Oh God! Watch out!" I'm no doctor but I'd have to say I was falling to pieces. Falling, why yes, that was one of my worst nightmares, everything falling away below me as I told myself I had a parachute somewhere, if only I could find it.

One man in the approach column, for good reason more skittish than Funaro, was the lead man, point man or first scout. Stalking forty yards ahead of everyone, bent from the waist with rifle at high ready port, finger within the trigger guard, safety off, one in the chamber, the ready pose of a tense grouse hunter, moving his head from side to side to widen his view, listening intently through the silently drying mist, taking furtive glances at the ground ahead for trip wires or sunken ground, sign of a personnel mine.

Now and then he stopped abruptly, cocking his head like a robin listening for movements of a worm, to catch in the antenna bucket of his steel helmet any noise at all that might warn him in time. Somebody or bodies up there ahead wanted to shoot him down like *he* was the game. Meanwhile, drip and drizzle of slow rain was a disruptive waterfall to ears searching for certain guarded, most sinister sounds.

We relieved our point men frequently. One of the stories rear echelon soldiers tell at Veterans of Foreign Wars bars is how they put goof-offs on point to punish them. Liars, that spot is held by men with whom you must trust your lives.

Suddenly the mysterious mist went from ominous to dangerous to horror as early morning came awake abruptly with the ugly canvas-ripping sounds of deadly burp guns blazing. Corporal Brand of the Banzai Third was point at the time and as the file of us anxious men stopped, I ran hunching, scooting, zigzagging, charging up to assistant squad leader, Sergeant Tree, to find Brand laying on his back in a small depression behind a tree, his shoulders pulled up under his helmet. As Tree began to crawl toward him, Brand rolled over on his stomach and got cautiously to his knees, pointing where the sudden fire came from.

"About ten gooks dug in right there, sar. . . ."

S-s-s-zlapt! blood splattered from Brand's right shoulder and shuddering, weakened by the heavy hit, trembling from the powerful physical shock, he rolled over and over into a shell hole away from the point of contact. Thousand to one he's finished, went through my mind; then quickly modified, "for a week, anyway, and if he got a stateside wound, a bone or a nerve, say good bye, Brand'll never be back, the lucky bum."

"Lead man right of the trail," Tree yelled. "Get us moving. Off the trail, José, now; chogee."

Private Joseph ran past, bent double, zigzagging from boulder to another, tree to tree, scrub pine to scrub pine, as someone yelled for the company Doc to clear out. Third Platoon medic Myles came scurrying up and I stopped him with urgent hand signals.

"That's suicide. For the love'a Christ, Doc, wait. Brand's red-hot. See if he can't stop bleeding himself."

Disregarding our yells, Doc Singleton, company medic, reached the wounded buddy and tugged open the stiff snap of Brand's first aid pouch. Brand attempting to sit, pushing up with the hand of his good arm, like a drunken man in a forward slump, still shaking, rocked half unconscious from the shock he slumped back.

"You'll both be killed!" someone shouted. "Get back! Get back! Grab his feet, pull him to cover!"

"What's the situation up there?" I yelled.

After a silence of two or three minutes, "All right here," Brand said, scarcely heard above the angry barking of rifles, staccato of machine guns.

"Except for Brand, my squad's under cover," Sergeant Tree responded.

"Anyone else hit?" I asked.

"None of mine," Sergeant Zigerfoose said.

"We're all right," Pop Miller sounded.

"Okay here," came from Sergeant Olsen.

"All okay?" I yelled. "We're going after them now. Who's leading point?"

"Brand's up moving, sir," Pop shouted with evident joy.

"Brand? Brand?" I yelled. "Hear me, Brand? Can you move us out?"

There was no answer.

"Brand, get us moving," I repeated, getting a little teed off, assuming from Brand's "All right here," and "Brand's up moving," he was only nicked.

Still no answer.

"What's the matter, Brand?" I shouted, crawling up on my belly past Pop Miller.

Doc Singleton, ignoring the warning to pull Brand by his feet to safety, worked quietly and efficiently, hunkered low as he could, had cut off Brand's fatigue jacket, working a bandage over a low, badly bleeding shoulder wound. Myles crawled up then to help Singleton drag Brand back behind cover and when the company medic scampered back for his aid kit, preoccupied with his job, he made the mistake of standing part way and a bullet went sh-u-u-umft! straight through his helmet, throwing it off his head liner and through the air. Flopping from momentum down a steep slope, Doc's quivering body turned over twice in a rapidly decreasing motion, limp arms and legs flopping down a two-foot drop off through the air like a rag doll. Ski, near where he landed, went crazy, standing in full view, yelling his lungs out at the gooks, screaming for them to show themselves. It took three soldiers to get him down and hold him and two slid with him down the slippery trail to a slight hollow where bullets couldn't reach, where Pop sat on the gangly Pole and held him with one of the men, like talking to calm a frenzied horse; "C'mon, buddy, get hold of yourself. Calm down, Ski, or get killed. Steady, steady, boy. There, there take a deep breath. We'll get them bastards, don't worry. . . . C'mon there, that's my buddy, take a deep breath."

Ski, not as bright as most guys, never tried to hide his feelings and although he calmed his body so Pop didn't have to worry any more, he started sobbing like a little kid, growing softer and softer until, as Pop scooted up the trail to the rest of his squad, he sat there staring with a little whimper. Ski felt things deeper.

The platoon cursed savagely reverberating pure hate throughout Love company, spreading from cover to cover, with the bad news that one of our Christ-like medics, sainted savior, chief of company medics, was gone. An enemy machine gunner became active and immediately the battle was rejoined.

Doc Singleton had not had time to give Brand morphine and evidently the slug hit a bone, probably the collar bone for it was observed from a distance from Brand's face he was in great pain. After

Doc's sudden death, we were too occupied with the enemy to check Brand and, indeed, most of us having witnessed Doc working on him assumed he was taken care of medically. No one got to Brand for an hour and when one did, Brand's blood was gone. One glance in his face told me shock. Damn sonofabitch anyway, where were you, Gould, when Brand died? Where was God?

We were in the flurry and the din of furious battle, each sergeant thinking he led the attacking squad, platoon size though it grew. Dying was all around, engulfing us with lead and jagged steel. To us it was all we could withstand. All our dead put down from National memory in black bags with no one to applaud their supreme sacrifice, or ever remember it in that Forgotten War, not even their mothers gone today knew how their loved sons died, no one save a handful of old guys like me all alone at a typewriter trying to commemorate. Shit!

Very few of us know how they were wasted. I don't suppose there are more than five in this world anymore even can talk first hand about that battle for Hill 1243. Goodbye forever and ever Corporal Brand. Excuse me, I do not remember your first name. And Specialist E-5 Doc Singleton, your first name escapes me too for which I apologize. After all these forgotten lonely years, only the God of War remembers it, thrown away young warriors, brave as any who have been discarded, ever lived in whatever age, used up, unidentified.

Above the wamp wamp and woompt woompt of grenade and mortar explosions, the snappy individual bark of rifles, were my frantic calls of encouragement as I estimated and directed changing situations: "Over there; c'mon, you! . . . yes, YOU! . . . Sergeant Roundtree. *Tree,* don't look at me, look up! Watch it! Christ, watch it! . . . WATCH IT! WATCH IT, I SAID! . . . Goddamn gook there! . . . Can't you see him by the tree? . . . Get the sonofabitch! SKI! . . . WHERE ARE YOU, SKI? . . . All right, watch that side over there! . . . WAKE UP! . . . WAKE UP! . . . HERE THEY ARE AGAIN! . . . UP AND AT 'EM. . . . Funaro, good boy, another Edsel Turner! . . . YOU, YES YOU! GET SOME HEAVY FIRE IN THERE FAST cover that BAR! . . . ON THE DOUBLE! . . . NOW LET 'EM HAVE IT AGAIN! . . . ATTA' BOY, KARL. LET 'EM HAVE IT! . . . Rose, Lieutenant Rose, work your men through. That's the way!

. . . Hey, you. What's your name, man? . . . Well, put that guy behind rocks and get your ass back up. . . . We can't spare anyone. . . . He's hit in the arm? Call your platoon medic! He isn't going to die. . . . HEAR ME? I SAID STOP HIS BLEEDING AND DROP THAT GUY AND GET BACK FIRING. . . . Catch up, WE'RE GOIN' OVER! . . . Hey, *you*, get your BAR over here. . . . WATCH IT, MILLER! . . . HEY, POP, WATCH IT! THERE'S TWO BEHIND THAT LITTLE PINE TREE . . . NOW GET 'EM. GET 'EM BOTH . . . THAT LITTLE ONE THERE! . . . TOSS 'EM A GRENADE! . . . GO AHEAD, GIVE 'EM ANOTHER."

And leading in all outbursts of E-e-e-e de-e wa-a and other desperate battle cries were the sergeants and Red Rose yelling their lungs out. We drove the enemy before us so close we clearly heard the hollow-tube CHOOOMP of their mortar rounds leaving tubes from a ravine hidden to the north of us. We drove an advanced enemy back up to their permanent position. This, mixed with sharp, barking rifles; metallic sounds, tinny peeee-w-w-wink! of empty M1 clips flying from the automatically-locked-back ready to be reloaded actions of rifles; the resounding metal-plate-clattering of empty burp gun ammo drums dropping on rocks; and the frantic jingle-jangle of war materiel hanging from cartridge belts or loose in fatigue pockets of men running up against fire that blue-smoked morning.

"Aim low," came a calm but loud voice. "Keep your ass down and fire up and we'll have 'em on the run." Warren Milligan, baptized at the abbey at Cassino in Italy January 1944, Master Sergeant volunteer replacement from Division for Sergeant Eppler's spot.

When the brief commotion was over, King and Item closed and blended in behind us to help beat back a stiff gook counterattack. The enemy was stubborn, however, fell back orderly across a saddle and dug in swiftly before the permanent installations atop 1243, concentrating small arms fire, forcing Lieutenant Rose to slide back, abandoning three dead.

When the yelling subsided and all were under cover and silent again, in clear English came the order shouted from a gook bunker further up the hill for Red to "Throw it in!" "GI, quit now! Go way!" Red took it for a while and then responded, without realizing it, with

308

Zachary Taylor's noble answer to the Mexican surrender ultimatum as the furious Battle of Buena Vista turned against the Fourth Infantry: "My wounded are behind me and I'll never pass them alive," except Red prefaced his with "fuck you, gook bastard!" as old Zachary might well have done with strong profanities of his own times.

Nearing the critical grenade line, guys in front bogged down under a sustained burst from an enemy machine gun which, with unappreciated flippancy, closed with the braggadocio burst 'shave and a hair cut, Bay Rum.' Horsing around like that was momentarily confusing. Plain gooks, of rice fields, weren't supposed to know that diverting jingle nor have a sense of humor, or maybe they knew only that it was a tune coming from an American gunner somewhere and thought it daring to reproduce.

As I turned to cheer on my men, several coordinated burp guns opened up from a hitherto unknown suicide emplacement down the hill from the large bunkers on the very crest of 1243. Out of the corner of my eye, behind me, I watched horrified as Tree, forward of his squad, slumped to the ground, then stood halfway unsteadily and began to stumble and fall the second time, pawing air with his right arm for support. Tree's face drained of blood turning ashen gray-brown, his constant hateful symbol of comparison, color, nearly gone; that token black we in Love learned to respect and, yes, love in a masculine way.

"God! God! What a sight. No, God, NO!"

Those who watched the swift drama stopped, shook and shocked, their faces pallid too, stricken with abject disgust, hate and remorse.

"My God," someone said. "Look how white Tree is."

There went our buddy, self-proclaimed 'token nigger' who sang and hummed us to sleep, lying face up, smiling as usual—like he always did and dead often do.

I stumbled forward, completely out of myself, upward in blind fury standing tall, screaming: "Bastards! . . . sonsofbitches!" and choked out uncontrolled ineffective words. There suddenly weren't any in infantry jargon strong enough to fit the occasion and from my throat came meaningless animal growling sounds and aggressive curses used in mortal anger since caveman days. Moving ahead and upward, waving my carbine, temporarily out of ammo and my mind as blank, I yelled: "Get 'em! Ee-dee-waa, yellow cunts!"

At the bitter end it was always cunts! Never evil North Korean soldiers, or dirty enemy, but something down below in a woman every man who is a man cherishes and vies for in perpetual heat. Why? Why not: "Lousy shot!" or "Murderer, you"? Why did we call those we would kill cunts? Don't tell us we were simply sex-crazed. Women were furthest from our thoughts.

Heavy Weapons let loose behind us with a steady tirade of water-cooled machine guns, recoilless rifles and salvoes of 81mm mortars as I swung around waving my empty carbine over my head with one hand.

"Get over it! Kill the bastards! You can't live forever! . . . Let's go! Let's go! They got Tree! Blow 'em up! Bayonets! "

We crawled and ran stumbling up the last steep grade through soft artillery churned soil, every man yelling like a banshee, welded into a mobile foray of fury, forlorn hope of screaming madmen running enemy off with the shear blast of voices, Jericho trumpets of our own, inspired to commit suicide over the death of an outstanding buddy; assaulting with the spirit, crying for vengeance of the brave heroes of all wars.

Hell, man, neither we nor our dead were ever to be known outside battalion; actions not even mentioned after a single day anywhere but to fill space in the Far East edition of *Stars & Stripes*. Our heroics were so expected as they were asked for, they were usually unknown even to regiment except as unique tragedies traveling on grapevine for days. We struggled and died anonymously, unsung, unknown to all but our combat buddies, only our true, transient brothers in blood knew and applauded our efforts, respected and loved us the manly way.

King moved into our immediate rear behind Item and warriors of both companies within earshot stopped briefly, stared disbelievingly as they passed Tree's tumbled body where, after a glance, in an electrifying second, they took up our angry cries, "Get 'em! Get 'em! Kill the cocksuckers!" "Bastards got Tree!" Sergeant E-5 Roundtree, known to every man and officer in the battalion just for being black. In those days he was, indeed, our token black, humorously declared by himself in mock slave jargon, "Yeah, man, I'se yo' token nigger."

"You heard the lieutenant!" Sergeant Burris yelled. "They got Tree. Let's go!"

Surmounting 1243, I yelled myself hoarse. This was my most successful assault, I, with the largest number of guys up with us, contributed greatly to revenging Tree. Usually only a handful go all the way over the grenade line—the critical moment that spells success or failure. The number swells as soon as intermediate bugouts see you've taken the hill. They want to be classed with heroes so you got to have them for a quick defense.

We smashed through the grenade line and stumbled on and took the summit about 1430 in the afternoon and beat back the first counterassault half an hour later, eight or ten suicidal enemy emptying burp gun drums, running up as close as they could to die. We dug holes to protect our bodies until our strength was gone and laid on our arms for hours as we answered radio queries from the rear. By 1700 we could no longer transmit to battalion over our dying batteries, although sitting in the setting sun worrying we continued to faintly receive and made out a weak, surrealistic voice over the air—

Buzzard Seven? Buzzard seven? . . . Buzzard Five? Buzzard Six? Anyone up there? Report your situation. . . . This is Buzzard One, Buzzard One . . . Buzzard Seven? Buzzard Seven?

My second known-for-sure victim, came suddenly in back of me in the second counter attack against 1243 just at dusk, balanced on the outside of his right foot suddenly about twenty feet away, right shoulder and arm stretching his body back to throw a grenade at me, an easy target. I squeezed my carbine trigger in two short bursts. His grenade dropped and blew up two or three feet behind him as he fell.

As we crested, five or six badly scared gooks ran silently, unburdened, through tree stumps down the saddle path leading north from 1243. All ten or fifteen of us almost out of ammo were too pooped to bother these runaways, good targets though they were. Sand gritting my teeth, sweat from my scalp smarting my eyes, and my throat and mouth were parched by my hot, rasping breath. I yelled hoarsely, "We made it. Sonofabitch, we made it!"

Soon Pop Miller came over to my portable company command post with a proud look as he urged along four bloody prisoners. "Al's got more," he told me.

The spongy, artillery loosened ground at the top was barren of debris of battle comparable to 1181 – empty American cloth bandoleers, a bullet-punctured helmet, ours, since Chinks or gooks had none. Empty burp gun drums, clumsily soldered cans of grenade fuses and sacks of gunpowder with which to assemble their frag grenades on location, empty cardboard mortar tubes of 60mm rounds captured from ROKs, bloody cloth dropped by wounded. A rifleman stooped to recover a meaningful item beside a square yard of blood-soaked earth.

"Ain't this Pete's old harmonica?"

It sure was, his name scratched on it. Pete Simpson of King, who entertained us some evenings with a buddy playing a banjo before a movie, dropped MIA, taken off with a capture team several weeks back from a staked-out night patrol.

Everywhere, always after every battle, debris scattered in the ruins from pilfered pockets of looted enemy. Whoever so much as touched a downed buddy could expect a beating by more than one of his friends including even Philip Funaro.

In trampled mud – a small, happy Japanese doll good luck charm, brought from R&R, a jackknife with a broken plastic handle, an unexplained blood-splattered legionnaire roll, and a yo-yo, all taken from Americans. One of Pop Miller's men picked up a rain-soaked booklet of instructions in English on how to take successful pictures with a Russian camera. Having tried to thumb apart the wet pages, he flung it into the bushes.

There was little enemy loot, nothing personal. Two or three large canvas bags of frag grenade hulks with leather carrying straps, rolls of gook Army-issue tobacco leaves, and twenty or thirty white cloth bags of NKA issue unroasted peanuts. Why they hadn't assembled the grenades we'll never know, unless they were newly arrived. One guy recovered a US Army-issue forty-five caliber pistol.

Dropped here and there in that litter, twisted bodies of gooks

312

killed mostly by artillery.

While the chogee train which slaved for our battalion took a break, shivering, wrinkled old carriers scrambled about to salvage what they could from the wreckage. One papa-san slipped, with guilty glances about him, into the blood-stained fatigue jacket a medic had peeled from a man, and tied to his crude rope belt a cloth toilet kit someone had foolishly brought along. The old gentlemen pawed eagerly for rare scraps of rations and poked through broken litters, empty machine gun ammo metal boxes, spent gook assault wire reels, and other junk of battle.

As soon as new batteries reached us, Buzzard One wanted our casualty report. In addition to one MIA, rumored to have fallen down a cliff off a ridge trail, I was surprised to learn we had only four killed aside from Corporal Brand, Doc Singleton, and Sergeant Tree and nine wounded, three seriously, already well on their happy ride down, one, unconscious from an ominous head wound. We seldom understood how they were MIA, missing in action, although in those wild mountain ways there were plenty of half-hidden gorges and precarious drop-offs.

A young King Company Korean interpreter interrogated the prisoners in an intimate circle squatting on their haunches safe from gook fire behind a rock formation. Shaggy conqueror Sergeant Eppler stood over them. One, obviously an officer, was the most disappointed man I'd ever seen. Noticing the silver bar on my collar, he stood and faced me, straightened smartly to attention, slapped his moldy tennis shoes together, bowed low from the waist, and then proceeded with surprising candor to tell me in good English his "American foe" were pretty good fighters, but their firing didn't scare his men half as much as the sudden yelling at the very end. Using third person, he gave no inkling he was describing us directly in case it was taken wrong.

"Americans, you had? . . . has? . . . cigarette?" he asked, searching for the correct tense, at the same time making a motion of pulling a cigarette from his mouth and coolly blowing smoke into the interpreter's face.

The interpreter scolded the captive's boldness and as the POW grinned broadly in turn, I lit him up.

313

"Hey, Kim," I said, "Ask this cocky guy how come they never wear officer insignia?"

Side-stepping a direct answer in English, the honcho jabbered back and forth with our interpreter for five minutes before an answer was produced.

"He say North Korean People's Army real democratic and he say. . . ."

"Shit," Eppler scolded the King Company Korean interpreter, "tell him he's full of shit."

"No shit!" the POW spoke up indignantly.

"Yeah," came from someone in back of us, "if bullshit was music, he'd be a brass band."

Enemy bunkers, the usual suicide apertures facing south, were of no use to us and we had to hurriedly dig foxholes facing the threat from the north side of the pinnacle. First, we took care to hunt down booby traps, duds and all-wood, shoebox mines. Many a soldier was maimed or killed by merely touching a dud or jostling it with his toe. Dud is, of course, a word I'm sensitive to. What usually causes a dud is an activated firing pin released to strike a primer to set off a charge hanging in its shaft part way to the primer, with its spring energy held back. The pin is bound or caught or hung up, to one degree or another, to one side of the shaft in which it rides and may take only a slight jar to dislodge it to complete its strike, stepping heavily on the ground beside it, picking it up.

It became obvious that someone at division expected many casualties for a special, impressed carrying party approached us late in the afternoon, pale-faced, pussy-footing men of the Second Division Band and sundry 38th regimental headquarters personnel under a Graves Registration master sergeant, with twenty unhappy Korean civilians and their recently emptied A frames and litters ready for hauling down wounded and dead, had they litters enough.

"We've been waiting back down the trail since yesterday afternoon," the bandmaster admitted.

I warned him about becoming their own casualties and demonstrated to his musicians how to creep bent over.

314

I found myself thinking that since Brand and Funaro were in the same squad, why couldn't it have been Funaro, immediately apologizing to the delinquent Italian-American gang member. Shit, it's fate that's all, and Funaro's got every right to live. He's better than any ass-kissing rear echelon. He's no prize, but he's earned his right just by surviving this far and is part of a fire team, riflemen and BAR, whether always up with us or not. He's one of our banzai gang for sure.

Light of a setting sun dimmed over the badly-maimed trees below as I scurried along the perimeter of 1243, checking the guys of Love Company, encouraging them, pulling them as tightly together as I dared, covering the contested ground mindful of the age-old threat of infantrymen: "One round will get you all."

Early fall chill was with us, arriving with gray darkness. Digging like woodchucks turning over freshly plowed dirt, some brought white phosphorous to air that caught fire again and, burning quietly, stunk like skunks.

The band carriers and the regular bearers gone, leaving behind empty litters, while settling for the night, a heavy artillery fire opened on us. We dove for cover and I bellied behind a large rock waiting to hear what would transpire. Burp gun racket would mean they were attacking in force but there was no small arm fire and as the second terrible air-rush-screech came in, we realized it was coming from the south where our friends were, so-called 'friendly fire'; on the wrong elevation, one wrong digit, failed to understand his forward observer, or trouble reading elevation on his own map, a simple, mistake at Fire Direction Center way down the valley behind us.

We could never call our own artillery but it had to go through several stages and then we had no control over it and rounds could not be corrected until radioed back by their own forward observer, wherever he was. A dastardly crime never atoned by the observer who called for it across the valley with the Marines, or the guilty air control man who misjudged elevations. Fear in me equaled the night in May playing dead in that impact area, except that few of my guys were in a protecting declivity. This artillery, long tom 155's, I learned much later as I was writing my journal, was intended to sail high above us on its way to support Marines attacking from Death Valley.

While most rounds pass on over, some, notably proximity fuses set to explode so many feet from an object as determined by returning radar waves, will sometimes prove to be shorter than they should be, and at times difficult for gunners dependent on their maps and the accuracy of forward observers to calculate the correct clearance of their shells passing over terrain features such as a newly conquered mountain top. Our tactical maps were hurried US Army Engineer copies of old Japanese civilian maps of Korea, sometimes with faulty or no elevation markers.

"Third squad! Pop! Hey, Pop Miller," I heard Sergeant Eppler yell. "You guys all right?"

"Okay over here!" Pop replied.

There was still confusion as to whose fire it was and I shouted, "Brown? Keep the machine gun where you can get it out from under. That goes for all three platoons."

Those around me in Love Company headquarters on a shrunken enemy side of 1243, down from the ridgeline digging a defense, were untouched.

"Short of us, sir; on friendly side."

"Ziggy? Speedy? . . . You guys all right?"

"Okay," Ziggy yelled and Gonzales's affirmative was relayed up to me.

Suddenly it was landing behind us again, on the friendly side, a short TOT, time on target, barrage of angry salvoes. One minute they were living, upright, warmed by their blood, talking animals, human beings, shouting warnings and encouragements, closely bonded to face any danger, a second later human parts strewn about the ridge top torn, unrecognizable broken, bloody remnants of fury as salvo after salvo, screeching 155 shells from one of our own artillery battalions, no longer angel kisses but flying packages of magma. My forward portion of the crest was spared and as soon as rounds stopped crashing in, giving a five-minute safety wait as was customary, I ran up and over the crest to where many of my Banzai Third platoon used to be.

As I neared, a private volunteered, "Mostly dead, sir."

"Pop!" I shouted, "where are you? Pop?"

"Sergeant Miller's over here!" a voice croaked and I found my old buddy, old timer, fellow WWII vet, like me, fellow dogface, lightweight, pale, sickish, bloodless yellow face of him, suddenly transformed by raging pieces of jagged hot steel into a terribly hurt, broken up, prone, blood-covered man doll, chest pumping cherry-red spurts soaking your fatigues, the blood-soaked glimpses of an exposed shiny white shattered bone, the shredded stump of an arm. Fast as blood flows you quickly lose all hold of yourself, all contact with dying parts. Say goodbye to yourself, search your personal history fast as you can, if you can in a flash, and goodbye to everything living.

In writing this, I could discover only one sergeant who claims to have survived that disaster, 1243, and it is not strange that I do not recall him; I have talked to some who though we have proof we served together do not remember me. This is normal I've discovered, over half a century the most engaged in combat have to forget or learn to sleep less.

Exactly when my buddy Pop Miller left I do not know, I know only that I ended up holding him.

"Medic! Medic! Hurry," I yelled as I pulled Pop onto my lap and pressed into the unbandaged chest puncture that was sucking air, hoping to slow some of the bleeding long enough to clot. Pop's face was yellowish-green, eyes closed limp as Ich when I handled him.

"Damn you! Doc! Singleton, Singleton! Hurry!"

"Doc?" a voice demanded. "Dead! Gone. Doc's gone, remember?"

"Get an aid kit, hurry!"

"Lieutenant Rose got hit trying to fix one of his men and his medic's using it."

The awful short time it took Pop to die, looking back, most probably instantly, the terribly short while anything could have been of help, drowning in so much blood as I held him in my arms, keeping his head up holding by his hair, pushing in on the chest puncture, trying to stop the still pump from spurting, assuring him all the while he was doing well, when I knew it was over. "Okay, old buddy, don't worry." I knew he was gone but I so wanted him to be alive. I could do no more than push in over his chest wound, that had been, I thought, pumping erratically or convulsing, pulling in bloody air from outside his chest straight into his lungs in spasms, only seconds, eventually drowning in blood. And his half-severed arm? Oh God, fix it, someone hurry. Put it back together.

"Someone help! Get bandages, hurry! A tourniquet! . . . Stop bleeding! My God, he's all blood, bleeding everywhere." His blood was all gone but I thought still bleeding; some chance of saving him if only I tried hard enough.

The hysterical pleading of a nearby rifleman, "I'm hit? Doc! Please, Doc! Running down my leg."

"Blood? You pissed yourself."

Pop and I were together on our own and as his blood drained killing him on my lap or maybe before, vomit from a short C ration supper and bitter bile rose in my throat together. I was beyond short-winded; suffocating from stomach bitterness, my throat burning from acid, searing stomach acid. Sucking cold air, my chest pained as it too sagged on my aching lungs and expanded slowly, painfully as well. It seemed I breathed a weak eighth inch in, eighth inch out, spitting stringy, sticky, bitter slime from my mouth, gagging, choking on bitter bile and coughing, rasping desperately for air. I could drown in my own puke with no air in me, as I was just sitting there, Pop on my lap, giving me his blood.

Time in death, passed Pop and me and it grew very dark so I could barely see. I remember dimly two men from Item Company, I believe, one an officer, bending down taking Pop off me, their hands slippery with his blood—God, he's bled gallons— and I watched him slip out of their grasp crossing the large, smooth rock ledge formation we were lying on, to lay his bloodless body on a litter soon painted red.

Without sense of time or where I was, I lost normal feelings and reactions and entered a world wherein myself was referred to as 'him' and only occasionally. I could never recall exactly when Pop's heart and breathing stopped in those seconds that were one.

When my breathing returned to a livable rhythm and depth and I rose from where I had been with Pop, a small coagulating pool of his blood ran slowly off my lap down the outside of my pant leg, disappearing in the porous cloth of my fatigues. I remembered scolding as we would kid each other, "Old fart. Yes, you, Pop, you know me and you are too damn old for this sort of thing. Let's get to the rear before something bad happens."

One man, a medic or an officer, wanted to know what I was saying, talking patiently to me as with a drunk, finally seizing my chin in one hand, raising my head back, forcing me to swallow from his canteen and I coughed up more bitter bile to my mouth and spit it out with sticky stuff.

My waist, right side of my fatigues and right sleeve were soaked, black, where blood dried, making my fatigues stiff, my hands sticky while tears flowed like rain of salt water down my cheeks for the terrible thing I was part of, holding that poor butchered animal, old buddy Pop.

"How about that lieutenant?" a distant voice asked as another man stood towering over me. "Must be hurt bad. Look at the blood."

"Someone else's."

"Someone else's blood; again, someone else's blood; someone else's blood," I repeated over and over. "Someone else's blood. You had your chance to bleed, now Pop's made up for us both."

We were in that slaughterhouse, foliage red abattoir, forever before Item Company finished passing through, relieving what was left to Love. Firing, some far away it seemed, and unimportant, as Item beat back a small probing counterattack. Still later that black night, a strange language was talking above me as the Dutch, back from Pusan with green replacements, climbed from the Pia-ri Valley with orders to relieve Item, passing me by, all staring at someone else's blood drying black on me.

During a long, moonless, starless night, the remnants of Love were withdrawn carefully back down the ridge, ushering me tied by commo wire around the waist of a soldier of Item carefully down to the broad valley from where we started two months, or was it a year or so ago? Aside from dozens of litter cases were forty stumbling wounded, including a very rattled me with what I thought was a broken arm, in single file, eight to be triaged serious, mute, riding before us, solid lumps of bloody Army fatigues tied to litters.

I stumbled along more forlorn than I've ever been under the

319

perpetual scream of a bad dream to a beat-up cane bottom chair by the entrance to the Dutch aid station, unnoticed in the general low-toned medical urgency and bustle, favoring my arm, watching a grim parade of ambulatory passing with bowed heads and litter-borne and un-wounded in shock, heads bowed, shuffling zombies—quiet and grim, one young soldier crying.

A medic, doctor or aid man, I was unable to differentiate, asked me routinely, "How're you, lieutenant? Hit? Hurt? Where's your tag?"

"Hurt, not hit," pointing to my unmovable right arm.

It seemed he knew me or of me and then one of our men gave a Dutch medic my first and last name and helped him write a tag, for what I couldn't decipher, and I remember trying to be normal, joking that even doctors' assistants wrote so they couldn't be read. "Broken or fractured arm." I thought it should read. A Dutch chaplain passed by, a Catholic; our eyes met and he looked away quickly and went in search of needy believers.

From there for many months, or years—time lost to me—my life was weak; its sick residue badly out of tune, or, you might say, discombobulated, if you know what I mean. Months or maybe even years, or could have been just many hours, was a big blank in which I shot the breeze with Dorn and Tree and now with Pop, and less with J C Rodriguez who, you recall, was a quiet guy, and, yes, especially that heroic, cocky, little commo guy, with the wire reel forever on his back, Sergeant Miller's young assistant wire man—"you and asshole divvy up my Medal of Honor"— whose terrible dying ended convulsing bleeding inside, fast-growing goiter, which memory hurts so I try consciously never to remember and skip right by that painful part of my sorry life without thought, blank when I try hard to recall, come unexpectedly in nightmares at times well organized by a mysterious self that dwells inside just to blame me. "I've done my best, dammit, I've tried. I didn't kill them, now for the last time, get out of my head!"

A medic, doctor or aidman, whomever, went by me before I could tell him how I felt. When he came back I told him my arm was broken. He picked it up and moved it about carefully and said, I think he said, he'd seen such cases, not to worry, it's mental . . . will heal itself. What is mental, a broken arm is mental?

I was in the center of deathly concern for hours or maybe nights and as morning, or even days or an afternoon, as an old horned war devil chased me around and around mountain tops and tripped me and broke my right arm again and sat on me so I couldn't escape. His awful stinking self like shit, is again waiting by me, I sense less patiently, another cannon perhaps with off-center sights, a big mortar with unmatched bubbles. Shit! Understand? Plain shit. Fred said it—shit. In fact, stink I smelled came from me— I sat in it.

My dead lay on Kach'il-Bong all night and I was still at the Dutch forward aid station with other ambulatory when they brought down the rest of the cold bodies early in the morning. How carelessly Dutch mortician helpers loaded them as we had done so many times; two men swinging each rigid body by head and feet alternating slabs of wood, skin-covered meat, onto the hard bed of a truck, one man climbing inside to pull the bodies forward. Like we disposed of those courageous young gooks who penetrated our line, flinging them back down the steep hill.

"Where's their bags?" I yelled at a sergeant. "Don't throw them away. They don't breathe doesn't mean they're nothing."

"No say English," the Dutchman apologized.

They were stiffened together in death, Pop's right hand, the good one, pointed skyward in the pile over Ski's bloody, broken knee. Ski's blood-caked head flopped back over someone's torn boot, and Ski, who out of combat wouldn't hurt a flea, glared, eyes frozen wide open in terror at the pitiless sky at what they did to him. At last lost soul, you've found a home equal to any—no more orphan place—as intelligent and worldly-wise as any piled above or below you. You have truly arrived at the common goal, equal to any man.

Forever out of combat, the last day for so many wonderful guys who loved life but were killed in Love. And Sergeant Ray Martin, old dogface First Sergeant now and forever, didn't have to be there that late afternoon. Stand your last retreat, old pro. This time Old Glory salutes and weeps for you; joking as usual how you came along because someone had to show us how to do it right, a violent battle curse set forever on your lips. Funaro, too, most reluctant soldier who forever denied signing RA. Back in South Bronx they used to say he'd succumb to a zip gun the way he was headed, already belonging to a dangerous street gang. Instead, he was killed legally in Uncle Sam's large-scale gang war.

Slowly, with no one suggesting or me even realizing what I did, my fingertips went together on my tired, cracked lips, ready for a Buddhist or a Christian prayer.

> and if I die before I wake, I pray
> the Lord my soul to take.

9
The Casualty

I awoke clawing my way out of a sticky cocoon on a cot in the mental hygiene ward of the 11th Evacuation Hospital feeling I should be angry at some one or some thing, yet anger was a debilitating luxury; instead, I collapsed on the floor at the foot of my cot and cried again that our own artillery killed us. I sobbed and shook uncontrollably trying to let it all out of me. Yes, I was hurt enough to die but instead I cried, reaching round about for my death. When I most needed a death philosophy, a belief instead of a doubt, it wasn't there, no pity or promise in Agnosticism, nothing soft, mysterious or at all comforting; nowhere to go just when you're all ready. It's easy to live an Agnostic if you're hard, so lonely but hard to die alone, for fellow Agnostics are never there when you need them.

There at the 11th Evac, Lieutenant Colonel Watson convinced me my arm wasn't hurt, a trick of my mind to force the rest of me out of danger. Army doctors have a name for it. I was, all of me, a lost one, off by myself again and found me cleaned of my shit, talking to a warrant officer case worker to prepare me for a hot shower, clean fatigues, shave, haircut and warm spicy food, plus a shot of pentothal.

There, them, we, maybe just me, planned revenge, threatening to press manslaughter, court-martial charges. But first off, there was no recognizable guilty ones. Early on it would have been heard by 'my friend' Walter Winchell, but just who, asked the warrant officer, could I finger? Who's to blame, give me a name, 'They,' whomever those guys might be. He suggested I let it pass as officialdom does, a horrible accident. Nothing could or would be done at my level anyway, for I was a mere rifle soldier, bound over without rights of citizens or generals, who could I complain to, some rear-echelon sonofabitch colonel who'd white-wash?

I thought a lot, too much, and stretched and yawned and sucked on one weed after another, slept early and up late, accepting the peaceful promises of the day, but days brought no mitigation to my wicked dreams. Eyes red-rimmed and watery, I arose unwillingly, stooped over to lace my muddy old combat boots and found soft hospital slippers instead and straightened up only part way to face another ordeal called day and they kept me in the 11th Evac as though they owned me for weeks it seemed, against my understanding.

Why, for Christ sake ... what's happening now? They put me under, with my permission, to see what they could find and if they ever found anything I was never told. Sleep was so illusive I dreamed without it. I'd sometimes be up in the still of a late hour, in my robe and over through the damp, thick darkness of the open ward to chat with second shift cooks. Once I dreamed I hoofed the five miles alone at night down a dark, winding footpath of a wild hill I recall marching down to an eerie valley of dead civilians and once bivouacked where we slept in rain in the July monsoon, ancient Korean mounds where their ancestors were buried sitting up on the hillside where rice could not be grown, clasping their hands in front of their knees.

Could it have been another dream? It was so rocky we couldn't dig in either, and I rested against a grave feeling at home, to think deep, solemn thoughts of life and death and eternity. Silently, in half light, one by one my dead walked before me in sand bag bathrobes out in a circle around me. I was surrounded by my dead; yes, *my* dead, I ordered them. It was all my fault; they have every right to stare at me; I let them down ... down, down. "Lieutenant," they seemed to say, "why don't you join us?"

I might have died too had I stayed in the 11th Evac had not someone somewhere exclaimed: "Why, Lieutenant Gould, where've you been?" and they jeeped me to battalion headquarters, fated never to return to the mountains along the Punchbowl except in flashbacks that came when I closed my eyes, times when I saw or heard something terrible to remind me.

A replacement captain took over Love, former rifle platoon

sergeant field commissioned in the First Division during their retreat in 1943 in Algeria. We didn't hit it off at all. He neglected to say anything friendly like my guys were proud of me or anything, or that he knew I got a Silver Star leading and a Bronze Star training them. I think he was probably jealous and probably said things about me behind my back for trying to lead a rifle company in combat as an untrained Sunday soldier. I wouldn't put it past him.

What to do with Gould was Mighty Mouse's big worry, compounded by Lieutenant Colonel Watson, the 11th Evac's head shrink, telling him it would take time for me to recover from the 'unusual' trauma suffered on Magpie Mountain, that probably would always be a nightmare.

Guided by Watson's insistence that I be kept out of combat, Duncan interviewed me and after reminding me that Roy Carse filled the only slot in battalion that because of the provision in his records positively couldn't involve combat, and my little respect for an assignment in the rear echelon anyway, my sharp tongue and predisposition for a court martial, he asked me what training I had in demolition.

"Not much," I told him.

"Well," the colonel said, "I'm sending you to a ten-day refresher course at X Corps EOD, explosive ordnance demolition, and since you did heavy lifting on your foundry job and have a lot of experience with hard-working guys, I'm giving you P&A Platoon [pioneer, meaning in advance of the main body, and ammunition]. I understand you're still a little shook, but Doctor Watson's keeping an eye on you."

"And I'll keep an eye on him."

"Smart talk again, Gould."

"Speaking of smart talk, colonel, where's my captaincy and DSC?"

"I was waiting for you to mention that, sorry I went out of my way. As I told you at the time, stuck my neck out to let you know what I heard. If you really want to know, I did it to let you feel proud of yourself because odds were damn high you wouldn't survive. Don't hold me to it, it was talk I heard from Colonel Mildren."

He looked away a second and went on: "It might still be coming, after all, it's less than two weeks. Give him time. Boatner's on

325

TDY [temporary duty] to UN to straighten out POW riots at Koje-do. He took the 23rd with him."

I was given a cot in the crowded officers' tent at Headquarters and Headquarters Company and settled my pack with what little stuff I had, and was introduced to master sergeant, platoon sergeant, Bill Hipp, and the P&A bunch.

When I got back from a ten-day X Corps demolition crash course, Woody, our mailman, brought me a letter from Kitty and one from Gordy, my so-called best friend, who asked me how it was going and how many I nailed; how sorry he was for not having time to answer my letter from Fox Company.

"I've had a new job, Dud, busy as hell." Shirley, his wife, had been sick a lot. "They don't seem to know what's wrong with her; know how aggravating those things are. I bumped into Kitty the other day on the Square; she doesn't look so hot either. I got to go, Dud, drop me a line. Them Chinese on your ass all the time? Watch it. If anyone can handle them, it's you."

PFC Woody, who kept close track of our correspondence, wanted to know who was *Catherine* Gould, my daughter?

Kitty's letter was the second since right after 1179 and of course I lost the first and hadn't written either. I was afraid to open it for fear it was a dear john. "Dudley," she began, seriously. Not Dud or stud, shit pot or any other affectionate nickname. "This is hard to write and you know I'm no whizz at English. You should be right here to talk face-to-face. I worry about us, but enough about us, Dickie has had a chronic cough and knowing how bad it was with your mother, I took him to Doctor Montgomery who gave our Dick a skin test and x-ray. Nothing like TB he said. The test was negative but he's having his tonsils out Thursday and he's got mastoiditis and where are we getting the money? I don't know, but is it possible to borrow more on your pay? It would be nice."

She began Dudley which she never called me and signed Catherine which I never called her. It was always Kitty or honey, or sweetheart or something funny but nice. At least she didn't call me dirty rat again, but no more I love you honey. It didn't matter to her if I got killed tomorrow afternoon. What does she know or want to know about

326

what I have to do? Later, I learned from her sister she worried all the time about me, days and lonely nights she worried. "You could be dead now, this afternoon, she would worry," Betty said, "all the times you know you're in no trouble; with her you're in trouble all the time."

I never realized that.

After that I got just one letter, in which she did call me honey. "Honey," she wrote, "Why do this to us, hurt me and make me cry? Dickie starts crying when he hears his mother cry. Don't you love us anymore; you never ask about Dickie. My mother thinks he takes after you. Honey, what's the matter? Don't you love us anymore?"

I didn't know just how to answer that and I didn't find time.

I married Kitty three weeks after coming home from three years overseas during World War II. At the ripe old age of twenty-six, I worried my hair was coming out because my father was partially bald at twenty. I was fast becoming an unwanted old man; I must get married while I still had a chance to attract someone pretty. On first sight, Kitty was the one for me. She was nineteen, humorous, high-spirited, at odds with her mother and stepfather, living with her older sister, as eager as me to marry someone and start a family. Besides, she often told me, forcing on a kiss, I was her hero, the most manly man in Watertown, a uniformed officer. We were fabulously in love, in a hurry. In less than a week we up and eloped with two fifty dollar rings. Only her mother, stepfather, sister and brother-in-law were with us; my father, in so many words, disowned me for not finishing college for free on the GI Bill.

After I took the ten-day demolition course, Captain Benson, supply officer, and I took a jeep back to quartermaster depot for a three-day cold weather school to be outfitted with sets of cold-weather gear, heavy zipper lined parka with wolverine fur around the face under a hood, heavy lined mittens with separate soft leather trigger fingers, a long, heavy cord inside the parka around your shoulders like with little kids' mittens fixed to each other so you couldn't lose one; thermal underwear with a large buttoned flap when you have to take a crap and a long fly with buttons instead of zipper so you won't have to worry about them freezing; two pairs of arctic socks and thermal-lined snow boots and wool overalls with suspenders, without a belt so as not to cut off circulation.

Back in January at Hoengsong in thin cotton fatigue jackets, some wounded froze to death, just as sometime after I left they issued bulletproof vests, which all of us could have used.

We visited the companies, the captain talking up the benefits while one by one I demonstrated what they would soon be issued. As I took it off and showed each piece, some guys would yell from the rear: "Take it off, take it all off," like I was a strip teaser. Too bad we didn't have a real stripper. With no sense of humor, the captain then had me do it the other way, put the cold weather gear on one by one.

One thing none of us ever heard before was anyone sounding off how dangerous smoking is in cold weather. "Lieutenant Gould, take notice," our physician instructor at Pusan QM Depot said, seeing me light one from another. I told him I was from up north and never heard such a thing. "No serious study has been made before," he told me, "and now the tobacco industry is fighting us tooth and nail. We now know for certain that nicotine, formerly used as an insecticide in Black Flag, causes small blood vessels to collapse in your extremities and without circulation, arms and legs grow colder and colder and easily frost bitten and even death from hypothermia."

Psychologists will probably understand when I say I began to lose self-respect. I mean without my proud dangerous job up there what am I, a rear echelon P&A platoon leader? Plain labor far from combat. I'll go to pieces in the rear all the time while my guys keep dying up there. Up where you don't dare stand up. Nobody back here understands just what I can do, my potential—how valuable and what I can do, and what I've done already. Back here they have a different way of judging guys— how polite and modest you are, how prompt, how servile, how clean and uniform and 'military,' like West Pointers. Only once did I feel good back here, when an E-5 hospital returnee on limited duty came up after a class to ask if I wasn't *the* Lieutenant Gould who took Fools Mountain and 1243.

"Sure am," I told him without any damn apology.

328

Our P&A platoon was three squads, most important being what gung-ho guys wanted to be assigned to, demolition men, led by SFC Tim Regis. The EOD people at division did the same damn thing as P&A demolition squads with no fear of enemy fire and drew 50% more in hazardous duty pay.

We took our jeeps with trailers and weapons carrier loaded with supplies and equipment over to the Mundung-ni Valley northwest of Heartbreak Ridge past Satae-ri to help demolition platoons of the Second Division Engineer Battalion, Company C, lay long lines or chains of blocks of explosives at twenty-foot intervals to blow mines. We wired them together with primer cord and fuses and blew them in long lines where each track of a tank would run approaching Mundung-ni to lay preparatory fires.

Most trouble were Chink wooden box mines held together by dove-tailing and glue. With existing shell fragments, the area having been fought over before, our sweeps, mine sweeper SCR 625, would be singing all the time, and because of the time element, probing was out of the question. We simply blew tracks all the way up. Of course we had to be especially observant probing with a long steel rod where we went laying primer cord and charges.

I was surprised to learn that the old juggernaught companies, Item, Love and King, were in harness again at Mundung-ni, Love leading with that professional captain of the Regular Army. Much later, after I got back to the States, former medic, Bill Maddox of North Little Rock, Arkansas, told me that our Sergeant Tony Burris won a Congressional Medal of Honor at Mundung-ni the hard way. Grapevine told me the very day when Tony was among those who got it but the citation wasn't written while I was still in Korea. Colonel Duncan authored it and it was endorsed up the line to the Armed Forces Committee of Congress.

The Chinks were using their own 82mm mortar shells for mines because American mortar shells had as a safety device a throw-out pin that had to spin loose outside of the shell as it swirled beyond the tube to arm by centrifugal force only upon leaving the tube. Because of it, it could not explode in the tube or within short distance from the firing. Russian mortar shells, with no such safety blow-out pin necessary to arm them, were planted in groups of three about two feet apart, either with a nose fuse sensitive to the weight of a foot or tire pressure, or armed with trip wire to pull fuses.

Being of metal they were easily detected by minesweepers; nearly impossible to detect with the sweeper were wooden box mines. All they required to activate a fuse was for an unsuspecting rifleman to step down on a hidden light piece of wood and break it to arm the fuse. Anti-vehicle box mines had larger charges and thicker wood requiring a jeep or other vehicle to break a piece of trigger wood.

One of my demolition guys found a mine with his prod in a dry rut on an access road, alerted by the fact that the area above the box was sunk by repeated rains. Here was my chance to show I had what it takes. I wouldn't have any of them do something I was scared to do so I came up to the guy clearing it and motioned him aside, which he did gladly enough. Platoon Sergeant Hipp stepped between us: "That's all right, lieutenant, it's his job."

"It's mine too, anything you guys do I'm supposed to do better."

He smiled and stepped aside. "Be our guest, sir; be careful, we ain't had no officer since the ground thawed last April."

I drew my carbine knife and dug carefully, flipping the soil up and throwing it out of the way with my left hand until I finished clearing the box all around to the bottom and then reached two finger joints underneath all across the foot-square box.

"Careful to clear all around the sides, sir. There's wires to pull fuses. What you got there is a big one planted for jeeps or small trucks."

"I know, sarge, I know, they taught me at Corps."

"In a week?"

"It was ten days and we worked some nights and it was thorough."

I took a deep breath and went at it again. Certain that there were no trip wires to the box from the sides, I grabbed hold of its upper sides and proceeded to lift about ten pounds of explosive out of the rut when there was a sickening tug and a dull, broken wire snap sound, re-

330

sistance that warned me in a second that there was a trip wire connected to something below the box in hand. It broke as I pulled. I held the box, not knowing, as the saying goes, whether to shit or wind my watch. My knees quivered like jelly as I fought to keep my legs in the same position, the box suspended at the same level and turned my torso to face Sergeant Hipp who kept a safe distance as they all did, telling him in what I was embarrassed to say was a cracked, almost whimpering little voice: "Sarge, I think there's something underneath, I noticed the tug when you lifted. Now don't panic, gently set the box down and step away and back up to me."

I turned back slowly, and as Hipp said, slowly set the mine down and backed away. He went forward, knelt beside the hole where the box mine was and pushing down with a steel prod found two more mines, one on top of the other. By placing three anti-vehicle mines together they hoped to blow up a six-by or tread off a tank. By the time Sergeant Hipp was through setting a charge to blow them in place, a small crowd had gathered a safe distance and when he told them what I did they cheered. One told me that's how they'd lost their last lieutenant, a guy named Roderick. All that saved me, Sergeant Hipp explained, was the fact that the mines had been planted months ago and the cotter pin of that top mine was not squeezed close enough together to allow an easy pull out and gave resistance enough to break the rusted iron wire to the box mine fuse immediately below.

For the short remainder of my assignment with P&A they were careful to dig under mines far enough to loosen them for easy pulling and rig gin poles, a pyramid of three heavy crossed sticks and commo wire run back about thirty feet and either lifting them out or blowing them in place. The story of my narrow escape got around battalion headquarters and Lieutenant Colonel Duncan chided me for barnstorming. "To begin with, as an officer, you had no business doing the work." His attitude toward me had for some reason cooled. I wondered if that wasn't because he no longer had to depend on me to take objectives now he had an orthodox regular army captain.

On Mundung-ni we remained over several nights in hastily dug foxholes down below in no-man's land. We and demolition squads of the division's Second Engineer Battalion C stayed until we were through blowing tracks but the powerful tanks which offered protection in daylight and for whom we were clearing the track were helpless after dark without a full perimeter of riflemen rumbled behind the MLR back up the Satae-ri Valley before sunset. Otherwise, enemy could sneak in, plant satchel charges or take direct shots with captured 3.5 rockets that would drill and burn through armor over a foot to explode molten metal within. Tankers were justifiably afraid of tank hunters.

Leading a P&A platoon wasn't counted as combat but like other engineer projects, combat or not, has dangerous moments with its demolition squad. Generally, however, we were a labor group, working like division engineers getting heavy rolls of barbed wire, tactical wire, it's called, as opposed to communications 'commo wire,' pickets to snap it onto, burlap bags; all kinds of ammo from an ordnance dump where big ordnance trucks unloaded it; build and maintain secondary roads as best as possible, construct small bridges and fords and clear pads for helicopters. Primarily, of course, we kept ammo stockpiled, including mortar flares and willie peter and delivered it to company supply points.

It was especially dangerous clearing areas occupied by UN or ROK forces, especially ROKs, who failed to map fields to keep track of the mines, laid mines up the ass, and planted deadly grenade booby traps in empty C rations cans all over the place. Anyone could and did do it. Take a frag grenade, set it in an empty C ration can resting on the spring handle with the cotter pin and the ring to arm it pulled, the handle under spring tension would remain in the can and not fly off to set off the grenade until someone kicked the can or pulled a trip wire to dislodge the handle. It was said that ROKs killed more friendly troops relieving them than they did enemy.

Kitty never mentioned divorce in her second letter and I certainly never did. Underneath random dirty thoughts I knew I loved her very much. My men were gone every which way and she was all I had left in the world, although I didn't appreciate it then. Of course, there was Dick. I loved her every bit as much as always and could never forget her risking her life coming to comfort me, in the most terrifying time of my life, 15th of May; forget any of her for that matter. How "don't worry, honey," patting my head, "Everything will be all right," instantly put me in a deep sleep that saved my life.

Kitty once wrote several reasons she was unhappy; first she had no reason to feel good or be proud; was she part of a great national effort as I was? Did she have a lot of comrades to pass time with? No! She was all alone in a strange apartment in an old made-over mansion in the snobby part of town with no friendly neighbors or baby sitters which she couldn't afford and her mother and stepfather worked all day and I never talked it over with her about my volunteering to run off to be a big hero. Hero? Certainly not to she and Dickie. "Run off by your lonesome, right out of our lives to be a big hero and leave us all alone and that Silver Star and Bronze Star you sent home, stick them up your you know what."

I stewed a lot about whether our bad letters, our misunderstandings, were more the result of her miseries or mine. Who was the more miserable? Wasn't it mostly circumstance because of the housing shortage in Watertown following WWII that she couldn't find a decent apartment we could afford, then she had to move in without my help and find and buy furniture from Epstein's Secondhand Furniture Store what with less than $1000 we got left for selling our house. Look at the beatup Maytag Epstein gave her such a big deal on. "Oh yes, Mrs. Gould," they told her, "you have our word. It won't cost a red cent to run, trust us. Would we lie to you with your husband off in Korea fighting for democracy?"

It sunk in that to Kitty, I was responsible for everything bad that happened simply because I volunteered for Korea. I guessed I might be at fault; I had no right being married when I felt such a deep urge to have my mettle tested. It's not wrong to go off fighting for your country, just don't be married and have other responsibilities.

I didn't mind being P&A leader. Not that the work wasn't too much rear echelon, which it was, although compensated by being real physical. I always liked muscle work in the sun and open air; you feel like a goddamn man. I took turns with thick leather gloves hauling coils of barbed wire off tail gates, helping build a log bridge over a stream near headquarters and a rock ford down the way in what should have been engineer battalion territory but Duncan asked me to do it without work orders and the lot of stalling you got from division. "C'mon guys," I said, "we'll show 'em how to do it" and almost caught my death of cold, being wet all one chilly December afternoon winching huge flat rocks in place with our weapons carrier.

I don't know exactly when my 'personality problems' began, slowly sliding off the deep end, ornery with the guys for instance, finding it hard to sleep, awakening often, startled sometimes even though we were a good ten miles from gooks. One time I woke up past midnight thinking it my time to pull guard as I did in the platoon, or run the company line, checking holes to be sure somebody was awake and once woke officers in our tent talking in my sleep and, they complained, I even shouted once like when I was a little boy, this time banzaiing. The rear echelon officers didn't say boo to my face but bitched to Colonel Duncan and I was asked to take my cot to a spare supply tent, "Nothing personal, Lieutenant Gould, we know you can't help it." Never Dud anymore.

One night Master Sergeant Ulriche and I were sitting in the rain under parkas laughing at something Ski said the wrong way. He was noted for mispronouncing and putting common sayings ass-end backwards. "Get off the pot, dummy, if you want to shit." As the guys mocked him he'd snicker to himself trying to believe he was funny on purpose and that's why they laughed and was therefore socially acceptable; looking for an approval he normally got only from Pop and me. Damn, he was the most innocent guy I ever met, the least harmful of any and it was good he didn't slug anyone when he was mad. He was only eighteen but could just hold a guy in his arms and squeeze him until he recanted and he embarrassed guys because he, alone, was so lacking in guile.

I'd wake up at times three or four in the morning sobbing softly to myself thinking or dreaming of Pop and Ski together. Pop was much closer to Ski than my father ever was to me, with manly love to give. What a pair they were, Pop disdained by women, feeling helpless about it; Ski who never had anyone to love, a father, a mother, a girl, a puppy, anything. Ironical that Pop worried so about Ski being on his own after Korea, no orphanage to return to at his age to help him forget his terrible experiences. And Pop trying to impress Ski with the simple fact that he had to keep re-enlisting in the same company, and take as long an enlistment as possible until he got his twenty in, if they'd let him, and he hoped Ski could find some sergeant like himself for a new friend. Now, worry and helplessness were of no account, thrown t-ogether to eternity onto the bed of a six-by for their last ride in fresh air before being lonely eternally in brown Army coffins, buried deep, white tombstone crosses apart.

Neither Kitty nor I mentioned divorce again after the brief blowout over the washing machine, but we both seemed to get our kicks taking pot shots at each other, me much more than her, vicious accusations, devoid of common sense. According to her I actually enjoyed Korea, "acting important, being a big hero must be lots of fun. I've been asked to show those Silver Star and Bronze Star citations to the *Times*, but that would just make you more anxious to stick your neck out and Dickie— remember him?—needs you home."

Although I accompanied Sergeant Hipp and the guys on four major mine-clearing jobs after Mundung-ni, most of the time was spent delivering ammo, burlap bags, tactical wire, pickets and other heavy equipment, sweeping and probing for land mines, etc. The guys really didn't need me, they worked together for at least six months without an officer and one good thing about the rear, you didn't go losing buddies all the time. As for an officer, most couldn't remember having one and Bill Hipp was probably better than most officers, certainly knew his business better than I did. Who needed me anymore?

I passed too much free time smoking and fretting about what Kitty might be doing while I was stuck in that asshole of the world. With more time on my hands I wrote more often, but her letters didn't increase. She inferred a lot but never complained she was having a hard time with Dickie. Her letters weren't as hateful as at the beginning but I tried to find them that way. I was as nervous as an old hen, as we used to say; crazy thoughts and weird daydreams I fed along with bad ideas took over and I felt myself slipping away as I did when Love was ended for me by short rounds. Who, I sometimes thought, was I fighting now? Back at cold-weather training, Captain Benson once had to tell me to shape up, demanding: "Who do you think you're talking to?" Being rear echelon as he was, I suppose I had been a little contemptuous. I had to apologize.

The weather was changing fast; strong winds blew our way, as mountain leaves changed color to greet winter. As I became an old-timer, closer and closer to having my own rotation number, it cooled down at night and a new winter descended ominously. Spoils from our diggings stiffened with cold air from Manchuria and Siberia. Thin layers of frost formed and the sky darkened earlier and earlier and stern, unfriendly clouds covered the gray-blue northern sky. Back in Watertown, hunting season over, we'd look up and say: "It's like for snow."

Some religious guys sent home for Christmas decorations for the mess hall tent and our cold weather issue was doled out. It began to get real cold and one morning as we were about to go to the ordnance depot for a load of ammo, Colonel Duncan sent for me and excused his runner and sergeant major and told me to take a seat and instead of chewing me out for going unshaven and sometimes, I'll confess, without washing every day, as I figured he would, he told be bluntly: "Dud, you're going home!"

Crimus, I thought, just like that! I knew something was wrong. That's just what I need, that'd suit me fine. Everyone knows I've done more than my share over here; soft-pedaling it with this P&A job. No one deserves it more than me after all I've been through.

"You don't seem surprised, Lieutenant."

"It's only fair," I told him. "I've done a lot more than my share."

"Modest, aren't you."

"That depends on what others have done. Modesty becomes people with no reason to be proud."

He wouldn't let it go but kept pounding away at my attitude until I was raising my voice to him and had to be warned to control myself. He made me suspicious and I studied his face and suddenly figured he wasn't any more understanding than Major Wilkes, trying to get something out of me he could humiliate me with. I cautioned myself to watch out, be careful what I said anymore. Sure enough, soon he was trying to talk me into seeing Colonel Watson again.

"Never mind me," I told him. "Goddammit, colonel, where's all you promised to get me to stick my neck out on 1243? The promotion and DSC?"

Suddenly no longer nice, he snapped. "Gould, I don't have to kiss your ass to get you to do anything. I order you, understand? You're still a lieutenant and I happen to be a lieutenant colonel!" He paused to settle a flash of anger and continued, "Now something's terribly wrong, lieutenant, and we want to find out so we can help you."

"Everything's bugging me, sir. I'd like to get back to combat, at least you know who your friends are. At least you're with real men."

"Master Sergeant Hipp and the platoon aren't men? Cut the crap, lieutenant. Shape up!"

"Where's the DSC and captaincy you promised?"

Duncan raised his voice: "Damn it, Gould, I didn't promise you anything and what sort of captain do you think you'd be? Look at you, lose your razor, forget where the shower point is? I told you I was taking a big chance telling you what Colonel Mildren told me General Boatner said. In the first place, it's too early for anything. Bull has been on Koje Island since we got 1243, straightening out rioting POWs. And you haven't a right to demand anything."

The way I figured it, Duncan no longer needed me with that First Division combat veteran captain over Love Company. I told him this point blank and made him mad again and we talked angrily for a few minutes, then suddenly calmed down and sounded almost friendly and in a lower voice called me Dud again and told me he had no choice but send me back to the 11th Evac where "they have your case history."

I might've been pissed off that he was trying to pull a fast one but suddenly it seemed just the right thing. I didn't argue. I was actually relieved of a heavy burden of paranoia, realizing I could use some help with controlling my sick thinking and it was the only place to get it. Suddenly what had sarcastically always been *shrinks* were badly needed mental doctors. I could tell I could use one of those shots again

337

and some understanding and if my painful, evil, sickening mental condition, which I was beginning to recognize as such, wasn't enough there's my damn athlete's foot acting up again, reason enough to go back for a visit.

I was more than a little suspicious, however, when they had me turn in my combat equipment and my old buddy, my carbine and all the new cold-weather stuff.

In the first three days back at 11th Evac, I got shots to make me sleep which I was happy to do all the way to the next noon. Man, I didn't even realize how I'd been missing a good night's sleep.

I snuck a peek at the warrant officer's paperwork—

Subject officer underwent the traumatic sudden loss of eighteen of his men to friendly artillery which he is unable to resolve satisfactorily. He has so far avoided a complete breakdown but his personality has suffered. Subject evinces an adult situational maladjustment to the death of his mother twenty-six years ago. He seems to be suffering from a marginal identity premorbid personality, an inability to adjust to a father/son hostility permitting him to exist only in the role of wrongdoer. He deludes himself that his wife is unfaithful, based upon a lack of affection in their correspondence. He has nothing to support this belief. For unstated reasons, he scorns rear echelon personnel.

I was held in the 11th Evac over a week and put on a pound or two until I got really loud about getting back so I could go home. "That aggressive attitude, lieutenant, is why we can't release you just yet. Have you been taking your medicine regularly or do we have to give you something stronger to calm you down? Lieutenant Gould, you are going to end up in serious depression if you don't learn to relax. Now take in some deep breaths and unwind." When they did release me with warnings about mental hygiene, unhealthy thinking, and a prescription for what I believed were antidepression pills, I reported to Colonel Duncan as ordered. Before he could say anything, I demanded: "I thought you said I was going home, sir."

"I told you, Dud, but you were skating too close to the edge again, and we had to get you under control. Now's the time," and he held up a message from Division so I could see the Red Cross letterhead. "The Watertown, New York Red Cross has been in contact with the Second Division Red Cross representative. Don't worry, Dud; it's not serious, only potentially, and they recommend you be returned to your family before it is serious. Chaplain Johnson and I agree you have earned a long rest and the situation between you and your wife is apt to become progressively worse. You have only a few months to go before rotation anyway; we are requesting your transfer to the zone of interior and after an emergency leave stationed as near possible to your home town."

"What situation with my wife?" I blurted. "I thought I was going home on my own account. It's me you're worried about; I'm the one taking the beating. What does a damn chaplain know? He hasn't even talked to me, and what's this about my wife? I got a right to read what the Red Cross said."

"Sorry, Dud, it's confidential. Believe me, she's not critical, only that the situation, if allowed to continue, could get out of hand. Major Johnson has seen it happen time and again, the cruel breakup of families during wartime separations. The letter is only one paragraph addressed to battalion commander recommending compliance, which the Division Red Cross Representative endorses action we have already decided on. Your orders are being cut at division transferring you to the Ninth Infantry Division at Fort Dix from where you will be processed and transferred to Camp Drum, seven miles from Watertown."

All I could think was something bad is wrong with Kitty. "What situation could get out of hand?" That's all I could think, and I argued with Duncan but not until I teared up a little did he give in, afraid I'd break up right there.

"Dud, if I tell you what's in this letter I can get my ass in a sling." His decision sounded familiar, "I must swear you to keep it to yourself. I'm making a career in this man's Army."

"You say they're cutting my orders now; I won't be around to tell anyone. If there was anything wrong with your wife, wouldn't you want to know?"

"All right, not a word to anyone, your wife is suffering from severe depression. Do you know a Doctor Montgomery?"

"Our family doctor; delivered our little boy, but what's *she* depressed about? *I'm* the guy's taking pills."

"Well, he's still taking care of your wife and son. He's not a specialist but says she's worrying herself into some serious mental sickness and strongly recommends your presence."

"She never wrote about anything serious, except I didn't love her."

It was a sixteen-day voyage back to Seattle where I was bused with other guys from the docks to Fort Lawton and had the steel security bands snipped from my B-4 bag. Another infantry lieutenant, George Easly from Charleston, and I grabbed a taxi to the airport where we learned since it was getting close to Christmas all flights east were booked for the weekend. As we turned away from the last airline, a broker for nonscheduled lines caught up to us. He knew one line, a nonscheduled, Coast to Coast Special, had four seats available, leaving about seven that night for New York.

Not needing to worry about cost, I was traveling compassionate reassignment on an Army travel voucher, it turned out to be cheaper on the nonscheduled flight than on scheduled airlines.

Waiting for our unknowable takeoff time, which we learned couldn't be too long with only two seats unsold, I got plastered. Easly, assistant personnel officer of the 23rd Infantry, doing the buying had to listen to my battle tattle.

I got worrying about seeing Kitty and talking to her face-to-face, almost too excited and tense to go through with it worrying what our relationship would be after our ugly separation, I mean the nasty things I wrote her, listening in the waiting room with a good glow on to Christmas carols, colored lights blinking, my uncontrolled meanness, the unjust things I wrote, I admitted entirely my fault for the first time how cruel and cowardly I'd been and after two more drinks got a bunch of quarters and called her on a pay phone.

She sounded surprised to hear my voice, first, she said, it reminded her of the weird connection we had from Pusan back in May. She was strangely subdued and cool and when I told her I had to take a nonscheduled plane she didn't sound worried. She didn't say much at all. She might have shown some concern that her husband, after all the combat he went through, was flying nonschedule, the stinking reputation they had. One crashed a week earlier right in the center of Brooklyn and a few weeks before that in Buffalo.

Dickie was doing "well as expected" she volunteered before I could ask and sobbed a little just as the operator told me to drop in more quarters, which I didn't have and I was cut off without a chance to say good bye. It was more unsettling than my earlier call from Pusan and I worried when I hung up what she meant "well as expected."

The plane we flew in was an Army surplus C46, its large white star painted over but faintly visible under the light blue. Bucket seats facing the aisle were replaced by comfortable upholstered seats facing front, one row each side. As the pilot came over the loud speaker for us to prepare for takeoff—how to prepare he failed to say—our flight attendant came down the aisle telling us to buckle up because it was a law. She neglected to add what we knew she must have been thinking: "That's an order and don't you forget it!" Who would be brave enough to forget it despite the fact that being brave was a prerequisite for flying nonscheduled. A regular Wagnerian opera singer she was without her steel helmet—tall, chesty and blonde. Lieutenant Easly was astonished: "I just saw her outside handing up the luggage."

He passed me a pony of Seagram Seven for myself and we decided to take our minds off it. I was half in, half out of a drunken stupor in the middle of the night when we dropped down in the blackness of a moderately light snow storm rather suddenly on a ranch in the middle of Montana, a single floodlight guided us in as we landed in a foot of powder snow. "We're lucky," the intercom told us, "a big blizzard's coming close behind us." We taxied up to an old barn sporting Christmas lighting and gassed up at a Shell aviation pump. We made it up again blowing a snow screen behind and after another drunken, snoring sleep, landed at LaGuardia where Easly and I parted company.

There was nothing headed toward Syracuse, the nearest airport to Watertown and no trains until morning. I was lonely in that large almost empty Christmas lighted airport waiting room at 0200, rehearsing over and over what to say to Kitty, until an off duty American Air-

341

line flight attendant stopped to tell me I looked lonely. I think she had other plans than I but we chatted and when she found out my case, a sick little boy, she left and came right back excited, telling me to hurry with my bag, a special plane was leaving Newark for Syracuse with an extra crew to fly out a grounded plane. I was hustled to an American Airline transfer station wagon and got to Newark with the extra crew with fifteen minutes to spare, thanks to deserted streets. I was taken aboard, courtesy of the war effort, with a "Merry, Merry Christmas, you guys sure deserve one," a soldier in uniform returning home in distress, as a nonpaying passenger (no one asked for my US Army travel voucher) signing a statement absolving American Airlines of any claims.

We arrived at Syracuse's Hancock Field about 0430, 23 December. I remember blinking, colored Christmas lights and an unlit manger scene. There was no train or bus headed north because of a dangerous blizzard off Lake Ontario. I took a cab to the Greyhound depot and was sitting in the waiting room feeling sorry for myself, trembling off and on with excitement and the thrill of being almost home after all those 'years' (it seemed) in a treacherous wasteland, when two guys in their early twenties came over and asked where I was headed. "Good," they said, "we're trying to get to Ogdensburg and need a little help with the gas; there's no stations open this early in the morning going north. We can use your weight for better traction and might need help pushing out."

Snow was light until Pulaski halfway to Watertown where a sheriff pulled us over to tell us the highway north was closed. One of the guys pleaded: "Sir, we got a hero from Korea back there. He's on emergency leave and it's almost Christmas and his wife's very sick and they've been separated two years. We're trying to make it to Ogdensburg where a cousin's getting married tomorrow."

"Okay, okay, okay," the sheriff, an older man with a pot belly advised, throwing up his hands in mock defense. "There's two plowmen having coffee in the Star Diner up ahead. It's thirty miles to Watertown, they're pushing a big rotary and if you keep close in their wake, up close to their taillights, you got a chance, good luck. Wouldn't pay to lose their taillights; you'd be a snowplow yourself.

Now you didn't hear me say nothing. I didn't see you sneak by."

Driving along with tons of snow blown high into the air over our right front reminded me of hugging taillights of the 155mm howitzers with their huge tractors on that liaison job to the Seventh Division.

Before I knew it, we were coming down Washington Street, main drag through Watertown ending at Public Square. I counted blocks starting with South Junior High School where I used to go, until Paddock, five blocks, and got my B-4 bag from their trunk and handed over the twenty agreed on and a five spot with the trunk key. They told me to keep the five and buy something for the kid but I refused to take it back. We were already old friends; like guys in a foxhole sweating out gooks, surviving the terror of that blizzard made us buddies. We'd been through one of life's tensest times together, a trip through a dangerous blizzard. Had the driver made a slip off a shoulder, a second's lack of attention losing the taillights, we'd have ended in a ditch and maybe, dressed the way we were, frozen to death before anyone found us.

"Dammit," I told them, "if it wasn't for you I'd still be on my ass in the waiting room. If there's anything I can ever do for either of you, let me know. You've got my phone number and address."

They swore the same and we waved, parting company in a blizzard which was petering out some.

Sinking each step into a three-foot snow bank with snow filling my low-cut shoes and even down my shirt front, I struggled half a block with my bulging B-4 bag banging against my thigh and passed Kitty's apartment and came back two houses. Covered with snow, I entered the cellar vestibule of the garden apartment I'd never seen, thinking about the blizzard we had a year ago when I was young and patriotic and left her folks house across Black river. When I tried my key which I wore on my dog tag chain along with my C ration can opener, it wouldn't go all the way. I banged softly and then louder and louder until a weak little voice asked: "Who's there? What do you want?"

"Me," I told her, "remember I called?"

"Me who?"

"Dud. Don't you recognize my voice?"

343

"What do you want?"

Want? What does that mean, I thought, what do I want? She lost her marbles?

"Let me in. I'm cold."

It didn't sound like my Kitty, so weak and mild, and low, somehow very sick or beaten.

"Is this Mrs Dudley C Gould? Kitty?" I said, raising my voice.

"Yes."

She was there yet so far away, like being slugged in the gut; something terrible happened all right to lose her strong, youthful voice, happy lady of twenty-five. She sounded scared and beaten down like an old woman, or something worse.

"This is your husband, Dud. Please, honey, open up. It's cold and there's a big blizzard and my key won't fit."

The door of the apartment across the hall opened ten inches and a man's face demanded, "Who's there? Her husband's in Korea. Now get out of here. People are sleeping." He closed the door but, I felt, kept an ear to it.

"I *am* her husband," I told him over my shoulder. . . . "Honey, don't leave me standing here; my key won't fit."

"I know."

She opened the door slowly, and stood way back out of the draft and let me push it all the way as she backed further away, standing barefoot in a long pink flannel nightgown, eyes down, arms crossed tightly, squeezing herself, bent forward, covering her breasts, hiding them as she shivered. I realized how cold her . . . that is, our . . . apartment was. I set my B-4 bag down on a cold air register by the door to let the snow melt. Kitty was a shock; hardly recognizable, so terribly gaunt, dark shadows under her eyes, her hair unkempt. She'd lost about fifteen pounds—twenty, I found out. Her depression, if that's what it was, was very apparent and how drab the chilly place, spiritless, as places you dislike immediately. This was no home. There was no warmth or happiness there, not one Christmas decoration; much the opposite, cold and dark like a full body bag lying in the rain; and the thrill and excitement of anticipation and returning home turned suddenly to despair. My god, I asked myself, what's happened? How terribly haggard she is.

Dickie coughed and cried, "Mommy," from his small bedroom down the hall. Kitty disappeared and returned reluctantly, it seemed, with him, as though she wasn't sure that she should let me see him. Tucking a blue and white striped child's blanket around him, she hoisted him to her shoulder, his bare belly to her breasts, his face away from me, thumped his back rather vigorously, rhythmically, shaking back and forth, purring in a low monotone: "Honey, honey, honey, your mommy loves you. Mommy loves you, honey. There. There. There."

His coughing ceased; he kept sobbing quietly as he pulled on a little pink thumb with his lips.

"What's the matter with the boy?" I asked, immediately biting my tongue, realizing how cold and aloof 'the boy' was. As an infantry company commander in the throes of combat I knew how to be a tough-love father; how to push and lead them, to comfort them, wounded and dying men, but until trained by my wife I was worthless at home with a sick little boy.

I felt awkward. Damn it, it's not the boy, it's our Dickie, two-year-old baby. I needed to redeem myself, say sweety or honey, be a natural father. Instead I was an outdoor lout standing there, a cold utter stranger to Kitty and Dickie, inside their home, a brutal senseless killer in this joyless, rear echelon, somehow feminine place. I had to say something that sounded like I really loved my son and wife but the shock at the signs of her suffering choked me.

Avoiding eye contact or addressing me, Kitty pulled her grandmother's old rocking chair away from the bookcase with one hand and sat down with Dickie, tucking his blanket to her body tightly all around and rocked. Several of our books, including a large, fairly expensive world atlas, that is to us expensive, I bought after hearing of Korea, and several 45 record albums on the bottom shelf had spines scraped off by her rocker, rocking, rocking rhythmically harder and harder, sliding backward into the bookshelf.

"Mommy loves you, honey. Honey, mommy loves you," and when she rocked harder, she began to cry softly in a patterned little whimper: "There, there, there, honey, mommy loves you. Don't worry, mommy loves you. Just you never mind. Everything will be all right."

Suddenly, she faced me and I thought I heard her again: "Don't worry, honey, everything will be all right."

"Honey, honey," I blurted. "Honey."

My god, I thought, looking at the scraped book spines, how many cold nights like this, lonely, worried hours, did she have to rock that hard to keep her sanity? And it all hit me hard.

"Honey," I sobbed tearfully, "I'm awfully sorry for what I've done. I didn't realize I was killing you, too. What happened to me? I was crazy. Didn't mean anything I wrote, sweety. I'm awful sorry," and, eyes full of regret, I collapsed forward on my knees and reached to stop her rocker and bent over to kiss away tears on the back of the hand that held our sick little boy to her bosom.

Korea, 1951. The Punch-bowl is north of the 38th Parallel in central, eastern Korea while Seoul, the capital of South Korea, is south of that famous line in central, western Korea.